Human Capital, Trade and Public Policy in Rapidly Growing Economies

ACADEMIA STUDIES IN ASIAN ECONOMIES

Series Editor: Sheng-Cheng Hu, *Director, Institute of Economics, Academia Sinica, Taiwan*

Titles in the series include:

Economic Efficiency and Productivity Growth in the Asia-Pacific Region
Edited by Tsu-Tan Fu, Cliff J. Huang and C.A. Knox Lovell

Food Security in Asia
Economics and Policies
Edited by Wen S. Chern, Colin A. Carter and Shun-Yi Shei

The Economic Analysis of Substance Use and Abuse
The Experience of Developed Countries and Lessons for Developing Countries
Edited by Michael Grossman and Chee-Ruey Hsieh

Productivity and Economic Performance in the Asia-Pacific Region
Edited by Tsu-Tan Fu, Cliff J. Huang and C.A. Knox Lovell

The Economics of Health Care in Asia-Pacific Countries
Edited by Teh-Wei Hu and Chee-Ruey Hsieh

Monetary Policy and Taiwan's Economy
Edited by Gerald P. Dwyer, Jr., Jin-Lung Lin, Jia-Dong Shea and Chung-Shu Wu

Global Warming and the Asian Pacific
Edited by Ching-Cheng Chang, Robert Mendelsohn and Daigee Shaw

Human Capital, Trade and Public Policy in Rapidly Growing Economies

From Theory to Empirics

Edited by

Michele Boldrin

Professor, University of Minnesota, Minneapolis, MN, USA

Been-Lon Chen

Professor, Academia Sinica, Taipei, Taiwan

Ping Wang

Professor, Vanderbilt University, Nashville, TN, USA and NBER, New York, USA

ACADEMIA STUDIES IN ASIAN ECONOMIES

Edward Elgar
Cheltenham, UK • Northampton, MA, USA

Published by
Edward Elgar Publishing Limited
Glensanda House
Montpellier Parade
Cheltenham
Glos GL50 1UA
UK

Edward Elgar Publishing, Inc.
136 West Street
Suite 202
Northampton
Massachusetts 01060
USA

A catalogue record for this book
is available from the British Library

Library of Congress Cataloguing in Publication Data
International Conference on Economic Growth (2000 : Academia Sinica, Taipei, Taiwan)
Human capital, trade, and public policy in rapidly growing economies : from theory to empirics / edited by Michele Boldrin, Been-Lon Chen, Ping Wang.
p. cm.
A collection of original papers, the majority presented at the International Conference on Economic Growth held at the Institute of Economics, Academia Sinica, Taipei, in December 2000.
Examines the forces underlying economic growth in the East Asian newly industrialized countries of Hong Kong, South Korea, Singapore, and Taiwan.
Includes bibliographical references and index.
1. East Asia—Economic conditions—Congresses. 2. Human capital—East Asia—Congresses. 3. International trade—East Asia—Congresses. 4. East Asia—Foreign economic relations—Congresses. 5 East Asia—Economic policy—Congresses. I. Boldrin, Michele, 1956– II. Chen, Been-Lon, 1961– III. Wang, Ping, 1957 Dec. 5– IV. Title.

HC460.5.I5595 2000
330.95—dc22 2004047147

ISBN 1 84376 883 6

Printed and bound in Great Britain by MPG Books Ltd, Bodmin, Cornwall

Contents

PART III PUBLIC POLICY

Figures

Tables

Contributors

Michele Boldrin, Professor, Department of Economics, University of Minnesota, Minneapolis, MN, USA.

Ching-Cheng Chang, Research Fellow, Institute of Economics, Academia Sinica, Taipei, Taiwan.

Wen-ya Chang, Professor, Department and Graduate Institute of Economics, Fu-Jen Catholic University, Taipei County, Taiwan.

Been-Lon Chen, Research Fellow, Institute of Economics, Academia Sinica, Taipei, Taiwan.

Yeong-Yuh Chiang, Professor, Department of Money and Banking, National Chengchi University, Taipei, Taiwan.

Theo Eicher, Associate Professor, Department of Economics, University of Washington, Seattle, WA, USA.

Amy Jocelyn Glass, Associate Professor, Department of Economics, Texas A&M University, College Station, TX, USA.

Wai-Hong Ho, Assistant Professor, Economics Programme, Faculty of Social Sciences and Humanities, University of Macau, Macao.

Ming-Feng Hung, Assistant Professor, Department of Industrial Economics, Tamkang University, Taipei County, Taiwan.

Sang Choon Kim, Student, Department of Economics, University of Washington, Seattle, WA, USA.

Ching-chong Lai, Research Fellow, Institute of Economics, Academia Sinica, Taipei, Taiwan.

Carol Lehr, Associate Professor, Department of Economics, School of Business, Virginia Commonwealth University, Richmond, VA, USA.

Yeun Yeun Lim, Assistant Manager, Commercial Department, PSA Corporation, Singapore.

Kazuo Mino, Professor, Graduate School of Economics, Osaka University, Toyonaka, Japan.

Theodore Palivos, Professor, Department of Economics, University of Macedonia, Greece.

Daigee Shaw, Research Fellow, Institute of Economics, Academia Sinica, Taipei, Taiwan.

Jhy-yuan Shieh, Assistant Professor, Department of Economics, Chinese Culture University, Taipei, Taiwan.

Koji Shimomura, Professor, Research Institute for Economics and Business Administration, Kobe University, Kobe, Japan.

Chung Yi Tse, Associate Professor, School of Economics and Finance, The University of Hong Kong, Hong Kong, PRC.

Henry Wan, Professor, Department of Economics, Cornel University, Ithaca, NY, USA.

Ping Wang, Professor, Department of Economics, Vanderbilt University, Nashville, TN, USA and Research Associate, Health Economics Program, National Bureau of Economic Research, New York, USA.

Foreword

In addition to the introductory chapter, this volume gathers together 12 original contributions to theoretical and empirical analyses of economic growth, with a primary focus on human capital (Part I), trade (Part II) and public policy (Part III). In particular, the forces underlying the long-lasting growth experiences in East Asian newly industrialized countries (Hong Kong, South Korea, Singapore and Taiwan) are examined from various angles, which will be of interest to a broader set of developing countries.

Most of the chapters were first presented at the International Conference on Economic Growth held at the Institute of Economics, Academia Sinica, Taipei, in December 2000. Every contribution has been through a careful refereeing process (by at least one anonymous external reviewer and by one of the editors). The editors would like to thank Jess Benhabib, Eric Bond, Thomas Cooley, Peter Howitt, Sheng-Cheng Hu, Rody Manuelli, Kazuo Nishmura, B. Ravikumar and Karl Shell for their help in putting together an outstanding conference program and/or their participation in the meeting. We would also like to thank Robert Lucas and Nancy Stokey for their inputs at the early stage of planning in an NBER conference held in Chicago. We are grateful to Zsolt Becsi, Eric Bond, John Fender, Gerhard Glomm, Neville Jiang, Edwin Lai, Derek Laing, Rody Manuelli, Kazuo Nishmura, Thomas Olson, Chris Papageorgiou, B. Ravikumar, Ellis Tallman, Robert Tamura, Danyang Xie and Chong K. Yip for their willingness to serve as referees, and their comments and suggestions. We acknowledge financial support by Academia Sinica, the Bank of China (Republic of China, ROC), the Council for Economic Planning and Development (Executive Yuan, ROC), and the National Science Council (Executive Yuan, ROC). Finally, excellent assistance from Ya-Ping Yeh, Hung-Lin May Chen and Hsien-Tang Eric Yen is also acknowledged.

1. Introduction: A Quick Reference to Growth Theory

Michele Boldrin, Been-Lon Chen and Ping Wang

Why do some economies rise and others fall? What are the major determinants of long-term growth and development? Is human capital the main driving force? Does international trade play a crucial role? Of particular interest to us is the question, what are the forces underlying the long-lasting growth experiences in East Asian newly industrialized countries (NICs, that is, Hong Kong, South Korea, Singapore and Taiwan)? Can public policy help in breaking down any barriers towards becoming rich? If so, what would be the optimal design of such a development policy to remedy the existing distortions or market failure problems? The main purpose of this volume is to provide theoretical and empirical analyses towards addressing these important issues.

1 EMPIRICAL REGULARITIES

Kaldor (1961) summarized some important stylized facts concerning long-run economic growth:

1. (great ratios) ongoing increase in capital–labor ratio and output per worker over time;
2. (factor returns) ongoing increase in real wages in conjunction with stationary real interest rates; and
3. (factor shares) stationary labor and capital income shares.

More recently, the availability of the Summers–Heston international data set (Summers and Heston, 1991) accompanied by the Barro and Lee (1993) data set enables numerous cross-country studies. Several additional empirical regularities have been documented (for example, see Maddison, 1982; Barro, 1991; Barro and Sala-i-Martin, 1992; Levine and Renelt, 1992; Mankiw et al., 1992; Alesina and Rodrik, 1994; Quah, 1996):

1. (club convergence) developing countries starting above a particular threshold level of development tend to catch up with the advanced countries, whereas those below the threshold fall into a low-growth trap;
2. (growth acceleration) the rate of per capita output growth of the leading country has been increasing over the past three decades (from −0.07 percent between 1700 and 1785 in the Netherlands, to 0.5 percent between 1785 and 1820 in the United Kingdom, to 1.4 percent between 1820 and 1890 in the United Kingdom, to 2.3 percent between 1890 and 1970 in the United States);
3. (determinants of long-run growth) while educational attainment has consistently contributed to higher growth, the growth effects of the investment ratio, government size, the rule of law and political institutions and the state of financial development are insignificant at the time; moreover, the scale effect (that is countries with a larger labor force grow faster) is absent, whereas inequality is usually harmful for economic growth; and
4. (East Asian miracle) the NICs have overtaken their former peer countries (such as Argentina, Brazil, Mexico and the Philippines), moving along a rapid growth path and catching up with the advanced economies.

2 THE DEVELOPMENT OF GROWTH THEORY: FROM RAMSEY TO ROMER

Formal theories of economic growth can be traced back at least to Harrod (1939). An unpleasant feature of the Harrod model is the knife-edge equilibrium concept where by long-run steady state is determined by a relationship depending on three exogenous parameters: the capital–output ratio, the population (or employment) growth rate and the saving rate. To remedy this inherent instability problem, three theories have been developed:

1. the neoclassical model which allows a capital–output ratio based on the neoclassical production theory (compare Solow, 1956; and Swan, 1956);
2. the labor choice model which endogenizes employment growth (compare Nagatani, 1969); and
3. the Keynes–Wicksell model, which considers endogenous propensity to save (compare Kaldor, 1957; and Stein, 1966).

Since the labor choice model relies crucially on a permanent gap between the rates of growth of employment and population and the Keynes–Wicksell model depends on *ad hoc* saving behavior, it is not surprising that the Solow–

Swan neoclassical growth model comes to the fore Yet, despite its popularity, this neoclassical growth model lacks an optimizing behavior – the long-run path of capital accumulation is entirely driven by the mechanics of the aggregate production technology. This problem is partially rectified by von Neumann (1937), Allais (1947) and Phelps (1966), where a golden rule solution (or a 'maximum maximorum') is proposed to maximize the steady-state level of consumption per worker. Not until Cass (1965) and Koopmans (1965) was close attention paid to a much ignored seminal work by Ramsey (1928). Since then, this optimal exogenous growth model has become the predominant framework to evaluate the long-term performance of economic development.

Three main predictions of the optimal exogenous growth model are summarized as follows:

1. In contrast with the Solow–Swan model, the saving rate in the optimal exogenous growth model is endogenous – it rises (or falls) with the effective capital–labor ratio if the intertemporal elasticity of substitution is sufficiently lower (or higher) than the capital income share.
2. The golden rule solution of the steady-state accumulation of capital is dynamically inefficient.
3. The rate of growth of output per worker is exogenously pinned down by the rate of technical progress and other preference/technology parameters. As in the Solow–Swan model, the optimal exogenous growth model predicts conditional convergence where the growth effect of the initial level of development (measured by output per effective unit of worker) depends on the steady-state value of output per (effective) worker.

In spite of their wide recognition and substantial influence, the exogenous growth models have several shortcomings:

1. the rate of exogenous technical progress is the sole driving force of steady-state economic advancement, which offers little help in understanding the determinants of long-run growth;
2. the convergence path is monotonic, thus ruling out the possibility of overtaking or lagging behind the development process; and
3. policy or economic behavior does not matter in the long run unless it can affect the rate of technological changes.

These problems give birth to the endogenous growth theory, stimulated by the seminal contributions of Romer (1986) and Lucas (1988).

The main feature of endogenous growth models is that the total marginal product of all reproducible factors is bounded below by a positive constant, thus requiring the production function to exhibit constant, asymptotic constant or increasing returns with respect to all reproducible factors. Accordingly, we can briefly summarize the literature as shown in Table 1.1.

Table 1.1 Classification of Endogenous Growth Models

Returns to scale	One sector	Multi-sector
Constant or asymptotically constant	Rebelo (1991) Jones and Manuelli (1990)	Lucas (1988) Bond, Wang and Yip (1996)
Increasing	Romer (1986)	Lucas (1988) Boldrin and Rustichini (1994) Benhabib and Perli (1994) Xie (1994) Benhabib, Meng and Nishimura (2000) Grossman and Helpman (1991) Aghion and Howitt (1992)

It is useful to note that early works by Pitchford (1960), Arrow (1962), Uzawa (1965) and Shell (1966) are the building blocks of the modern endogenous growth theory. In particular, Pitchford observed the property of asymptotically positive marginal product of reproducible capital under constant elasticity of substitution between capital and labor. Arrow emphasized how learning by doing creates knowledge that can exhibit positive spillovers to the entire economy and in turn encourage income growth. While Uzawa highlighted the role of human capital in economic advancement, Shell formalized Schumpeter's (1911) idea that positive rent encourages incentive activity and capital accumulation.

The simplest form of the production function satisfying the required property is the so-called AK model developed by Rebelo (1991), in which output is linear in a 'general capital' input. This AK technology can be appended to the conventional diminishing return production function to permit well-defined transitional dynamics (compare Jones and Manuelli, 1990). The two-sector version of constant-returns endogenous growth models has been elaborated by Lucas (1988) and Bond, et al. (1996), where the latter completely characterizes the dynamics of the system with requiring explicit functional forms of production technologies. Two major predictions arise in this class of endogenous growth models:

1. Any economic factor or policy instrument that affects the level of the scaling factor of the production or human capital accumulation technology will generate a long-run growth effect.
2. A polarization property holds regardless of the factor intensity rankings: when the goods sector is physical capital intensive, price dynamics is stable but quantity dynamics is unstable; when the goods sector is human capital intensive, price dynamics is unstable but quantity dynamics is stable. As a consequence, the unique balanced growth path is a saddle.

By allowing for uncompensated positive knowledge or human capital spillovers (compare Romer, 1986; Lucas, 1988), the increasing-returns version of endogenous growth models has added much more complex dynamics. In particular, increasing returns give rise to the possibility of dynamic indeterminacy in the sense that there is a continuum of transition paths converging to a unique long-run balanced growth path. This property is helpful in explaining overtaking/lagging-behind development experiences (see discussions in Benhabib and Perli, 1994; Boldrin and Rustichini, 1994; and Xie, 1994). Alternatively, one may follow the spirit of Schumpeter to consider imperfect market structure, either monopolistic competition (compare Grossman and Helpman, 1991) or monopoly (Aghion and Howitt, 1992), thus permitting positive rent and incentives to investment in research and development (R&D). Complex dynamics may exist in these types of setup, including multiplicity of equilibria as well as limit cycles. Finally, it is noteworthy that even under constant returns, models with distortionary taxes or externalities such that private returns to scale differ from social returns can lead to dynamic indeterminacy (see Bond, et al., 1996; and Benhabib et al., 2000, respectively).

3 A CRITICAL SURVEY OF THE LITERATURE ON HUMAN CAPITAL, TRADE, PUBLIC POLICY AND GROWTH

To focus on the main issues addressed by contributors to this volume, we next turn to a critical survey of the endogenous growth literature in the areas of human capital, international trade and public policy.

3.1 Human Capital

Barro (1991), Mankiw et al. (1992) and Benhabib and Spiegel (1994) document using cross-country regressions that educational achievement accounts for 5–28 percent of output growth; in a case study of Taiwan, Tallman and Wang (1994) find the contribution of human capital up to 45 percent. To account for the positive effect of human capital on long-run growth, one may consider formal schooling (compare Lucas, 1988) or on-the-job learning (compare Stokey, 1988) with or without the peer-group knowledge spillover effect. With regard to formal schooling, Glomm and Ravikumar (1992) compare private versus public education in the dimensions of long-run growth and inequality and determine the education system based on majority voting. Focusing on on-the-job learning, Laing et al. (1995) explore the relationship between unemployment and growth in which workers choose their schooling effort prior to engaging in job search in the labor market, finding that education is deemed to affect each worker's stock of knowledge as well as their ability to accumulate additional human capital once employed (on-the-job learning). In Becker et al. (1990), the quantity and quality trade-off in fertility choice is reexamined, in which the interrelationships between childbearing and human capital investment are explicitly modeled. Eicher (1996) analyzes education decision in an endogenous growth setup allowing for dynamic interactions between human capital and technological advancements. While De Gregorio (1996) studies how exogenous credit constraints may affect human capital accumulation and the rate of economic growth, Lloyd-Ellis (2000) examines the role of public education in a dynamic general-equilibrium framework endogenous occupational choice (between the skilled and the unskilled).

Recently, there has been a growing literature on education and growth by emphasizing the inalienability of human capital in the presence of an imperfect capital market. Zeira (1991) and Galor and Zeira (1993) recognize this to derive endogenous credit constraints that limit individuals' educational choice and hence influence growth and income distribution (between the educated and the uneducated). Following this avenue of research, Tsiddon (1992) argues that the presence of moral hazard behavior in educational investment may lead an economy to a low growth trap. Both Zeira and Tsiddon assume that all agents are *ex ante* the same and take the same decision (whether to become educated or not); *ex post* they may differ because of luck in the outcome of education. In Galor and Zeira, agents differ in their initial wealth (but not ability), which serves as the main driving force for the evolution of income distribution. Fender and Wang (forthcoming) revisit this issue by permitting *ex ante* heterogeneity in ability in which agents make endogenous educational decision and choice between borrowing and lending. They find that the presence of the moral hazard problem leads to lower education and a lower real interest rate, both of which widen the inequality between the skilled and unskilled. They also study the role of public policy in remedying the inefficiency arising from credit market imperfections and examine whether public education can improve upon the credit-constrained equilibrium.

While the empirics are generally subject to data limitation with regard to precise measurement of human capital, the theoretical literature largely overlooks the dynamic evolution of human capital and the dynamic interactions between human capital and other labor market decisions. While the former is crucial for understanding the pattern of income inequality over time, the latter is important for assessing household welfare and evaluating government education and immigration policies.

3.2 International Trade

While openness to trade has been found to promote economic growth (compare Barro, 1991), one of the fundamental propositions of the comparative advantage theory of trade, the Heckscher–Ohlin theorem, has not gained much empirical support (compare Leamer, 1984) without incorporating international productivity differences (see Trefler, 1993). Findlay and Kierzkowski (1983) study the dynamic trade theory in a framework differentiating between skilled and unskilled labor and endogenizing the choice of whether to become skilled or to remain unskilled. It was not until Grossman and Helpman (1991, Chapter 5), that issues concerning international trade and endogenous growth were thoroughly studied. They consider the case in which there are external effects from the development of new products and examine accumulation of two 'factors': technology and a general capital. Van and Wan (1997), advance a new interpretation of the rapid growth experiences in several East Asian economies where trade in intermediate goods is prominent. By linking trade to growth through technical progress, they find that a developing country lacking R&D efforts may still enjoy a sequence of gains from trade without reducing the technology gap.

In the benchmark perfect competition setup, Ventura (1997) constructs a two immediate-goods model in which factor supply convergence emerges when goods production exhibits constant returns in the reproducible factor. He also demonstrates that with diminishing returns in the reproducible factor and with long-run exogenous labor supply permitting differences in productivity growth, a priori preferences over different capitals can be eliminated. In Bond et al. (forthcoming), a two-country endogenous growth model with accumulation of both physical and human capital is constructed, showing that balanced growth equilibria satisfy a static and dynamic version of the Heckscher–Ohlin theorem, whereas the existence of unbalanced growth equilibria leads to violation of both the static and dynamic versions of Heckscher–Ohlin theorems.

Young (1991) stresses the role of externalities from learning by doing played in international trade. Under a Ricardian framework, Young considers that more sophisticated goods have higher unit labor requirements but generate greater gains from learning by doing. As a result, international trade may actually harm growth when trade opportunities encourage resource reallocation toward less sophisticated sectors. A similar conclusion is made in the work by Stokey (1991), in which human capital is accumulated via learning by producing high-quality goods and free trade tends to slow down this learning process in the South, thus suppressing output growth. Ishikawa (1992) extends Stokey by allowing the industrial composition (agricultural versus manufacturing) to be endogenously determined. The study of trade and sectoral shift can also be found in a recent study by Wan (2002), where an interesting example is provided to illustrate that learning in quality control and production scheduling may lower production cost and hence enable a shift towards heavy industry. Along these lines, Bond et al. (2001) explicitly model the dynamic general equilibrium consequences of learning from exporting in economy with a traditional (agricultural) sector, an import competing and endogenous array of modern export sectors. They find that knowledge capital (from learning) and physical capital play very different roles in the evolution of industrial transformation and wage disparity between the skilled and the unskilled.

While the significant role of international trade in long-run growth has been widely accepted, the reason why the development experiences between East Asian and Latin American economies diverge has largely been unexplored. For example, why can the Taiwanese machine tool firms stand on the shoulder of the knowledge giant and why are the emperor's new clothes not made in Colombia? Moreover, the existing literature remains silent on (i) what are the underlying channels through which trade may affect investments in human and physical capitals and (ii) how to isolate these indirect effects from the direct effect of trade on economic advancements.

3.3 Public Policy

In the process of economic development, preexisting distortions and market failures are often present. For example, there exist free-rider problems associated with education, international trade barriers in the forms of tariff and import restrictions, financial market imperfections as a consequence of asymmetric information, and market incompleteness in goods and asset transactions. These give rise to a positive role of public policy. While a carefully designed development policy is widely believed essential to the East Asian Miracle (compare Amsden, 1989; and Lucas, 1993), examples of unsuccessful public policy programs abound (such as the Akosombo Dam in Ghana, the Morogoro Shoe Factory in Tanzania, and the failed aid program in Zambia; see Easterly, 2001).

The role of government industrial policy in East Asia's economic development has long been a matter for popular debate. One strand thinks that the government has a role to play. In studying the origin of success in East Asia, Amsden (1989) and Wade (1990) emphasized the role of government in strengthening and governing the function of markets, and Rodrik (1997) stressed the government's role in correcting market failures. Another strand believes that industrial policy itself is of no use. For example, in documenting East Asia's high-growth performance, the World Bank (1993) concludes that the success in economic development lies in their governments, proper macroeconomic stabilization policies, including the maintenance of an open trade regime and stable prices.

Among the four East Asian tigers, however, the degree of government intervention differs. Except for Hong Kong, the governments in these countries design industrial policies to intervene in their economy. Yet, constrained by the small domestic markets, they rely on the international market in order to reach efficient production scales. International market forces in turn feed back to the domestic market. Because of dependency on the global market, the ability of East Asian governments to dictate economic development is restricted by international market mechanisms, in particular by the world institutions such as the GATT (General Agreemert on Tariffs and Trade) and their regulations (compare Chen et al., 2001). Given the international constraints, East Asian governments intervene in their economies by designing industrial policies to kick-start those industries without indigenous firms, provided that the government thinks it necessary to develop them.

In Taiwan, the government's industrial policies have been implemented through setting up new institutions (especially public enterprises and non-governmental organizations) to activate a new industry, and through intervening at the industry level (compare Wang and Xie, 2001; Chen and Hsu, 2002). In South Korea, the government has usually kicked off a new industry by subsidizing conglomerates to set up firms in the new area, and by intervening at the firm level (compare Kang, 2001). Notably, while the protection of these new enterprises provides investment incentives, the resulting barriers to potential competitors would hurt long-term development. This situation has not yet occurred in Korea and Taiwan (compare Chu et al., 2001). The basic reason for this is that these small economies rely heavily on the global market (Lau and Wan, 1994). As a consequence, external conditions force governments to allow local competitors to enter; otherwise, once the local market is open and foreign competitors come in, the incumbents would be forced out due to lack of efficiency. Such pressures have thus restricted the government to market-oriented intervention.

Rapid human capital accumulation is considered to be one of the primary engines for economic growth in East Asia (see Tallman and Wang, 1994). Two kinds of problem emerge for human capital investment. First, human capital creates positive externalities and individuals tend to underinvest by free-riding on their peers' knowledge. Second, human capital is inalienable and informational frictions cause underinvestment as a result of credit constraints. These problems induced the East Asian governments to intervene in human capital formation by offering public education. According to the UNDP (1991), in 1960, public expenditure on education as a percentage of GDP was higher in East Asia than in other developing countries.

Financial policies may also affect economic growth, as argued by King and Levine (1993). In particular, Fernandez and Galetovic (1994) document that the positive relationship between financial development and output growth within the OECD (Organization for Economic Cooperation and Development) countries has been much weaker than that within the developing economies. One way that financial policies influence economic growth is to promote savings, which is crucial for physical capital accumulation at the early stage of economic development. Of particular interest, the Taiwanese government accomplished this in two steps. First, as early as 1950, the government set interest rates for time deposits so that its real return was always positive. This policy was in contrast to the experiences in Latin America in the 1960s and the 1970s when most countries there depressed the financial sector so that the real interest rate was negative (compare McKinnon, 1973). Following Tsiang's recommendations (see Tsiang, 1979), the interest rate for one-month time deposits was set at 7.5 percent, that is compound annual rates at 125 percent. Second, the unique interest income tax exemption for time deposits was introduced in 1960. In 1980, about 98 percent of depositors received interest income less than the exemption cap.

Finally, fiscal policy in the forms of government spending and taxation may generate long-run growth effects. King and Rebelo (1990) are among the first to illustrate such growth effects. In an endogenous growth model with public capital, Barro (1990) obtains a positive optimal income tax rate at the second-best optimum. By allowing public investment to build up infrastructure, Fugatami et al. (1993) still reconfirm Barro's finding. Later,

Turnovsky (1996a, b) extends the Barro model and Chen (2002) extends Futagami et al., by considering both consumption and capital income taxation. They both find positive capital income and consumption tax rates for the first-best as well as the second-best optimum. This result is in contrast to what Chamley (1986) finds that the optimal capital income tax rate is asymptotically zero in a Ramsey-type exogenous growth model. Although theoretically important, fiscal policy may be quantitatively unimportant to long-run economic growth (compare Lucas, 1990). Indeed, current research has not yet reached an agreement on this matter. For example, while Jones et al. (1993) find that factor taxation can generate a strong effect on output growth, Rebelo and Stokey (1995) find it quantitatively inessential.

4 A BRIEF SUMMARY OF THIS BOOK

We shall now summarize the contributions collected in this volume. Chapters 2–5 in Part I address issues concerning human capital. In Chapter 2, Eicher and Kim analyze a horizontal R&D model with the introduction of heterogeneous technologies, production costs and market shares. They find that increased competition benefits firms at the technological frontier, while laggard firms experience accelerated product obsolescence. Their finding confirms empirical inverted-U relationships between monopoly power and innovation. In Chapter 3, Mino studies the relation between patterns of long-term economic growth and indeterminacy in an endogenous growth model with human capital formation. By introducing sector-specific externalities and a non-separable utility into the Lucas model, he shows that indeterminacy may emerge even in the absence of social increasing returns. In Chapter 4, Lehr and Palivos empirically examine and test the relationship between public education expenditures and fertility rates across countries, while in Chapter 5, Chang and Chen identify the sources of productivity growth in 70 less-developed economies using the distance-function-based Malmquist productivity index.

Chapters 6–9 in Part II focus on international trade-related issues. In Chapter 6, Lim and Wan elaborate four types of systematic bias in the growth accounting leading to understating the efficiency gains in the newly industrialized economies. They introduce a performance measure that is the proportional rate of income gap reduction. In Chapter 7, in a two-country, two-tradable goods, dynamic general equilibrium, international trade model, Shimomura shows that indeterminacy is possible without assuming any source of distortions such as technological externalities, increasing returns, government intervention or market imperfections. In Chapter 8, Tse evaluates quantitatively three effects of trade restrictions on aggregate output in a neoclassical growth model: (i) dulling the protected firms' incentives to invest in new technologies and expand employment; (ii) magnifying the adverse effects of taxing capital equipment; and (iii) drying up the foreign exchange earning available for financial capital investment. He finds that only (iii) is quantitatively important. In Chapter 9, Glass explores and finds several implications of reductions in tariffs or transport costs on the rate of innovation in a quality ladders model, where firms from both countries innovate.

Chapters 10–13 in Part III discuss the effectiveness of public policies. While Chapters 10 and 11 are about financial policy, Chapters 12 and 13 elaborate on fiscal and environment policies. In Chapter 10, Chen, Chiang and Wang study an overlapping generations model with human capital and an active financial sector, and evaluate the long-run growth effects of three financial policies — a reserve requirement policy, a loan rate control policy, and a deposit rate ceiling policy. In Chapter 11, Ho investigates the role of public borrowing in a financial market with credit-rationing problems and finds a positive growth effect. In Chapter 12, Shieh, Chang and Lai employ a two-sector endogenous growth model with a wealth-induced social status to examine the linkage between government expenditure and economic growth. They find that the effect of government expenditure on economic growth depends on the presence of the social status effect and production externality of public goods. Finally, in Chapter 13, Hung and Shaw use panel data and a simultaneity model between per capita income and air pollution to empirically examine the environmental Kuznets curve relationship between per capita income and air pollution, where they confirm such a relationship for NO_2 and CO.

5 AVENUES OF FUTURE RESEARCH IN GROWTH THEORY

Finally, we would like to provide our own views on fertile avenues of future research. For brevity, we shall mention only five:

1. from representative-agent to heterogeneous-agent setups (such studies may be built on the existing models in Glomm and Ravikumar, 1992; Benabou, 1996; and Aghion and Bolton, 1997) — this will be useful for studying an old but important issue in development, growth versus inequality, as well as a new problem in the United States concerning widened wage disparities both between groups and within a particular

skill group;

2. from aggregative models to frameworks taking more explicit account of the underlying microeconomic behaviors (for example, see an attempt made by Berliant et al., 2002, in understanding the economics of knowledge spillovers) — this will be helpful in understanding several 'black boxes' in the existing literature;
3. from canonical Walrasian economy to frictional labor/goods markets (by extending the search and matching structures developed by Aghion and Howitt, 1994 and Laing et al., 1995 and forthcoming, on the labor market or Chen et al., 2002, and Laing et al., 2002, on the goods market) — this will enable a systematic analysis of the interrelationships between growth, unemployment and technological diffusion;
4. from balanced to unbalanced growth (which is largely unexplored, with only two very recent research outputs by Rebelo and Xie, 2002, and Bond et al., 2001) — this will be crucial for examining the dynamics of industrial transformation and sector shifts;
5. from the study of individual incentives to analysis of economic institutions and organizations (which is still virgin territory as pointed out by Jovanovic, 2000) — this will synthesize the two distinctive branches of research in economic development and economic growth, leading to better assessments of policy effectiveness and social efficiency.

REFERENCES

Aghion, Philippe and Patrick Bolton (1997), 'A Theory of Trickle-down Growth and Development', *Review of Economic Studies*, **64**, 151–72.

Aghion, Philippe and Peter Howitt (1992), 'A Model of Growth Through Creative Destruction', *Econometrica*, **60**, 323–51.

Aghion, Philippe and Peter Howitt (1994), 'Growth and Unemployment', *Review of Economic Studies*, **61**, 477–94.

Alesina, Alberto and Dani Rodrik (1994), 'Distributive Politics and Economic Growth', *Quarterly Economic Review*, **109**, 465–90.

Allais, Maurice (1947), *Economie et Intérêt*, (Economy and Interest), Paris: Imprimerie Nationale.

Amsden, Alice (1989), *Asia's Next Giant: South Korea and Late Industrialization*, New York: Oxford University Press.

Arrow, Kenneth J. (1962), 'The Economic Implications of Learning by Doing', *Review of Economic Studies*, **29**, 155–73.

Barro, Robert J. (1990), 'Government Spending in a Simple Model of Endogenous Growth', *Journal of Political Economy*, **98**, S103–S125.

Barro, Robert J. (1991), 'Economic Growth in a Cross Section of Countries',

Quarterly Journal of Economics, **106**, 363–94.

Barro, Robert J. and Xavier Sala-i-Martin (1992), 'Convergence', *Journal of Political Economy*, **100**, 235–51.

Barro, Robert J. and Jong-wha Lee (1993), International Comparisons of Educational Attainment, *Journal of Monetary Economics*, **32(3)**, 363–94.

Becker, Gary S., Robert Barro and Robert Tamura (1990), 'Human Capital, Fertility, and Economic Growth', *Journal of Political Economy*, **98** (5), part II, S12–S37.

Benabou, Roland (1996), 'Heterogeneity, Stratification and Growth', *American Economic Review*, **86**, 584–609.

Benhabib, Jess, Q. Meng and Kazuo Nishimura (2000), 'Indeterminacy under Constant Returns to Scale in Multisector Economies', *Econometrica*, **68**, 1541–9.

Benhabib, Jess and Roberto Perli (1994), 'Uniqueness and Indeterminacy: On the Dynamics of Endogenous Growth', *Journal of Economic Theory*, **63**, 113–42.

Benhabib, Jess and Mark M. Spiegel (1994), 'The Role of Human Capital in Economic Development: Evidence from Aggregate Cross-country Data', *Journal of Monetary Economics*, **28**, 143–73.

Berliant, Marcus, Shin-Kun Peng and Ping Wang (2002), 'Production Externality and Urban Configuration', *Journal of Economic Theory*, **104**, 275–303.

Boldrin, Michele and A. Rustichini (1994), 'Indeterminacy of Equilibria in Models with Infinitely-lived Agents and External Effects', *Econometrica*, **62**, 323–42.

Bond, Eric W., Ronald Jones and Ping Wang (2001), 'Economic Take-offs in a Dynamic Process of Globalization', Working Paper, University of Rochester, Rochester, NY.

Bond, Eric W., Kathleen Trask and Ping Wang (forthcoming), 'Factor Accumulation and Trade: Dynamic Comparative Advantage with Endogenous Physical and Human Capital', *International Economic Review*.

Bond, Eric W., Ping Wang and Chong Yip (1996), 'A General Two-sector Model of Endogenous Growth with Human and Physical Capital: Balanced Growth and Transitional Dynamics', *Journal of Economic Theory*, **68**, 149–73.

Cass, David (1965), 'Optimal Growth in an Aggregative Model of Capital Accumulation', *Review of Economic Studies*, **32**, 233–40.

Chamley, Christopher (1986), 'Optimal Taxation of Capital Income in General Equilibrium with Infinite Lives', *Econometrica*, **54**, 607–22.

Chen, Been-Lon (2002), 'Optimal Taxation in a Growth Model with Public Capital Stock and Adjustment Costs', mimeo, Taipei: Academia Sinica.

Chen, Been-Lon and Mei Hsu (2002), 'Coordination Failures and Catchup: Experiences of Manmade Fiber in Taiwan', in Peter Chow (ed.), *Taiwan in a Global Economy: From an Agrarian Economy to an Exporter of High-tech Products*, Westport: CT Greenwood, 39–75.

Chen, Been-Lon, Jie-Ping Mo and Ping Wang (2002), 'Technology Adoption, Matching and Economic Growth with Market Frictions', *Journal of Economic Dynamics and Control*, **26**, 1927–54.

Chen, Tain-Jy, Been-Lon Chen and Yung-Peng Chu (2001), 'The Development of Taiwan's Electronics Industry', in Poh-Kam Wong and Chee-Yuen Ng (eds), *Industrial Policy, Innovation and Economic Growth*, Singapore: Singapore University Press, 245–282.

Chu, Yung-Peng, Tain-Jy Chen and Been-Lon Chen (2001), 'Rethinking the Development Paradigm: Lessons from Taiwan — The Optimal Degree of State Intervention', in Poh-Kam Wong and Chee-Yuen Ng (eds), *Industrial Policy, Innovation and Economic Growth*, Singapore: Singapore University Press, 197–244.

De Gregorio, Jose (1996), 'Borrowing Constraints, Human Capital Accumulation, and Growth', *Journal of Monetary Economics*, **37**, 49–71.

Easterly, William (2001), *The Elusive Quest for Growth: Economists' Adventures and Misadventures in the Tropics*, Cambridge, MA: MIT Press.

Eicher, Theo (1996), 'Interaction between Endogenous Human Capital and Technical Change', *Review of Economic Studies*, **63**, 127–44.

Fender, John and Ping Wang (forthcoming), 'Educational Policy in a Credit Constrained Economy with Skill Heterogeneity', *International Economic Review*.

Fernandez, David G. and Alexander Galetovic (1994), 'Schumpeter Might Be Right — But Why? Explaining the Relation between Finance, Development and Growth', Working Paper, Johns Hopkins University, Baltimore, MD.

Findlay, Ronald and Henry Kierzkowski (1983), 'International Trade and Human Capital: A Simple General Equilibrium Model', *Journal of Political Economy*, **91**, 173–91.

Fugatami, Koichi, Yuichi Morita and Akihisa Shibata (1993), 'Dynamic Analysis of an Endogenous Growth Model with Public Capital', *Scandinavian Journal of Economics*, **95** (4), 607–25.

Galor, Oded and Joseph Zeira (1993), 'Income Distribution and Macroeconomics', *Review of Economic Studies*, **60**, 35–53.

Glomm, Gerhard and B. Ravikumar (1992), 'Public versus Private Investment in Human Capital: Endogenous Growth and Income Inequality', *Journal of Political Economy*, **100**, 818–34.

Grossman, Gene and Elhanan Helpman (1991), *Innovation and Growth in the Global Economy*, Cambridge, MA: MIT Press.

Harrod, Roy F. (1939), 'An Essay in Dynamic Theory', *Economic Journal*, **49**, 14–33.

Ishikawa, Jota (1992), 'Learning by Doing, Changes in Industrial Structure and Trade Patterns, and Economic Growth in a Small Open Economy', *Journal of International Economics*, **33**, 221–44.

Jones, Larry E. and Rodolfo E. Manuelli (1990), 'A Convex Model of Equilibrium Growth: Theory and Policy Implications', *Journal of Political Economy*, **98** (5), 1008–1038.

Jones, Larry E., Rodolfo Manuelli and Peter Rossi (1993), 'Optimal Taxation in

Models of Endogenous Growth', *Journal of Political Economy*, **102** (3), 485–513.

Jovanovic, Boyan (2000), 'Growth Theory', NBER Working Paper, No. 7468, National Bureau of Economic Research, Cambridge, MA.

Kaldor, Nicolas (1957), 'A Modoel of Economic Growth', *Economic Journal*, **67**, 591–624.

Kaldor, Nicolas (1961), 'Capital Accumulation and Economic Growth', in Friedrich A. Lutz and Douglas C. Hague (eds), *The Theory of Capital Proceedings of Conference Held by the International Economics Association*, London: Macmillan, 177-222.

Kang, Hojin (2001), 'The Development Experience of South Korea — The Role of Public Policy', in Poh-Kam Wong and Chee-Yuen Ng (eds), *Industrial Policy, Innovation and Economic Growth*, Singapore: Singapore University Press, 323-96.

King, Robert G. and Ross Levine (1993), 'Finance and Growth: Schumpeter Might Be Right', *Quarterly Journal of Economics*, 153, 717–38.

King, Robert G. and Sergio Rebelo (1990), 'Public Policy and Economic Growth: Developing Neoclassical Implications', *Journal of Political Economy*, **88** (5), S126–S150.

Koopmans, Tjalling C. (1965), 'On the Concept of Optimal Economic Growth', in Salviucci Pietro (ed.), *The Econometric Approach to Development Planning*, Amsterdam North-Holland, 225-300.

Laing, Derek, Theodore Palivos and Ping Wang (1995), 'Learning, Matching and Growth', *Review of Economic Studies*, **62**, 115–29.

Laing, Derek, Theodore Palivos and Ping Wang (2002), 'Endogenous Pricing and Product Diffusion with Goods Market Frictions', *Economic Theory*, **19**, 707–36.

Laing, Derek, Theodore Palivos and Ping Wang (forthcoming), 'The Economics of New Blood', *Journal of Economic Theory*.

Lau, Man-lui and Henry Wan, Jr. (1994), 'On the Mechanism of Catching-up', *European Economic Review*, **38**, 952–63.

Leamer, Edward (1984), *Sources of International Comparative Advantage: Theory and Evidence*, Cambridge, MA: MIT Press

Levine, Ross and David Renelt (1992), 'A Sensitivity Analysis of Cross-country Growth Regressions', *American Economic Review*, **82**, 942–63.

Lloyd-Ellis, Huw (2000), 'Public Education, Occupational Choice, and the Growth —Inequality Relationship', *International Economic Review*, **41**, 171–201.

Lucas, Robert E., Jr. (1988), 'On the Mechanics of Economic Development', *Journal of Monetary Economics*, **22**, 2–42.

Lucas, Robert E., Jr. (1990), 'Supply-side Economics: An Analytical Review', *Oxford Economic Papers*, **42**, 293–316.

Lucas, Robert E., Jr. (1993), 'Making a Miracle', *Econometrica*, **61**, 251–72.

Maddison, Angus (1982), *Phases of Capitalist Development*, Oxford: Oxford University Press.

Mankiw, N. Gregory, David Romer and David Weil (1992), 'A Contribution to the Empirics of Economic Growth', *Quarterly Journal of Economics*, **107**, 407–38.

McKinnon, Ronald (1973), *Money and Capital in Economic Development*, Washington, DC: Brookings Institution.

Nagatani, Keizo (1969), 'A Monetary Growth Model with Variable Employment', *Journal of Money, Credit and Banking*, **1**, 188–206.

Phelps, Edmund S. (1966), *Golden Rules of Economic Growth*, New York: Norton.

Pitchford, John D. (1960), 'Growth and the Elasticity of Substitution', *Economic Record*, **26**, 491–504.

Quah, Danny (1996), 'Twin Peaks: Growth and Convergence in Models of Distribution Dynamics', *Economic Journal*, **106**, 1004–55.

Ramsey, Frank (1928), 'A Mathematical Theory of Saving', *Economic Journal*, **38**, 543–59.

Rebelo, Sergio (1991), 'Long-run Policy Analysis and Long-run Growth', *Journal of Political Economy*, **99**, 500–521.

Rebelo, Sergio and Nancy Stokey (1995), 'Growth Effects of Flat-rate Taxes', *Journal of Political Economy*, **103** (3), 519–50.

Rebelo, Sergio and Danyang Xie (2002), 'Beyond Balanced Growth', *Review of Economic Studies,* 68(4), 869-82.

Rodrik, Dani (1997), 'Trade Strategy, Investment and Exports: Another Look at East Asia', *Pacific Economic Review*, **2** (1), 1–24.

Romer, Paul (1986), 'Increasing Returns and Long-Run Growth', *Journal of Political Economy*, **94**, 1002–37.

Schumpeter, Joseph (1911), *Theory of Economic Development*, Cambridge, MA: Harvard University Press (Reprinted 1934).

Shell, Karl (1966), 'Toward a Theory of Incentive Activity and Capital Accumulation', *American Economic Review*, **61**, 62–8.

Solow, Robert (1956), 'A Contribution to the Theory of Economic Growth', *Quarterly Journal of Economics*, **70**, 65–94.

Stein, J. (1966), 'Money and Capacity Growth', *Journal of Political Economy*, **74**, 451–65.

Stokey, Nancy (1988), 'Learning by Doing and the Introduction of New Goods', *Journal of Political Economy*, **96**, 701–17.

Stokey, Nancy (1991), 'Human Capital, Product Quality, and Growth', *Quarterly Journal of Economics*, **106**, 587–616.

Summers, Robert and Alan Heston (1991), 'The Penn World Table (marks): An Expanded Set of International Comparisons, 1950–1988', *Quarterly Journal of Economics*, **106** (2), 327–68.

Swan, Trevor W. (1956), 'Economic Growth and Capital Accumulation', *Economic Record*, **32**, 334–61.

Tallman, Ellis W. and Ping Wang (1994), 'Human Capital and Endogenous Growth: Evidence from Taiwan', *Journal of Monetary Economics*, **34**, 101–24.

Trefler, D. (1993), 'International Factor Price Difference: Leontief Was Right!', *Journal of Political Economy*, **101**, 961–87.

Tsiang, S.C. (1979), 'Fashion and Misconceptions in Monetary Theory and Their Influences in Finance Banking Policies', *Zeitschrift für die gesamte Staatwissenschaft*, **135**, 584–604.

Tsiddon, Daniel (1992), 'A Moral Hazard Trap to Growth', *International Economic Review*, **33**, 299–321.

Turnovsky, Stephen J. (1996a), 'Optimal Tax, Debt, and Expenditure Policies in a Growing Economy', *Journal of Public Economy*, **60**, 21–44.

Turnovsky, Stephen J. (1996b), 'Fiscal Policy, Adjustment Costs and Endogenous Growth', *Oxford Economic Papers*, **60**, 21–44.

UNDP (United Nations Development Programme) (1991), *Human Development Report*, New York: Oxford University Press.

Uzawa, Hirofumi (1965), 'Optimal Technical Change in an Aggregative Model of Economic Growth', *International Economic Review*, **6**, 18–31.

Van, Pham Hoang and Henry Y. Wan (1997), 'Interpreting East Asian Growth', in Bjarne S. Jensen and Kar-yiu Wong (eds), *Dynamics, Economic Growth, and International Trade*, Ann Arbor, MI: University of Michigan Press, 265–86.

Ventura, Jamune (1997), 'Growth and Interdependence', *Quarterly Journal of Economics*, **112**, 57–84.

von Neumann, John (1937), 'A Model of General Economic Equilibrium', *Review of Economic Studies*, **13**, 1–9.

Wade, Robert (1990), '*Governing the Market: Economic Theory and the Role of Government in East Asian Industrialization*', Princeton, NJ: Princeton University Press.

Wan, Henry Jr. (2002), 'Why Trade Matters to Development: A Learning Model', in A.D. Woodland (ed.), *Economic Theory and International Trade: Essays in Honour of Murray C. Kemp*, Cheltenham, UK and Northampoton, MA, USA: Edward Elgar, 295–310.

Wang, Ping and Danyang Xie (2001), 'Activation of a Modern Industry', IMF Working Paper, International Monetary Fund, Washington, DC.

World Bank (1993), *The East Asian Miracle: Economic Growth and Public Policy*, New York: Oxford University Press.

Xie, Danyang (1994), 'Divergence in Economic Performance: Transitional Dynamics with Multiple Equilibria', *Journal of Economic Theory*, **63**, 97–112.

Young, Alwyn (1991), 'Learning by Doing and the Dynamic Effects of International Trade', *Quarterly Journal of Economics*, **106**, 369–406.

Zeira, Joseph (1991), 'Credit Rationing in an Open Economy', *International Economic Review*, **32**, 959–72.

Part I

Human Capital

2. Market Structure and Innovation Revisited: Endogenous Productivity, Training and Market Shares

Theo Eicher and Sang Choon Kim

1 INTRODUCTION

The empirical literature documents positive, negative and even 'inverted-U' relationships between monopoly power and innovation/growth. Such findings are intuitive since insufficient market power prevents firms from reaping the benefits of up-front research and development (R&D) investment, while excessive market power reduces the need for further innovations. Most growth models imply, however, that greater market power should unambiguously increase innovation and growth. This chapter highlights the forces that can generate the non-monotonic relationship between market power and growth that is observed in the data.

We introduce heterogeneous technologies, production costs and market shares into a conventional product variety model to allow for positive effects of competition on technological change and growth. Increased competition is then shown to benefit firms at the technological frontier, while laggard firms experience accelerated product obsolescence. Since skills and technologies are both endogenous, we can also address the 'research intensity puzzle'. We provide a mechanism by which increases in the share of skilled workers in R&D do not automatically increase the growth rate – a key counterfactual implication of R&D-based growth models. We suggest that how growth responds to changes in the share of labor in R&D depends on the level of development.

A key feature of R&D-based growth models is the relationship between market power and rates of innovation/growth. The models imply unequivocally that greater monopoly power increases returns to investment and thus R&D and growth.[1] The voluminous empirical literature contradicts this implication, as it documents both positive and negative relationships between monopoly power and innovation.[2] Scherer (1967) and Levin et al. (1985) even find an 'inverted-U' relation. Such findings are intuitive since insufficient market power prevents firms from reaping the benefits of up-front R&D investment, while excessive market power reduces the need for further inventions.

In this chapter we introduce heterogeneous technologies, production costs and market shares into the conventional product variety model to allow for the possibility of positive effects of competition on technological change and growth. While maintaining symmetric consumer preferences over all goods, we permit innovators to reduce production costs by employing new technologies. As producers with newer technology have lower per unit costs, they can charge lower prices to capture larger market shares. Since new technologies arrive continuously, each innovator's proximity to the technological frontier eventually erodes. The change in the productivity (and hence price) differentials between existing firms and cutting-edge firms generates time-varying market shares.

Increased competition then has two effects on firms. First, the increased elasticity of demand lowers the markup each firm can charge. Second, the increased ability to substitute one good for another allows consumers to allocate more purchases to relatively cheaper goods. As a result, recent innovators find that overall profits increase because the shift in the demand toward their products compensates for their reduced markup. Firms using old technologies suffer as competition increases, not only because of lower markups, but also because of reduced demand. As new innovators find their profits and market share increased by competition, more R&D is undertaken and greater positive spillovers from technological change increase the aggregate growth rate. Interestingly, a corollary result exposed by the model is that this mechanism functions only in economies that are sufficiently developed.

Previous models find similar results. Aghion et al. (1997b) and Kletzer (1997) find that competition and/or imitations may be growth enhancing in an industry if step-by-step innovation is assumed. This approach postulates limited knowledge spillovers, where followers must first catch up to the leader before being able to overtake. The results in our model do not require step-by-step innovation. Adding richer microfoundations, Aghion et al. (1997a) introduce agency considerations into a model of innovation. This structure may imply a positive effect of competition on innovation, if increased competition raises managerial discipline. Nickell et al. (1997) provide empirical support for this approach. Finally, Aghion and Howitt (1998) decompose R&D into creation and adoption of new blueprints to show that endogenous product-line upgrading may lead to higher growth if competition increases. This mechanism is similar to our model where the driving force is the accelerated obsolescence of old lines as demand shifts to new technology products. Neither Aghion and Howitt (1998) nor Aghion et al. (1997a) feature our result that the effect of competition on firm profits is asymmetric, favoring advanced firms and accelerating obsolescence for laggards.

Horizontal and vertical integration have been examined by the industrial organization literature (see, for example, Economides, 1993 and Smulders and van de Klundert, 1995). These models do not replicate a negative relationship between market power and growth. Previous product variety models rely on *identical* productivities of technologies and feature *symmetry* between new and old technologies and goods. Caballero and Jaffe (1993) rely on symmetric technologies, while retaining asymmetric consumer preferences in order to generate asymmetric demand for products. Alternatively, Lai (1998) allows for exogenous reduction in the cost of innovation. In contrast, we specify that productivities of new and old technologies differ and that endogenous production cost advantages allow new varieties to capture larger market shares. Instead of relying on asymmetric productivities, Kletzer (1997) models spatial competition and product characteristics, which allows for endogenous and asymmetric research effort across firms.

If we follow Romer (1990) and Grossman and Helpman (1991) and interpret the proliferation of one industry's product line as the performance of a country, the model addresses the 'research intensity puzzle' which is at the core of previous R&D-based growth models. These models carry the implication that the growth rate is either positively, or not at all related to the share of workers allocated to R&D (for example, Romer, 1990 and Jones, 1995a, respectively). Both implications are counterfactual (see Jones, 1995b). We show that when market shares, technologies and human capital are modeled to be endogenous, the impact of increased research intensity on growth depends on the *level of development*. Specifically, we find that increased research intensity in high-growth countries may be associated with lower growth rates (as in OECD (Organization for Economic Cooperation and Development) countries), while increased research intensity is shown to be the key to increased growth in developing countries. Essentially we show that the profit destruction effect, due to increased research intensity, may be sufficiently smaller in the low-growth countries, to allow the positive effects of higher rates of innovation and increased demand for skilled labor to dominate.

2 ENDOGENOUS PRODUCTIVITY AND TRAINING IN A PRODUCT VARIETY MODEL

We embed endogenous technology, training and market shares into a product variety model. Previous product variety models that rely on *identical* technologies and *symmetry* between new and old goods (technologies) imply that all goods are priced equivalently and hence consumed in equal proportions. Below we extend a product variety model to allow newer technologies to be more productive, hence cutting-edge firms face lower unit costs. Since agents have preferences over varieties, but technologies and unit costs are heterogeneous, asymmetric price reductions generate distinct market shares. This renders the model a hybrid between product variety and quality ladder models.

We follow Eicher (1996) and specify that ever more sophisticated technologies cannot be absorbed into production by agents with stationary knowledge. To this end we endogenize the training decision by firms and specify that firms determine not only how much research should be undertaken, but also how much training workers should receive. The positive side effect of firm-specific training is a positive externality to the general pool of knowledge.

2.1 Tastes

At time t, a representative consumer maximizes utility:

$$U(t) = \int_t^{\infty} e^{-\rho(\tau-t)} \log\left[\int_{-\infty}^{n(t)} x_i(t)^{\frac{\varepsilon-1}{\varepsilon}} di\right]^{\varepsilon/\varepsilon-1} d\tau, \quad \varepsilon > 1 \tag{2.1}$$

that extends over the set of products produced, $n(t)$, and they maximize (2.1) subject to the intertemporal budget constraint:

$$\int_t^{\infty} e^{-[R(\tau)-R(t)]} E(\tau)d\tau \leq \int_t^{\infty} e^{-[R(\tau)-R(t)]} h(\tau)d\tau + B(t), \tag{2.2}$$

where ρ represents the discount rate, ε the elasticity of substitution, $R(t) = \int_0^t r(\upsilon)d\upsilon$ the discount factor, $B(t)$ the individual assets (ownership shares in enterprises), $E(t) = \int_{-\infty}^{n(t)} p_i(t)x_i(t)di$ the expenditures and $p_i(t)$ the price of good i. Through normalizations the wage rate of effective labor is one, hence $h(t)$ is both the stock of effective labor in the economy and labor income. Assuming the elasticity of substitution exceeds unity, the introduction of new goods erodes existing varieties' market share. Taking p_i as given, the demand for a good i is:

$$x_i(t) = \frac{E(t)p_i(t)^{-\varepsilon}}{\int_{-\infty}^{n(t)} p_i(t)^{1-\varepsilon} di}. \tag{2.3}$$

While equation (2.3) is standard for product variety models, it highlights that comparatively lower-priced goods command a relatively higher market share, and that the introduction of cheaper goods reduces the demand for all existing products. These price and market share dynamics are a key component of this model. Using (2.3), we can rewrite the utility index in (2.1) as

$$E(t)\left[\int_{-\infty}^{n(t)} p_i(t)^{1-\varepsilon} di\right]^{-1/(1-\varepsilon)}.$$

2.2 Production of Final Goods

Firms undertake three activities: creating new technologies, training workers and producing varieties of final goods. Assume there exist $i \in [-\infty, \infty]$ technologies, of which $i \in [-\infty, \ldots, N(t)]$ have been discovered at time t, the rest are yet to be invented. Technologies are arranged in the order of increasing technological sophistication, so that the latest invention at t, $N(t)$, is also the most productive. Before firms can realize the productive potential of their technologies, workers must learn about firm-specific technologies. Let s_i denote the amount of training that is provided by a firm using technology i. Once training is completed, production can take place. Let $S(t)$ be the total number of firms that are engaged in training at time t. Thus, $n(t) = N(t) - S(t)$ is the most sophisticated good produced at time t, since N is the newest technology and S is the number of firms engaged in training.[3]

Much like fixed costs, the training cost and the cost of the blueprint must be incurred before production of the final goods commences. Hence we can separate the maximization decision of how much to produce, how much training to provide and how much to pay for a blueprint.[4] The production of final good, x_i, requires firm-specific technology, i, effective labor, h_{Pi} and firm-specific training, s_i. How productive workers are after experiencing s_i periods of training depends on the workers' constant training efficiency, q:

$$x_i = e^i s_i^q h_{Pi}, \tag{2.4}$$

where e represents the exponential function. *Ceteris paribus*, equation (2.4) indicates that labor productivity increases when workers are matched with more sophisticated technologies. We assume decreasing returns to training and restrict the training efficiency to $q<1$. The size of the labor force and the wage rate are normalized to unity, there is no population growth, and hence the production wage at time t is simply $h_{P_i}(t)$. The production function implies that firms using newer technologies are more productive and can thus charge a lower price.

Firms utilize the demand for good i, (2.3), to maximize production profits (excluding training and R&D costs):

$$\underset{p_i}{\text{Max}}\ \pi_i = p_i x_i - h_{Pi}, \tag{2.5}$$

which results in the following pricing rule:

$$p_i = \frac{\varepsilon}{\varepsilon - 1} \frac{1}{s_i^q e^i}. \tag{2.6}$$

This pricing rule is crucial, as it incorporates the distinct feature of the model. In contrast to previous product variety models that rely on homogeneous technologies, our heterogeneous productivities of technologies introduce asymmetric changes in the marginal cost. As technologies increase in sophistication, labor productivities also increase, which lowers the marginal costs to new firms. Hence, while the pricing rule is standard in that it represents the usual fixed markup over marginal cost, marginal costs and hence prices differ.

Within the monopolistically competitive framework, firms pass on lower prices to consumers to capture a larger share of the market and maximize profits. Substituting (2.6) into (2.3) yields the derived demand for good i:

$$x_i = \frac{\varepsilon - 1}{\varepsilon} \frac{E(s_i^q e^i)^\varepsilon}{\int_{-\infty}^{n} (s_{i'}^q e^{i'})^{\varepsilon - 1} di'}. \tag{2.3'}$$

Clearly, market shares increase in the technological sophistication of the product. We can now combine (2.6), (2.3′), (2.4) and (2.5), to find the production profits of firm i:

$$\pi_i = \frac{1}{\varepsilon} \frac{E(s_i^q e^i)^{\varepsilon-1}}{\int_{-\infty}^{n} (s_{i'}^q e^{i'})^{\varepsilon-1} di'}. \tag{2.7}$$

Note again that profits increase in the level of technological sophistication, so that newer technologies and goods command higher profits.

2.3 R&D

We assume with Jones (1995a) and Segerstrom (1998) that research is subject to aggregate *fishing-out* problems. ‘Fishing out’ refers to the notion that easy inventions occur early with little effort. Fewer, harder problems are solved later, requiring considerably more research intensity, cost and effort. Caballero and Jaffe (1993) and Kortum (1993) provide evidence for fishing-out problems at the industry level. This research function has also received strong empirical support from Jones (1995b) who proves that such congestion externalities in research must exist to explain OECD long-run growth performances. The form we employ is fundamentally identical to Segerstrom (1998), but more general functional forms can be applied as shown in Eicher and Turnovsky (1999).

We define $A(t)$ as the economy-wide R&D congestion externality at t, such that the research function can be written as:

$$\dot{N} = \frac{h_R}{A}, \tag{2.8}$$

where h_R represents the aggregate share of labor devoted to R&D at time t. To quantify the congestion externality, we assume that the difficulty index increases linearly in the aggregate research effort, or:

$$\dot{A} = h_R. \tag{2.9}$$

Equations (2.8) and (2.9) imply that a constant rate of innovation requires increasing amounts of effective labor devoted to R&D. Firms finance their research efforts by issuing equity and are awarded infinitely lived patents for their inventions. There is free entry into research and development. After inventing technology and after completing training, firms engage in monopolistic competition with all other patent holders.

Whenever a firm innovates, it has devoted h_{RN} units of labor to the research sector, (2.8), to gain the cutting-edge blueprint, N. The cost of the research effort is the scientists' wage, h_{RN}. From the profit condition, (2.7), we know the instantaneous profits of a firm with technology N, which we can utilize to calculate the stock market value of the firm, given by the discounted net present value of the new technology:

$$V(N,t) = \int_{t+s_N}^{\infty} e^{-r(\tau-t)}\pi_N(\tau)d\tau - \int_{t}^{t+s_N} e^{-r(\tau-t)}h_{TN}(\tau)d\tau. \qquad (2.10)$$

The net present stock market value of the current innovator is a function of the profits that accrue to the firm using technology N minus the discounted value of wages paid to train h_{TN} workers for s_N periods.

Given the net present value of the blueprint as described in equation (2.10), a firm that invests h_{RN} units of labor for dt units of time, generates a value of $V(N,t)h_{RN}/A$. Free entry thus implies that research will be undertaken whenever $V(N,t) \geqq A$, which constitutes the incentive condition in R&D. Since $V(N,t) > A$ implies infinite research activity, $V(N,t) = A$ must be the equilibrium condition. Free entry, thus, prevents firms from earning excess returns and relates the value of new technology to the cost of market entry. Also, as R&D difficulty increases, the value of a new technology must rise to induce positive R&D activity.

2.4 Training

The training decision is similar to an investment in firm-specific capital that the firm must acquire as it is specific to the technology the firm purchases. This capital, much like the blueprint, must be procured before production can begin. Hence the profit stream derived from production must cover not only the cost of the blueprint, but also the cost of training (as shown in (2.10)). Once the training cost has been incurred, firm-specific capital also fixes the capacity of the innovator.

The second stage of the firm's problem is to determine whether and how much training should be provided to maximize the value of a blueprint, given profits derived from final good production, (2.7), and given the cost of training h_{Ti} workers. Substituting the labor demand derived from (2.3′) and (2.4) into (2.10), the firm can determine the optimal training duration by simply maximizing $V(N,t)$ with respect to s_N. Differentiating (2.10) with respect to s_N we find that the optimal training duration s_N^* for technology N is given implicitly by:

$$\begin{aligned}&\int_{t+s_N}^{\infty} \frac{E_{(\tau)} q (s_N^q e^N)^{\varepsilon-1} e^{-r_{(\tau-t)}} (\varepsilon - 1)}{s_N \int_{-\infty}^{n_{(\tau)}} (s_{i'}^q e^{i'})^{\varepsilon-1} di' \varepsilon} d\tau - \frac{E_{(t+s_N)} (s_N^q e^N)^{\varepsilon-1} e^{-r_{(s_N)}}}{\int_{-\infty}^{n(t+s_N)} (s_{i'}^q e^{i'})^{\varepsilon-1} di'} \\ &- \int_{t}^{t+s_N} \frac{E_{(\tau)} q (s_N^q e^N)^{\varepsilon-1} e^{-r_{(\tau-t)}} (\varepsilon - 1)^2}{s_N \int_{-\infty}^{n_{(\tau)}} (s_{i'}^q e^{i'})^{\varepsilon-1} di' \varepsilon} d\tau = 0,\end{aligned} \tag{2.11}$$

where the first term represents the return to training, the second term is the cost of training and the third term represents the production profits forgone during the training period.

In addition, we assume a spillover from firm-specific training to the general pool of knowledge. The rationale is twofold. First, Kletzer (1998) reports strong evidence of this effect in the empirical literature. One can motivate such spillovers with intergenerational spillovers, or simply through job turnover. Second, from a modeling point of view it is impossible to track the various heterogeneous (firm-specific) levels of human capital in the population, hence the spillover also returns a homogeneous labor force to new firms. As in Lucas (1988) effective labor, $h = h_p + h_T + h_R$ grows

$$\dot{h} = \varphi h_T, \tag{2.12}$$

where h_T represents the share of the total labor force engaged in training. The productivity parameter, φ, scales the spillovers from training to the general human capital pool. Despite the spillover, however, workers are unable to use more sophisticated technology without further training.[5] The continuous increases in the levels of general human capital and technology that drive the steady increase in effective labor, are the factors that ultimately allow for ongoing growth in our model. Without the human capital spillover, growth would ultimately cease, as firm-specific investment would only be a sunk cost to the firm, with no effects on effective labor.

The endogeneity of skills is essential to the results of the model. Recent models of non-scale growth (Jones, 1995a) rely on exogenous rates of population growth to determine long-run growth. In our model, changes in the firms' incentives to educate endogenously alter the growth rate of effective labor (2.12). We show in the next section that the growth rate is indeed equal to the growth rate of effective labor. Hence it is exactly the endogeneity of skills that cause *variation* in the rate of firm-specific training (due to, for example change in competition) to translate into changes in growth rates.

3 BALANCED GROWTH

Equation (2.11) renders the dynamic analysis about the equilibrium intractable, hence we focus on the properties of the stationary state. Using equations (2.1) and (2.2), the consumer's problem reduces to choosing an optimal expenditure path. Solving the current-value Hamiltonian for $E(t)$ renders the standard optimal condition:

$$\hat{E}^* = r^* - \rho, \tag{2.13}$$

where '^' denotes proportional changes and '*' values represent equilibrium quantities. The absence of uncertainty renders stocks and bonds perfect substitutes in equilibrium.

3.1 Training

Using the condition for optimal training duration, (2.11), we employ the implicit function theorem to show that the optimal training duration is *independent* of technological sophistication,

$$\frac{\partial s_N^*}{\partial N} = 0. \tag{2.14}$$

This implication seems surprising at first, as one might suspect that greater leaps in productivity generate more incentives for training. The intuition will become clear when we generalize the optimal training rule to:

$$s_N^* = s_i^* = s^*, \tag{2.15}$$

which simply says that, since *all* firms possess the cutting-edge technology at *some* point in time, and since the incremental increases in technology are constant along the balanced growth path, all firms train for the identical periods in equilibrium. Alternatively, equations (2.14) and (2.15) simply state that today's cutting-edge firm invests as much in training as did the cutting-edge firm ten years ago. Further intuition can be derived by solving the optimal pricing rule, (2.6) for the training duration, $s_i = \left[(\varepsilon - 1)\, p_i e^i / \varepsilon\right]^{-1/q}$. The constancy of s^* simply restates the profit- maximization condition for the monopolistically competitive firm: in equilibrium new firms lower the price at the rate of the productivity increase. The stationary training decision, $s_N^* = s_i^* = s^*$, is novel in that explicit, firm-specific training is seldom introduced into growth models, especially in conjunction with endogenous R&D decisions. The implication that the training does not increase in the level of technology does not follow from the assumptions, it is an equilibrium condition for a balanced growth path.

Given the optimal training rule, (2.15), a positive return on innovation, $V[.] > 0$, implies the incentive condition $e^{-[p+g(\varepsilon-1)]s^*} > (\varepsilon - 1)/\varepsilon > 0$, which imposes bounds on the market power necessary to induce the firm to invest in training. The bounds are more restrictive than in previous models of innovation *without* training, since firms must recapture additional training costs that are absent in previous models. We assume hereafter that the condition is satisfied.

Since all new innovator firms train for equal periods in equilibrium, the number of firms that provide training in the economy at any time t is given by:

$$S^*(t) = \int_{t-s}^{t} \dot{N}(\tau)d\tau , \tag{2.16}$$

since the equilibrium rate of technical change, (2.16), (which is constant and equal to the economy-wide growth rate, $\dot{N}^* = g$) implies that the number of firms engaged in training increases in the growth rate and in the training duration, $S^* = gs^*$. With accelerated technical change there is simply more need for training, and more longer training periods imply that more firms at each period of time are engaged in training.

3.2 Profits

Once the training duration has been established, we can rewrite the profit condition for final goods as:[6]

$$\pi_i^* = E^*\left(\varepsilon - 1\right)e^{(i-n^*)(\varepsilon-1)} \big/ \varepsilon. \tag{2.7'}$$

Equation (2.7′) immediately implies that production profits increase with technological sophistication, because the increased productivity associated with new invention generates ever greater cost reductions for firms at the technology frontier. This allows firms to lower the price of their product, and capture a greater market share. In addition, (2.7′) implies that the greater the number of firms involved in training at each point in time, the lower the competition in the product market, which drives up production profits. An increase in the product frontier, n, on the other hand, hurts profits due to the profit destruction and reduced market share, very much as in the quality ladder models.

Equation (2.7′) clearly outlines the profit destruction and loss in market share that occurs when new goods are introduced. Since each firm's distance to the technology frontier is distinct, the introduction of new goods affects firms differently. Differentiating (2.7′) with respect to the elasticity of substitution, we find that there is a critical technology level $\tilde{i} = n^* - [\varepsilon(\varepsilon - 1)]^{-1}$. For all firms with technologies $i > \tilde{i}$, more competition increases profits. If the firm is sufficiently far from the technology frontier, an increase in competition aggravates the impact of their high production costs, which accelerates obsolescence through profit destruction. Inevitably, each firm's technology distance to the leader widens as new products are introduced, and the technology falls below the critical level, $i < \tilde{i}$. The profit function thus features dramatic product cycle behavior, in contrast to previous variety models.[7]

The intuition to the result is that more competition allows for more substitution between goods. All goods suffer as their markup declines. However, the increased substitution allows consumers to substitute away from pricey goods towards newer, cheaper products. Hence old goods (those sufficiently far away from the technological frontier) face not only a decline in the markup, but also a decline in demand. New goods, however, find that the shift in demand towards their cheaper products more than compensates for the decline in markup. The more sophisticated the technology, the lower the costs and the greater the shift in demand towards the product. Firm $\tilde{i}$ is the firm where the loss in markup equals the gain in increased demand to render profits unaffected.

3.3 Labor Markets

Integrating the firms' labor demands, derived from (2.3′) and (2.1), over all goods produced yields the stock of effective labor in production:

$$h_P^* = \int_{-\infty}^{n} h_{i'}^* di' = \frac{E^*(\varepsilon - 1)}{\varepsilon}, \qquad (2.17a)$$

which implies that the labor engaged in training is:

$$h_T^{\ *} = \int_{N-S}^{N} h_{i'}^{\ *} di' = \frac{E^*\left[e^{S^*(\varepsilon-1)} - 1\right](\varepsilon - 1)}{\varepsilon}. \tag{2.17b}$$

The research equation (2.8), together with the incentive condition in R&D, determines the number of R&D workers:

$$h_R^{\ *} = \dot{N}^* A^* = \dot{N}^* V^*[.], \tag{2.17c}$$

which then implies a total labor demand of:

$$h^* = h_p^{\ *} + h_T^{\ *} + h_R^{\ *} = \frac{E^* e^{S^*(\varepsilon-1)}(\varepsilon - 1)}{\varepsilon} + \dot{N}^* V^*[.]. \tag{2.17d}$$

In stationary equilibrium three conditions must be fulfilled. Labor demand must equal labor supply (2.12) and the proportion of labor allocated to each activity must be constant. Second, expenditures, (2.13), labor income, (2.12), and the value of the firm, (2.10), must grow at equal rates. Third, the amount of labor devoted to R&D and the R&D difficulty index must grow at the same rate, or $\hat{h}_R = \hat{A}$. These conditions imply:

$$\begin{aligned} \hat{h}^* &= \hat{h}_R^* = \hat{h}_P^* = \hat{h}_T^* = \hat{E}^* = \hat{V}^* = \hat{A}^* \\ &= \dot{N}^* = g = \frac{h_T}{h}\varphi = \frac{\varphi\left[1 - e^{-gs^*(\varepsilon-1)}\right][\rho + g(\varepsilon - 1)]}{\rho + g\varepsilon e^{-[\rho+g(\varepsilon-1)]s^*}}. \end{aligned} \tag{2.18}$$

As written, the growth rate is still a function of s^*. We can substitute the equilibrium conditions (2.15) and (2.13) into the optimality condition for the training duration (2.11) to derive the equilibrium training duration condition:

$$(\varepsilon - 1)q - \left[\rho + g(\varepsilon - 1)\right]s^* - \frac{q(\varepsilon - 1)^2 e^{[\rho+g(\varepsilon-1)]s^*}}{\varepsilon} = 0, \tag{2.19}$$

which then allows us to determine s^* and g jointly. Equation (2.19) is in essence the individual firms' optimal training decision, given the underlying parameters of the economy. Equation (2.18) is the aggregate growth rate as determined by the sum of activities of all firms.

4 PROPERTIES OF THE BALANCED GROWTH PATH

Most noticeably, the *size* of effective labor, h, does not appear in either of the two equilibrium conditions (2.18) and (2.19). This implies that the scale of the economy does not affect long-run growth, just as in the recent R&D-based growth models (for example, Jones, 1995a, Segerstrom, 1998; and Young, 1998). The crucial difference to the previous literature is that the growth rate is not exogenous as for example in Jones, but jointly determined by the rates of investment in training and R&D. This implies that, even if R&D investment did take place, the absence of training would drive the growth rate to zero. We can summarize the characteristics of the investment in training and the growth rate with the following propositions:[8]

Proposition 1 More competition increases both training, s^*, and growth, g^*.

Increased competition, as measured by an increase in the substitutability among goods, ε, generates three separate effects relating to (a) labor demand, (b) training duration, and (c) profit destruction. Since increased competition allows consumers to switch more easily between goods, they substitute from expensive (old) products to cheaper (new) goods. This generates a larger market share for cutting-edge firms. To satisfy the greater demand for their products, the cutting-edge firms increases their labor demand. Hence more workers receive training.

Aside from the fact that more workers receive training, the increase in competition forces new innovators to reoptimize their training duration decision. For all firms with technologies $i > \tilde{i}$, more competition increases profits (2.7′), and the value of the firm (2.10) indicates that an increase in production profits not only compensates for increased training costs, but also creates greater incentives to invest in more training, which boosts productivity. As both the number of workers trained and the training duration increase, the economy-wide growth rate also increases, (2.12).

The third effect is the profit destruction effect. As the rate of technological change increases, each firm's proximity to the technological frontier is eroded faster, (2.19). This implies that high-tech firms lose their frontier status earlier and see their market shares dissipate sooner. This profit destruction effect reduces the incentives to train, because the time to recoup outlays has been reduced.

In models that abstract from training or an endogenous size of the labor force, the positive labor demand effect is offset by the profit destruction effect. This is because in such models the long-run growth rate depends entirely on the R&D activity of firms seeking monopoly profit. Here, however, the positive training duration effect combines with the positive labor demand effect to dominate the adverse effects of profit destruction. Note the importance of the training component to the analysis. With exogenous population growth, the economy could overcome the decreasing returns in research (see Jones, 1995a), but the economy would not exhibit higher growth because the factor that is used intensively in the R&D process is exogenous.

Proposition 2 (a) Greater training efficiency, q, increases both investment in training and long-run growth. (b) Greater spillovers from specific to general knowledge, φ, increase the long-run growth rate, but decrease the amount each firm invests in training.

Greater training efficiency, q, increases the marginal returns to training relative to the marginal cost of training (2.11). As each firm increases its training period, the number of firms engaged in training, S^*, rises together with the number of workers receiving training (2.17b). As the fraction of the labor force that receives training increases, so do the spillovers to the general human capital pool. This subsequently raises the aggregate growth rate.

Greater spillovers from specific to general knowledge increase the growth rate (2.18) via an increased rate of effective labor growth (2.12). Greater spillovers, however, also accelerate the rate of profit destruction for individual firms since new goods are introduced at a faster rate and each firm's proximity to the technological frontier erodes faster (2.7′). This causes each firm to train for shorter periods of time to reduce the training cost, and to start producing final goods earlier to compensate for the accelerated contraction in production profits (2.10). The combined effect of greater knowledge spillovers on the growth rate is positive, since the increased growth of effective labor dominates the negative effect of reduced training investment on an individual firm basis.

Since the growth rate of general human capital equals the growth rate of the economy (see 2.18), proposition 2b implies that an increase in the spillover parameter reduces firm-specific learning, but through the increased spillover from specific to general knowledge, the growth rate of general knowledge in the economy increases.

Proposition 3 How the growth rate is affected by a change in the share of labor devoted to R&D, $\gamma_R \equiv h_R/h$, depends on the industry characteristics or the level of development. A threshold growth rate, $\tilde{g}$, determines whether an increase in the share of labor increases or decreases the growth rate.

$$\left.\frac{dg}{d\gamma_R}\right|_{g=g^*} \lesseqgtr 0 \text{ as } g^* \lesseqgtr \tilde{g}, \text{ where } \tilde{g} \equiv \frac{\rho}{q(\varepsilon-1)^2}.$$

Proposition 3 might be the most interesting result of the model where training and R&D compete for resources, and where market power decreases the rate of growth. Conventionally, product variety models have two interpretations. The model may describe a particular industry in the economy, or, alternatively, it has frequently been used to describe the performance of an entire country (for example, Romer, 1990; and Grossman and Helpman, 1991). The proposition adds an additional dimension, as it implies that an increase in the share or researchers devoted to R&D may increase or *decrease* the economy-wide growth rate depending on whether the country is a high- or a low-growth country.

As the share of labor allocated to the R&D sector increases, the rate of innovation and the introduction of new goods increase, (2.8). This increases both the growth rate and the fishing-out problem in research. From equation (2.16) we know that this increases the total number of firms that are engaged in training at any moment in time, which increases the share of the population that receives training, (2.17b), and the growth rate. However, the higher rates of innovation also have a negative impact on existing firms. The profit destruction effect increases as faster innovations and product introductions wash out the market share of yesterday's high-tech firm at a faster rate. As each firm's market share declines, the observed training duration will also decline to lower the share of workers trained in the economy and thus the rate of general human capital accumulation and growth.

To dissect which effect dominates, we start with the case of a high-growth country, $g^*>\tilde{g}$, a country with a high productivity in research, elasticity of substitution, and worker quality (see propositions 1 and 2). In this country the profit destruction effect described above is high because of the high elasticity of substitution and the high worker quality. Hence the net outcome is a decrease in the growth rate. In the laggard, or low-growth country, however, where $g^*<\tilde{g}$, the low productivity in research combines with a low-quality workforce to lead to a weak profit destruction effect. Greater research effort in laggard countries does not cause such powerful effects since a high discount rate generates sluggish responses in the firms' training decisions. Hence subsequent, low spillover from firm-specific to general human capital leads to a slower increase in the rate of innovation.

5 CONCLUSIONS

We constructed a model that incorporates costly technology absorption efforts of firms and dynamic decreasing returns to scale in R&D technology into a Schumpeterian framework to explore their implications for long-run growth. The objective was to construct a model that is consistent with the empirical evidence that shows a non-monotonic relation between innovation and market power.

We propose that the main factor affecting the allocation between investment in R&D and investment in the technology absorption is the elasticity of substitution between products. Our model is capable of asymmetric effects of competition of firms. We find that more competition in product markets spurs innovation in high-tech industries, but it accelerates obsolescence for low-tech firms, those that are sufficiently far from the technological leader.

On an aggregate level, a higher degree of substitutability may be growth enhancing if the positive effects of profit creation for high-tech firms outweigh the profit destruction experienced by laggard companies. Interestingly this translates into a non-monotonic relationship between research intensity and growth. We find that a threshold growth rate determines whether higher research effort will generate positive, negative or no growth, which qualifies the strong implications regarding scale effects in the previous R&D literature.

Our framework may be useful to examine a number of related issues. One extension may be to allow for international trade with or without imitation. We conjecture that such a model would allow for true product cycle dynamics, with dynamic changes in the production depending on not only demand and competitive conditions, but also the level of human capital and time preference in a country.

APPENDIX 2A

Properties of the Balanced Growth

Taking total differentials of equations (2.18) and (2.19), we can find:

$$\begin{bmatrix} a_{11} & a_{12} \\ a_{21} & a_{22} \end{bmatrix} \begin{bmatrix} dg \\ ds \end{bmatrix} = \begin{bmatrix} a_{13}d\varphi + a_{14}d\varepsilon + a_{15}d\rho \\ a_{23}d\varepsilon + a_{24}dq + a_{25}d\rho \end{bmatrix}$$

$$\begin{aligned} a_{11} = {} & g(\varepsilon-1)e^{-\left[\rho+g(\varepsilon-1)\right]s}\left[1-gs(\varepsilon-1)\right] \\ & + \frac{(\varepsilon-1)\varphi\rho}{g\varepsilon}\left[1-e^{-gs(\varepsilon-1)}\right] \\ & - \frac{(\varepsilon-1)^2\varphi s}{g}\left[\rho+g(\varepsilon-1)\right]e^{-gs(\varepsilon-1)} > 0 \end{aligned}$$

$$a_{13} = [\rho + g(\varepsilon-1)][1-e^{-gs(\varepsilon-1)}] > 0$$

$$\begin{aligned} a_{14} = {} & \frac{g}{\left[\rho+g(\varepsilon-1)\right]} \times \\ & [\, g\rho\left\{1-e^{-[\rho+g(\varepsilon-1)]s}\right\} + g^2\left\{1+\varepsilon s\left[\rho+g(\varepsilon-1)\right]\right\}e^{-[\rho+g(\varepsilon-1)]s} \\ & + \varphi s\left[\rho+g(\varepsilon-1)\right]^2 e^{-gs(\varepsilon-1)} > 0] \end{aligned}$$

$$a_{15} = g^2\varepsilon s e^{-[\rho+g(\varepsilon-1)]s} + g\left\{\frac{\varphi}{g}\left[1-e^{-gs(\varepsilon-1)}\right]-1\right\} > 0$$

$$a_{21} = -\left\{(\varepsilon-1)s + \frac{(\varepsilon-1)^3}{\varepsilon}qse^{[\rho+g(\varepsilon-1)]s}\right\} < 0$$

$$a_{22} = -\left\{\left[\rho+g(\varepsilon-1)\right] + \frac{(\varepsilon-1)^2}{\varepsilon}q\left[\rho+g(\varepsilon-1)\right]e^{[\rho+g(\varepsilon-1)]s}\right\} < 0$$

$$a_{23} = -\frac{1}{\varepsilon(\varepsilon-1)}\left\{\rho s\left[\varepsilon+1+gs\varepsilon(\varepsilon-1)\right] - (q-gs)(\varepsilon-1)\left[1+gs\varepsilon(\varepsilon-1)\right]\right\} < 0,$$

for $\Psi(.) > 0$

$$a_{24} = -\left\{(\varepsilon-1) - \frac{(\varepsilon-1)^2}{\varepsilon}e^{[\rho+g(\varepsilon-1)]s}\right\} < 0,$$

$$a_{25} = s\left\{1 + \frac{(\varepsilon - 1)^2 q}{\varepsilon} e^{[\rho + g(\varepsilon - 1)]s}\right\} > 0.$$

The determinant, $D = a_{11}a_{22} - a_{12}a_{21} < 0$, which implies that stability in g-s space.

Proof of Proposition 1

$$\frac{dg^*}{d\varepsilon} = \frac{1}{D}(a_{14}a_{22} - a_{23}a_{12}) > 0.$$

Given stability in the g-s space,

$$\frac{ds^*}{d\varepsilon} = \frac{1}{D}(a_{11}a_{23} - a_{21}a_{14}) > 0.$$

Proof of Proposition 2

$$\frac{dg^*}{dq} = \frac{1}{D}(-a_{24}a_{12}) > 0, \quad \frac{ds^*}{dq} = \frac{1}{D}(a_{11}a_{24}) > 0, \quad \frac{dg^*}{d\varphi} = \frac{1}{D}(a_{13}a_{22}) > 0,$$

$$\frac{ds^*}{d\varphi} = \frac{1}{D}(-a_{21}a_{13}) < 0.$$

Proof of Proposition 3

From (2.18),

$$\gamma_R = \left(g\varepsilon\left\{e^{-[\rho + g(\varepsilon - 1)]s} - (\varepsilon - 1)/\varepsilon\right\}\right)\Big/\left\{\rho + g\varepsilon e^{-[\rho + g(\varepsilon - 1)]s}\right\},$$

which implies:

$$\frac{d\gamma_R^*}{dg^*} = \frac{\varepsilon\left[\rho + g(\varepsilon - 1)\right]se^{-[\rho + g(\varepsilon - 1)]s}}{\left\{\rho + g\varepsilon e^{-[\rho + g(\varepsilon - 1)]s}\right\}^2}\left[\frac{\rho}{q(\varepsilon - 1)} - g(\varepsilon - 1)\right] \lesseqgtr 0.$$

ACKNOWLEDGMENT

We thank Charles Engel, Fahad Khalil, Lillian Lyons, Carme Riera Prunera, Steve Turnovsky and seminar participants at Nuffield College, and the universities of Copenhagen, Rotterdam, Tilburg, Dortmund, Tübingen and Munich for helpful suggestions. We also thank the Royalty Research Fund and the DFG Mercator Grant for financial support.

NOTES

1. Product variety models imply unequivocally that industries with greater degrees of monopoly power should generate more innovations and higher growth rates. Quality ladder models do not address the issue because they assume unitary elasticity of substitution, see Aghion and Howitt (1992, 1998).
2. See Cohen and Levin (1989) for a summary. More recently, Blundell et al. (1995), Nickell (1996), Nickell et al. (1997) and show unambiguously negative correlations.
3. Below we suppress time subscripts unless required to avoid confusion.
4. Training and final good maximizations could be combined. However, to render a cleaner exposition of the separate decisions of the firm, we present them separately in Sections 2.2 and 2.4.
5. Training to learn a firm-specific accounting program generates general familiarity with computers and accounting. However, the individual still requires training if he/she changes jobs and works with a different firm's more sophisticated accounting program.
6. The profit condition is similar to Caballero and Jaffe (1993), who assume that consumers value new products better by an exogenous amount. As indicated in the introduction, in our model the productivity and cost differential between firms is endogenous.
7. See Lai (1997) for an alternative specification of product cycles in a product variety model.
8. The proofs of the propositions are provided in Appendix 2A.

REFERENCES

Aghion, P., M. Dewatripont and P. Rey (1997a), 'Corporate Governance, Competition Policy and Industrial Policy', *European Economic Review*, **41** (3–5), 797–805.

Aghion, P., C. Harris and J. Vickers (1997b), 'Competition and Growth with Step-by-step Innovation: An Example', *European Economic Review*, **41** (3–5), 771–82.

Aghion, P. and P. Howitt (1992), 'A Model of Growth through Creative Destruction', *Econometrica*, **60**, 323–51.

Aghion, P. and P. Howitt (1998), *Endogenous Growth Theory*, Cambridge, MA: MIT Press.

Blundell, R., R. Griffith and J. Van Reenen (1995), 'Dynamic Count Data Models of Technological Innovation', *Economic Journal*, **105** (429), 333–44.

Caballero, R.J. and A.B. Jaffe (1993), 'How High Are the Giant's Shoulders: Empirical Assessment of Knowledge Spillover and Creative Destruction in a Model of Economic Growth', in O.J. Blanchard and S. Fischer (eds), *NBER Macroeconomics Annual 1993*, Cambridge, MA: MIT Press.

Cohen, W.M. and R.C. Levin (1989), 'Empirical Studies of Innovation and Market Structure', in R. Schmalensee and R.D. Willig (eds), *Handbook of Industrial Organization*, **II**, New York: Elsevier.

Economides, N. (1993), 'Quality Variations in the Circular Model of Variety Differentiated Products', *Regional Science and Urban Economics*, **23**, 235–57.

Eicher, T.S. (1996), 'Interaction between Endogenous Human Capital and Technological Change', *Review of Economic Studies*, **63**, 127–44.

Eicher, T.S. and S.J. Turnovsky (1999), 'A Generalized Model of Economic Growth', *Economic Journal*, **109**, 394–415.

Grossman, Gene M. and Elhanan Helpman (eds) (1991), *Innovation and Growth in the Global Economy*, Cambridge, MA: MIT Press.

Jones, C.I. (1995a), 'R&D-based Models of Economic Growth', *Journal of Political Economy*, **103**, 759–84.

Jones, C.I. (1995b), 'Time Series Tests of Endogenous Growth Models', *Quarterly Journal of Economics*, **110**, 495–525.

Kletzer, K. (1997), 'Growth with Endogenous Product Innovation and Differentiation', University of California Santa Cruz Working Paper, Santa Cruz, CA.

Kletzer, L.G. (1998), 'Job Displacement', *Journal of Economic Perspectives*, **12** (1), 115–36.

Kortum, S.S. (1993), 'Equilibrium R&D and the Patent – R&D Ratio: US Evidence', *American Economic Review*, **81**, 450–57.

Lai, E.L.C. (1997), 'Product Cycles with Endogenous Cost of Imitation', Vanderbilt University Working Paper, Nashville, TN.

Lai, E.L.C. (1998), 'International Intellectual Property Rights Protection and the Rate of Product Innovation', *Journal of Development Economics*, **55** (1), 133–53.

Levin, R.C., W.M. Cohen and D.C. Mowery (1985), 'R&D Appropriability, Opportunity and the Market Structure', *American Economic Review Proceedings*, **75**, 20–24.

Lucas, R.E. (1988), 'On the Mechanics of Economic Development', *Journal of Monetary Economics*, **22** (1), 3–42.

Nickell, S.J. (1996), 'Competition and Corporate Performance', *Journal of Political Economy*, **104** (4), 724–46.

Nickell, S.J., D. Nicolitasas and N. Dryden (1997), 'What Makes Firms Perform Well?', *European Economic Review*, **41** (3–5), 783–96.

Romer, P.M. (1990), 'Endogenous Technological Change', *Journal of Political Economy*, **98**, 71–102.

Scherer, F.M. (1967), 'Market Structure and the Employment of Scientists and Engineers', *American Economic Review*, **57**, 524–31.

Segerstrom, P.S. (1998), 'Endogenous Growth without Scale Effects', *American Economic Review*, **88**, 1290–1310.

Smulders, S. and T. van de Klundert (1995), 'Imperfect Competition, Concentration and Growth with Firm-specific R&D', *European Economic Review*, **39**, 139–60.

Young, A. (1998), 'Growth without Scale Effects', *Journal of Political Economy*, **106**, 41–63.

3. Human Capital Formation and Patterns of Growth with Multiple Equilibria

Kazuo Mino

1. INTRODUCTION

This chapter studies the relation between patterns of long-term economic growth and indeterminacy of equilibrium in an endogenous growth model with human capital formation. By introducing sector-specific externalities and a non-separable utility function into the Lucas–Uzawa model, we show that multiple balanced growth equilibria and indeterminacy of converging paths may emerge even in the absence of social increasing returns. Our results indicate that the standard endogenous growth model with small modifications would be useful to consider the reason why we often observe diverse growth performances among countries with similar economic environments.

This chapter examines a model of endogenous growth with multiple equilibria. Our main concern is to demonstrate that growth models with multiple converging paths may present a useful analytical framework to consider various growth patterns among countries that have similar economic environments. Of course, it is not novel to use growth models with multiple equilibria for describing diverse growth patterns. The presence of low-growth trap generated by multiplicity of long-run equilibria has been a popular idea in development economics. In particular, the argument about 'history versus expectations' emphasized by Krugman (1991) and Matsuyama (1991) has been discussed extensively. A common feature in this class of study is that indeterminacy holds under the assumption of a strong degree of increasing returns.[1] However, the recent empirical investigations suggest that the degree of increasing returns may not be so large as many theoretical studies have assumed. This implies that the exposition of non-convergence of per capita income and diverse patterns of growth based on indeterminacy of equilibrium would be empirically dubious.

In this chapter we demonstrate that the presence of increasing returns is not necessary for generating indeterminacy of equilibrium. By using one of the prototype models of endogenous growth, we show that multiple equilibria and complex patterns of transitional dynamics can emerge even under social constant returns. The main purpose of examining such a model is to emphasize that we do not need extreme assumptions to show diverse growth performances among countries with similar technologies and preferences. If we make a small modification of the base model in which equilibrium should be unique, the model will display various patterns of growth dynamics.

More specifically, we analyze a generalized version of the two-sector endogenous growth models *à la* Lucas (1988). We show that if the utility function of the representative family is not additively separable between consumption and leisure and if there are sector-specific externalities, then the Lucas model may produce indeterminacy of equilibrium even if technologies of the final good and the new human capital production sectors satisfy social constant returns. In order to clarify the analysis, we impose specific conditions on the parameter values involved in the model. This enables us to examine the global dynamic behavior of the model. We demonstrate that in this specific case the balanced growth equilibrium may be locally indeterminate. Additionally, the model may involve dual balanced growth equilibria. If the economy involves dual long-run equilibria, the balanced growth equilibrium with a higher growth rate is locally determinate, while the other with a lower growth rate may be locally indeterminate. In this case, the global dynamics of the model economy is rather complex: under the same initial condition, the identical economies will follow completely different growth processes depending on expectations of the economic agents.

In the existing literature, Benhabib and Perli (1994) and Xie (1994) explore indeterminacy in the Lucas model. Xie (1994) presents a detailed analysis of transitional dynamics in the presence of indeterminacy by setting specific conditions on parameter values of the model. Since he presents a model without labor–leisure choice, indeterminacy needs strong increasing returns. Benhabib and Perli (1994) consider endogenous labor supply and show that indeterminacy can be established with a relatively small degree of increasing returns. They use an additively separable utility function, so that indeterminacy stems from a specific production structure assumed in their model. In contrast to these contributions, this chapter emphasizes the role of preference structure in generating indeterminacy.

It is to be noted that Benhabib et al. (1999) and Mino (2001) also examine indeterminacy in the two-sector endogenous growth models with social constant returns. A key assumption in their models is that both the final good and the new human capital-producing sectors use human as well as physical capital. In this setting, they show that local indeterminacy holds, if the final good sector is more human capital intensive than the new human capital producing sector from the private perspective but it is more physical capital intensive from the social perspective.[2] Since the Lucas model used in this chapter assumes that the education sector employs human capital alone, there is no factor intensity reversal between the social and the private technologies (the final good sector always uses a more physical capital-intensive technology than the education sector). Therefore, the cause of indeterminacy with social constant returns in this chapter comes mainly from the preference structure rather than from the production technology emphasized by Benhabib et al. (1999) and Mino (2001).[3]

The rest of the chapter is organized as follows. Section 2 sets up the model. Section 3 derives the dynamical system and examines local dynamics. Based on the simplified model, Section 4 characterizes global dynamics and presents some economic implications of our main results. Section 5 points out the limitation of our analysis and the issues to be explored to strengthen the empirical plausibility of our claims.

2 THE MODEL

2.1 Production

Consider a competitive economy with two production sectors. The first sector produces a final good that can be used either for consumption or for investment on physical capital. The production technology is given by:

$$Y_1 = K^{\alpha} H_1^{\beta_1} \bar{K}_1^{\varepsilon} \bar{H}_1^{\phi_1}, \quad \alpha, \beta_1 > 0, \qquad \alpha + \beta_1 + \varepsilon + \phi_1 = 1, \tag{3.1}$$

where Y_1 denotes the final good, K is stock of physical capital and H_1 is human capital devoted to the final good production. $\bar{K}^{\varepsilon}$ and $\bar{H}_1^{\phi_1}$ represent sector-specific externalities associated with physical and human capital employed in this sector.[4] The key assumption in Human Capital Formation and Patterns of Growth with Multiple Equilibria 63 is that the production technology is socially constant returns to scale. The second sector is an education sector that produces new human capital. Following the Lucas – Uzawa setting, we assume that new human capital production needs human capital alone and its technology is specified as:

$$Y_2 = \gamma H_1^{\beta_2} \bar{H}_2^{\phi_2}, \qquad \gamma, \beta_2, \phi_2 > 0, \qquad \beta_2 + \phi_2 = 1. \tag{3.2}$$

Here, Y_2 is newly produced human capital, H_2 is the stock of human capital used in the education sector, and $\bar{H}_2^{\phi_2}$ stands for sector-specific externalities. Again, the production technology of new human capital is exhibit social constant returns.

The firms in each sector maximize their profits under given external effects. Thus the value of marginal product of each private capital is equal to its nominal rent:

$$R = p_1 \alpha K^{\alpha-1} H_1^{\beta_1} \bar{K}_1^{\varepsilon} \bar{H}_1^{\phi_1} \tag{3.3}$$

and

$$W = p_1 \beta_1 K^{\alpha} H_1^{\beta_1 - 1} \bar{K}_1^{\varepsilon} \bar{H}_1^{\phi_1} = p_2 \gamma \beta_2 H_2^{\beta_2 - 1} \bar{H}_2^{\phi_2}, \tag{3.4}$$

where R, W, p_1 and p_2, respectively, denote the nominal rent on physical capital, the nominal rent on human capital, the price of final good and the price of new human capital. Note that since the private technologies exhibit decreasing returns, the firms may earn positive profits. We assume that entire stocks of physical and human capital are owned by the households so that the profits are distributed back to them.[5]

2.2 The Household

The representative household maximizes a discounted sum of utilities:

$$U = \int_0^{\infty} u(C,l) e^{-\rho t} dt, \quad \rho > 0,$$

where C is consumption and l is the length of leisure time. We specify the instantaneous utility function as follows:[6]

$$u(C,l) = \begin{cases} \dfrac{\left[C\Lambda(l)\right]^{1-\sigma} - 1}{1-\sigma}, & \sigma > 0, \ \ \sigma \neq 1 \\ \ln C + \ln \Lambda(l), & \text{for } \sigma = 1. \end{cases}$$

Function $\Lambda(l)$ is assumed to be monotonically increasing and strictly concave in l. We also assume that:

$$\sigma \Lambda(l) \Lambda''(l) + (1 - 2\sigma) \Lambda' \ (l)^2 < 0. \tag{3.5}$$

This assumption, along with strict concavity of $\Lambda(l)$, ensures that $u(C,l)$ is strictly concave in C and l.

Since lH unit of human capital is not used for production activities, the wage income of the household is $W(1-l)H$. Hence, the flow budget constraint for the household is given by:

$$p_1\left(\dot{K}+\delta K\right)+p_2\left(\dot{H}+\eta H\right)+p_1 C=RK+W(1-l)H+\pi_1+\pi_2,$$

where δ and η are depreciation rates of physical and human capital, and π_i $(i=1,2)$ denotes the distributed profits earned by the ith sector. Define the total wealth of the household as:

$$A=p_1 K+p_2 H. \tag{3.6}$$

Then the flow budget constraint can be written as:

$$\begin{aligned}\dot{A}=&\left[\frac{R}{p_1}+\frac{\dot{p}_1}{p_1}-\delta\right]p_1 K\\&+\left[\frac{W(1-l)}{p_2}+\frac{\dot{p}_2}{p_2}-\eta\right]p_2 H+\pi_1+\pi_2-p_1 C.\end{aligned} \tag{3.7}$$

The household maximizes U subject to (3.6), (3.7) and the given initial level of wealth (A_0) by controlling C, l, K and H. In so doing, the household takes sequences of prices and profits, $\{p_1(t), p_2(t), R(t), W(t), \pi_1(t), \pi_2(t)\}_{t=o}^{\infty}$, as given.

The current-value Hamiltonian for the household's optimization problem can be set as:

$$\begin{aligned}\mathcal{H}=&\frac{\left[C\Lambda(l)\right]^{1-\sigma}-1}{1-\sigma}\\&+q\left[\left(\frac{R}{p_1}+\frac{\dot{p}_1}{p_1}-\delta\right)p_1 K+\left[\frac{W(1-l)}{p_2}+\frac{\dot{p}_2}{p_2}-\eta\right]p_2 H+\pi_1+\pi_2-p_1 C\right].\\&+\lambda\left(A-p_1 K-p_2 H\right).\end{aligned}$$

Under the given sequences of prices and distributed profits, the necessary conditions for an optimum are the following:

$$C^{-\sigma}\Lambda(l)^{1-\sigma} = qp_1 \tag{3.8}$$

$$C^{1-\sigma}\Lambda'(l)\Lambda(l)^{-\sigma} = qWH \tag{3.9}$$

$$q\left(\frac{R}{p_1} - \frac{\dot{p}_1}{p_1} - \delta\right) = \lambda \tag{3.10}$$

$$q\left[\frac{W(1-l)}{p_2} - \frac{\dot{p}_2}{p_2} - \eta\right] = \lambda \tag{3.11}$$

and

$$\dot{q} = q\rho - \lambda, \tag{3.12}$$

together with (3.6), (3.7) and the transversality condition:

$$\lim_{t\to\infty} e^{-\rho t} qA = 0. \tag{3.13}$$

Note that (3.10) and (3.11) yield:

$$\frac{R}{p_1} + \frac{\dot{p}_1}{p_1} - \delta = \frac{W(1-l)}{p_2} + \frac{\dot{p}_2}{p_2} - \eta, \tag{3.14}$$

which shows the non-arbitrage condition between holding physical and human capital.

2.3 Market Equilibrium Conditions

The equilibrium conditions in product markets are given by:

$$Y_1 = C + \dot{K} + \delta K \tag{3.15}$$

and

$$Y_2 = \dot{H} + \eta H. \tag{3.16}$$

The full-employment condition for human capital is:

$$H_1 + H_2 + lH = H. \tag{3.17}$$

Denoting $H_1/H = v$, (3.1), (3.2), (3.15), (3.16) and (3.17) yield the accumulation equations of physical and human capital:

$$\dot{K} = K^{\alpha}(vH)^{\beta_1}\bar{K}^{\varepsilon}\bar{H}_1^{\phi_1} - C - \delta K \tag{3.18}$$

and

$$\dot{H} = \gamma(1 - v - l)^{\beta_2}H^{\beta_2}\bar{H}_2^{\phi_2} - \eta H. \tag{3.19}$$

3 GROWTH DYNAMICS

3.1 The Dynamical System

For analytical simplicity, the following discussion assumes that $\Lambda(l)$ is specified as:

$$\Lambda(l) = \exp\left(\frac{l^{1-\theta} - 1}{1-\theta}\right), \quad \theta > 0,\ \theta \neq 1, \tag{3.20}$$

where $\Lambda(l) = l$ for $\theta = 1$. Given this specification, when $\sigma = 1$, the instantaneous utility function becomes:

$$u(C,l) = \ln C + \frac{l^{1-\theta}}{1-\theta}.$$

Under this specification, the concavity condition (3.5) reduces to:

$$(1-\sigma)l^{1-\theta} - \sigma\theta < 0. \tag{3.21}$$

If we assume that the number of households is normalized to one, in equilibrium it holds that $\bar{K}(t) = K(t)$ and $\bar{H}_i(t) = H_i(t)$ $(i = 1,2)$ for all $t \geq 0$. Thus, keeping in mind that $\alpha + \beta_1 + \varepsilon + \phi_1 = 1$ and $\beta_2 + \phi_2 = 1$, (3.3), (3.4), (3.18) and (3.19), respectively, become:

$$R = p_1 \alpha K^{\alpha+\varepsilon-1} (vH) H^{1-(\alpha+\varepsilon)} \tag{3.3'}$$

$$W = p_1 \beta K^{\alpha+\varepsilon} (vH)^{-(\alpha+\varepsilon)} = p_2 \gamma \beta_2 \left[(1-v-l) H \right]^{-(\alpha+\varepsilon)} \tag{3.4'}$$

$$\dot{K} = K^{\alpha+\varepsilon} (vH)^{1-(\alpha+\varepsilon)} - C - \delta K \tag{3.18'}$$

and

$$\dot{H} = \gamma (1-v-l) H. \tag{3.19'}$$

Similarly, (3.8) and (3.9) yield:

$$\frac{C \Lambda'(l)}{\Lambda(l)} = \frac{p_2 \gamma \beta_2 H}{p_1}.$$

Given (3.20), the above becomes:

$$C = (p_2/p_1) \gamma \beta_2 l^{\theta} H. \tag{3.22}$$

Let us denote the factor intensity in the final good sector as $x = K/vH$. From (3.4) we obtain:

$$\frac{p_2}{p_1} = \frac{\beta_1}{\gamma \beta_2} x^{\alpha+\varepsilon}. \tag{3.23}$$

Equations (3.22) and (3.23) give $C = \beta_1 l^{\theta} x^{\alpha+\varepsilon} H$ Hence, using $x = K/vH$ and denoting the capital ratio by $K/H = k$, the commodity market equilibrium conditions (3.18′) and (3.19′) yield the following growth equations of capital stocks:

$$\frac{\dot{K}}{K} = x^{\alpha+\varepsilon-1} - \frac{\beta_1 l^{\theta} x^{\alpha+\varepsilon}}{k} - \delta \tag{3.18''}$$

and

$$\frac{\dot{H}}{H} = \gamma\left(1 - l - \frac{k}{x}\right) - \eta. \tag{3.19''}$$

On the other hand, (3.3′) and (3.4′) can be written as:

$$R/p_1 = \alpha x^{\alpha+\varepsilon-1}$$

and

$$W/p_2 = \gamma\beta_2(1-l).$$

Using the expressions derived above and keeping in mind that $\delta = \eta$, (3.14) presents the following:

$$\frac{\dot{p}_2}{p_2} - \frac{\dot{p}_1}{p_1} = \alpha x^{\alpha+\varepsilon-1} - \gamma\beta_2(1-l). \tag{3.24}$$

As a result, in view of (3.18″), (3.19″) and (3.24), we find that $x(=K/vH)$ changes according to:

$$\frac{\dot{x}}{x} = \frac{1}{\alpha+\varepsilon}\left[\eta - \delta + \alpha x^{\alpha+\varepsilon-1} - \beta_2\gamma(1-l)\right]. \tag{3.25}$$

From (3.20), equation (3.8) is expressed as:

$$C^{-\sigma}\exp\left[(1-\sigma)\frac{l^{1-\theta}-1}{1-\theta}\right] = qp_1.$$

Substituting (3.22) into the above and taking time derivatives of both sides, we obtain:

$$\left[(1-\sigma)l^{1-\theta}-\sigma\theta\right]\frac{\dot{l}}{l}=(1-\sigma)\frac{\dot{p}_1}{p_1}+\sigma\left(\frac{\dot{p}_2}{p_2}+\frac{\dot{H}}{H}\right)+\frac{\dot{q}}{q}.$$

This equation, together with (3.10), (3.12) and (3.24), yield the dynamic equation of leisure time, l:

$$\frac{\dot{l}}{l}=\Delta(l)\cdot\left\{\alpha(1-\sigma)x^{\alpha+\varepsilon-1}+\sigma\gamma\frac{k}{x}-\sigma\gamma(1-\beta_2)(1-l)-\rho-(1-\sigma)\delta\right\} \tag{3.26}$$

where $\Delta(l)=\left[\sigma\theta-(1-\sigma)l^{1-\theta}\right]^{-1}$, which has a positive value under the concavity assumption (3.21). Finally, (3.18″) and (3.19″) mean that the dynamic equations for the behavior of $k\ (=K/H)$ is given by:

$$\frac{\dot{k}}{k}=x^{\alpha+\varepsilon-1}-\frac{\beta_1 l^{\theta}x^{\alpha+\varepsilon}}{k}-\delta+\eta-\gamma\left(1-l-\frac{k}{x}\right). \tag{3.27}$$

Consequently, we find that (3.25), (3.26) and (3.27) constitute a complete dynamic system with respect to $k(=K/H)$, $x(=K/vH)$ and l.

3.2 A Simplified System

Since the complete dynamic system derived above is rather complex, three-dimensional one, it is hard to conduct a precise analysis of transition dynamics. A conventional strategy to deal with such a situation is to linearize the system around the steady state and to focus on the local behavior of the model. In what follows, rather than concentrating on the local analysis, we impose specific conditions on parameter values in order to clarify the global dynamics of the model. First, we assume that $\theta=1$ (so that $\Lambda(l)=l$). Second, following Xie's (1994) idea, we focus on the special case where $\sigma=\alpha$. As shown below, these assumptions enable us to reduce the three-dimensional dynamic system to a two-dimensional one.[7] Finally, we also assume that $\delta=\eta$, that is, physical and human capital depreciate at the identical rate. This assumption is made only for notational simplicity and the main results obtained below are not altered when $\delta\neq\eta$.

The assumptions $\sigma=\alpha$ and $\theta=1$ simplify the argument as the following can be held:

Lemma 1 If $\sigma = \alpha$ and $\theta = 1$, then the consumption–capital ratio, C/K, is constant over time even out of the steady state.

Proof Let us define $z = \beta_1 x^{\alpha+\varepsilon} l/k\left(= C/K\right)$. If $\sigma = \alpha$ and $\theta = 1$, then (3.25) becomes:

$$\frac{\dot{x}}{x} = x^{\alpha+\varepsilon-1} - z - \gamma(1-l) + \gamma\frac{k}{x}.$$

Therefore, keeping in mind that $\delta = \eta$, from (3.26) and (3.27) we obtain:

$$\frac{\dot{z}}{z} = (\alpha+\varepsilon)\frac{\dot{x}}{x} + \frac{\dot{l}}{l} - \frac{\dot{k}}{k} = z - \frac{\alpha + (1-\alpha)\delta}{\alpha}.$$

Since this system is completely unstable, on the perfect-foresight competitive equilibrium path the following should hold for all $t \geq 0$:

$$z\left(= \frac{C}{K}\right) = \frac{\rho + (1-\alpha)\delta}{\alpha}.$$

Hence, consumption and physical capital always change at the same rate during the transition process.

The above result means that on the equilibrium path x is related to k and l in such a way that:

$$x = \left\{\left[\frac{\alpha + (1-\alpha)\delta}{\alpha}\right]\frac{k}{l}\right\}^{\frac{1}{\alpha+\varepsilon}}. \tag{3.28}$$

Substituting this into (3.26) and (3.27), we obtain the following set of differential equations:

$$\frac{\dot{k}}{k} = \left(\lambda\frac{k}{l}\right)^{1-\frac{1}{\alpha+\varepsilon}} + \frac{\gamma}{\lambda}\left(\lambda\frac{k}{l}\right)^{1-\frac{1}{\alpha+\varepsilon}} l - \gamma(1-l) - \lambda$$

and

$$\frac{\dot{l}}{l} = (1-\alpha)\left(\lambda\frac{k}{l}\right)^{1-\frac{1}{\alpha+\varepsilon}} + \frac{\gamma}{\lambda}\left(\lambda\frac{k}{l}\right)^{1-\frac{1}{\alpha+\varepsilon}} l - \gamma(1-\beta_2)(1-l) - \lambda.$$

where $\lambda = \left[\rho + (1-\alpha)\delta\right]/\alpha$. To simplify further, denote:

$$q = (\lambda k/l)^{1-\frac{1}{\alpha+\varepsilon}}. \tag{3.29}$$

Then the above system may be rewritten in the following manner:

$$\frac{\dot{q}}{q} = \left(\frac{1-\alpha-\varepsilon}{\alpha+\varepsilon}\right)\left[\gamma\beta_2(1-l) - \alpha q\right] \tag{3.30}$$

$$\frac{\dot{l}}{l} = \left(1-\alpha+\frac{\gamma}{\lambda}l\right)q - \gamma(1-\beta_2)(1-l) - \lambda. \tag{3.31}$$

Under the conditions where $\sigma = \alpha$ and $\theta = 1$, this system is equivalent to the original dynamic equations given by (3.25), (3.26) and (3.27).

3.3 The Balanced Growth Equilibrium

First, consider the steady state in (3.30) and (3.31). When $\dot{q} = \dot{l} = 0$, (3.29) shows that k stays constant over time. Thus from (3.28) x does not change in the steady state, which means that $v = x/k$ stays constant as well. Accordingly, in the steady state K, H, C and Y grow at a common, constant rate of:

$$g = \gamma\left(1-\bar{l}-\bar{v}\right) - \delta,$$

where $\bar{l}$ and $\bar{v}\left(=\bar{x}/k\right)$ denote steady-state values of l and v.

As for the existence of the balanced growth equilibrium, we find the following:

Proposition 1 Under $\sigma = 1$ and $\theta = 1$, there exists a unique, feasible balanced growth equilibrium if and only if:

$$\gamma(\beta_2 - \alpha) - \rho - (1-\alpha)\delta > 0. \tag{3.32}$$

and there may exist dual balanced growth equilibria if:

$$\gamma(\beta_2 - \alpha) - \rho - (1-\alpha)\delta < 0. \tag{3.33}$$

Proof Condition $\dot{q} = 0$ in (3.30) yields $q = (\gamma\beta_2 l\alpha)(1-l)$. Thus conditions $\dot{l} = \dot{q} = 0$ are established if the following equation is satisfied:

$$\xi(l) = \frac{\gamma\beta_2}{\alpha}\left(1 - \alpha + \frac{\gamma}{\lambda}l\right)(1-l) - \gamma(1-\beta_2)(1-l) - \lambda = 0.$$

Note that:

$$\begin{aligned} \xi(0) &= (\gamma\beta_2/\alpha)(1-\alpha) - \gamma(1-\beta_2) - \lambda \\ &= (1/\alpha)\left[\gamma(\beta_2 - \alpha) - \rho - (1-\alpha)\delta\right] \\ \xi(1) &= -(1/\alpha)\left[\rho + (1-\alpha)\delta\right] < 0. \end{aligned}$$

If condition (3.32) is met, $\xi(0) > 0$ and $\xi(l)$ is monotonically decreasing with l for $l \in [0,1]$. Hence, $\xi(l) = 0$ has a unique solution in between 0 and 1. If (3.33) is satisfied, then $\xi(0) < 0$. Since $\xi(l) = 0$ is a quadratic equation, if $\xi(l) = 0$ has solutions for $l \in [0,1]$, there are two solutions.

To consider numerical examples, suppose that $\alpha = \sigma = 0.3$, $\varepsilon = 0.1$, $\beta_2 = 0.7$, $\rho = 0.03$, $\delta = \eta = 0.04$ and $\gamma = 0.2$. Those parameter magnitudes satisfy (3.32) so that the balanced growth equilibrium is uniquely determined. Given those values, we find that the steady-state level of leisure time is $\bar{l} = 0.3731$ and the balanced growth rate is $\bar{g} = 0.0151$. If we set β_2 and γ as 0.6 and 0.15, respectively, and keep the other parameter values at the same levels shown above, we see that condition (3.33) is met. In this case, the steady-state values of l are 0.118 and 0.512. In the steady state with the lower l the balanced growth rate is 0.083, while it is 0.0021 at the steady state with the higher l.[8]

3.4 Local Determinacy and Indeterminacy

Before analyzing the dynamic properties of (3.30) and (3.31), let us relate the stability conditions of the simplified system to those of the original system consisting of (3.25), (3.26) and (3.27). First, note that (3.29) gives the relationship between q, l and k. Since the initial value of k $(= K/H)$ is predetermined, (3.29) implies that the initial levels of q and l cannot be freely selected. For example, if the steady-state of (3.30) and (3.31) where $\dot{q} = \dot{l} = 0$ is a source, then the original system is totally unstable. This is because, in view of (3.29), there is no way to select the initial values of q and l at their steady-state levels simultaneously, unless the initial value of k happens to be its steady-state level, $\bar{k}$. If (3.30) and (3.31) exhibit a saddle-point property, there (at least) locally exists a one-dimensional stable manifold around the steady state. Hence, the relation between q and l on the stable manifold can be expressed as $q = q(l)$. By depicting phase diagrams of (3.30) and (3.31), it is easy to confirm that if the stationary equilibrium is a saddle point, the stable arms have negative slopes. Thus we find that $q'(l) < 0$ (see Figures 3.1, 3.2 and 3.3). Substituting $q = q(l)$ into (3.29), we obtain:

$$k = lq(l)^{\frac{\alpha+\varepsilon}{\alpha+\varepsilon-1}}.$$

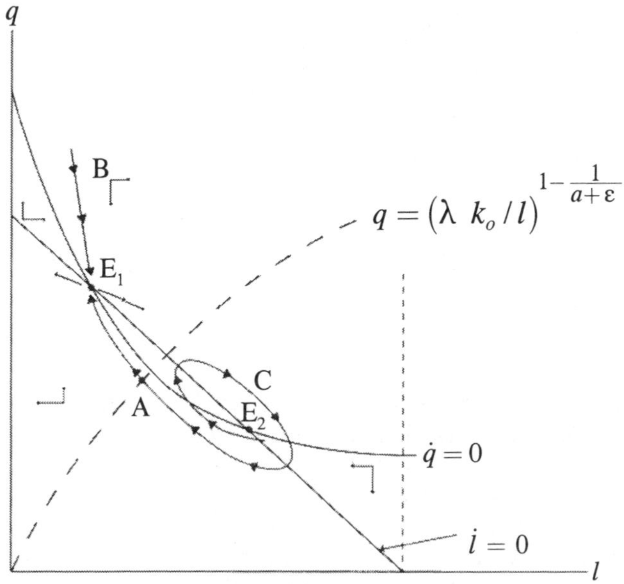

Figure 3.1 *The high-growth equilibrium (point* E_1*) is a saddle point and the low-growth equilibrium (point* E_2*) is a source*

Since the right-hand side of the equation monotonically increases with l, the relation is invertible and thus we have:

$$l = l(k),\ l'(k) > 0. \tag{3.34}$$

Using (3.25), (3.27) and (3.34), we obtain a two-dimensional system with respect to x and k. It is easy to confirm that this reduced system has a saddlepoint property, which means that the original system exhibits determinacy around the steady-state equilibrium.

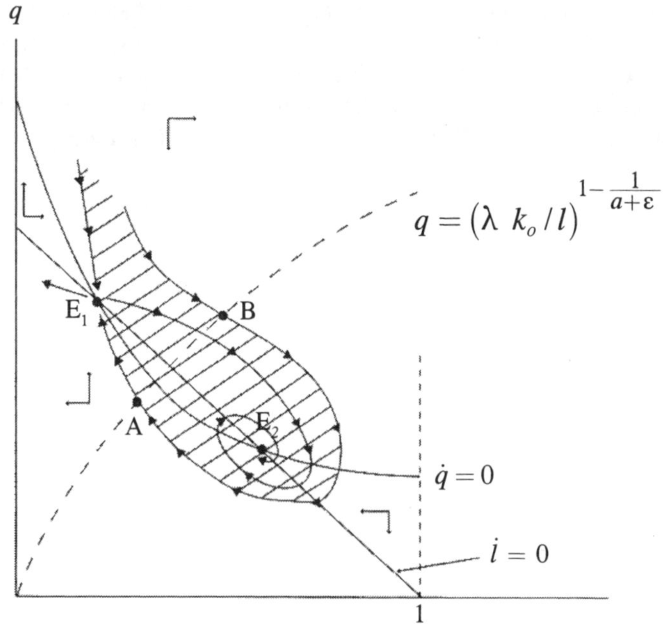

Figure 3.2 The high-growth equilibrium (point E_1*) is a saddle point and the low-growth equilibrium (point* E_2*) is a sink*

In contrast, suppose that the steady state of (3.30) and (3.31) is a source and hence there is a continuum of converging paths. In this case, unlike (3.34), the relation between k and l on the converging trajectories is not uniquely determined. This shows that, under a given initial value of k, a unique converging path cannot be selected in the original system either.

To sum up, if (3.30) and (3.31) involve a feasible steady state and it is a saddle point, then the original system consisting of (3.25), (3.26) and (3.27) satisfies local determinacy. In contrast, if the steady state of (3.30) and (3.31) is asymptotically stable, then (3.25), (3.26) and (3.27) exhibit local indeter minacy. More precisely, by inspection of the eigenvalues of the coefficient matrix of (3.30) and (3.31) linearized around the steady state, we find the following results:

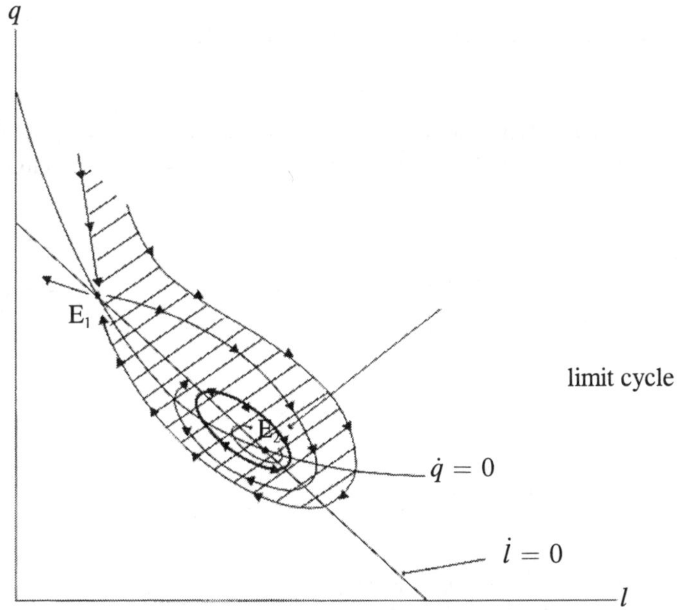

Figure 3.3 The presence of a limit cycle around the low-growth equilibrium

Proposition 2 Suppose that $\sigma = \alpha$ and $\theta = 1$. Then the balanced growth equilibrium is locally determinate, if and only if:

$$\beta_2 - \alpha + \frac{\alpha\gamma\beta_2}{\rho + (1-\alpha)\delta}(2\bar{l} - 1) < 0, \tag{3.35}$$

while it is locally indeterminate, if and only if the following holds:

$$\left[1 - \beta_2 - \frac{\beta_2(\alpha + \varepsilon - 1)}{\alpha + \varepsilon}\right]\bar{l} + \frac{\beta_2(\alpha + \varepsilon - 1)}{\alpha + \varepsilon} + \frac{\rho + (1-\alpha)\delta}{\alpha} < 0 \tag{3.36}$$

and

$$\beta_2 - \alpha + \frac{\alpha\gamma\beta_2}{\rho + (1-\alpha)\delta}\left(2\bar{l} - 1\right) > 0, \tag{3.37}$$

where $\bar{l}$ denotes the steady-state value of leisure time.

Proof Linearizing (3.30) and (3.31) at the stationary point and using the steady-state conditions that satisfy $\dot{l} = \dot{q} = 0$, we find that signs of the trace and the determinant of the coefficient matrix of the linearized system fulfill:

$$\begin{aligned} &\operatorname{sign}(\text{trace}) \\ &= \operatorname{sign}\left\{\left[1 - \beta_2 - \frac{\beta_2(\alpha + \varepsilon - 1)}{\alpha + \varepsilon}\right]\bar{l} + \frac{\beta_2(\alpha + \varepsilon - 1)}{\alpha + \varepsilon} + \frac{\rho + (1-\alpha)\delta}{\alpha}\right\} \end{aligned}$$

and

$$\operatorname{sign}(\det) = \operatorname{sign}\left\{\beta_2 - \alpha + \frac{\alpha\gamma\beta_2}{\rho + (1-\alpha)\delta}\left(2\bar{l} - 1\right)\right\}.$$

If (3.36) and (3.37) hold, then the trace and the determinant, respectively, have negative and positive values. This means that the linearized system has two stable eigenvalues. On the other hand, if (3.35) holds, the system involves one positive and one negative eigenvalue, while there are two eigenvalues with positive real parts when (3.36) holds but (3.37) does not. In the former, the steady state is locally determinate and in the latter it is totally unstable. Thus the original system consisting of (3.25), (3.26) and (3.27) satisfies local determinacy under (3.35), while it is locally indeterminate under (3.36) and (3.37).

Using the same examples shown in Section 3.3, we find that when $\alpha = \sigma = 0.3$, $\beta_2 = 0.7$, $\rho = 0.03$, $\delta = 0.04$ and $\gamma = 0.2$, in the unique balanced growth equilibrium, we find that (3.36) and (3.37) hold. Thus the balanced growth path is locally indeterminate. In the presence of dual balanced growth equilibria that holds when $\alpha = \sigma = 0.3$, $\beta_2 = 0.6$, $\rho = 0.03$, $\delta = 0.04$ and $\gamma = 0.15$, it is shown that the balanced growth path with a lower l satisfies (3.35), while that with a higher l fulfills (3.36) and (3.37). As a consequence, the steady state with a higher growth rate is locally determinate, but the other steady state with a lower growth rate exhibits local indeterminacy

4 PATTERNS OF GROWTH

4.1 Global Dynamics

Since interesting global dynamics can be shown in the case of dual balanced growth equilibria, in this sector we assume that system (3.30) and (3.31) has two steady states.[9] In the presence of dual steady states, we find:

Proposition 3 If the system has dual steady states, it holds that: (i) the steady state with a higher growth rate is locally determinate; and (ii) the steady state with a lower growth rate is locally intermediate if (3.36) and (3.37) are satisfied, while it is totally unstable if (3.36) holds but (3.37) does not.

It is easy to confirm the above proposition by depicting the phase diagrams of (3.30) and (3.31). Figure 3.1, 3.2 and 3.3 display typical phase diagrams when there are dual steady-state equilibria. First, we should confirm that in these figures, the stationary point with a lower l and a higher q (point E_1 in the figures) attains a higher growth rate. To see this, first note that from (3.34) the steady-state level of k increases with l. On the other hand, (3.28) and (3.29) give:

$$\bar{v} = \frac{\bar{x}}{\bar{k}} = \lambda^{\frac{1}{\alpha+\varepsilon}} \left[\frac{\alpha + (1-\alpha)\delta}{\alpha} \right]^{-\frac{1}{\alpha+\varepsilon}} \bar{k}\bar{q}^{\frac{1}{\alpha+\varepsilon}-1}.$$

Since $0 < \alpha + \varepsilon < 1$, the above means that a lower l and a higher q yield a lower $\bar{v}$. As a result, the balanced growth rate, $g = \gamma(1 - \bar{l} - \bar{v}) - \delta$, attained at equilibrium E_1 is higher than that at E_2 which associate with a higher l and a lower q. We see that (3.35) and (3.26), respectively, hold at E_1 and E_2. In addition, E_2 is a sink under (3.37) and it is a source if (3.37) does not hold.

In Figure 3.1, the steady state with a lower growth rate is a source, so that there is no converging path around E_2. Since E_1 is a saddle point, there are two converging paths towards E_1 Given the initial level of capital ratio, k_0, the economy's initial position is on the broken line which expresses equation (3.29). In the figure, the initial levels of l and q are uniquely determined by point A on the converging saddle path. If the economy starts from point A, it converges monotonically towards E_1. During the transition, l decreases and q increases monotonically. Thus, as pointed out above, v also decreases monotonically in the transition process, which means that the accumulation rate of human capital continues increasing. In contrast, if the economy starts from point B, then l and q, respectively, increases and decreases on the converging path. Hence, the accumulation rate of human capital decreases monotonically during the transition. The monotonic convergence, however, does not hold, if the economy starts from a point close to E_2 (point C, for example).

Figure 3.2 illustrates the case where the low-growth steady state is a sink: there is a continuum of converging paths around E_2. The phase diagram indicates that not only local indeterminacy but also global indeterminacy can be observed in this case. If the initial level of k gives the broken line (equation (3.29)), any point between A and B would be a feasible initial position of the economy. For example, if point A is the initial point, the economy converges to the higher-growth steady state monotonically. But the economy may leave from point B towards E_1 If this is the case, the converging process is not monotonic (the growth rate of human capital first rises and then decreases during the transition towards point E_1). However, taking the starting position on point A or B is almost coincidental, if the initial position of the economy is randomly chosen: there are a continuum of feasible initial points on the line between A and B that lead the economy to the low-growth steady state, E_2. Unless the agents anticipate that their destiny will be the high-growth steady state, the economy almost always converges to the low-growth steady state. In this sense, the dynamic system exhibits global as well as local indeterminacy.

Such global indeterminacy may emerge even though the low-growth steady state is not locally indeterminate. In Figure 3.3, the low-growth steady state, E_2, is again assumed to be totally unstable. Thus unless the initial position is E_2 itself, any trajectory around E_2 will diverge. We should note that in this figure one of the unstable saddle paths diverging from the high-growth steady state, E_1, tends to converge to the low-growth steady state. However, since E_2 is a source, the unstable saddle path cannot converge to E_2. In addition, we see that any path starting from the hatched area will remain in this area. Consequently, in view of the Poincaré–Bendixson theorem, there exists at least one stable limit cycle around E_2. In other words, any trajectory within the hatched area eventually converges to the stable limit cycle. This indicates that the destiny of the economy is either the balanced growth equilibrium with a higher growth rate or the cyclical growth path around the low-growth steady state. Again, the dynamic system displays global indeterminacy.

4.2 Implications

The graphical analyses conducted above make three points. First, when there are dual steady states, two economies that have the identical technology and preference may display completely different growth performances even though they start with the same levels of physical and human capital. Additionally, even when the economy converges to the same steady state that is locally determinate, the convergence trajectory may not be monotonic. If the economy starts from the position such as point A in Figure 3.1, the economy monotonically converges to the balanced growth equilibrium as does the standard Lucas model. However, when the economy starts from point C in Figure 3.1, the growth rate of human capital first decreases and then increases up to the higher balanced growth rate. Hence, when we focus on the determinate equilibrium, the long-term growth pattern would depend on the initial level of capital stocks. It is to be noted that this kind of non-monotonic converging behavior of human capital formation has already been pointed out by Xie (1994).

Second, in the case of dual steady states, the possibility of realization of the low-growth steady state is much higher than that of the high-growth steady state. This is because, if the low-growth steady state is locally indeterminate (or locally unstable but there exists a stable cycle around it) and if the initial position of the economy is randomly selected, the economy will almost always converge to the steady state with a lower growth rate. This means that the destiny of the economy can be the steady state with a higher growth rate only when the economic agents share an optimistic view about the future of their economy. In other words, the conventional growth-promoting policies would not be enough to make the economy converge to the high-growth steady state.

Third, our result shows that the economy converging to the low-growth steady state tends to be more volatile than the economy that converges to the steady state with a higher growth rate. Since the high-growth steady state is locally determinate, the economy converging to it will not display fluctuation if there is no fundamental, technological shock. In contrast, when the low-growth steady state is locally indeterminate, we may find sunspot fluctuations caused by extrinsic uncertainty that affects the agents' expectations. Although the relation between volatility and growth is still a controversial issue in the empirical literature, our discussion suggests that the relation between growth and volatility would not be examined properly if the researchers presume that the fundamental shocks are only sources for economic fluctuations.

In his much cited essay on the growth miracle of East Asian countries, Lucas (1993) states that multiplicity of equilibria may present a useful insight as to why countries with similar economic conditions can display diverse growth performances in the long run. As a typical example, he mentions comparative growth performances between South Korea and the Philippines. In the early 1960s, per capita income of both countries was about the same. In addition, they shared many common features such as population size, degree of urbanization, rates of school enrollment and the like. After three decades, the per capita income of South Korea became more than three times as large as that of the Philippines. If we stick to the idea that economies with the same economic conditions must follow the same growth process, we should seek more fundamental differences between South Korea and the Philippines that economic theory usually dismisses, that is, the differences in political stability, religion, climate, social atmosphere and so on. In contrast, if we consider the possibility of multiple equilibria, we may explain the reason for income divergence without considering those non-economic conditions. Obviously, we cannot claim that divergence of per capita income between South Korea and the Philippines has been generated by multiplicity of equilibrium alone. However, from the viewpoint of economic theory, it is insightful to use the growth models with multiple equilibria when we explore the reasons as to why some East Asian countries have attained extremely good performances in growth but the countries in South Asia with similar economic fundamentals have shown relatively poor growth performances.

5 CONCLUDING REMARKS

This chapter has examined indeterminacy of equilibrium in a two-sector model of endogenous growth with human capital formation. We have shown that if the utility function of the household is not additively separable between consumption and labor, the model economy may exhibit indeterminacy of equilibrium even under social constant returns. In particular, under a specific set of parameter values, the model economy involves dual steady states and global indeterminacy may emerge.

An obvious limitation of our discussion is that the main analytical results concerning the global dynamics of the economy hinge on the particular specification of the parameter values involved in the model. In particular, we have assumed that $\sigma = \alpha$, which means that the intertemporal elasticity of substitution in the felicity function, $1/\sigma$, is close to 3.0 if we assume that the income share of physical capital, α, is around 0.35. Namely, establishing indeterminacy under social constant returns requires that the preference structure satisfies weak convexity. The foregoing studies on indeterminacy in growth models have generally shown that there exists a trade-off between non-convexity of production technology and convexity of preferences to hold indeterminacy: in order to find out indeterminacy conditions, the model with convex technology tends to need weak convexity of preferences, while the models with strong convex preferences should assume the presence of strong non-convexity of technology. As emphasized earlier, our model is free from the criticism claiming that the growth models with indeterminacy of equilibrium should assume an empirically implausible degree of increasing returns. On the other hand, the high degree of intertemporal substitutability of consumption assumed in our discussion would lack plausibility.[10]

We should, however, note that further generalization may weaken the restrictive assumptions in our model. For example, it has been known that introducing distortional taxes on factor income or endogenizing capital utilization can substantially lower the required degree of increasing returns in the models with indeterminacy. Those kinds of extension would also be useful to hold indeterminacy in the model of constant returns with weaker restrictions on the parameter magnitudes. As stated in the introduction of the chapter, our main purpose is to present an example demonstrating that complex dynamics may emerge in the standard models with small modifications. Hence, to make such a claim more convincing, further extensions of the model seem to be necessary. This is a relevant topic in future investigations.

NOTES

1. See, for example, Benhabib and Farmer (1994) and Boldrin and Rustichini (1994).
2. Since they assume that there is no labor–leisure choice, the balanced growth equilibrium is uniquely determined in Benhabib et al. (1999) and Mino (2001).
3. Pelloni and Waldmann (2000) emphasize the role of non-separable utility function for generating indeterminacy in a one-sector endogenous growth model based on Romer (1986). In a one-sector economy, endogenous growth can be sustained in the presence of a large degree of increasing returns, so that not only non-separability of utility function but also increasing returns are crucial for showing indeterminacy in Pelloni and Waldmann (2000).
4. The role of sector-specific externalities was first analyzed by Benhabib and Farmer (1996).
5. As pointed out by Benhabib and Farmer (1999), the presence of positive profits means that the production technology of an individual firm satisfies some type of increasing returns to prevent entry. The issue in this chapter is whether or not the aggregate technologies exhibit constant returns.
6. As is well known, if the utility function involves pure leisure time as an argument, the functional form should be the following in order to define feasible balanced growth equilibrium. Bennett and Farmer (1998) also introduce this form of utility function into the model in Benhabib and Farmer (1994). They reveal that the non-separable utility function reduces the degree of increasing returns that is necessary to produce indeterminacy. The similar result can be obtained, if we consider home production which needs capital as well as labor: see Perli (1998).
7. The key condition for simplification of the dynamic system is that $\sigma = \alpha$. The assumption $\theta = 1$ is not essential for our results but it is useful for analytical convenience.
8. Ladrón-de-Guevara et al. (1999) show that if labor–leisure choice is allowed in the Lucas model, multiple steady states could be obtained even without externalities. However, the Lucas model without externalities is an optimal growth model, and therefore indeterminacy is not the issue in their study.
9. Xie (1994) also conducts transitional analysis of the Lucas model with multiple equilibria. Since his model involves a unique steady state, patterns of dynamics are simpler than in our model.
10. If we use a simpler model that does not involve physical capital, we may obtain essentially the same conclusions shown in this chapter without assuming that $\sigma = \alpha$: see Mino (2001). Thus the main results in this chapter would be established for a wider class of parameter values.

REFERENCES

Benhabib, J. and R.E. Farmer (1994), 'Intermediacy and Growth', *Journal of Economic Theory*, **63**, 19–41.

Benhabib, J. and R.E. Farmer (1996), 'Indeterminacy and Sector Specific Externalities', *Journal of Monetary Economics*, **37**, 397–419.

Benhabib, J. and R.E. Farmer (1999), 'Indeterminacy and Sunspots in Macroeconomics', in J.B. Taylor and M. Woodford (eds), *Handbook of Macroeconomics*, **1**, Amsterdam: North-Holland, 387–443.

Benhabib, J., Q. Meng and K. Nishimura (1999), 'Indeterminacy under Constant Returns to Scale in Multisector Economies', *Econometrica*, **68**, 1541–8.

Benhabib, J. and R. Perli (1994), 'Uniqueness and Indeterminacy: Transitional Dynamics', *Journal of Economic Theory*, **63**, 113–42.

Bennett, R.L. and R.E. Farmer (1998), 'Indeterminacy with Nonseparable Utility', *Journal of Economic Theory*, **93**, 118–43.

Boldrin, M. and A. Rustichini (1994), 'Indeterminacy of Equilibria in Models with Infinitely-lived Agents and External Effects', *Econometrica*, **62**, 323–42.

Krugman, P. (1991), 'History versus Expectations', *Quarterly Journal of Economics*, **106**, 651–67.

Ladrón-de-Guevara, A., S. Ortigueira and M.S. Santos (1999), 'A Two-Sector Model of Endogenous Growth with Leisure', *Review of Economic Studies*, **66**, 609–31.

Lucas, R.E. (1988), 'On the Mechanics of Development', *Journal of Monetary Economics*, **22**, 3–42.

Lucas, R.E. (1993), 'Making a Miracle', *Econometrica*, **42**, 293–316.

Matsuyama, K. (1991), 'Increasing Returns, Industrialization, and Indeterminacy of Equilibrium', *Quarterly Journal of Economics*, **106**, 617–50.

Mino, K. (2001), 'Indeterminacy and Endogenous Growth with Social Constant Returns', *Journal of Economic Theory*, **97**, 203–222.

Pelloni, A. and R. Waldmann (2000), 'Can West Improve Welfare?', *Journal of Public Economics*, **77**, 45–79.

Perli, R. (1998), 'Indeterminacy, Home Production and the Business Cycles: A Calibrated Analysis', *Journal of Monetary Economics*, **41**, 105–25.

Romer, P.M. (1986), 'Increasing Returns and Long Run Growth', *Journal of Political Economy*, **94**, 1002–34.

Xie, D. (1994), 'Divergence in Economic Performance: Transitional Dynamics with Multiple Equilibria', *Journal of Economic Theory*, **63**, 97–112.

4. On the Relationship Between Fertility and Public Education in Different Stages of Development

Carol Lehr and Theodore Palivos

1 INTRODUCTION

This chapter examines the relationship between public education expenditures and fertility rates across countries. While conventional wisdom holds that increasing the share of output devoted to public education increases educational attainment and lowers fertility, we find that for a set of developing countries, the former prediction holds while the latter does not. In fact, increases in the share of output devoted to public education tend to increase fertility in developing economies. This non-monotonicity may result from one or a combination of factors, some of which have previously been noted in the literature. However, we do not attempt to pin down the causal factors. We present a theoretical model that is sufficiently general to accommodate a number of complementary explanations. The construct allows us to investigate the behavior of a dynamic general equilibrium economy with endogenous fertility when the latter is affected by education differently across economies of different income levels. The empirical conclusions are subject to a battery of sensitivity analysis tests including a version that, guided by the theory, jointly estimates the parameters of fertility and education equations.

This chapter examines the link between public education expenditures and fertility outcomes. According to conventional wisdom, increasing educational effort (particularly female education) will lower fertility rates. Indeed, the unconditional correlation between public education expenditures as a share of gross domestic product (GDP) and fertility rates across 88 countries provides preliminary albeit crude support for the allegation.[1] Figure 4.1(a) illustrates a scatter plot of the data points and the estimated unconditional relationship. The slope coefficient is negative (with a point estimate of −47.74 and *t*-statistic of −8.22), although the fit is clearly imprecise as would be expected from a one-variable explanation of fertility rates.

However, a different story emerges if one breaks the sample into high and low-income countries. Figure 4.1(b) depicts the fertility-education expenditures

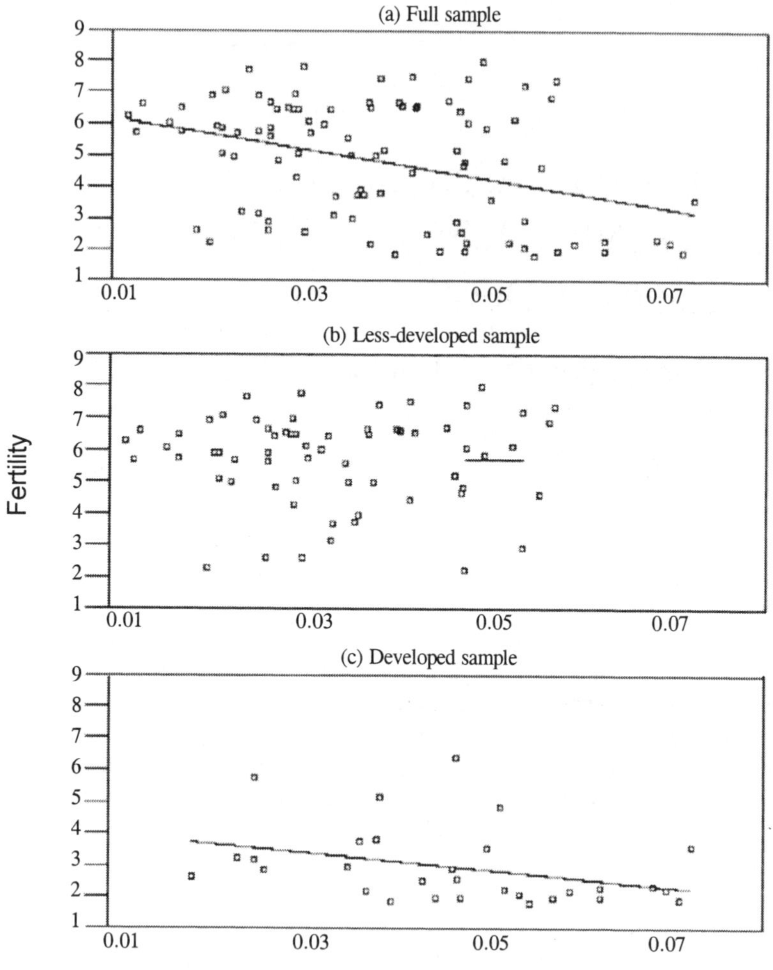

Figure 4.1 Fertility vs. education expenditure share

share relationship for the 33 'rich' countries whose initial income level exceeded the mean for the sample, while Figure 4.1(c) shows the same for the remaining 55 'poor' countries. The negative relationship between the education expenditures ratio and fertility remains for the rich countries (yielding a slope estimate of −27.42 with a *t*-statistic of −4.28), and with the exception of a few high-fertility countries, the estimated correlation is a fairly good fit considering the absence of any other conditioning variables. However, the 'poor' countries, as a group, exhibit no systematic tendency for higher public education expenditure shares to be associated with lower fertility rates. In fact, the estimated correlation is positive, although it is numerically small and statistically insignificant (the slope estimate is 0.58 with a *t*-statistic of 0.08). Therefore, this exploratory excursion suggests that there should be a more rigorous examination of the impact of public education provision on fertility across countries in different stages of development. This chapter accepts that task.[2]

First, we shall examine whether the unconditional correlations hold up under closer scrutiny (as a conditional relationship). Section 2 presents results using the cross-section, time-series (five-year averages) data for the 88 countries mentioned above. Our empirical implementation uses cross-country data because the preliminary evidence suggests that increases in the public education expenditure share affect fertility differently in economies with different income levels. An investigation of these implications could not be accomplished with micro-level data within any one country or between countries of similar development status. We find that, after accounting for country-specific fixed effects, time-specific effects and other determinants of aggregate fertility rates (female and male educational attainment, infant mortality and income per adult), the public education expenditure share explains a significant portion of fertility variations across countries and over time. Moreover, increases in the public education expenditure share yield declines in fertility in rich countries and *increases* in fertility in developing countries.

There have been other allusions to this positive relationship between education and fertility at low education or income levels. For example, the *World Development Report*, 1984 states: 'It is true that, in poorer countries, women with a few years of primary schooling have slightly higher fertility than do women with no education at all, especially in rural areas' (p. 109). The report briefly speculates that 'some education may be associated with a lower rate of sterility, and it often leads to a decline in breast-feeding not offset by greater use of contraceptives'. The lower sterility rate is likely associated with the increased awareness of health and sanitation issues that some exposure to education engenders. Also, several demographic studies have noted the possible positive correlation between education and fertility at low education levels. Cochrane (1983) presents a review of these studies. However, by and large, the possibility of non-monotonicity in the fertility-education nexus has been overlooked by the economics profession.[3] Furthermore, there does not exist a theoretical underpinning for the empirical relationship within a general equilibrium framework.[4]

What could cause an increase in education expenditures to increase fertility in less-developed economies? The World Development Report (1984) and Schultz (1981) suggest that health improvements may be the causal factor. Dasgupta (1995) points to a possible decline in sexual post-partum taboos as female education levels rise, particularly in parts of Africa. Trussel et al.

(1992) find that breast-feeding declines as education levels rise in developing countries (breast-feeding triggers natural contraceptive tendencies). Goldin (1995) shows that female labor force participation initially *decreases* with increases in income. She attributes the probable cause of the decline to the existence of norms and stigmas that discourage female participation in market activity outside of the domicile during a time when labor effort is shifting from traditional to industrial markets. At higher-income levels, norms begin to change and/or the types of available work shift (for example, from factory to clerical) and female labor force participation begins to increase. The initial decline in labor force participation may be accompanied by a fertility increase.[5]

We present a theoretical framework in Section 3 to explore how these sorts of explanation fit into a general equilibrium model of growth and development with an endogenous fertility choice. To accommodate any of the explanations put forth above, we postulate that education increases productivity both in the market and at home where the home activity is child-bearing. The increase in productivity of child-bearing can be a result of increased health awareness, the decline in taboos, or even from a stigma associated with female labor force participation. However, we also stipulate that education can influence home productivity only up to a point. After a critical amount of education is achieved, further increases in education influence only market productivity.

Therefore, the reaction of fertility to increases in the public education expenditure share to output depends upon the contribution of education to raising home productivity relative to its positive effect on market productivity. In developing countries, the home productivity effect of education is operative and can therefore lead to fertility increases. On the other hand, developed countries may experience fertility declines and unbounded output growth as the education expenditures share rises because the home productivity effect of more education has already been exhausted.[6]

The final phase of the investigation revisits the empirical results. The model presented in Section 3, as with many models of endogenous fertility, has both an endogenous fertility and education choice. Section 4 presents a simultaneous equation model that also presumes fertility and education are jointly determined. After allowing for the simultaneity of the education and fertility decision, the results presented in Section 2 remain intact. Less-developed countries respond to a higher public education expenditure share with higher fertility while developed countries respond with lower fertility. Overall, the results indicate that in this sample, the market productivity effects of educational advances do not outweigh the home productivity (fertility-enhancing) effects for the majority of less-developed countries .[7]

2 BASELINE EMPIRICAL MODEL

In this section we use the panel data sets assembled by Barro and Lee (1993 and 1996) to estimate how fertility is related to changes in the share of output devoted to public education. Panel data have an obvious advantage over strictly cross-sectional data in increasing the number of observations, but more importantly, the panel data also allow us to take into account country-specific effects on fertility. Since child-bearing can be heavily influenced by cultural norms, societal beliefs and other unobserved country-specific effects, the ability to at least partially account for those factors is especially helpful.[8] The panel consists of 88 countries and spans the years from 1960 to 1984.[9] Each time-series observation is a five-year average, thereby yielding five points for every country. The use of five-year averages helps to smooth variations due to business cycle phenomena and facilitates the discovery of underlying secular relationships.

In estimating the fertility relationship, we use national total fertility rates which are derived from age-specific birth rates and represent how many children a woman would bear in her lifetime if she experienced the current age-specific birth rates.[10] This measure is intended to minimize the effects on fertility due to changes in the age structure of the population and the percentage of women in the total population. Other more simple measures of fertility, such as crude or net birth rates, would be subject to those demographic variations. The independent variables include (i) the ratio of public education expenditures to GDP, (ii) real GDP per equivalent adult, (iii) the infant mortality rate, (iv) average years of female and male education (primary, secondary, higher or total) and (v) time dummies for the last four of the five 5-year time periods.[11]

Clearly, the first independent variable is the major focus of the empirical investigation. The income variable is scaled by the adult population, rather than the entire population to avoid simultaneity with the dependent variable and is included to capture the net impact of the wealth and substitution effects of higher adult incomes. The substitution effect acts through the opportunity cost of having children, given that child-rearing is time-consuming. The wealth effect acts by pushing out the budget constraint and allowing the household to consume more of all goods, including children. The infant mortality rate affects fertility because some children will not live past the age of five and it is presumed that parents care about the number of children that reach adulthood.

Government spending on education may affect fertility decisions partly through educational attainment.[12] Therefore, placing female education in the regression equation presents two concerns: (i) its inclusion will bias the coefficient estimate on government education expenditures toward zero and (ii) it may be simultaneously determined with fertility and, therefore, present an endogeneity problem. However, there are other factors driving educational attainment such as employment opportunities, urbanization and government regulation that argue in favor of keeping the education variables in the empirical specification. In light of the above considerations we proceed with the empirical study by first estimating the impact of government spending on fertility conditional on female education. By so doing, if we find statistically significant results, we have done so under conditions which were not favorable to that conclusion. In another section to follow, we also investigate the robustness of the results in face of a simultaneity bias by estimating a simultaneous equation system that allows for the joint determination of fertility and education decisions.

We utilize measures of average years of education for primary, secondary and higher education, and average total years of education for females over 15 years of age. Since no particular version of these measures stands out as the obvious choice, we estimate each fertility equation four times, each time using one of the four different education measures. As discussed below, the results are not overly sensitive to the specific choice of the education variable.

Note that there will obviously be heterogeneity in both educational quality and private education expenditures across countries, and to the extent that these differences are not captured by the included variables, their impact will be part of the error term. However, we do not believe that these factors will alter our conclusions with respect to the relationship between the public education expenditure share and fertility in the less-developed economies. To see this, consider two poor countries with the same public education expenditure share, but one has higher-quality education and/or more private education investment. Now suppose both of these countries raise their share of government spending on education. The country that has higher private education spending and/or higher educational quality is more likely to have surpassed the threshold that would encourage an increase in fertility. Therefore, the existence of these cross-country differences would bias the coefficient estimate on the public education expenditure share toward zero in the less-developed sample. This leads us to conclude that our findings of a positive coefficient on the public education expenditure shares is robust to those cross-country differences. Also, conditioning the estimates on education levels helps to eliminate some of these cross-country differences since countries with similar government spending ratios but higher quality and/or private investment are likely also to have higher education levels. Finally, note that the public education expenditure share may help to measure quality of public education and it is partially through the quality channel that the proposed link may operate.

Proceeding with the estimation, we divide the sample of 88 countries into two subsamples, which we label 'developed' and 'less-developed' countries. Countries are assigned to a particular category based upon their initial (1960–64 average) income levels per adult. Specifically, we split the sample into those countries whose initial income levels exceed the mean and those whose income levels are below the mean. This procedure yields 56 low-income countries and 32 medium- to high-income countries. While this selection criteria is admittedly arbitrary its choice diminishes the chances of falsely accepting our null hypothesis of differential fertility influences across samples. Specifically, we have included in our sample of less-developed countries not only the poorest of economies, but also some countries that may have reached and passed the threshold over the sample period. We have also examined the robustness of our results with respect to sample selection by re-estimating the results using subsamples based on the uppermost and lowermost quartiles of income distribution as well as by dividing the sample into high- and low-education countries. The outcome using these alternative specifications is discussed below, but in general, the results remain intact.

The panel structure of the data allows us to account for unobserved country-specific effects on fertility. Our prior belief is that the fixed-effects model is the most appropriate because it seems probable that the unobserved effects might be correlated with the regressors, implying that the random effects specification would be undesirable. However, for the sake of robustness, we also estimate a random effects specification. The results are not significantly affected by the choice.[13]

2.1 Results

Table 4.1 presents the estimation results for the fixed-effects specification.[14] The different versions of the model (that is different columns in the table) arise from the use of a different measures for educational attainment within each subsample. Columns (a)–(d) display results for average years of primary, secondary, higher and total years of education, respectively. In the sample of developed countries, increases in the public education expenditure share are associated with declines in fertility rates and the estimated coefficients are statistically significant at the 5 percent level or better in every case. On the other hand, in the sample of less-developed countries, the estimated coefficients on the public education expenditure share are positive. All versions in the less-developed sample, with the exception of the equation using average higher education years, yield statistically significant coefficient estimates at close to the 5 percent level or better. Yet, while the estimated coefficients are positive, the magnitude of the coefficients is rather small.

To interpret the findings, we focus on the coefficient estimates from the version using total years of education, columns (d), when it is convenient to use a numerical example. These results indicate that if a less-developed country with an education expenditure share of 1.2 percent of GDP (the lowest time average in the sample) increased the education expenditure share to 4 percent of GDP (a 233 percent increase), its fertility rate would rise by 13 percent.[15] The magnitude of the negative effect in the developed country sample is larger. If a country in that sample increased its education expenditure share from 4 percent of GDP to the developed country average of 4.6 percent of GDP (a 15 percent increase), its fertility rate would fall by 3.5 percent.

Table 4.1 Fixed-effects regression estimates (dependent variable: log of total fertility rate)

Explanatory variables	Less-developed sample				Developed sample			
	(a)	(b)	(c)	(d)	(a)	(b)	(c)	(d)
	Primary	Sec.	Higher	Total	Primary	Sec.	Higher	Total
Educ. Exp./Output	0.058 (0.03)*	0.074 (0.03)**	0.046 (0.02)*	0.057 (0.03)*	−0.210 (0.08)**	−0.260 (0.09)**	−0.198 (0.10)**	−0.235 (0.08)**
Output/Equiv. Adult	−0.091 (0.05)*	−0.097 (0.05)**	−0.057 (0.05)	−0.099 (0.05)**	−0.281 (0.10)**	−0.174 (0.10)*	−0.123 (0.10)	−0.276 (0.10)**
Infant mortality rate	0.481 (0.06)**	0.470 (0.06)**	0.462 (0.07)**	0.471 (0.06)**	0.323 (0.08)**	0.322 (0.08)**	0.372 (0.08)**	0.320 (0.08)**
Yrs female educ.	−0.17 (0.07)**	−0.105 (0.05)**	−0.012 (0.02)	−0.134 (0.07)**	0.496 (0.15)**	0.200 (0.07)**	0.124 (0.04)**	0.542 (0.14)**
Yrs male educ.	0.165 (0.07)**	0.081 (0.05)	0.027 (0.03)	0.118 (0.08)	−0.254 (0.19)	−0.152 (0.08)**	−0.122 (0.05)**	−0.348 (0.16)**
Dummy variables								
1966–1970	0.001 (0.02)	−0.001 (0.02)	0.020 (0.02)	0.001 (0.02)	0.048 (0.03)	0.065 (0.03)**	0.063 (0.03)**	0.052 (0.03)*
1971–1975	−0.004 (0.02)	−0.005 (0.02)	0.009 (0.02)	−0.003 (0.02)	0.011 (0.02)	0.008 (0.02)	−0.002 (0.03)	0.017 (0.02)
1976–1980	0.005 (0.02)	0.014 (0.02)	−0.010 (0.02)	0.003 (0.02)	−0.045 (0.02)	−0.060 (0.02)**	−0.062 (0.02)**	−0.046 (0.02)**
1981–1985	−0.009 (0.02)	−0.007 (0.02)	−0.024 (0.02)	−0.008 (0.02)	−0.054 (0.03)	−0.071 (0.03)**	−0.050 (0.03)	−0.067 (0.03)**
Adjusted R-squared	0.69	0.69	0.64	0.69	0.82	0.79	0.79	0.81

Notes:
* Indicates signficance at the 10% level or better.
** Indicates significance at the 5% level or better.
All non-binary regressors are in natural logs.

Table 4.2 Random-effects regression estimates (dependent variable: log of total fertility rate)

Explanatory variables	**Less-developed sample**				**Developed sample**			
	(a) Primary	(b) Sec.	(c) Higher	(d) Total	(a) Primary	(b) Sec.	(c) Higher	(d) Total
Educ. Exp./Output	0.089 (0.03)**	0.095 (0.03)**	0.050 (0.03)	0.087 (0.03)**	−0.099 (0.07)	−0.101 (0.08)	−0.082 (0.07)	−0.095 (0.07)
Output Equiv. Adult	−0.020 (0.04)	−0.018 (0.04)**	−0.108 (0.04)**	−0.028 (0.04)	−0.039 (0.09)	−0.040 (0.09)	−0.019 (0.08)	−0.045 (0.09)
Infant mortality rate	0.540 (0.04)**	0.535 (0.04)**	0.488 (0.04)**	0.533 (0.04)**	0.348 (0.05)**	0.333 (0.05)**	0.353 (0.06)**	0.342 (0.06)**
Yrs female educ.	−0.074 (0.04)*	−0.052 (0.03)	−0.013 (0.02)	−0.046 (0.05)	0.202 (0.10)**	0.125 (0.04)**	0.096 (0.04)**	0.227 (0.11)**
Yrs male educ.	0.106 (0.06)*	0.044 (0.04)	0.045 (0.03)	0.057 (0.07)	−0.173 (0.12)	−0.098 (0.04)**	−0.117 (0.04)**	−0.209 (0.14)
Dummy variables								
1966–1970	−0.020 (0.03)	−0.013 (0.03)	0.013 (0.03)	−0.017 (0.03)	−0.023 (0.04)	−0.032 (0.04)	−0.025 (0.04)	−0.025 (0.04)
1971–1975	−0.040 (0.03)	−0.031 (0.03)	−0.004 (0.03)	−0.036 (0.03)	−0.090 (0.04)**	−0.111 (0.04)**	−0.106 (0.04)**	−0.091 (0.04)**
1976–1980	−0.042 (0.04)	−0.022 (0.04)	0.004 (0.04)	−0.040 (0.04)	−0.154 (0.05)**	−0.184 (0.05)**	−0.169 (0.05)**	−0.157 (0.05)**
1981–1985	−0.062 (0.04)	−0.046 (0.05)	−0.027 (0.04)	−0.040 (0.04)	−0.153 (0.06)**	−0.191 (0.06)**	−0.166 (0.06)**	−0.158 (0.06)**
Constant	3.416 (0.19)**	3.422 (0.19)**	3.217 (0.20)**	3.415 (0.19)**	2.423 (0.37)**	2.453 (0.34)**	2.493 (0.38)**	2.448 (0.37)**
Adjusted R-squared	0.52	0.52	0.56	0.51	0.75	0.75	0.75	0.75

Notes:

* Indicates signficance at the 10% level or better.

** Indicates significance at the 5% level or better.

All non-binary regressors are in natural logs.

Comparing other coefficient estimates between the developed and less-developed countries, it is interesting to note that while the subsamples are generated by income differences, there may still be important income effects within each sample. In all cases, the coefficient estimates are negative and often statistically significant. Interestingly, the coefficient estimates in the developed sample are two to three times as large as the estimates from the less-developed-country sample. By far the most important factor in lowering fertility in developing countries is a lower infant mortality rate. The second most important factor in less-developed countries is female education. Raising total years of female education from one to three years (a 200 percent increase), would lower fertility by 26.8 percent. A curious result in the developed-country sample is the statistically significant positive sign on female education and the statistically significant negative coefficient estimate on male education.

Table 4.2 displays the estimates from a random-effects model (where the unobserved country-specific effects are specified as part of the error structure). In the less-developed sample, the magnitude of the coefficient on the public education expenditure share rises and the magnitude of the coefficient on female education falls (in absolute value), relative to the fixed-effects specification. Also, the coefficient on the public education expenditure share loses its statistical significance in the developed sample. However, as mentioned above, it is unlikely that unobservable country-specific influences on fertility are not correlated with the regressors.

To ensure that the results shown in Table 4.1 were not driven by mis-specification, we also re-estimated the results under the following alternative specifications: (i) dividing the sample by income categories and by education, (ii) using average female enrollment rates rather than average total years of schooling, and (iii) allowing lagged income per equivalent adult to proxy for its contemporaneous value.

In one alternative sample division we culled countries in the top and bottom quartiles of the income distribution and labeled the first group 'rich' and the second group 'poor'. Since the rich distribution is practically identical to the developed-country sample above, all of the results for that group remain unchanged. For the poor group, the positive statistically significant relationship between the public education expenditure share and fertility remain but the magnitude of the coefficient falls. In the second alternative split we divided the countries by their education levels rather than income levels. In theory, the two samples should be very similar because of the high theoretical correspondence between human capital and income per capita. However, we initially chose to split the sample by income levels because it is often asserted that the existing education data do not adequately proxy for human capital. For that reason our preferred sample split is by income level; however, to check for robustness, we re-estimated the model dividing the countries into those whose initial average years of total female education lie above the full sample mean ('high-education' subsample) and those whose average years of total female education fall below the sample mean ('low-education' subsample). In this alternative, the low-education sample results are similar to the poor sample above. The high-education sample produced a small negative coefficient on the public education expenditure share that is statistically insignificant.

We also estimated the model using enrollment ratios for female education measures in lieu of the stock measures of years of education attained. The stock measure better matches in timing with the fertility variable, and is therefore our preferred measure, but we recognize that enrollment rates may influence fertility through the education/schooling choice. Conditioning the coefficient estimates on the public education expenditure share with female enrollment rates, yields coefficients on the former variable that are nearly identical (and statistically significant) to those calculated in the income-generated subsamples (our baseline model).[16]

Finally, we wanted to address the issue of the possible endogeneity of income in the model. We chose to include income per adult in the model rather than income per capita to minimize the possible endogeneity problem with this variable. That is, if fertility increases, this will, by definition lower output per capita but not output per adult. However, it is also possible for current fertility to lower current work effort and, therefore, fertility may be endogenous with respect to current output. Therefore, we also re-estimated the model using lagged output as an instrument for current output to diminish the possibility of endogeneity. In the less-developed sample, the magnitude of the coefficient on the public education expenditure share does not change and its statistical significance increases, while the coefficient estimates on the education variables decline in magnitude and lose their statistical significance. In the developed-country sample, the magnitude of all coefficient estimates declines and the coefficients on both output and the public education expenditure share become statistically insignificant.

In summary, the finding of a positive correlation between the public education expenditure share and fertility in less-developed countries survives a battery of sensitivity analyses. This contrasts with the negative correlation between the same variables in developed countries. The following section presents an overlapping generations model with endogenous fertility and education choices. The model predicts that countries with low initial levels of human capital will settle into a steady state with high fertility and low education while high initial human capital countries will experience unbounded output and human capital growth and a low fertility rate. Moreover, the low human capital countries will increase fertility when the public education expenditure share rises while high human capital countries will lower fertility. The features that drive this result are a (i) human capital technology that has increasing returns to scale in its inputs (average aggregate human capital and public education expenditures) and (ii) fertility behavior that is increasing in public education expenditures while the latter remain below a critical value.

3 THE MODEL

Our theoretical predictions are drawn from a three period overlapping generations model with an endogenous fertility choice. More specifically, at each period of time, $t \in N$, a new generation appears (is born). $N(t)$ members of this generation survive and spend the first period of life as children (making no economic decisions). In the second period of life, agents are young adults and start with a minimum level of productive skills, h_{min}, which they were born with or acquired during childhood. They are also endowed with one unit of time, which they allocate between human capital accumulation (schooling or training) and child-rearing.

We follow the standard 'demand' model of fertility choice in assuming that agents enjoy parenthood; however, since time is scarce, agents face a trade-off between raising children and augmenting their own skill level. We adopt this formulation to capture in the sharpest and simplest way the deferment of marriage and child-bearing that characterizes the average individual pursuing secondary and higher education. (Table 4.3 presents cross-country data on women's fertility rate, average age at first marriage, years of schooling and secondary and tertiary education enrollment[17].) For convenience, we also assume that individuals do not consume in the first two periods of life, although the case where they consume a fixed amount of output (endowed from their parents) can readily be introduced.

Table 4.3 Regional average statistics for fertility, female schooling and marital age

	Sub-Saharan Africa	Least developed	OECD	Nordic
Total fertility rate	6.1	6.5	1.8	1.9
Age at first marriage	19.0	18.7	25.3	28.7
Years schooling	1.0	0.9	11.0	11.2
Secondary enrollment rate	15.0	12.0	85.0	88.0
Tertiary enrollment rate	1.1	0.9	47.0	55.0

Notes:
Total fertility rate and years of schooling are the average for 1992, the enrollment rates are averages from 1990, age at first marriage is the average from 1980–90. Years of schooling is the average years of schooling for women over 25 years of age.

Source: UNDP, *Human Development Report*, 1994 and 1995.

Finally, in the last period of life, old people supply labor inelastically (the time endowment is again normalized to one) and enjoy consumption of a single good. Naturally, the higher is the individual's human capital acquired in the previous period, the more consumption he/she will command this period. The lifetime preferences of an individual born at time $t-1$ are given by the simple utility function:

$$U_{t-1} = \phi ln(n_t) + (1-\phi) ln(c_{t+1}), \qquad \phi \in [0, 1/2] \tag{4.1}$$

where n_t represents the number of children and c_{t+1} denotes consumption in the last period of life.

Young individuals at time t accumulate human capital according to the following learning technology, which is similar to the technology adopted by Glomm and Ravikumar (1992):[18]

$$h_t = h_{min} + E_t^{\alpha} H_{t-1}^{\gamma} e_t, \qquad \alpha \in [0,1], \ \alpha + \gamma > 1, \tag{4.2}$$

where E_t, H_{t-1} and e_t denote, respectively, public provision of education services per old person (or as explained below per taxpayer), the average level of human capital of the previous generation ($H_{t-1} = \sum_{i=1}^{N_{t-2}} (h_{it-1}/N_{t-2})$) and time devoted to education by the young adult.[19] The fact that $\alpha + \gamma > 1$ is important for dynamic properties of the model. It can be justified in a variety of ways (see, for example, Romer, 1986; Boldrin, 1992b; and Azariadis, 1996, especially Sections 4.1, 4.4 and 4.5). Finally, note that human capital accumulation is linear in e_t purely for convenience; it allows us to obtain a closed-form solution of the model.

The empirical results presented above indicate that fertility responds to increases in the public education expenditure share positively in less-developed countries and negatively in developed countries. As discussed in the introduction, the positive reaction of fertility may be a result of increased health (World Development Report, 1984 and Schultz, 1981), decreased breast-feeding (Trussel et al., 1992 and Appleton, 1996), the diminution of taboos (Dasgupta, 1995), or the persistence of norms against female participation in market activity (Goldin, 1995).[20] The empirical results do not distinguish between these different mechanisms nor will the mechanism below. We simply view the increase in education at low levels of human capital as creating higher home productivity (where the major activity is assumed to be child-bearing). The increase in home productivity may be a result of any one or combination of the above factors. We suspect that different channels may be more prominent than others in specific regions or countries, but this does not deny the main conclusion that at low levels of human capital, increasing education tends to increase home productivity as well as market productivity. Because the positive effect of public education expenditures on fertility seems to be exhausted (or at least much less important) in developed countries, we presume that public education expenditures increase home productivity only at low levels of expenditures and human capital. On the other hand, increases in public education expenditures increase market productivity at all levels of expenditures and human capital.[21]

Thus, we presume the existence of a threshold level of public education expenditures, $\overline{E}$, after which increases in E will no longer be accompanied by increases in the number of children per household. The positive effects on fertility are fully exploited at lower levels of expenditures and fertility is governed by the following formulation:

$$n_t = \begin{cases} E_t^{\beta}(1-e_t) & \text{if } E_t < \overline{E} \\ \overline{E}^{\beta}(1-e_t) & \text{otherwise} \end{cases}, \qquad \beta \in [0,1]. \tag{4.3}$$

Finally, the consumption good is produced with a constant returns to scale production technology:

$$y_{t+1} = Ah_t, \tag{4.4}$$

where $A > 0$ is a positive constant.

The government finances its spending with a proportional income tax on the working generation (old adults).[22] Thus, $E_t = \tau W_t h_{t-1}$, where τ, $\tau \in [0,1]$, is a constant tax rate and W_t represents the wage rate in period *t*.

Agents maximize their lifetime utility (equation (4.1)) subject to the learning technology (equation (4.2)), the 'technology' for child-rearing,

$$n_t = [(1-j)E_t + j\overline{E}]^{\beta}(1-e_t) \tag{4.5}$$

and the private budget constraint,

$$c_{t+1} = (1-\tau)W_{t+1}h_t \tag{4.6}$$

where $j = 0$ if $E_t < \overline{E}$ and $j = 1$ otherwise.

Firms maximize their profits subject to the production technology (equation (4.4)) by choosing labor in effective units (h_t) employed.

A competitive equilibrium for our economy consists of a set of sequences $\{e_t\}_{t=1}^{\infty}$, $\{n_t\}_{t=1}^{\infty}$, $\{h_t\}_{t=1}^{\infty}$, $\{c_{t+1}\}_{t=1}^{\infty}$, $\{E_t\}_{t=1}^{\infty}$, $\{N_t\}_{t=1}^{\infty}$, $\{W\}_{t=1}^{\infty}$, such that given $H_0 > h_{min} > 0$ and N_1, $N_0 > 0$, (i) each person's lifetime utility is maximized given H_{t-1}, E_t, W_t, (ii) firms maximize profits, (iii) the labor market clears, (iv) the government budget constraint is balanced every period, (v) $N_t = N_{t-1}n_t \ \forall \ t \geq 0$ and (vi) $H_t = h_t \forall t.$

The first-order necessary conditions with respect to n_t, e_t, h_t and c_{t+1}, for the agent's problem are:

$$\frac{\phi}{n_t} = \lambda_{2t} \tag{4.7}$$

$$\lambda_{1t} E_t^{\alpha} H_{t-1}^{\gamma} = \lambda_{2t}\left[(1-j)E_t + j\bar{E}\right]^{\beta} \tag{4.8}$$

$$\lambda_{1t} = \lambda_{3t+1}(1-\tau)W_{t+1} \tag{4.9}$$

and

$$\frac{1-\phi}{c_{t+1}} = \lambda_{3t+1} \tag{4.10}$$

where λ_{1t}, λ_{2t} and λ_{3t}, $t = 1,2,...,$ are the Lagrangian multipliers associated with equations (4.2), (4.5) and (4.6), respectively. These conditions equate the marginal product of its activity to its marginal cost.

The firm's maximization problem, on the other hand, yields $W_t = A \forall t \geq 1$. Also, the resource constraint for this economy, obtained by combining (4.6) with the government constraint, is:

$$E_t + c_t = Ah_{t-1}.$$

Using the first-order conditions, the resource constraint and the equilibrium condition $H_{t-1} = h_{t-1}$, one can get:

$$e_t = 1 - \frac{\phi}{1-\phi}\frac{h_t}{\tau^{\alpha} A^{\alpha} h_{t-1}^{\alpha+\gamma}} = 1 - \frac{\phi}{1-\phi}\frac{h_t}{h_t - (1-\phi)h_{\min}}. \tag{4.11}$$

Furthermore, equations (4.2) and (4.5) can be rewritten as:

$$h_t = (1-\phi)\left(h_{min} + \tau^{\alpha} A^{\alpha} h_{t-1}^{\alpha+\gamma}\right) \tag{4.12}$$

$$n_t = [(1-j)\tau A h_{t-1} + j\bar{E}]^{\beta}(1-e_t). \tag{4.13}$$

Equation (4.12), together with the initial condition ($H_0 \geq h_{min} > 0$), describes the evolution of human capital. Given the dynamic path of h, (4.11) and (4.13) determine the evolution of e and n. Note that (4.12) implies that, for a wide range of parameter values, there is a poverty trap (see Figure 4.2).[23] Economies that start with an initial level of human capital between h_{min} and $\bar{h}$ converge to the human capital level h^*. On the other hand, economies that start with an initial level of human capital above (the unstable steady-state level) $\bar{h}$ experience persistent growth.

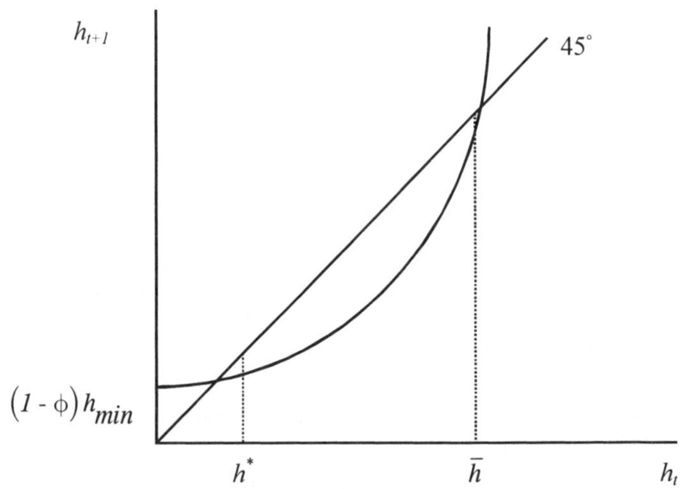

Figure 4.2 Poverty trap

3.1 Less-developed Economies

Consider first the case of less-developed economies, that is, economies that are initially endowed with a low level of human capital. For these economies we assume that $j = 0$. The stationary levels of human capital, fertility rate and education effort, h^*, n^* and e^*, are given by the following simultaneous equation system:

$$h^* - (1-\phi)A^\alpha \tau^\alpha (h^*)^{\alpha+\gamma} = (1-\phi)h_{min} \tag{4.14}$$

$$e^* = 1 - \frac{\phi}{1-\phi}\frac{1}{\tau^\alpha A^\alpha (h^*)^{\alpha+\gamma-1}} \tag{4.15}$$

and

$$n^* = (E^*)^\beta (1-e^*) = \frac{\phi}{1-\phi} A^{\beta-\alpha} \tau^{\beta-\alpha} (h^*)^{1+\beta-\alpha-\gamma}. \tag{4.16}$$

It follows that if the government of a less-developed economy were to increase the percentage of GDP devoted to public education (that is, $\tau \equiv E/y$ increases), then its steady-state levels of human capital, output and education effort would rise.[24] However, the effect on fertility is ambiguous and is given by the following expression:

$$\frac{dn^*}{d\tau} = \frac{\phi}{1-\phi} A^{\beta-\alpha} \tau^{\beta-\alpha-1} (h^*)^{\beta-\alpha-\gamma} \cdot \left[(\beta-\alpha)h + (1+\beta-\alpha-\gamma)\frac{dh^*}{d\tau} \right]. \tag{4.17}$$

The ambiguity arises from the two competing effects on fertility engendered by the increase in the public provision of education. On the one hand, at low levels of education, increases in government-provided services will tend to raise home productivity and, therefore, augment fertility. However, on the other hand, the increase in education also adds to market productivity and thereby enhances the incentives for an individual to pursue more education (lower the time spent raising children $1-e$) and a higher consumption level in the following period. Nevertheless, it follows from (4.17) that if public spending on education is equally or more effective in contributing to home rather than market activity and the external effect of human capital is small then fertility will unambiguously rise. Put differently, $\beta \geq \alpha$ and $1 \geq \gamma$ are sufficient conditions for $dn^*/d\tau > 0$.

3.2 Developed Economies

We next consider the case where an economy spends at least $\bar{E}$ on public education.[25] The evolution of h_t, e_t and n_t is described by (4.11), (4.12) and (4.13), where $j = 1$. In this case, economies experience persistent growth. Furthermore, e_t and n_t converge asymptotically to $(1-2\phi)/(1-\phi)$ and $\bar{E}^{\beta}\phi/(1-\phi)$, respectively.

Note that an increase in the percentage of GDP devoted to education (increase in τ) tends to increase the returns to education and therefore raises the entire paths of human capital and education effort. Moreover, the dynamic path of the number of children per household shifts down as the opportunity cost of child-rearing increases. That is, $dh_t/d\tau > 0$, $de_t/d\tau > 0$ and $dn_t/d\tau < 0$, $\forall t$.

Summarizing, in less-developed economies when the initial level of human capital is low, an increase in the public education expenditure share will tend to raise human capital and output and increase fertility if the home productivity effect is strong relative to the market productivity effect. That is, at low levels of education, there is a positive relationship between the public education expenditure share and fertility, contrary to some popular beliefs. On the other hand, the negative relationship between fertility and public education expenditure shares does hold in developed economies. The dichotomy results from the dual contribution of education to both market and home productivity. In the presence of fertility threshold effects, developed economies have initial education and human capital levels that are sufficiently high so that increases in government-provided education do little to improve home productivity. Therefore, in developed economies only the effect on market productivity prevails and increases in public education expenditure shares raise the opportunity cost of child-bearing and lower fertility, while in less-developed economies, increases in government-provided education will increase fertility if the effect on home productivity dominates. Indeed, we saw in the previous section that the empirical evidence bears out the threshold effect of government-provided education and supports the dichotomous effect in developed versus less-developed economies. We now return to the empirical evidence and add a bit of structure that is guided, in part, by theory.

4 SIMULTANEOUS EQUATION ESTIMATES

The above theoretical section illustrates a potential problem in the single-equation baseline regressions, namely, the possible endogeneity of the female education measures with respect to fertility rates. A woman's education and fertility decisions may occur within the same period of life and, therefore, the desire to pursue more education is very likely to result in postponed and reduced fertility. Thus, while the female education rates do proxy for time costs (in terms of wages) as well as other important influences on fertility, there may also be a simultaneity issue in the statistical estimation. The theory also predicts that changes in the public education expenditure share will increase education, again implying that education may not be strictly exogenous. Therefore, we also re-estimated the model as a simultaneous equation system with the two endogenous variables being fertility and female education measures.

The seemingly unrelated regression (SUR) technique is used to jointly estimate parameter values for this two-equation system. The system is 'identified' (i) by using the share of investment in income to proxy for the return to labor under the common assumption of a positive cross-product between labor and capital in the production function, and (ii) by assuming that the infant mortality rate only affects female education decisions through its impact on fertility. So, the fertility equation contains the same set of conditioning variables as in the baseline model, while the education equation includes the fertility rate, the public education expenditure share, output per equivalent adult, the investment share and years of male education as independent variables.

Tables 4.4 and 4.5 show the results for the less-developed and developed subsamples, respectively, using the fixed-effects specification. Focusing first on the less-developed sample (Table 4.4), any simultaneity bias present in the baseline results (Table 4.1) seems not to have distorted the main findings with respect to the effect of the public education expenditure share on fertility. In most cases, the magnitude of the coefficient estimates are quite similar to the baseline model, as are the standard errors. In the simultaneous equation system, female education has a stronger negative impact on fertility relative to the baseline results and are estimated a bit more precisely. The same can be said for the positive influence of male education on fertility, while the coefficients on output per adult are similar to the baseline model. Turning to the education equation, the model suggests that increases in public education expenditure share should increase educational attainment. The data bear out this prediction with the strongest impact of higher spending occurring in secondary and higher years of education. Also note that the investment share is positive and statistically significant in all education equations except higher education (there is very little female higher educational attainment in the less-developed-country sample.) This is consistent with the motivation for its placement in the education equation: to capture higher returns to education engendered by industrialization. In fact, in the less-developed sample, investment share is more strongly related to female educational attainment than is output per adult. Finally, as suspected, fertility is negatively related to female educational attainment. In summary, the above evidence suggests that the simultaneous equation system for the less-developed sample may have allowed for more precise estimates of the impact of education on fertility. However, the conclusions with respect to the impact of public education expenditures on fertility are unchanged.

The system estimation of the fertility equation for the developed-country sample (Table 4.5) also yields coefficient signs and magnitudes for the public education expenditure ratio that are very similar to the baseline single equation results, although they are estimated a bit more precisely in the systems estimation. Output per adult has a much stronger negative impact on fertility relative to the baseline single equation model. And, as for the less-developed sample, the magnitudes (in absolute value) of the education variables rise and the standard errors fall. Yet, the signs still remain positive and negative, respectively, for female and male education. The education equation also shows that output per adult is strongly positively associated with female educational attainment and, unlike the less-developed sample, is much more important than the investment share for explaining female educational attainment. Surprisingly, fertility is positively related to female educational attainment in the developed-country sample. So that, after conditioning on income per adult and public education expenditure shares, fertility and female education tend to be positively related. Of course, this is consistent with the positive coefficient estimate on female education in the fertility equation.

While our preferred specification is fixed effects, we also estimated the system using the random effects specification. (See Tables 4.6 and 4.7) In the less-developed sample, the public education expenditures ratio becomes more important and female education becomes less important in explaining fertility. In the education equation, almost all of the variation in female educational attainment is accounted for by variations in output per adult and male education. In the developed-country sample, the coefficient estimates on the public education expenditure share remain negative and are statistically significant in the equations using higher and total years of education. The coefficient estimates on female and male education remain, respectively, positive and negative in the fertility equation and the coefficient estimate on fertility and in the education equation remains positive in three of the four versions.

5 CONCLUSION

Our work has shown that increases in the share of output devoted to public education do not monotonically lower fertility rates as conventional wisdom might suggest. We believe that this occurs because education not only increases market productivity but also has far-reaching effects on the evolution of norms, beliefs as well as implications for health and well-being. We have used the catch-all term 'home productivity' to refer to the set of mechanisms that shifts

Table 4.4 Simultaneous regression estimates (less-developed sample: fixed effects)

Dependent variable:	*Primary years*		*Secondary years*		*Higher years*		*Total years*	
	Fertility	Educ.	Fertility	Educ.	Fertility	Educ.	Fertility	Educ.
Regressors								
Fertility rate		−0.376 (0.13)**		−0.557 (0.15)**		−0.752 (0.32)**		−0.472 (0.13)**
Educ. exp./output	0.051 (0.03)*	0.020 (0.07)	0.074 (0.03)**	0.187 (0.08)**	0.072 (0.02)**	0.252 (0.12)**	0.051 (0.03)*	0.033 (0.07)
Output/equiv. adult	−0.084 (0.04)**	−0.026 (0.10)	−0.089 (0.04)**	0.086 (0.12)	0.003 (0.04)	0.075 (0.21)	−0.091 (0.04)**	0.051 (0.10)
Infant mortality rate	0.490 (0.05)**		0.467 (0.06)**		0.564 (0.05)**		0.475 (0.06)**	
Yrs female educ.	−0.246 (0.06)**		−0.139 (0.04)**		−0.048 (0.02)**		−0.203 (0.06)**	
Investment share		0.077 (0.03)**		0.153 (0.04)**		−0.038 (0.05)		0.079 (0.04)**
Yrs male educ.	0.199 (0.07)**	0.027 (0.02)	0.78 (0.04)*	0.064 (0.02)**	0.039 (0.02)*	0.089 (0.02)**	0.141 (0.08)*	0.025 (0.02)
Dummy variables								
1966–1970	−0.007 (0.02)	−0.137 (0.05)**	−0.009 (0.02)	−0.201 (0.05)**	−0.005 (0.01)	−0.026 (0.09)	−0.007 (0.02)	−0.151 (0.05)**
1971–1975	−0.004 (0.02)	−0.059 (0.04)	−0.006 (0.02)	−0.040 (0.04)	0.001 (0.01)	0.130 (0.09)	−0.004 (0.02)	−0.072 (0.05)
1976–1980	0.012 (0.02)	0.008 (0.04)	0.026 (0.02)	0.221 (0.04)**	0.008 (0.01)	0.422 (0.10)**	0.010 (0.02)	0.010 (0.05)
1981–1985	0.006 (0.02)	0.129 (0.05)**	0.008 (0.02)	0.274 (0.05)**	0.018 (0.01)	0.545 (0.11)**	0.009 (0.02)	0.137 (0.06)**
Adjusted R-squared	0.76	0.45	0.75	0.71	0.77	0.55	0.75	0.52

Notes:
* Indicates signficance at the 10% level or better.
** Indicates significance at the 5% level or better.
All non-binary regressors are in natural logs.

Table 4.5 Simultaneous regression estimates (developed sample: fixed effects)

Dependent variable:	*Primary years*		*Secondary years*		*Higher years*		*Total years*	
	Fertility	Educ.	Fertility	Educ.	Fertility	Educ.	Fertility	Educ.
Regressors								
Educ. exp./output	−0.192 (0.06)**	0.140 (0.09)*	−0.297 (0.08)**	0.541 (0.20)**	−0.197 (0.07)**	0.460 (0.21)*	−0.153 (0.06)**	0.090 (0.08)
Output/equiv. adult	−0.428 (0.08)**	0.790 (0.09)**	−0.237 (0.09)**	0.745 (0.21)**	−0.316 (0.08)**	0.704 (0.22)**	−0.518 (0.08)**	0.875 (0.09)**
Infant mortality rate	0.283 (0.06)**		0.306 (0.07)**		0.318 (0.06)**		0.289 (0.05)**	
Yrs female educ.	0.653 (0.12)**		0.263 (0.05)**		0.187 (0.03)**		0.721 (0.12)**	
Investment share		−0.002 (0.02)		0.140 (0.05)**		0.146 (0.06)**		0.042 (0.02)*
Yrs male educ.	−0.183 (0.14)	0.009 (0.02)	−0.156 (0.06)**	0.054 (0.03)	−0.139 (0.04)**	0.140 (0.03)	−0.278 (0.13)**	0.024 (0.02)
Dummy variables								
1966–1970	0.042 (0.02)**	−0.051 (0.04)	0.074 (0.02)**	−0.325 (0.08)**	0.05.42 (0.02)**	−0.187 (0.10)*	0.038 (0.02)**	−0.118 (0.04)**
1971–1975	0.021 (0.02)	−0.058 (0.04)	0.015 (0.02)	−0.151 (0.05)**	0.019 (0.02)	0.141 (0.10)	0.030 (0.02)	−0.114 (0.04)**
1976–1980	−0.043 (0.02)**	0.014 (0.04)	−0.062 (0.02)**	0.116 (0.05)**	−0.056 (0.02)**	0.664 (0.10)**	−0.047 (0.02)**	−0.002 (0.04)
1981 – 1985	−0.057 (0.02)**	0.075 (0.05)	−0.089 (0.03)**	0.421 (0.07)**	−0.042 (0.03)	0.925 (0.11)**	−0.063 (0.03)**	0.100 (0.05)**
Adjusted R-squared	0.81	0.50	0.81	0.72	0.79	0.76	0.79	0.66

Notes:
* Indicates signficance at the 10% level or better.
** Indicates significance at the 5% level or better.
All non-binary regressors are in natural logs.

Table 4.6 Simultaneous regression estimates (less-developed sample: random effects)

Dependent variable:	*Primary years*		*Secondary years*		*Higher years*		*Total years*	
	Fertility	Educ.	Fertility	Educ.	Fertility	Educ.	Fertility	Educ.
Regressors								
Educ. exp./output	0.084 (0.03)**	0.015 (0.06)	0.078 (0.03)**	0.087 (0.07)	0.068 (0.02)**	0.106 (0.08)	0.077 (0.03)**	0.066 (0.05)
Output/equiv. adult	−0.016 (0.04)	0.147 (0.08)**	0.009 (0.04)	0.253 (0.09)**	−0.004 (0.03)	−0.004 (0.11)	0.009 (0.04)	0.149 (0.07)**
Infant mortality rate	0.553 (0.04)**		0.521 (0.04)**		0.478 (0.04)**		0.525 (0.04)**	
Yrs female educ.	−0.097 (0.05)**		−0.002 (0.02)		−0.046 (0.02)**		−0.013 (0.04)	
Investment share		−0.013 (0.04)		−0.001 (0.03)		0.021 −0.04		−0.022 (0.03)
Yrs male educ.	0.135 (0.06)**	1.377 (0.06)**	−0.010 (0.03)	1.110 (0.04)**	0.044 (0.02)**	0.835 (0.05)**	−0.008 (0.06)	1.460 (0.06)**
Dummy variables								
1966–1970	−0.033 (0.03)	−0.017 (0.08)	−0.025 (0.02)	−0.001 (0.08)	−0.007 (0.02)	−0.092 (0.10)	−0.026 (0.02)	−0.037 (0.07)
1971–1975	−0.051 (0.03)	−0.041 (0.09)	−0.029 (0.03)	−0.065 (0.09)	−0.014 (0.02)	0.020 (0.11)	−0.031 (0.03)	−0.084 (0.07)
1976–1980	−0.050 (0.03)	−0.058 (0.09)	−0.032 (0.03)	−0.017 (0.09)	−0.016 (0.03)	0.173 (0.12)	−0.034 (0.03)	−0.108 (0.08)
1981–1985	−0.069 (0.04)*	−0.128 (0.09)	−0.041 (0.03)	−0.033 (0.10)	−0.017 (0.03)*	0.181 (0.12)	−0.039 (0.03)	−0.145 (0.08)
Constant	3.462 (0.20)**	−0.521 (0.53)	3.35 (0.17)**	−0.77 (0.57)	3.106 (0.15)**	0.444 (0.58)	3.383 (0.17)**	−0.234 (0.51)
Adjusted R-squared	0.48	0.74	0.61	0.83	0.85	0.74	0.62	0.78

Notes:

* Indicates signficance at the 10% level or better.

** Indicates signficance at the 5% level or better.

All non-binary regressors are in natural logs.

Table 4.7 Simultaneous regression estimates (developed sample: random effects)

Dependent variable:	*Primary years*		*Secondary years*		*Higher years*		*Total years*	
	Fertility	Educ.	Fertility	Educ.	Fertility	Educ.	Fertility	Educ.
Regressors								
Educ. exp./output	−0.064 (0.07)	0.127 (0.07)*	−0.080 (0.07)	0.093 (0.12)	−0.245 (0.08)**	0.008 (0.13)	−0.164 (0.07)**	0.107 (0.08)
Output/equiv. adult	−0.110 (0.09)	0.018 (0.06)	−0.128 (0.09)	0.498 (0.14)**	−0.021 (0.08)	0.396 (0.12)**	−0.301 (0.09)**	0.328 (0.09)**
Infant mortality rate	0.333 (0.06)**		0.286 (0.06)**		0.331 (0.07)**		0.266 (0.06)**	
Yrs female educ.	0.436 (0.13)**		0.287 (0.05)**		0.166 (0.05)**		0.551 (0.10)**	
Investment share		−0.041 (0.03)		−0.060 (0.05)		0.042 (0.06)		−0.100 (0.03)**
Yrs male educ.	−0.415 (0.41)**	1.268 (0.06)**	−0.233 (0.06)**	0.937 (0.07)**	−0.092 (0.06)	0.47 (0.06)**	−0.369 (0.13)**	1.227 (0.07)**
Dummy variables								
1966–1970	−0.029 (0.04)	0.087 (0.06)	−0.052 (0.04)	0.201 (0.12)*	0.012 (0.04)	0.008 (0.14)	0.010 (0.04)	0.184 (0.07)**
1971–1975	−0.090 (0.04)**	0.058 (0.06)	−0.142 (0.04**)	0.293 (0.13)**	−0.073 (0.05)	0.238 (0.15)	−0.023 (0.05)	0.145 (0.08)*
1976–1980	−0.158 (0.05)**	0.071 (0.07)	−0.233 (0.05)**	0.421 (0.14)**	−0.172 (0.07)**	0.456 (0.16)**	−0.110 (0.06)**	0.184 (0.09)**
1981–1985	−0.157 (0.06)**	0.054 (0.07)	−0.253 (0.06)**	0.463 (0.15)**	−0.203 (0.08)**	0.583 (0.17)**	−0.137 (0.07)**	0.163 (0.09)*
Constant	2.677 (0.36)**	−0.916 (0.38)**	2.729 (0.35)**	−3.390 (0.75)**	2.212 (0.42)**	−2.267 (0.61)**	2.264 (0.35)**	−1.776 (0.48)**
Adjusted R-squared	0.69	0.80	0.69	0.79	0.70	0.92	0.74	0.85

Notes:
* Indicates signficance at the 10% level or better.
** Indicates significance at the 5% level or better.
All non-binary regressors are in natural logs.

female activity toward child-bearing as education rises from initially low levels. In less-developed economies, the home productivity effect outweighs the market productivity effect and increases in the public education expenditure share tend to increase fertility. In more-developed economies, however, the market productivity effect dominates and increases in the public education expenditure share decrease fertility.

Of course, this does not imply that the optimal government action is to withdraw support for education. On the contrary, the empirical results show that most less-developed economies have not yet reached levels of education where the fertility-decreasing impact dominates. Clearly, education, no matter what its estimable impact on output and fertility may be, promotes literacy and other social cohesion skills that are desirable in their own right. In fact, our results suggest that macroeconomists should devote more effort toward understanding the channels through which education influences macroeconomic outcomes. It is our intention to focus on the changing norms and institutions that education may promote and to explore their implications for macroeconomic growth, fertility and development.

ACKNOWLEDGMENTS

We would like to thank Bill Easterly, Oded Galor, Chris Papageorgiou, Peter Pedroni, Ping Wang and especially Michele Boldrin for helpful comments on earlier versions of the chapter. Of course, any remaining errors and shortcomings are of our own doing.

NOTES

1. From here on, 'public education expenditure share', means as a share of GDP.
2. We do not argue that governments of low-income economies should decrease expenditures on education. On the contrary, the results reported below show that there is insufficient spending on education. That is, most less-developed countries have not yet achieved the education level where market productivity effects dominate.
3. An exception is Dasgupta (1995) who notes the 'curious' relationship in passing. Also, Barro and Sala-i-Martin (1995) estimates a fertility equation that generates a positive coefficient on primary education. There is also a recognition of a possible increase in fertility in some recent work on the demographic transition (for example, Galor and Weil, 1996, 2000).
4. Schultz (1981), in a partial equilibrium setting, argues that 'the supply [of children] schedule may be upward sloping [with respect to education], perhaps because more educated mothers are healthier and have greater fecundity, and their offspring have enhanced survival prospects' (pp. 127–8). He then proceeds to make a case for an empirically estimable inverse '*U*' curve. Our chapter contains elements of this argument within the context of public policy toward education. There is also an attempt to theoretically account for the fertility transition in Galor and Weil (1996, 2000).
5. Another possibility is that the positive relationship between the education expenditure ratio and

fertility in developing countries is driven by reverse causation. That is, as fertility rises, governments devote a larger share of national income toward education. However, we discarded that notion for several reasons. First, the differential response between rich and poor countries was not readily explained by the reverse causation argument. Second, the reverse causation argument relies on the ratio of public education expenditures to GDP rising with fertility. While it is sensible to argue that increases in fertility lead to increases in the level of public spending on education, over longer periods of time, the higher fertility also increases the level of GDP. Yet, the positive relationship in developing countries holds for long-time averages as well (Figure 4.1(a)–(c)). Since, in long-time averages, the reverse causality explanation would increase both education expenses and GDP, one would not expect to see this if the entire explanation were due to reverse causality.

6. We shall use the term 'human capital' to refer to the human capital employed in market production rather than home production.
7. The presentation below is agnostic with respect to the welfare effects of high fertility. The research simply aims to illustrate that the relationship between government spending on education and fertility may not be negative for a substantial subset of economies.
8. Note that many studies on fertility and education have been conducted within one country. Certainly that approach holds country-specific effects constant. However, our goal is to examine the differential effects of government spending on education in high- and low-income countries. Therefore we need cross-country data and by utilizing these data in a panel form we can control for country-specific effects.
9. We began with Barro and Lee's (1993) sample of 98 countries. Ten countries had insufficient time-series data to be included in the sample. Also, note that their (1993) data end in 1985 and thus provide the end-constraint on the estimation period. Finally, since we are using five-year averages, the last five-year period spans 1980–1984.
10. These are live births and are not adjusted for child deaths during infancy.
11. The education measures for total years of schooling for women over the age of 15 comes from Barro and Lee (1996) while the other measures (with the exception of income per equivalent adult) comes from Barro and Lee (1993). The former data set covers more countries and extends the time range; however, it does not include total government spending on education as one of its variables. Income per equivalent adult was obtained directly from the Penn World Table version 5.6 assembled by Robert Summers and Alan Heston and described in Summers and Heston (1991).
12. It could also change the quality of education and influence fertility through that channel by raising the market return to education or by providing more thorough health education.
13. It seems natural to suspect that the relationship between fertility and other variables is non-linear since there is an upper bound on national fertility and this might be approached non-linearly. Therefore, we estimate the model in log–log form. If the variables are not logged, the results are similar, but statistical signficance in the poor sample declines.
14. We tested for statistical significance of the fixed effects and found that one could not eliminate the panel aspect of the data in favor of a pooled regression. Finally, we ran a battery of tests for heteroscedasticity using modified Breusch–Pagan tests. When the errors showed signs of heteroscedasticity, the method of weighted least squares was used.
15. Estimating the model over the full sample with total years of education to measure educational attainment and entering the public education expenditure share quadratically, indicates that the positive effect of public education on fertility peaks at about 4 percert of GDP. The coefficients on the linear and quadratic terms of the education share are 8.28 and −204.48, respectively, and both are significant at the 1 percent level.
16. Interestingly, when both female primary and secondary enrollment rates are entered into the same regression equation in the less-developed-country sample, the coefficient estimate on the primary enrollment rate is positive while that for the secondary enrollment rate is negative. This is not true in the developed-country sample. Again, this offers evidence that initial increases in primary education have a positive effect on fertility.
17. Cigno (1991) also discusses the evidence supporting later child-bearing for high-education females. Furthermore, evidence from developing countries suggests that increases in primary education are associated with an increase in the age of cohabitation. See Appleton (1996) and the references therein.
18. We use uppercase letters to denote variables which are outside the control of each agent and

lowercase letters to denote individual specific variables.

19. In an earlier version of the chapter we included education expenditures per person in school, $E_t(N_{t-2}/N_{t-1})$, in the human capital accumulation equation. Here, we adopt the current formulation because it simplifies the algebra considerably, without changing the main results of the chapter (since individual agents take education expenditures and the population size as given). An even more general formulation is the one where $E_t\left[N_{t-2}/(N_{t-1})^{\varepsilon}\right]$, $\varepsilon \in [0,1]$, enters in (4.2).
20. For example, Trussel et. al. (1992) find a nearly universal decline in breast-feeding with increases in education for those countries that participated in the World Fertility Surveys or the Deomographic Health Surveys. Appleton (1996) estimates that a woman with complete secondary education will reduce the duration of breast-feeding by eight months relative to a woman with no schooling. Also, Dasgupta (1995, p.9) states that '[i]n Sub-Saharan Africa, where polygyny is widely practiced, post-partum female sexual abstinence can last up to three years after birth'. The views of the *World Development Report* (1984) and Goldin (1995) were summarized in the introduction.
21. It will be discussed below that $\bar{E}$ will be linked to a critical level of human capital, $\bar{h}$. For levels of human capital below $\bar{h}$, the economy will converge to a low output (no growth) steady state, while for levels of human capital above $\bar{h}$, the economy will converge to a steady state growth path.
22. The analysis would be unchanged if the government financed expenditures with a consumption tax.
23. Boldrin (1992a) analyzes in detail the dynamic implications of external effects in a standard overlapping generations model with physical capital. He finds that a poverty trap always arises whenever persistent growth is possible.
24. We consider a change in τ from an arbitrary point. For a model of public education financed through income taxation, whose rate is determined by majority voting, see Boldrin (1992b).
25. $\bar{E}$ is assumed to be greater or equal to the level of public education expenditure that corresponds to $\bar{h}$, that is, $\bar{E} \geq \tau A\bar{h}$.

REFERENCES

Appleton, S. (1996), 'How Does Female Education Affect Fertility? A Structural Model for the Côte d'Ivoire', *Oxford Bulletin of Economics and Statistics*, February, 139–66.

Azariadis, C. (1996), 'The Economics of Poverty Traps. Part One: Complete Markets', *Journal of Economic Growth*, December, 449–86.

Barro, R.J. and Jong-Wha Lee (1993), 'International Comparisons of Educational Attainment', *Journal of Monetary Economics*, December, 363–94.

Barro, R.J. and Jong-Wha Lee (1996), 'International Measures of Schooling Years and Schooling Quality', *American Economic Review*, May, 218–23.

Barro, R.J. and X. Sala-i-Martin (1995), "Economic Growth" New York, McGraw Hill.

Boldrin, M. (1992a), 'Dynamic Externalities, Multiple Equilibria, and Growth', *Journal of Economic Theory*, May, 198–218.

Boldrin, M. (1992b), 'Public Education and Capital Accumulation', Discussion Paper 1017, Center for Mathematical Studies in Economics and Management Science. Northwestern University, Evanston, IL.

Cigno, A. (1991), *Economics of the Family*, New York: Oxford University Press.

Cochrane, S.H. (1983), 'Effects of Education and Urbanization on Fertility', in R. Bulatao and R. Lee (eds), *Determinants of Fertility in Developing Countries*, **II**, New York: Academic Press, 587–626.

Dasgupta, P. (1995), 'The Population Problem: Theory and Evidence', *Journal of Economic Literature*, December, 1879–902.

Galor, O. and D. Weil (1996), 'The Gender Gap, Fertility and Growth', *American Economic Review*, June, 374–87.

Galor, O. and D. Weil (2000), 'Population, Technology and Growth: From Malthusian Stagnation to the Demographic Transition and Beyond', *American Economic Review*, September, 806–28.

Glomm, G. and B. Ravikumar (1992), 'Public versus Private Investment in Human Capital: Endogenous Growth and Income Inequality', *Journal of Political Economy*, August, 818–34.

Goldin, Claudia (1995), 'The U-Shaped Female Labor Force Function in Economic Development and Economic History', in T.P. Schultz (ed.), *Investment in Women's Human Capital*, Chicago: University of Chicago Press, 61–90.

Human Development Report (1994), United Nations Development Programme, New York, Oxford University Press.

Romer, P.M. (1986), 'Increasing Returns and Long-run Growth', *Journal of Political Economy*, October, 1002–37.

Schultz, T.P. (1981), *Economics of Population*, Reading, MA: Addison-Wesley.

Summers, R. and A. Heston (1991), 'The Penn World Table (Mark 5): An Expanded Set of International Comparisons', *Quarterly Journal of Economics*, May, 327–68.

Trussel, J., L. Grummer-Strawn, G. Rodriguez and M. Vanlandingham (1992), 'Trends and Differentials in Breastfeeding Behaviour: Evidence from WFS and DHS', *Population Studies*, July, 285–307.

World Development Report (1984), World Bank, New York, Oxford University Press.

5. Productivity Growth and Catch-up in Less-developed Economies

Ching-Cheng Chang and Been-Lon Chen

1 INTRODUCTION

This chapter focuses on identifying the sources of productivity growth in 70 less-developed economies (LDEs) using the distance-function-based Malmquist productivity index following Färe et al. (1994a). The aggregate performance in Asia is found to be higher than non-Asian LDEs during the 1980s. We also found that efficiency improvements have played a more important role than technology changes in determining who the winners are. The cross-country regression results indicate that human capital accumulations and openness contribute to total factor productivity (TFP) growth, whereas the flow of advanced technology generated by foreign direct investment (FDI) and physical capital fails to enhance TFP growth. Governments' monetary involvement does not have a strong correlation with TFP growth, but debt financing and public consumption are detrimental.

Stimulated by Young's (1992) and Krugman's (1994) arguments that the miracle growth in Asia is mainly input driven, there has been 'a mushrooming of empirical papers trying to explain East and Southeast Asia's miracle' (Felipe, 1999, p. 1) In this chapter we attempt to compare the growth patterns among the LDEs and identify the differences and similarities between Asian and non-Asian economies using the Malmquist index and its decompositions.

The Malmquist index has gained considerable popularity in the measurement of TFP ever since Färe et al. (1994b) merged the ideas on measurement of efficiency from Farrell (1957) and on measurement of productivity from Caves et al. (1982) and applied the linear-programming approach to calculate the distance functions that make up the Malmquist index. There are three reasons for this increasing popularity. First of all, since the data envelopment type of analysis can be directly applied to calculate the index, the Malmquist index has the advantage of computational ease. Second, calculation of the Malmquist index does not require information on cost or revenue shares to aggregate inputs or outputs. Consequently, the Malmquist index is less data demanding than the Törnqvist index. Finally, the Malmquist productivity-change index is more general in that it allows for further decomposition of productivity into changes in efficiency and changes in technology. This further decomposition is important for facilitating a multilateral comparison that may help explain and characterize the differences and similarities in growth patterns for different regions. Our empirical results suggest that Asia's aggregate performance is indeed superior to that of non-Asian LDEs. Although we cannot identify a standardized growth pattern, efficiency improvements, in general, play a more important role than technology innovations in determining who the winners are.

Another interesting issue is the convergence of productivity growth among the LDEs. Strong patterns of convergence in TFP for Organization for Economic Cooperation and Development (OECD) countries are well documented in the literature (for example, Baumol, 1986; Dowrick and Nyugen, 1989). With the development of endogenous growth models, many intellectual debates concerning the convergence of the growth patterns between industrialized economies and LDEs have erupted. In general, a large and persistent productivity gap between industrialized economies and LDEs has been acknowledged (for example, World Bank, 1991; Parente and Prescott, 1993; Pritchett, 1997) and well accepted by economists. However, the reason why productivity growth differs so much and whether it is converging are still under debate.

King and Rebelo (1993) suggest that the neoclassical model's transitional dynamics cannot explain sustained cross-country differences in economic growth. Therefore, this chapter adopts the ideas of the endogenous growth school to identify the major determinants of TFP growth. The empirical outcomes suggest that the separation of human and physical capital accumulations and productivity growth as engines of economic growth may be improper. Our estimated results indicate that capital accumulations and trade foster productivity growth, but FDI and external debt do not. Our finding fails to support the idea that the flow of advanced technology generated by FDI enhances TFP growth in LDEs unless the LDEs have large stocks of physical capital. In addition, we can neither confirm nor deny the existence of divergence among the LDEs.

The remainder of the chapter is organized as follows. In the next section we give a brief review of the distance-function-based Malmquist productivity indices and the linear programming method outlined in Färe et al. (1994a). Section 3 describes the empirical data. Our multilateral comparison data comes from the Penn World Tables over the two decades 1970–80 and 1980–90. Section 4 presents the empirical results. Since the method constructs a best-practice frontier from the sample economies, the results allow us not only to compare the pattern of productivity growth and its components, but also to identify economies shifting the frontier over time (that is, the 'innovators'). Section 5 discusses the role of human capital and knowledge in TFP growth among these economies. Concluding comments are offered in the last section.

2 MALMQUIST INDEX AND ITS DECOMPOSITIONS

For each time period $t=1, \ldots, T$, the Malmquist index is based on the output distance function defined as: [1]

$$D^T\left(x^t, y^t\right) \equiv \inf\left\{\theta : \left(x^t, y^t/\theta\right) \in S^T\right\}, \tag{5.1}$$

where superscript T denotes the technology reference period, S^T is the technology set, x^t is a vector of inputs, and y^t is a vector of outputs. The output distance function is assumed to be closed, bounded and convex, and satisfies strong disposability properties. The distance θ is the ratio of the current level of outputs to its maximum potential level with given inputs. In other words, it calculates how far an observation is from the technology frontier. Therefore, the distance function is the reciprocal of the output-oriented measure of Farrell's (1957) technical efficiency. Note that $D^t(x^t, y^t) \leq 1$ if and only if $(x^t, y^t) \in S^t$, while $D^t(x^t, y^t) = 1$ if and only if (x^t, y^t) is on the boundary or frontier of technology. These concepts have been illustrated by Färe et al. (1994b) for the case of a single output and a single input in their Figure 1.

The Malmquist productivity index with technology in period t being the reference technology is defined as: [2]

$$M^t = \frac{D^t(x^{t+1}, y^{t+1})}{D^t(x^t, y^t)}, \tag{5.2}$$

where the distance function in the numerator, $D^t(x^{t+1}, y^{t+1})$, measures the maximal proportional change in output required to make (x^{t+1}, y^{t+1}) feasible in relation to the technology at t. Similarly, the Malmquist productivity index with technology in period $t+1$ as the reference technology is defined as:

$$M^{t+1} = \frac{D^{t+1}(x^{t+1}, y^{t+1})}{D^{t+1}(x^t, y^t)}. \tag{5.3}$$

Following Färe et al. (1994b), the Malmquist productivity-change index is defined as the geometric mean of two Malmquist productivity indices and is of the following form:

$$M(x^{t+1},y^{t+1},x^t,y^t)=\left[M^t\cdot M^{t+1}\right]^{1/2}$$
$$=\left\{\left[\frac{D^t(x^{t+1},y^{t+1})}{D^t(x^t,y^t)}\right]\left[\frac{D^{t+1}(x^{t+1},y^{t+1})}{D^{t+1}(x^t,y^t)}\right]\right\}^{1/2}. \quad (5.4)$$

This can be calculated relative to constant, increasing or decreasing returns to scale technology as alternative benchmarks. If we choose to calculate the index relative to the constant returns to scale (CRS) technology, then we can decompose the index in equation (5.4) into the change in relative efficiency and shift in technology over time (Färe et al., 1994b) as follows:

$$M(x^{t+1},y^{t+1},x^t,y^t)=\left[\text{Efficiency change}\right]\times\left[\text{Technical change}\right]$$
$$=\left[\frac{D_c^{t+1}(x^{t+1},y^{t+1})}{D_c^t(x^t,y^t)}\right]\times\left\{\left[\frac{D_c^t(x^t,y^t)}{D_c^{t+1}(x^t,y^t)}\right]\left[\frac{D_c^t(x^{t+1},y^{t+1})}{D_c^{t+1}(x^{t+1},y^{t+1})}\right]\right\}^{½} \quad (5.5)$$

where subscript c denotes the CRS benchmark technology.

The expression in the first brackets illustrates the change in relative efficiency and thus measures the extent to which observed production is getting closer (or farther) from the frontier. For a multilateral analysis, the frontier is a 'grand' or 'world' frontier, which is constructed by the best-practice economies that provide the most relevant reference technology with respect to each LDE. Thus, the efficiency change component captures the efforts needed (for example, changing input/output mixes) to catch up with the frontier given current technology status.

The geometric mean of the two ratios inside the second brackets in equation (5.5) is interpreted as the technical change component, which measures the shifts of the frontier with which an LDE wishes to catch up over time. Therefore, in our empirical analysis, how much the world frontier shifts at each economy's observed input mix is measured by this component. The improvements in this technical-change component can be interpreted as providing evidence of innovation (Färe et al., 1994b) for the economy that is considered. Further examination of this component thus allows for identifying the innovators.

If we calculate the output distance function based on a variable returns to scale (VRS) benchmark, then the ratio of $D_v^t(x^t,y^t)$ and $D_c^t(x^t,y^t)$ defines the scale efficiency in period t, where the v subscript represents the VRS technology. As a result, an enhanced decomposition of the Malmquist index can then be used to further decompose the efficiency component in equation

(5.5) into a pure efficiency-change component and scale component which captures changes in the deviation between the VRS and CRS technology as follows:

$$\begin{aligned} &\text{Efficiency change} \\ &= [\text{Scale efficiency change}] \times [\text{Pure efficiency change}] \\ &= \left[\frac{D_v^t(x^t, y^t)/D_c^t(x^t, y^t)}{D_v^{t+1}(x^{t+1}, y^{t+1})/D_c^{t+1}(x^{t+1}, y^{t+1})} \right] \times \left[\frac{D_v^{t+1}(x^{t+1}, y^{t+1})}{D_v^t(x^t, y^t)} \right]. \end{aligned} \tag{5.6}$$

Following Färe and Grosskopf (1996) and Färe et al. (1997), the technical change index can also be decomposed into the product of a magnitude index and bias index as follows:

$$\begin{aligned} &\text{Technical change} \\ &= [\text{Magnitude index}] \times [\text{Bias index}] \\ &= \left[\frac{D_c^t(x^t, y^t)}{D_c^{t+1}(x^t, y^t)} \right] \times \left[\frac{D_c^t(x^{t+1}, y^{t+1})}{D_c^{t+1}(x^{t+1}, y^{t+1})} \times \frac{D_c^{t+1}(x^t, y^t)}{D_c^t(x^t, y^t)} \right]. \end{aligned} \tag{5.7}$$

The magnitude index measures the magnitude of technical change along a ray using data for period t. The bias index measures the bias of technical change as a ratio of the magnitude of technical change along a ray through period $t+1$ data to that along a ray through period t data. Therefore, if the magnitude indices are the same during the two periods, then there would not be any contribution of the bias index to productivity change.

The Malmquist index can be calculated through the linear-programming approach outlined in Färe et al. (1994a). In our empirical work, for each economy, 12 linear programming problems are solved every two consecutive years. The mathematical programming software GAMS is used to solve these problems.

One caveat arises because the use of a programming approach to productivity measurement does not account for measurement error and statistical noise in the data. Banker (1996) and Grosskopf (1996) have discussed various available techniques to generate statistical inferences for the distance function estimates. In the case of the productivity-change index, the problem remains of how to take into account the data's possible time-dependent structure. For the individual distance function, the data noise may be a serious concern. However, for the productivity-change estimates, the overall statistical biases may be much less, because both the numerators and denominators contain a similar noise.

Therefore, we do not intend to examine the issues related to measurement uncertainty and instead give more attention to the explanation of the variations across countries.

3 DATA

Our sample includes 70 LDEs, 15 in Asia, 20 in Africa, 15 in Latin America and 13 in the Middle East and Europe, plus the G-7[3] as our references, over the 1970–90 period. For consistency, we examine only market economies and thus exclude communist and major oil-exporting economies. The data for our multilateral comparison come from the Penn World Tables, which are available through the internet website: http://www.bized.ac.uk/dataserv/datahome.htm. Details on the procedures used to create the data set can be found in Summers and Heston (1991). The method used involves constructing a best-practice frontier from the sample.

Our model is a simple two-input, single-output model. Real gross domestic product (GDP) is used as the output measure, whereas labor and non-residential capital are two aggregate input proxies.[4] The real GDP measure is real in the sense that it is measured in 1985 international prices. The two input proxies are not directly available from the data set. The labor variable is calculated by dividing real GDP (*RGDP*) with real GDP per worker (*RGDPW*).[5] The non-residential capital stock variable (K) is retrieved by multiplying non-residential capital stock per worker by labor. However, half of the sample economies do not have data on non-residential capital stock per worker. Therefore, they are calculated using the perpetual inventory method, that is,

$$K_t = I_t + (1 - \delta)K_{t-1}, \tag{5.8}$$

where I_t denotes non-residential gross investment at time t and δ is the depreciation rate. The non-residential investment is estimated by first multiplying the real investment share by real GDP. We have assumed a 10 percent depreciation rate for these five economies. Since their initial capital stock, K_{1970}, is also not available, it is estimated by 0.5 (which is the sample mean of the ratio of non-residential capital to real GDP in 1970) times their real GDP in 1970.

As some countries have explicit capital stocks while others are calculated using perpetual methods, the capital inputs may have measurement errors. Yet, if we use only explicit capital stock, then only half of the countries would be left in our sample. Moreover, since our perpetual methods are applied from 1970, the capital data in the 1980s should be a reasonable representation of the explicit capital stock. Nevertheless, the results for the 1970s should be interpreted with care.

We also note some other data problems. The aggregate capital stock data we use does not consider the relative price effects, although the effects are important and affect resource allocations. Moreover, data from different countries may have different compositions of capital intensity. Therefore, the general equilibrium effects of a given policy may be different. Furthermore, countries are different in institutional and other dimensions. All these have restrictions on our results. Nevertheless, given the data availability, we choose the input and output data that are most commonly used. We also incorporate continental dummies to capture a part of institutional and location differences.

The geometric means of the annual growth rates of real GDP, capital, and labor for each sample economy are reported in Table 5.1. To take into account possible structural changes, our discussion is based on two separate periods, that is, 1970–80 and 1980–90. As seen in Table 5.1, for all sample economies, real GDP growth over time was lower, on average, in the 1980s than in the 1970s. The average real GDP growth was 2.71 percent per year over the 1970s, whereas it was only 0.45 percent over the 1980s. It is worth noting that, for the second period, the economies having the highest average annual real GDP growth among the 70 economies are mostly located in Asia; the newly industrialized economies (NIEs) (Hong Kong, Korea, Singapore and Taiwan) and Thailand had the highest average annual growth rates in real GDP among the 70 sample economies. Capital exhibited a similar growth pattern with Indonesia, Singapore and Malta having the highest average growth rate over the second period. On the other hand, the average labor growth was rather modest and even across all sample economies.

Table 5.2 presents the average capital–labor ratios for both periods. The ratios increased over time for most of the economies. While only Singapore had a high (above 20) capital–labor ratio in the 1970s, 16 economies, of which half were located in the Middle East and Europe, emerged quickly into the high-ratio group in the 1980s. Singapore and Egypt had the highest ratios. The gap between the high-ratio and low-ratio economies also widened.

4 DECOMPOSITION RESULTS

Geometric means of the annual Malmquist productivity change and the two components for each sample economy are reported in 0. Positive values indicate an improvement in the relevant performance, whereas negative ones denote deterioration. From the regional perspective, it is clear that most of the Asian, Middle Eastern and European economies performed better during the 1980s than in the 1970s, with the exception of the Philippines, Indonesia, Jordan and

Table 5.1 Average annual growth rate of real GDP, capital and labor: 1970–80 and 1980–90 (%)

	Real GDP		Capital		Labor	
	1970–80	1980–90	1970–80	1980–90	1970–80	1980–90
Asia						
Bangladesh	−1.64	2.51	−0.28	0.90	−0.74	0.17
Fiji	3.37	1.05	16.33	2.43	1.07	0.33
Hong Kong	6.83	5.47	5.10	0.92	1.48	0.47
India	0.96	3.66	3.51	2.69	−0.48	0.15
Indonesia	6.00	4.42	16.95	10.59	−0.21	0.55
Korea, Rep.	6.29	7.99	10.50	7.11	0.76	0.75
Malaysia	5.84	3.04	19.78	7.87	1.33	0.53
Myanmar	1.91	3.14	7.95	4.75	0.04	0.07
Pakistan	0.76	2.30	7.24	4.72	0.03	0.17
Papua New Guinea	−0.63	−2.19	11.32	2.69	−0.50	−0.39
Philippines	2.96	−0.64	1.26	0.16	−0.08	0.16
Singapore	8.86	5.20	27.33	8.13	2.82	0.40
Sri Lanka	2.78	2.51	2.62	2.05	0.59	−0.08
Taiwan	7.38	6.10	11.48	7.20	0.71	0.64
Thailand	3.62	5.10	6.90	4.34	0.32	0.44
Latin America						
Argentina	1.44	−3.19	4.29	−0.75	−0.66	−0.39
Barbados	3.24	1.29	11.56	3.31	2.26	1.01
Bolivia	1.82	−1.80	6.24	−2.99	−0.47	0.00
Brazil	5.86	−0.62	19.65	2.99	1.04	0.03
Chile	0.77	1.09	1.80	3.96	0.80	0.80
Colombia	3.25	1.14	3.83	1.22	0.33	0.50
Costa Rica	2.50	−0.60	15.43	2.98	1.06	0.23
Dominican Rep.	4.31	−0.78	9.54	3.31	0.47	1.08
Ecuador	6.11	−1.60	6.06	1.50	−0.33	0.17
El Salvador	1.07	−0.99	8.84	0.94	0.03	0.06
Guatemala	2.41	−1.89	4.20	−1.16	−0.61	0.04
Guyana	0.60	−5.50	15.97	1.31	1.77	0.91
Haiti	2.16	−2.32	5.77	2.47	−1.42	−0.30
Honduras	2.07	−0.98	3.09	−2.56	−0.24	0.53
Jamaica	−1.13	0.75	0.58	−1.61	1.38	1.28
Mexico	4.27	−0.38	5.61	−0.19	1.24	0.70
Nicaragua	−2.39	−3.53	8.94	2.14	−0.10	0.43
Panama	2.76	−1.60	5.71	0.09	−0.03	0.72
Paraguay	6.16	−1.73	9.60	1.01	0.21	0.06
Peru	0.50	−2.69	1.57	0.10	0.57	0.32
Uruguay	2.14	−1.00	13.39	1.98	−0.13	−0.03
Venezuela	−0.46	−1.99	4.14	−1.24	1.30	0.50

	Real GDP		Capital		Labor	
	1970–80	1980–90	1970–80	1980–90	1970–80	1980–90
Africa						
Botswana	8.95	1.65	17.36	5.08	−0.84	−0.11
Central African Rep.	−0.56	−1.96	3.17	0.92	−0.81	−0.90
Ghana	−0.81	−0.79	3.35	0.16	−0.59	2.51
Kenya	4.51	0.00	0.81	−1.51	−0.37	1.48
Lesotho	9.02	−0.22	17.47	7.84	−0.30	−0.58
Malawi	2.33	−0.65	7.41	−2.30	−0.56	−0.63
Mali	2.42	−0.02	5.15	3.23	−0.36	3.91
Mauritius	5.22	3.88	4.43	4.44	1.09	0.52
Mozambique	−4.72	−1.92	−1.47	−2.57	−0.21	−1.56
Niger	−1.15	−3.87	8.11	−0.69	−0.59	−0.79
Senegal	−0.11	0.10	4.65	−0.10	−0.25	0.26
South Africa	0.72	−0.73	14.68	2.54	−1.00	0.24
Sudan	0.58	−1.34	5.55	1.93	−0.36	−0.06
Swaziland	1.91	−1.26	7.05	−2.98	−0.68	−0.44
Tanzania	1.25	1.37	10.68	3.06	−0.56	0.00
Togo	1.69	−1.31	16.29	1.22	−0.29	−0.73
Uganda	−1.90	0.37	−0.28	0.47	−0.29	0.31
Zaire	−3.59	−1.95	2.59	−0.30	−0.96	−0.69
Zambia	−1.39	−3.37	−0.35	−5.61	−0.29	−0.15
Zimbabwe	1.09	−0.20	0.68	−2.97	−0.43	1.82
Middle East & Europe						
Algeria	4.21	0.07	21.32	3.96	0.14	0.50
Egypt, Arab Rep.	3.53	1.52	29.20	6.71	−0.18	0.22
Greece	3.40	1.38	6.18	1.71	−0.21	0.05
Hungary	4.04	0.71	20.92	4.55	−0.86	0.16
Israel	2.78	1.65	3.96	0.43	0.14	0.47
Jordan	9.06	−1.47	19.54	5.14	−1.43	0.49
Malta	6.34	4.52	17.30	8.70	0.79	0.25
Portugal	4.19	4.14	5.59	4.06	1.16	0.20
Spain	2.35	2.63	6.58	4.01	−0.26	0.51
Syrian, Arab Rep.	6.89	−1.36	3.28	0.98	−0.08	−0.08
Tunisia	5.77	1.42	15.85	3.69	1.45	0.96
Turkey	2.70	2.67	6.25	1.63	−0.59	0.09
Yemen, Rep.	4.09	4.76	15.69	3.19	−1.18	0.04
Average	**2.71**	**0.45**	**8.75**	**2.09**	**0.08**	**0.30**

Table 5.2 Capital–labor ratio: 1970–80 and 1980–90 (%)

	1970–80	1980–90		1970–80	1980–90
Asia			Africa		
Bangladesh	2.08	2.30	Botswana	1.89	4.41
Fiji	11.31	21.11	Central African Rep.	0.89	1.09
Hong Kong	10.02	11.70	Ghana	1.70	1.84
India	1.27	1.72	Kenya	1.18	1.12
Indonesia	2.57	8.29	Lesotho	1.03	3.31
Korea, Rep.	6.64	12.72	Malawi	0.37	0.47
Malaysia	9.72	26.30	Mali	0.83	1.12
Myanmar	0.69	1.30	Mauritius	2.17	2.75
Pakistan	2.65	4.50	Mozambique	1.24	1.07
Papua New	4.14	6.82	Niger	1.13	1.75
Philippines	3.42	3.88	Senegal	1.62	1.96
Singapore	20.76	57.14	South Africa	12.29	22.92
Sri Lanka	6.53	8.19	Sudan	1.65	2.45
Taiwan	8.84	19.38	Swaziland	3.14	4.27
Thailand	2.45	4.05	Tanzania	0.79	1.41
Latin America			Togo	1.79	3.60
Argentina	9.45	11.88	Uganda	0.67	0.76
Barbados	10.42	17.46	Zaire	0.93	1.17
Bolivia	5.88	6.91	Zambia	2.61	1.83
Brazil	11.91	23.71	Zimbabwe	6.38	5.28
Chile	6.73	7.61	Middle East & Europe		
Colombia	10.35	12.53	Algeria	15.99	36.18
Costa Rica	11.12	20.14	Egypt, Arab Rep.	14.75	40.75
Dominican	3.38	5.34	Greece	15.71	22.01
Ecuador	10.26	15.41	Hungary	12.23	29.78
El Salvador	4.54	6.65	Israel	19.05	21.76
Guatemala	3.18	3.95	Jordan	9.30	27.69
Guyana	8.16	12.18	Malta	9.86	27.99
Haiti	1.14	2.05	Portugal	7.09	9.64
Honduras	4.61	4.57	Spain	14.99	22.36
Jamaica	5.25	3.83	Syrian, Arab Rep.	10.61	15.00
Mexico	11.68	13.88	Tunisia	6.80	12.68
Nicaragua	7.39	10.81	Turkey	4.90	7.09
Panama	13.14	16.16	Yemen, Rep.	3.73	9.48
Paraguay	0.51	0.88			
Peru	8.61	9.29			
Uruguay	10.56	21.68			
Venezuela	18.16	20.34			

Table 5.3 Annual growth in productivity, technology and efficiency: 1970–80 and 1980–90 (%)

	Annual growth in					
	Productivity		Technology		Efficiency	
	1970–80	1980–90	1970–80	1980–90	1970–80	1980–90
Asia						
Bangladesh	−1.0	2.1	2.5	−0.8	−3.4	3.0
Fiji	−7.1	−0.7	−1.5	0.7	−5.7	−1.4
Hong Kong	2.9	4.7	−1.1	2.0	4.1	2.7
India	0.4	2.8	3.5	−1.3	−3.0	4.1
Indonesia	0.3	−1.5	1.9	1.3	−1.6	−2.8
Korea, Rep.	−0.4	3.7	−0.6	1.6	0.2	2.1
Malaysia	−6.5	−2.4	−1.4	0.0	−5.2	−2.4
Myanmar	0.7	2.1	4.5	−1.6	−3.6	3.8
Pakistan	−2.1	0.1	1.8	0.3	−3.8	−0.1
Papua New Guinea	−5.6	−3.4	0.7	1.0	−6.2	−4.3
Philippines	2.4	−0.7	1.3	0.0	1.2	−0.7
Singapore	−6.2	4.8	−0.7	1.5	−5.5	3.2
Sri Lanka	0.9	1.4	−0.4	1.3	1.4	0.1
Taiwan	−0.5	1.3	−1.2	0.6	0.8	0.7
Thailand	0.8	2.9	2.0	0.1	−1.2	2.8
Latin America						
Argentina	−1.2	−2.5	−1.2	1.8	0.0	−4.3
Barbados	−4.9	−1.3	−1.3	1.0	−3.6	−2.3
Bolivia	−1.6	−0.1	−0.2	0.9	−1.4	−1.0
Brazil	−6.6	−2.6	−1.5	0.4	−5.2	−2.9
Chile	−0.7	−1.6	−0.5	1.2	−0.2	−2.8
Colombia	0.6	0.1	−1.1	1.9	1.8	−1.7
Costa Rica	−7.5	−2.5	−1.5	0.7	−6.0	−3.2
Dominican Rep.	−0.2	−2.9	1.2	0.6	−1.4	−3.5
Ecuador	2.1	−2.5	−1.3	1.5	3.5	−3.9
El Salvador	−3.4	−1.5	0.4	0.9	−3.8	−2.4
Guatemala	0.9	−1.4	1.4	0.0	−0.4	−1.4
Guyana	−9.1	−6.6	−1.0	1.9	−8.2	−8.3
Haiti	2.0	−2.6	3.7	−1.0	−1.6	−1.7
Honduras	0.6	−0.2	0.4	0.2	0.2	−0.4
Jamaica	−2.3	0.6	0.2	−0.1	−2.4	0.7
Mexico	0.1	−0.6	−1.4	1.9	1.5	−2.4
Nicaragua	−7.7	−4.9	−0.8	1.7	−6.9	−6.5
Panama	−1.1	−2.1	−1.5	1.4	0.4	−3.4
Paraguay	0.7	−2.3	0.7	−2.3	0.0	0.0
Peru	−0.8	−2.8	−1.0	1.5	0.2	−4.2
Uruguay	−6.4	−2.3	−1.6	0.6	−4.9	−2.9
Venezuela	−3.6	−1.4	−1.9	1.0	−1.7	−2.4

	Annual growth in					
	Productivity		Technology		Efficiency	
	1970–80	1980–90	1970–80	1980–90	1970–80	1980–90
Africa						
Botswana	4.6	−0.3	2.6	0.3	2.0	−0.6
Central Afri. Rep.	−0.6	−1.4	4.2	−1.8	−4.5	0.4
Ghana	−1.5	−2.5	2.9	−1.0	−4.3	−1.5
Kenya	4.6	−0.8	3.7	−1.6	0.9	0.9
Lesotho	5.9	−2.6	3.8	−0.2	2.0	−2.4
Malawi	−4.7	1.7	−3.1	−2.7	−1.6	4.5
Mali	1.8	−3.5	4.2	−1.6	−2.3	−1.9
Mauritius	2.9	1.4	2.3	−0.8	0.6	2.2
Mozambique	−4.3	−0.2	3.6	−1.7	−7.6	1.6
Niger	−2.4	−3.0	3.7	−1.1	−5.9	−1.9
Senegal	−1.3	0.0	3.0	−1.0	−4.2	1.0
South Africa	−8.1	−2.5	−1.5	0.5	−6.6	−3.0
Sudan	−0.8	−1.8	2.9	−0.7	−3.6	−1.1
Swaziland	−0.7	0.4	1.4	0.1	−2.1	0.3
Tanzania	0.0	0.8	4.3	−1.5	−4.1	2.3
Togo	−2.5	−1.3	2.7	−0.1	−5.1	−1.2
Uganda	−1.7	−0.3	2.5	−2.9	−4.1	2.7
Zaire	−3.3	−1.3	4.1	−1.6	−7.1	0.4
Zambia	−1.3	−1.7	2.0	−1.0	−3.2	−0.7
Zimbabwe	0.6	0.4	−0.3	0.5	1.0	0.0
Middle East & Europe						
Algeria	−8.2	−0.4	−1.1	1.5	−7.1	−1.9
Egypt, Arab Rep.	−12.1	1.2	−1.4	1.5	−10.9	−0.2
Greece	−1.0	0.2	−1.8	0.6	0.8	−0.4
Hungary	−8.3	−1.5	−1.6	0.7	−6.8	−2.2
Israel	0.1	1.1	−1.7	0.7	1.8	0.5
Jordan	−2.5	−5.2	−1.4	−0.1	−1.1	−5.1
Malta	−4.7	−0.4	−1.4	0.4	−3.4	−0.9
Portugal	0.1	1.4	−0.7	1.5	0.8	−0.1
Spain	−2.2	−0.1	−1.8	0.5	−0.5	−0.6
Syrian, Arab Rep.	4.6	−2.1	−1.3	1.4	6.0	−3.4
Tunisia	−3.8	−1.2	−0.6	1.8	−3.2	−2.9
Turkey	−0.4	1.7	0.2	1.0	−0.7	0.7
Yemen, Rep.	−2.0	2.8	1.0	1.5	−3.0	1.3

Syria. The progress in productivity can be attributed to improvements in either technology or efficiency. As can be seen from the table, efficiency improvements dominate in Asia while technological advances dictate in the Middle East and Europe. In Latin America and Africa, however, more than half of the sample economies experienced productivity slowdown in the 1980s with the slowdown coming from different causes. While the origins are mainly due to deterioration of efficiency for Latin American economies, most of the sample economies in Africa suffered from a huge setback in technology.

As for economy-to-economy comparisons, there are four top performers each with 5 percent or more average growth in productivity during the 1970s, including Lesotho, Botswana and Kenya in Africa, and Syria in the Middle East. High productivity growth of these African economies has been documented in Young (1994), but as with Young, we are not clear why they performed so well in the 1970s except for Bostwana whose diamond reserves generated massive export receipts and rapid economic growth. Their performances during the 1980s, however, are very disappointing due to deterioration in both technology and efficiency. The three top performers in the 1980s were Hong Kong, Korea and Singapore, all of which have a productivity growth rate above 4 percent. Singapore transformed from negative growth in the 1970s into positive growth in the 1980s. The worst performers were Guyana and Nicaragua in Latin America and Jordan in the Middle East. In the 1980s, Jamaica outperformed all others in Latin America due to its efficiency improvement. Similarly, in Africa, Malawi, Mauritius and Tanzania performed the best due to efficiency improvement.

Technology improvement, alternatively, played a more important role in the Middle East and Europe, which saw Greece, the Republic of Yemen, Portugal and Turkey go from negative or zero growth into positive territory. Basically, our empirical findings for the 1980s are in accordance with the general assertion that aggregate productivity growth in Asian economies is indeed higher than in other non-Asian LDEs. Our estimated results of productivity growth for Korea and Singapore contrast with Young (1995), who found negligible productivity growth for these two economies. On the other hand, the results complement the factor-price-based estimates of TFP growth found in Hsieh (1999). We also find that efficiency improvement played a more important role than technology in determining who the winners are.

The cumulative Malmquist productivity growth rates over the two decades (using 1970 as the base) and the two components for each sample economy are reported in Table 5.4. Again, it suggests that Asian economies outperform the non-Asian ones. More than 60 percent of the Asian economies experienced positive TFP growth, whereas only 9, 30 and 38 percent of the Latin American, African and Middle Eastern European economies, respectively, had positive TFP growth. The best performer among all the 70 sample economies was

Table 5.4 Cumulative productivity growth and decompositions: 1970–90 (%)

	Productivity	Technology			Efficiency		
		Total	Magnitude	Bias	Total	Pure	Scale
Asia							
Bangladesh	11.6	17.9	18.1	−0.1	−5.3	59.2	−40.5
Fiji	−55.4	−7.8	−6.8	−1.0	−51.7	−46.5	−9.6
Hong Kong	110.6	8.4	7.1	1.2	94.4	69.9	14.4
India	37.6	24.3	24.5	−0.2	10.7	−2.3	13.3
Indonesia	−11.8	37.7	39.2	−1.1	−36.0	−32.0	−5.8
Korea, Rep.	38.8	11.0	13.4	−2.1	25.0	38.0	−9.4
Malaysia	−59.7	−12.8	−12.3	−0.6	−53.8	−48.7	−10.0
Myanmar	32.0	32.0	33.0	−0.8	0.0	−12.9	14.8
Pakistan	−17.7	23.2	23.8	−0.4	−33.2	−17.3	−19.2
Papua New Guinea	−59.9	17.6	18.7	−0.9	−65.9	−72.5	23.8
Philippines	18.8	13.5	13.8	−0.3	4.7	4.4	0.2
Singapore	−15.5	7.8	9.3	−1.4	−21.6	−21.2	−0.6
Sri Lanka	25.4	8.7	8.9	−0.2	15.4	32.7	−13.0
Taiwan	8.9	−5.9	−4.5	−1.5	15.8	20.1	−3.6
Thailand	45.1	23.7	24.3	−0.5	17.3	−2.1	19.8
Latin America							
Argentina	−31.3	6.2	4.8	1.3	−35.3	−19.9	−19.2
Barbados	−46.5	−3.3	−3.6	0.2	−44.6	−42.9	−3.1
Bolivia	−15.7	7.3	8.4	−1.1	−21.5	−3.4	−18.7
Brazil	−61.2	−11.2	−10.3	−1.0	−56.3	−52.8	−7.5
Chile	−20.7	7.2	7.3	−0.1	−26.0	−16.2	−11.8
Colombia	7.9	7.6	7.6	0.0	0.3	27.0	−21.0
Costa Rica	−64.2	−7.6	−6.7	−1.0	−61.2	−57.5	−8.8
Dominican Rep.	−27.1	19.0	20.3	−1.0	−38.8	−30.4	−12.0
Ecuador	−4.7	1.4	0.6	0.8	−6.0	17.0	−19.7
El Salvador	−39.2	14.2	15.3	−1.0	−46.8	−36.7	−16.0
Guatemala	−4.4	15.1	15.9	−0.7	−17.0	8.8	−23.7
Guyana	−80.7	8.5	9.6	−1.0	−82.2	−79.7	−12.2
Haiti	−6.7	30.1	30.3	−0.2	−28.3	−45.2	30.8
Honduras	4.3	6.4	7.1	−0.6	−2.0	16.1	−15.6
Jamaica	−15.5	1.0	1.0	0.0	−16.3	−15.6	−0.9
Mexico	−4.9	5.3	5.1	0.2	−9.7	10.1	−18.0
Nicaragua	−72.7	9.4	10.5	−0.9	−75.0	−68.0	−21.9
Panama	−27.9	−1.5	−1.1	−0.3	−26.8	−13.3	−15.6
Paraguay	−14.9	−14.9	−52.1	77.5	0.0	0.0	0.0
Peru	−30.3	4.9	5.0	−0.2	−33.5	−18.4	−18.5
Uruguay	−59.3	−9.5	−9.0	−0.6	−55.0	−51.3	−7.6
Venezuela	−40.0	−9.5	−11.7	2.6	−33.7	−21.4	−15.6

	Productivity	Technology			Efficiency		
		Total	Magnitude	Bias	Total	Pure	Scale
Africa							
Botswana	52.4	33.4	34.6	−0.8	14.2	13.7	0.5
Central African Rep.	−18.0	25.9	25.8	0.1	−34.9	−46.6	21.9
Ghana	−32.9	20.1	20.9	−0.7	−44.1	−41.6	−4.3
Kenya	44.7	21.9	22.6	−0.6	18.7	27.8	−7.1
Lesotho	35.6	42.8	44.3	−1.0	−5.0	−33.8	43.6
Malawi	−27.2	−44.8	−44.8	0.0	31.9	217.9	−58.5
Mali	−16.2	29.0	29.7	−0.6	−35.1	−20.3	−18.6
Mauritius	52.9	16.6	14.3	2.0	31.1	11.8	17.3
Mozambique	−36.5	19.8	19.8	0.0	−47.0	−51.3	8.8
Niger	−42.2	28.2	28.6	−0.3	−54.9	−64.5	26.9
Senegal	−12.2	21.5	22.1	−0.5	−27.8	−35.3	11.6
South Africa	−66.6	−10.2	−9.5	−0.8	−62.8	−57.5	−12.5
Sudan	−23.4	24.1	24.5	−0.3	−38.3	−31.5	−9.9
Swaziland	−3.2	16.2	17.5	−1.1	−16.7	−27.9	15.6
Tanzania	8.1	31.1	31.6	−0.4	−17.5	−34.5	25.9
Togo	−31.8	29.5	31.3	−1.4	−47.3	−58.2	26.1
Uganda	−17.8	−4.5	−5.6	1.2	−14.0	−31.9	26.3
Zaire	−37.3	26.4	26.4	0.0	−50.4	−57.7	17.3
Zambia	−26.1	9.3	9.5	−0.2	−32.4	−31.6	−1.1
Zimbabwe	11.3	1.2	1.6	−0.4	9.9	8.0	1.8
Middle East & Europe							
Algeria	−59.3	3.5	0.2	3.2	−60.6	0.0	−60.6
Egypt, Arab Rep.	−68.9	0.7	−0.7	1.5	−69.2	−49.6	−38.8
Greece	−7.6	−11.9	−11.3	−0.6	4.9	11.4	−5.9
Hungary	−64.0	−9.0	−11.9	3.2	−60.5	−65.8	15.6
Israel	13.7	−9.8	−9.8	0.1	25.9	31.5	−4.2
Jordan	−54.1	−13.2	−11.1	−2.3	−47.1	26.4	−58.1
Malta	−41.1	−9.6	−11.0	1.6	−34.8	−20.6	−17.9
Portugal	16.7	9.2	9.3	−0.1	6.9	16.1	−7.9
Spain	−20.6	−12.0	−11.2	−0.9	−9.7	−0.5	−9.3
Syrian, Arab Rep.	26.4	0.0	−0.2	0.2	26.4	81.7	−30.4
Tunisia	−39.7	11.9	13.5	−1.5	−46.2	−38.4	−12.6
Turkey	13.4	13.3	14.1	−0.7	0.1	−6.4	6.9
Yemen, N. Arab	7.7	28.9	31.3	−1.8	−16.4	0.0	−16.4

Hong Kong. The main driving force behind its performance is pure efficiency growth. Mauritius ranked second, driven by efficiency growth as well, while Bostwana outperformed the other LDEs largely from technology progress. The growth patterns for the four East Asian tigers are quite similar, and are mainly governed by pure efficiency. On the other hand, the deterioration of pure efficiency is also the main factor for the TFP regression in other Asian economies such as Indonesia, Malaysia, Fiji and Papua New Guinea.

We also find a significant trade-off relationship between pure efficiency and scale efficiency in Asian economies. Most of the net gains in efficiency come from pure efficiency, not scale. A similar trade-off occurs in other non-Asian economies as well. Hong Kong, Mauritius and Israel are the only three exceptions to experience more than 10 percent growth in both pure and scale efficiencies. It seems that most of the LDEs have problems in catching up with the frontier when they try to improve their economies of scale at the same time. This type of substitution behavior is very interesting and deserves further investigation.

Another unique and interesting finding comes from Africa's decomposition results. Although scale efficiency moves in the opposite direction from pure efficiency, it is in the same direction as technology change. This complementary growth pattern between technology and scale can also be found in certain Asian economies (like Hong Kong, India, Myanmar and Thailand), but not in other regions. Whether this is related to a specific type of development also warrants further research.

An intra-regional comparison suggests that the TFP gap has widened among Asian economies due to the divergence in their efficiency performance. A similar TFP gap occurs in Africa and the Middle East, as well as in Europe, due to similar reasons plus some divergences in technology progress. For Latin American economies, the TFP gap is not as significant as in other regions, as most of the economies in this region experience similar progresses in technology, but a regression in efficiency. A lack of pure and scale efficiencies is the common reason for their poor TFP performances. Paraguay is the only exceptional case, where a huge progression from non-neutral (input-biased) technology change is observed.

Although the technical-change component informs us how the world frontier has shifted over time, it does not tell us which country actually causes the best-practice frontier to shift. As in Färe et al. (1994b), we use the following conditions to identify the innovators under two alternative benchmark assumptions:

$$TC^k > 1,$$
$$D^t\left(x^{k,t+1}, y^{k,t+1}\right) > 1$$

and

$$D^{t+1}\left(x^{k,t+1}, y^{k,t+1}\right) = 1.$$

Economies satisfying the three conditions outlined above can be regarded as having contributed to a shift in the frontier between periods t and $t+1$. Among the 17 OECD countries, Färe et al. (1994b) found that the United States was the sole innovator over the 1979–88 period. In the present study, we find that, beside the United States, Paraguay[6] was also an innovator during the 1970s while Hong Kong became the leader among the 70 LDEs in the 1980s. If we compare the engine of growth for these two innovators, then we find that Paraguay is driven by technology and Hong Kong by efficiency. Therefore, it seems that there is no standard model of innovation for the LDEs.

Under the assumption of CRS technology, Färe et al. (1994b) mention that the United States is the most technically efficient economy because it has the highest ratio of output to capital. In Figure 5.1, we plot the output–labor ratio against the capital–labor ratio to illustrate the formation of the frontier for the 70 LDEs plus G-7. The United States and the United Kingdom were located at the frontier during both decades, as were Paraguay and Mauritius at the lower end. Hong Kong emerged as a frontier economy during the 1980s with a medium level of output–labor ratio in the sample.

In Figure 5.2, we plot the cumulated TFP index and its decade-average growth rates against the capital–labor ratio. The figures show that the Malmquist index indeed smoothes out the fluctuations in inputs across countries to achieve a comparable measure of TFP. Both series appear to be random against the capital–labor ratio, which warrants our further investigation.

5 ROLE OF CAPITAL AND KNOWLEDGE

The empirical analyses in the previous section ignore the role of human capital, because only physical capital is considered. This section explores the implications of our results for the endogenous growth models that emphasize the importance of human capital and knowledge acquisitions in long-run growth (Romer, 1990). Our empirical framework is similar to those of Barro (1991), Barro and Lee (1994), and Borensztein et al. (1998) which relate the TFP growth to two sets of variables. The first set is the state variables, which include the initial GDP per capita, physical capital stock per capita (*Capital*[7]), stock of human capital in the form of educational attainment (*Schooling*), ratio of foreign direct investment to GDP (*FDI*), and the interactions of *Capital* and *Schooling* with *FDI*. In doing so, we assume that physical capital, education and FDI are the main vehicles to acquire knowledge and enhance productivity. The second set is the control (or policy) variables, which consist of the ratio of

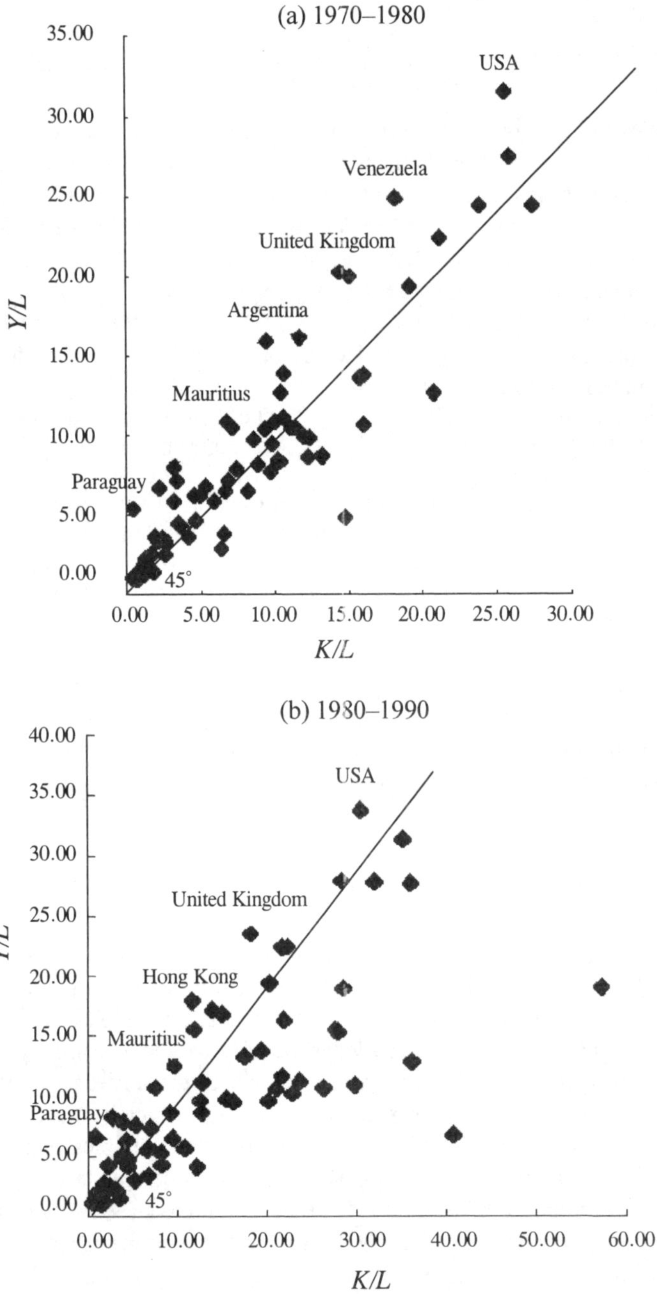

Figure 5.1 Output–labor ratio and capital–labor ratio, 70 LDEs and G-7

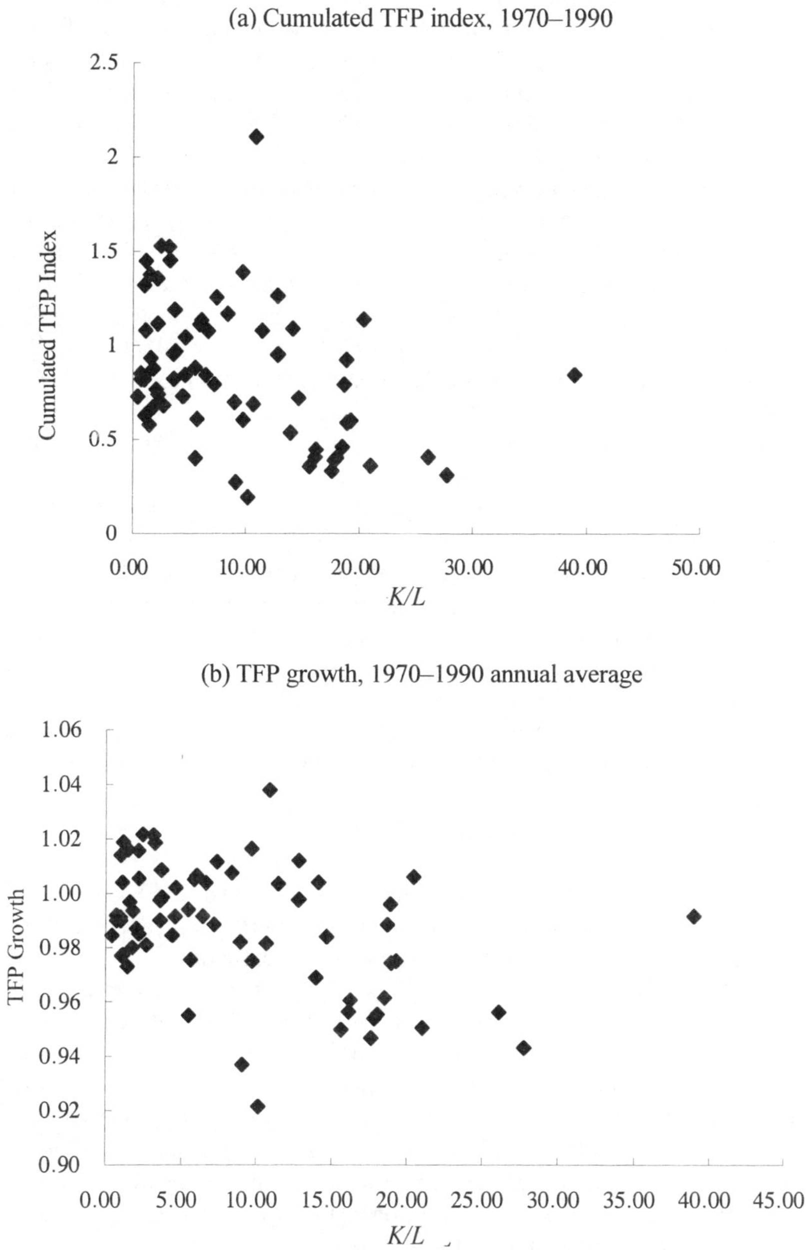

Figure 5.2 TFP and capital–labor ratio, 70 LDEs

real government consumption to real GDP, the ratio of external debt to real GDP, the degree of openness (ratio of exports plus imports to GDP), the ratio of quasi-money (M2) to GDP, the measure of civil liberty,[8] and other policies. To avoid the endogeneity problem, each period's initial values are used for the *Schooling*, the *FDI* and all the policy variables.[9] Three regional dummies are also added to represent other unknown socio-political factors.

Data on FDI and GDP come mostly from the *Balance of Payments Statistics Yearbook* and *International Statistics Yearbook* published by the International Monetary Fund.[10] We use the gross concept (that is, sum of inflows and outflows) on FDI, because both have the potential to close the technological gap. For the education variable, we use the average years of schooling of the total population that is over age 25 constructed by Barro and Lee (1993, 1994). Data for the policy variables come from Barro and Lee (1994) and Easterly and Yu (1999).

Our regressions are based on the panel data for the two decades 1970–80 and 1980–90.[11] The low-frequency growth rate of TFP matches the recent theories of growth which do not attempt to explain short-run business fluctuations. The Pearson correlation coefficients' matrix of explanatory variables is listed in Appendix 5A. The pair-wise correlation between initial GDP, schooling, and per capita capital seems to be rather high. Civil liberty also has a positive and high correlation with these three variables. These high correlations, to some extent, might render our estimation results insignificant.

Some of the sample economies were rejected out, because of the unavailability of data on either human capital or policy variables. Therefore, our sample includes either 58 or 65 LDEs, depending on the model specifications. The seemingly unrelated regression method (SUR) is adopted on the panel estimation.[12] The average Malmquist TFP growth rates over each decade (as listed in 0) are used as dependent variables. Each equation has a different constant term (not reported). Other coefficients are constrained to be the same for the two decades. The estimation allows for different error variances in each equation and for correlation of these errors across equations.

There are shortcomings for using this type of estimation method. One drawback is that it creates difficulties in measuring variables in a consistent and accurate way across countries and over time. In general, countries that are less developed tend to have more measurement errors in collecting data. The other empirical issue is the direction of causation. Many of the regressions are reactions to economic activities. One way to mitigate the causation problem is to use earlier values of explanatory variables that are thought to affect subsequent economic activities as we shall do below. However, this method may not always be valid in determining causation.

More than ten alternative regressions are performed to examine the sensitivity of the parameter estimates to model specifications and the robustness of these estimates. Eight sets of results are reported in Table 5.5. The adjusted-R^2 values range around 0.24 to 0.31. Our first finding is that schooling is positively and significantly associated with TFP growth, but its indirect interaction with FDI has negative and, in some cases, significant associations. Even though schooling may discourage productivity growth via interaction with FDI,[13] the net effects (evaluated at sample mean) are positive for all cases as its direct effect dominates the indirect effect. Conversely, physical capital and FDI do not have any significant association with TFP growth, nor do their interaction terms (except in model VII). In other words, our findings suggest that the flow of advanced technology brought along by FDI and physical capital may not be positively associated with TFP growth in the LDEs. These results are inconsistent with the theoretical and empirical studies on relative backwardness and technology diffusion from FDI postulated by Findlay (1978), Wang (1990) and others. They are also different from the results by Chang and Luh (2000) using the same methodology and database but a smaller sample size. In Chang and Luh's paper, FDI contributes to TFP growth in the Asian Pacific region either through catching-up or through technological progress, but the latter occurs only when a sufficient learning capacity is available in the host economy. In the current study, the LDEs as a whole can take advantage of neither the FDI nor their capital to accelerate TFP growth. Further research is needed to resolve this controversy.

Another factor that positively relates to TFP growth is the degree of openness. It is well known that trade and outward-looking policies are complementary to TFP growth during the 1960s and 1970s. This is still true as we move forward into the 1980s. The other significant policy variables are external debt and government consumption. Both are negatively related to TFP growth, which means that relying on foreign capital and government spending is detrimental to growth.

There are theoretically two important reasons for relying on external debts: to accumulate capital stock and to increase government expenditure. We ran regressions of the government consumption expenditure in GDP in 1970, the capital stock per capita in 1970, and both against the ratio of external debts to GDP. We find that the estimated coefficient on the government consumption expenditure is positive and statistically significant, whereas the estimated coefficient on capital stock is statistically insignificant. We next enter as a regressor in the TFP growth regressions the predicted ratios of external debts to GDP based on (i) the government consumption expenditure and (ii) both the government consumption expenditure in GDP and the capital stock per capita, and drop as the regressor the government consumption expenditure in GDP. We find that the results remain the same.

Table 5.5 Regression results for productivity growth: panel of two decades, 1970–80 and 1980–90

Independent variables	No regional dummy				With regional dummy			
	I	II	III	IV	V	VI	VII	VIII
Initial GDP per capita (*INIY*)	−0.02 (0.02)	−0.02 (0.02)	−0.01 (0.02)	−0.01 (0.02)	−0.00 (0.02)	0.00 (0.02)	0.01 (0.02)	0.01 (0.02)
Schooling (*SCH*)	57.70 (41.03)	70.51* (41.69)	119.39** (55.32)	129.86** (55.44)	41.99* (43.01)	47.60 (43.56)	95.85* (58.11)	94.83 (58.53)
Capital per capita (*CAPITAL*)	−0.53 (0.37)	−0.53 (0.37)	−0.59 (0.37)	−0.58 (0.37)	−0.34 (0.36)	−0.37 (0.36)	−0.39 (0.37)	−0.40 (0.37)
FDI (*FDI*)	28.03 (56.66)	10.80 (58.16)	35.18 (56.79)	18.30 (58.39)	31.25 (54.75)	12.61 (58.05)	38.20 (55.24)	22.53 (58.97)
Schooling* FDI (*SCH*FDI*)	−457.52 (334.85)	−349.74 (345.08)	−597.44* (344.92)	−489.05 (355.89)	−543.53* (321.10)	−406.82 (349.24)	−663.40* (334.22)	−541.34 (368.32)
Capital per capita* FDI (*CAPITAL*FDI*)	4.19 (3.76)	3.49 (3.79)	5.66 (3.85)	4.94 (3.89)	5.32 (3.61)	4.46 (3.72)	6.47* (3.73)	5.66 (3.88)
Government consumption (*GOV*)	−595.39 (410.86)	−470.89 (416.01)	−656.85 (412.27)	−534.67 (418.94)	−770.20* (413.80)	−692.72 (422.88)	−780.50* (415.27)	−717.57* (425.52)

External debt (*DEBT*)	−2.07***	−2.18***	−1.91***	−2.01***	−1.27**	−1.30**	−1.24**	−1.26**
	(0.54)	(0.54)	(0.55)	(0.55)	(0.59)	(0.60)	(0.60)	(0.60)
Openness (*OPEN*)	0.94*	1.22**	0.91*	1.18**	0.50	0.73	0.53	0.72
	(0.48)	(0.53)	(0.48)	(0.53)	(0.50)	(0.56)	(0.50)	(0.56)
M2		−2.22		−2.12		−2.00		−1.61
		(1.55)		(1.55)		(1.90)		(1.94)
Civil liberty (*CIVLIB*)			−35.43	−34.36			−29.47	−26.42
			(21.32)	(21.12)			(21.34)	(21.76)
Asia dummy					189.11**	196.76***	170.17**	178.31**
					(70.50)	(71.24)	(67.96)	(73.16)
Africa dummy					171.61**	165.91**	153.57**	150.88*
					(73.38)	(73.81)	(74.78)	(75.26)
Europe dummy					25.28	74.95	0.71	43.31
					(72.78)	(87.37)	(75.06)	(91.56)
Degree of freedom	107	106	106	105	104	103	103	102
Adjusted R^2	0.2361	0.2504	0.2547	0.2684	0.2919	0.3015	0.3043	0.3109

Notes: The standard errors are in parentheses. The constant terms are not reported. * Significant at 10% level. ** Significant at 5% level. *** Significant at 1% level.

As for the convergence issue, our results show that the initial real GDP level has mixed and insignificant associations with TFP growth. In other words, no significant evidence on TFP convergence can be found among the LDEs. Some existing empirical papers have found that the income levels among the LDEs have been diverging during the post-war period. Our results neither confirm nor deny whether the TFP divergence has also occurred among the LDEs since 1970. However, a strong divergent pattern has already been found in the previous section for the case of technological catching-up (that is, efficiency improvement). These divergent patterns signal that some of the LDEs may not take advantage of their 'backwardness' in accelerating TFP growth due to their lack of efficiencies.

As for the policy distortion variables, neither financial involvement (M2) nor civil liberty has any significant association with TFP growth.[14] However, the regional dummies for Asia and Africa enter with statistically significant positive coefficients, consistent with our expectations that these two regions outperform the rest of the LDEs in TFP growth after controlling the state and policy factors. Comparing models I–IV with models V–VIII, the overall explanatory power increases by about 5 percentage points by adding these regional dummies, but openness becomes insignificant. Therefore, part of the reason why Asian and African countries perform better may be due to their outward-looking policies. On the other hand, we ran a regression using as regressors only the three regional dummies and intercept and found the adjusted R^2 to be 0.13. Therefore, similar to findings in the classical development literature in the 1950s and 1960s, non-economic changes are still important determinants in the long-term growth process in LDEs for the 1970s and 1980s.

We also ran regression models for the two components of TFP growth separately, that is, technology changes (innovation) and efficiency improvements (adoption). The results are illustrated in Table 5.6. Obviously, the adjusted-R^2 values for technology changes are low, whereas those for efficiency improvements are mediocre. As can be seen from the estimates, schooling has positive and significant direct associations with both technology changes and pure efficiency improvements for which the estimated coefficient on efficiency improvements is more than twice that on technology changes. However, physical capital has a negative and significant association with efficiency improvement. There is also no direct association of FDI with any of the TFP components. In a recent paper explaining cross-country differentials in the growth rate of technical productivity, Benhabib and Spiegel (1994) found that human capital is positively associated with TFP growth both directly through domestic innovations and indirectly by affecting the speed of technological adoptions. Our above findings complement those of Benhabib and Spiegel, in spite of the differences in model specifications and the fact that our sample includes only LDEs whereas theirs involves both LDEs and developed economies.

Table 5.6 Regression results for productivity growth and its decomposition: panel of two decades, 1970–80 and 1980–90

Dependent variables / Independent variables	Productivity	Technology			Efficiency		
		Total	Magnitude	Input bias	Total	Scale	Pure
Initial GDP per capita (*INIY*)	0.01	0.02*	0.02**	−0.00	−0.01	−0.00	−0.02
	(0.02)	(0.01)	(0.01)	(0.00)	(0.02)	(0.01)	(0.02)
Schooling (*SCH*)	94.83	46.68*	58.19*	0.47	61.40	−39.82	90.23*
	(58.53)	(25.79)	(30.69)	(5.63)	(60.66)	(36.92)	(60.89)
Capital per capita (*CAPITAL*)	−0.40	0.13	0.30	−0.01	−0.67*	−0.24	−0.25
	(0.37)	(0.17)	(0.21)	(0.03)	(0.39)	(0.24)	(0.36)
FDI (*FDI*)	22.53	9.69	3.03	−3.02	31.54	29.28	16.84
	(58.97)	(27.01)	(31.60)	(4.89)	(62.33)	(40.09)	(59.34)
Schooling* FDI (*SCH*FDI*)	−541.34	−185.27	−222.95	20.93	−474.95	−39.46	−517.83
	(368.32)	(167.53)	(185.40)	(26.64)	(388.99)	(267.50)	(374.62)
Capital per capita* FDI (*CAPITAL*FDI*)	5.66	−1.87	2.72	−0.21	4.58	−0.09	5.29
	(3.88)	(1.80)	(2.06)	(0.29)	(4.12)	(2.69)	(3.87)
Government consumption (*GOV*)	−717.57*	−2.22	122.67	−24.88	−743.83*	−184.35	−619.58
	(425.52)	(177.93)	(210.86)	(45.69)	(430.20)	(264.85)	(465.90)

Table 5.6 (continued)

External debt (*DEBT*)	−1.26**	0.57*	0.78**	−0.02	−1.91***	−0.57	−1.25**
	(0.60)	(0.29)	(0.33)	(0.04)	(0.65)	(0.42)	(0.59)
Openness (*OPEN*)	0.72	0.33	0.39	0.02	0.22	0.32	0.28
	(0.56)	(0.26)	(0.31)	(0.05)	(0.60)	(0.37)	(0.55)
M2	−1.61	−1.21	−1.38	0.03	−0.35	−1.39	1.36
	(1.94)	(0.85)	(1.02)	(0.20)	(2.00)	(1.20)	(2.04)
Civil liberty (*CIVLIB*)	−26.42	−25.86***	−31.61***	1.80	−5.66	20.51*	−23.49
	(21.76)	(9.52)	(11.69)	(2.39)	(22.45)	(13.20)	(22.73)
Asia dummy	178.31**	41.03	68.27*	−2.80	128.28*	63.63	76.52
	(73.16)	(32.13)	(39.62)	(8.25)	(75.56)	(44.21)	(76.29)
Africa dummy	150.88*	−5.13	18.46	4.78	180.96**	104.84**	90.62
	(75.26)	(33.37)	(41.23)	(8.24)	(78.10)	(45.66)	(77.72)
Europe dummy	43.31	−6.39	14.99	4.56	12.63	−45.79	65.13
	(91.56)	(40.62)	(49.89)	(9.81)	(95.07)	(56.08)	(94.49)
Adjusted R^2	0.3109	0.0932	0.1259	0.0734	0.3028	0.2878	0.2302

Notes: The standard errors are in parentheses. The constant terms are not reported. * Significant at 10% level. ** Significant at 5% level. *** Significant at 1% level.

For policy variables, both government consumption and external debt are negatively associated with efficiency improvements. Nevertheless, external debts have a positive and statistically significant association with technology changes that is different from its associations with other components. Policies on financial involvement are not significantly related to all the TFP components, but civil liberty has a significantly negative association with technical changes and positive with scale efficiency. These results suggest that more borrowing and liberty may encourage technological innovation, but discourage catching-up. The positive association of the Asian dummy and African dummy with TFP growth mainly reflects efficiency improvements. This is also in accordance with Abramovitz (1986) and Landes (1990) in that the ability of poor countries to catch up with their richer counterparts by adopting modern technology is limited by social capabilities necessary to take advantage of such an adoption.

6 CONCLUDING COMMENTS

The eruption of the Asian financial crisis in July 1997 has stimulated another wide debate over the sources of Asia's rapid growth and its sustainability. Some point to a lack of technological progress and innovation, while others blame failure to achieve efficiency in the allocation of key resources. This chapter attempts to address these issues by identifying the determinants of productivity growth in 70 LDEs and NIEs. We calculate productivity growth and its components using distance-function-based Malmquist productivity indices and linear programming methods following Färe et al. (1994b). Consistent quantity data are collected from the Penn World Table (Mark 5) over the 1970–80 and 1980–90 periods. The productivity growth is decomposed into changes in efficiency and technical progress. Regression analyses are conducted to investigate the role of FDI and education in the TFP growth process.

Based on the findings of Young (1992, 1994, 1995) and Kim and Lau (1994), Krugman argues that TFP is of little importance in explaining the East Asian growth miracle, and therefore, East Asia's high growth rate is unlikely to be sustained in the future. In a more recent study, Kim and Lau (1996) confirm once again that TFP is relatively unimportant in the Asian Pacific economies, with Japan, Hong Kong and Singapore the only three exceptions in the region. However, TFP is found to be an important contributor to East Asian economic growth in other empirical studies. For example, Drysdale and Huang (1997) use the Penn World data to identify the sources of output growth in APEC (Asia-Pacific Economic Cooperation) economies.

In comparison to the existing literature on the East Asian miracle growth, our results shed light on some of the arguments over what Krugman (1994) stated. On the one hand, our results are in accordance with Krugman's argument in that NIEs as a whole outperform the others only in catching up with the frontiers. On the other hand, despite differences in methodology, sample size, data, assumptions on capital stock depreciation rates and so on, we find that the overall TFP growth in these East Asian economies during the 1980s is indeed better than in the other LDEs. We also find that the productivity divergence might have occurred since the 1970s due to discrepancies in catching-up capabilities. Accumulations of human capital cannot be separated from productivity growth; they are positively associated with the catching-up efficiency and thereby productivity growth.

From our Malmquist productivity index calculations and decompositions, we find that efficiency improvement has played a more important role than technology change in determining who the winners are. Aside from identifying the sources of TFP growth, and the strengths and weaknesses of each economy, our analysis delves further into the more fundamental issue of knowledge and human and physical capital accumulations. Our regression results indicate that education and openness to trade are beneficial to TFP growth while debt financing and government spending are detrimental. However, we fail to find any significant evidence that FDI and physical capital are positively associated with higher productivity growth.

Goodfriend and McDermott (1998, pp.1287) recently use a model which 'predicts that anything building a familiarity bridge from LDEs to industrial leaders helps the former to catch up' to explain Japan overtaking most Western nations and the miracle growth in Pacific Rim nations. Their paper concludes that the efficiency with which knowledge can be acquired is a primary determinant of relative per capita real income in the long run and that a country that opens its door to and gets familiar with others finds it easier to acquire know-how and will eventually catch up with or even overtake the more-advanced trading partners. In many aspects, our empirical results echo their theoretical arguments.

Two policy implications may be drawn from this study. First, outward-looking policies are critically associated with TFP growth and should be continued in the future. Second, economic growth can be sustained only if more investment in human capital is devoted to promote technological innovation and catching-up.

ACKNOWLEDGMENTS

We are grateful to an anonymous referee and Frank S.T. Hsiao for providing valuable comments and suggestions that have improved the quality of this chapter substantially. Please send all correspondence to: Dr. Ching-Cheng

APPENDIX 5A

Table 5A.1 Pearson correlation coefficients matrix of explanatory variables

	INIY	SCHOOL	CAPITAL	FDI	SCH*FDI	CAP*FDI	GOV	DEBT	OPEN	M2	CIVLIB
(I) 1970–1980											
INIY	1.00	0.48	0.64	−0.09	0.11	0.04	−0.31	−0.27	0.15	0.30	0.66
SCH	0.48	1.00	0.21	−0.08	0.37	0.00	−0.19	−0.18	0.33	0.37	0.71
CAPITAL	0.64	0.21	1.00	−0.10	−0.09	0.01	−0.35	−0.20	−0.33	−0.01	0.38
FDI	−0.09	−0.08	−0.10	1.00	0.74	0.70	0.24	−0.09	0.07	−0.06	−0.14
*SCH*FDI*	0.11	0.37	−0.09	0.74	1.00	0.74	0.03	−0.18	0.32	0.14	0.17
*CAPITAL*FDI*	0.04	0.00	0.01	0.70	0.74	1.00	0.08	−0.03	0.09	−0.03	0.01
GOV	−0.31	−0.19	−0.35	0.24	0.03	0.08	1.00	0.32	0.06	0.01	−0.27
DEBT	−0.27	−0.18	−0.20	−0.09	−0.18	−0.03	0.32	1.00	−0.03	−0.13	−0.24
OPEN	0.15	0.33	−0.33	0.07	0.32	0.09	0.06	−0.03	1.00	0.50	0.28
M2	0.30	0.37	−0.01	−0.06	0.14	−0.03	0.01	−0.13	0.50	1.00	0.39
CIVLIB	0.66	0.71	0.38	−0.14	0.17	0.01	−0.27	−0.24	0.28	0.39	1.00
(II) 1980–1990											
	INIY	SCHOOL	CAPITAL	FDI	SCH*FDI	CAP*FDI	GOV	DEBT	OPEN	M2	CIVLIB
INIY	1.00	0.66	0.50	−0.14	−0.14	−0.05	−0.45	−0.29	0.33	0.39	0.71
SCH	0.66	1.00	0.30	−0.17	−0.17	−0.14	−0.40	−0.20	0.14	0.33	0.82
CAPITAL	0.50	0.30	1.00	−0.09	−0.05	0.09	−0.37	−0.13	−0.16	0.04	0.35
FDI	−0.14	−0.17	−0.09	1.00	0.68	0.56	0.06	−0.04	0.03	−0.04	−0.19
*SCH*FDI*	−0.14	−0.17	−0.05	0.68	1.00	0.92	−0.17	0.08	0.13	0.15	−0.21
*CAPITAL*FDI*	−0.05	−0.14	0.09	0.56	0.92	1.00	−0.11	0.09	0.09	0.12	−0.11
GOV	−0.45	−0.40	−0.37	0.06	−0.17	−0.11	1.00	0.48	0.01	0.00	−0.34
DEBT	−0.29	−0.20	−0.13	−0.04	0.08	0.09	0.48	1.00	0.00	−0.02	−0.13
OPEN	0.33	0.14	−0.16	0.03	0.13	0.09	0.01	0.00	1.00	0.56	0.19
M2	0.39	0.33	0.04	−0.04	0.15	0.12	0.00	−0.02	0.56	1.00	0.28
CIVLIB	0.71	0.82	0.35	−0.19	−0.21	−0.11	−0.34	−0.13	0.19	0.28	1.00

Chang, Institute of Economics, Academia Sinica, 128 Academic Rd., Sec.2, Taipei 115, Taiwan. TEL: 886-2-2782-2791 ext 201. FAX: 886-2-2785-3946. EMAIL: Emily@econ.sinica.edu.tw.

NOTES

1. According to Färe and Lovell (1978), the distance functions are reciprocals of Debreu (1951)–Farrell (1957) technical efficiency measures. Either input or output distance functions can be used to define the Malmquist TFP index. For this chapter, we use the output distance function, which characterizes production technology by considering a maximum proportional expansion of outputs with given inputs.
2. This version of the Malmquist productivity change is from Caves et al. (1982).
3. The G-7 includes Canada, France, Germany, Italy, Japan, the United Kingdom and the United States. Their TFP growth results are not reported in this chapter but are available on request.
4. We do not incorporate human capital as an input here, because Benhabib and Spiegel (1994) discover that human capital is not a determinant of output growth, but 'of the magnitude of a country's Solow residuals' (Benhabib and Spiegel, 1994, p.167).
5. According to the appendix of Penn World Table 5.6, the worker for this variable is a census definition based on an economically active population. This definition implies that our labor variable is based on the total workforce rather than the actual number of employees. Thus, our study may overstate the actual amount of labor.
6. Paraguay's capital–labor ratio was among the lowest in our sample. We believe that this is the main reason why it is recognized as an efficient frontier as well as an innovator during the 1970s.
7. Although our scatter diagram shows that the TFP growth seems to be independent of the capital stock per capita, a large number of existing AK models consider physical capital to enhance productivity in a way described by Romer (1986) and documented by Caballera and Lyons (1990). We therefore include the capital stock per capita as a regressor. The human capital stock is included as a regressor for the same reason.
8. The measures for civil liberties are a subjective index from 1 (most freedom) to 7 (least freedom). Barro and Lee's (1994) data set does not report this index for Hong Kong, except the average of 1985–89. We assume here that there is no change during the period from 1970 to 1985 in Hong Kong.
9. External debt is the only exception, because using initial values causes a severe multi-collinearity problem in our regressions.
10. Data on FDI come from the table titled 'Direct Investment Abroad and Direct Investment in the Reporting Economy' in the *Balance of Payments Statistics Yearbook* (International Monetary Fund). However, data for Hong Kong and Taiwan are not available in the IMF publications. Therefore, the FDI data reported in the *World Investment Directory* (United Nations, 1992) is used for these two economies. The GDP data for Hong Kong comes from the *Key Indicators of Developing Asia and Pacific* (Asian Development Bank). Taiwan's GDP comes from the *Taiwan Statistical Data Book* (Council for Economic Planning and Development, 1997).
11. We use a decade's average data in all our regressions to avoid measurement problems on capital stock as mentioned earlier.
12. Alternatively, we merge the data with a period dummy, which is equal to one for the 1981–90 average and zero for 1971–80, and use ordinary least squares to conduct our estimations. The results are quite similar to those from the SUR estimations with cross-equation restrictions, but the R^2's are much lower. The period dummy is positive and significant, indicating that the average TFP growth rates are higher in the 1980s than in the 1970s.
13. We also separate the data into high (above sample average)-schooling and low (below or equal to sample average)-schooling groups, and then multiply the two groups with FDI to test whether the interaction between FDI and schooling should be differentiated by levels of schooling. The estimation results on the interaction terms are still insignificant for both groups, with all the remaining

results largely unaffected in terms of their significance and signs.

14. Note that although M2 does not have a significant association with TFP growth, removing it increases the explanatory power of both schooling and the interactions of schooling with FDI. Thus, M2 seems to be a sensitive factor in explaining the relationship between education and TFP growth.

REFERENCES

Abramovitz, M. (1986), 'Catching-up, Forging Ahead and Falling Behind', *Journal of Economic History*, **46**, 385–406.

Asian Development Bank (various issues), *Key Indicators of Developing Asia and Pacific*, Manila: Asian Development Bank.

Banker, R.D. (1996), 'Hypothesis Tests Using Data Envelopment Analysis', *Journal of Productivity Analysis*, **7** (2/3), 139–60.

Barro, R.J. (1991), 'Economic Growth in a Cross Section of Countries', *Quarterly Journal of Economics*, **106** (2), 407–43.

Barro, R. and J.W. Lee (1993), 'International Comparison of Educational Attainment', *Journal of Monetary Economics*, **32** (3), 361–94.

Barro, R. and J.W. Lee (1994), 'Sources of Economic Growth', *Carnegie-Rochester Conference Series on Public Policy*, **40**, 1–46.

Baumol, W.J. (1986), 'Productivity Growth, Convergence, and Welfare: What the Long-run Data Show', *American Economic Review*, **76** (5), 1072–85.

Benhabib, J. and M.M. Spiegel (1994), 'The Role of Human Capital in Economic Development: Evidence from Aggregate Cross-country Data', *Journal of Monetary Economics*, **34** (1), 143–73.

Borenszstein, E., J. De Gregorio and J.W. Lee (1998), 'How Does Foreign Direct Investment Affect Economic Growth?', *Journal of International Economics*, **45** (1), 115–35.

Caballero, R.J. and K.L. Lyons (1990), 'Internal versus External Economies in European Industries', *European Economic Review*, **34**, 805–30.

Caves, D.W., L.R. Christensen and W.E. Diewert (1982), 'The Economic Theory of Index Numbers and the Measurement of Input, Output, and Productivity', *Econometrica*, **50** (6), 1393–414.

Chang, C.C. and Y. H. Luh (2000), 'Efficiency Change and Growth in Productivity: The Asian Growth Experience', *Journal of Asian Economics*, **10** (4), 551–70.

Council for Economic Planning and Development (1997), *Taiwan Statistical Data Book*, Taipei: Council for Economic Planning and Development.

Debreu, G. (1951), 'The Coefficient of Resource Utilization', *Econometrica*, **19** (3), 273–92.

Dowrick, S. and D. Nyugen (1989), 'OECD Comparative Economic Growth 1950–85: Catch-up and Convergence', *American Economic Review*, **79** (5), 1010–30.

Drysdale, P. and Y. Huang (1997), 'Technological Catch-up and Economic Growth in East Asia and the Pacific', *Economic Record*, **73** (222), 201–11.

Easterly, W. and H.R. Yu (1999), 'Database for Global Development Network', http://www.worldbank.org/html/prdmg/grthweb/GDNdata.htm, Accessed 11/15/1999.

Färe, R., E. Grifell-Tatjé, S. Grosskopf and C. A. K. Lovell (1997), 'Biased Technical Change and the Malmquist Productivity Index', *Scandinavian Journal of Economics*, **99** (1), 119–27.

Färe, R. and S. Grosskopf (1996), *Intertemporal Production Frontiers: with Dynamic DEA*, Boston/London/Dordrecht: Kluwer Academic.

Färe, R., S. Grosskopf and C.A.K. Lovell (1994a), *Production Frontiers*, Cambridge: Cambridge University Press, Chapter 9.

Färe, R., S. Grosskopf, M. Norris and Z. Zhang (1994b), 'Productivity Growth, Technical Progress, and Efficiency Change in Industrialized Countries', *American Economic Review*, **84** (1), 66–83.

Färe, R. and C.A.K. Lovell (1978), 'Measuring the Technical Efficiency of Production', *Journal of Economic Theory*, **19** (1), 150–62.

Farrell, M.J. (1957), 'The Measurement of Productive Efficiency', *Journal of the Royal Statistical Society Series A: General*, **120**, 253–81.

Felipe, J. (1999), 'Total Factor Productivity Growth in East Asia: A Critical Survey', *Journal of Development Studies*, **35** (4), 1–41.

Findlay, R. (1978), 'Relative Backwardness, Direct Foreign Investment, and the Transfer of Technology: A Simple Dynamic Model', *Quarterly Journal of Economics*, **92** (1), 1–16.

Goodfriend, M. and J. McDermott (1998), 'Industrial Development and the Convergence Question', *American Economic Review*, **88** (5), 1277–89.

Grosskopf, S. (1996), 'Statistical Inference and Nonparametric Efficiency: A Selective Survey', *Journal of Productivity Analysis*, **7** (2/3), 161–76.

Hsieh, C.T. (1999), 'Productivity Growth and Factor Prices in East Asia', *American Economic Association Papers and Proceedings*, **2**, 133–8.

International Monetary Fund (various issues), *Balance of Payments Statistics Yearbook*, Washington, DC: IMF.

International Monetary Fund (various issues), *International Statistics Yearbook*, Washington, DC: IMF.

Kim, J. -I. and L. J. Lau (1994), 'The Source of Growth of the East Asian Newly Industrialized Economies', *Journal of Japanese and International Economics*, **8** (3), 235–71.

Kim, J. -I. and L. J. Lau (1996), 'The Sources of Asian Pacific Economic Growth', *Canadian Journal of Economics*, **29**, Special Issue, 448–54.

King, R. G. and S. T. Rebelo (1993), 'Transitional Dynamics and Economic Growth in the Neoclassical Model', *American Economic Review*, **83** (4), 908–31.

Krugman, P. (1994), 'The Myth of Asia's Miracle', *Foreign Affairs*, **73** (6), 62–78.

Landes, D. (1990), 'Why Are We So Rich and They So Poor', *American Economic Review*, **80**, 1–13.

Parente, S. L. and E.C. Prescott (1993), 'Changes in the Wealth of Nations', *Quarterly Review, Federal Reserve Bank of Minneapolis*, **17** (2), 3–16.

Pritchett, L. (1997), 'Divergence, Big Time', *Journal of Economic Perspectives*, **11** (3), 3–17.

Romer, P. M. (1986), 'Increasing Returns and Long-run Growth', *Journal of Political Economy*, **94**, 1002–57.

Romer, P. M. (1990), 'Endogenous Technological Change', *Journal of Political Economy*, **98** (5), Part 2, 71–102.

Summers, R. and A. Heston (1991), 'The Penn World Table (Mark 5): An Expanded Set of International Comparisons, 1950–87', *Quarterly Journal of Economics*, **106** (1), 1–41.

United Nations (1992), *World Investment Directory*, **1**, Asia and the Pacific, New York: United Nations.

Wang, J-Y. (1990), 'Growth, Technology Transfer, and the Long-run Theory of International Capital Movements', *Journal of International Economics*, **29** (3–4), 255–71.

World Bank (1991), *World Development Report: The Challenge of Development* New York: Oxford University Press.

Young, A. (1992), 'A Tale of Two Cities: Factor Accumulation and Technical Change in

Hong Kong and Singapore', in O. J. Blanchard and S. Fisher (eds), *NBER Macroeconomic Annual*, Cambridge, Ma: MIT Press, 13–54.

Young, A. (1994), 'Lessons from the East Asian NICs: A Contrarian View', *European Economic Review*, **38** (3–4), 964–73.

Young, A. (1995), 'The Tyranny of Numbers: Confronting the Statistical Realities of the East Asian Growth Experience', *Quarterly Journal of Economics*, **110** (3), 641–80.

Part II

Trade

6. Total Factor Productivity and the Catching-up Process

Yeun Yeun Lim and Henry Wan

1 INTRODUCTION

Growth accounting introduces four types of systematic bias that understate the efficiency gain in newly industrialized economies (NIEs) and cause a variety of unwarranted conclusions. For development studies, a better performance measure is the proportional rate of income gap reduction.

This chapter is part of a larger study. It serves three purposes: first, to reconsider the notion of total factor productivity growth (TFPG); second, to offer an alternative performance measure for economic development; and finally, to relate these two measures empirically. These issues are addressed in the next three sections. Some concluding remarks then follow.

2 ON TFPG

Today, TFPG is a ubiquitous empirical tool for economic growth and development. Debates raged in the early 1990s, when the measurement of the TFPG of the Asian NIEs led to four surprising conclusions, namely, these economies:

1. had insignificant and indifferent rates of technical progress,
2. gained merely a one-shot benefit from trade, at best,
3. owed their output growth only to increased input use (in particular, capital input), and
4. would suffer the same fate as that of the former Soviet economy (the 'Krugman hypothesis').[1]

According to Felipe (1999), these findings are supported by the 'fundamentalists' with additional estimates, but criticized by the 'assimilationists', because of contradicting measurements of TFPG and because growth accounting took no account of important facts from case studies, such as the assimilation of foreign technology. Yet, in the cited literature, almost no one had established any systematic bias in growth accounting,[2] or offered any alternative measurement for developmental performance.

These last two aspects are important from the historical perspective. TFPG was introduced by Solow (1957), using the aggregate production function. According to Solow (1966, 1257-60), the aggregate production function is not 'rigorously justifiable'. For him, it serves only as 'either an illuminating parable or a mere device to handle data, to be used so long as it gives good empirical results, and to be abandoned as soon as it doesn't, or as soon as something better comes along'. Under Solow's standard, the presence of either *systematic bias* or a *better alternative* would limit the application of TFPG. This will be so especially for the non-OECD economies, an application about which Solow (2000) has serious reservations.

Further digression is in order. The efficacy of growth accounting rests on three critical assumptions:

1. there is only one universal good,
2. the saving/income ratio is exogenously decided by behavioral factors, and
3. production technology is unaffected by influence outside the economy.

As we shall see later, the relaxation of these assumptions may invite systematic bias.

Solow (1957) was the first to apply growth accounting to a mature economy — America. As the leading industrial power at that time, America had little to learn from others. Thus, in his context, the third assumption is rather innocuous. Now, that growth accounting exercise was a complement to Solow (1956), which established the fact that given any substitutability between capital and labor, the Harrod–Domar model loses its 'knife-edge' property. To prove his point, Solow retained the first and second features. These came from the writings of Roy Harrod and John Maynard Keynes, where in the one-good economy, the saving behavior follows the 'Fundamental Psychological Law' and 'Animal Spirit' decides the investment. These assumptions were never the only consideration for Solow, for example, witness the theoretic investigation in Samuelson and Solow (1956), which offers a *many-good* version for the Ramsey model of *optimal saving*.

In this chapter, we take a different approach from the literature surveyed by Felipe. It may well be true that the 'Krugman hypothesis' makes no distinction between the former Soviet Union, an isolated victim of creative destruction, and Singapore, the host that benefited from the best high-tech multinational corporations (MNCs). It may well be true that the hypothesis stands on both the Kim and Lau (1994) study *and* the Young (1994) findings: the former concludes that statistically, the efficiency gain of Japan is significant and that of Korea is not; the latter ranks Korea higher than Japan in productivity gain. But our concern here is not how valid is a particular set of estimations, but, whether, as a method, growth accounting carries what kind of implicit, systematic bias about NIEs, wherever they are, in East Asia today, or in any other location at any other time.

By their nature, NIEs are in a process of becoming more industrialized, and they have only started doing so recently. This has systematic effects on individual, firm, sector and economy-wide levels.

2.1 Individual Level

At the *individual level*, agents with forethought usually save more to invest in the future, if industrialization presents more rewarding investment prospects. This causal chain is shown as the arrow with a question mark in Figure 6.1. It is not considered in growth accounting.

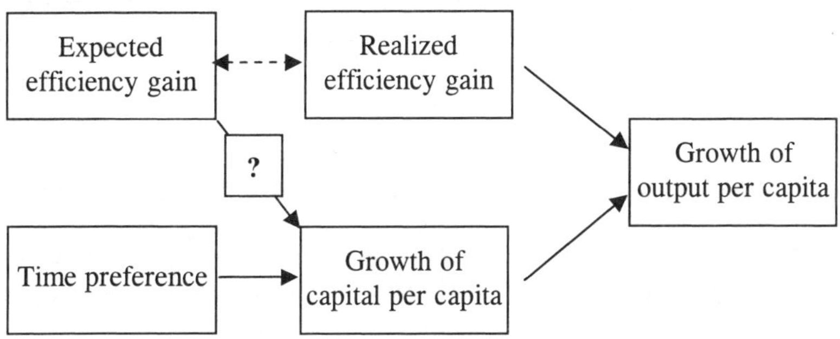

Figure 6.1 Causal chain in question: does efficiency gain matter to investment?

2.2 Firm Level

At the *firm level*, in an economy undergoing industrialization, enterprises more frequently make and implement long-term plans. For benefits in the long-haul they incur once-and-for-all investment in sunk cost. This situation is depicted in Figure 6.2.

One example is the well-documented entry of Hyundai Motors of Korea into the American market. This move was deemed crucial to Hyundai's viability (Stern et al., 1995). In preparation, for this move, Hyundai invested for years, and acquired the technology to meet the *American* standard for emission control. An allowance was made for a loss of $1,000 per car on its first American sales. Since both learning by exporting and the investment were indispensable to the whole project, clearly efficiency gain cannot be computed as a residual. Also trade must benefit growth. The project was planned in the 1970s, under President Park's Heavy-Chemical Industry

Drive. After a decade-long gestation period, the first American sales were made in 1986.

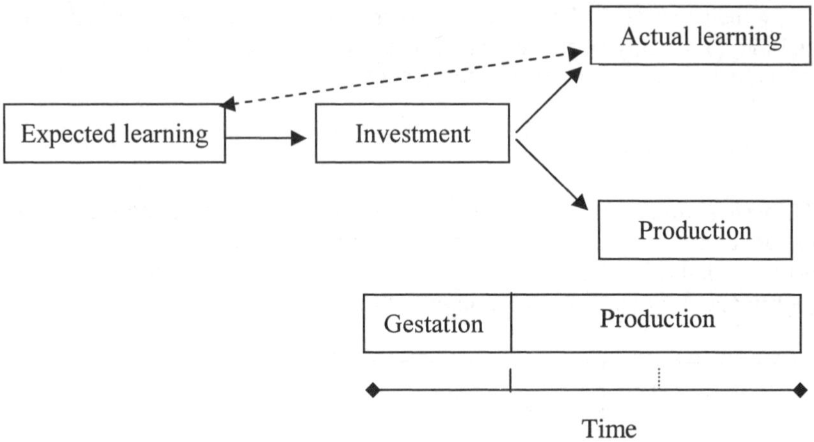

Figure 6.2 Phased production

The NIEs are, after all, economies that are *newly* industrialized. There tend to be proportionately more projects in the gestation phase. Because of such separation in time, growth accounting — based on the aggregate data from such economies — is likely to exaggerate the importance of increased capital spending during the early years.

Assuming that the production phase is twice as long as the gestation phase, a comparison between an NIE and a 'mature' industrialized economy is depicted in Figure 6.3 Proportionately speaking, the NIEs have fewer projects in the production phase but more in the gestation phase. According to traditional growth accounting, more capital spending means less efficiency gain, since the latter is regarded as a residual.

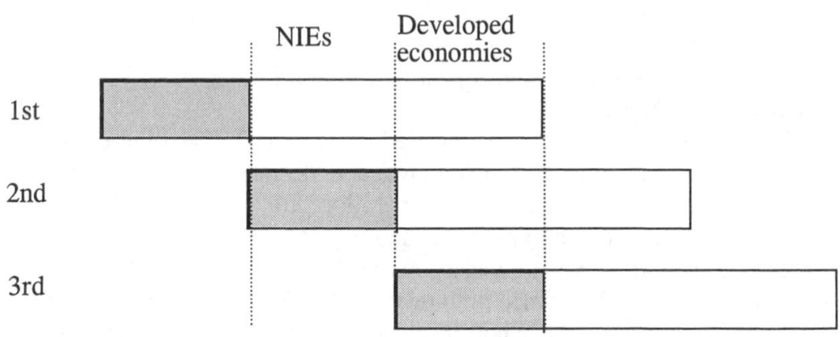

Figure 6.3 Economies and overlapping generations of projects

2.3 Sector Level

At the *sector level*, the first movers in a new industry make investments that provide information beneficial to the late-coming rivals. This discourages firms from being pioneers. In economic development, the justification for an industrial policy is its ability to remedy coordination failure. Whether due to government action (such as in Taiwan, Korea and Singapore) or a changing environment (such as in Hong Kong), new industries begin to emerge. Granted that for each firm, certain sunk cost is incurred in capital spending at the initial stage, and firms enter industries in all economies all the time, yet in a new industry, the firm making the first move must pay more in sunk cost. Proportionately there are more new industries in NIEs; therefore more capital spending is to be expected.

2.4 Economy Level

At the *economy level*, the process of industrialization provides valuable experience, both improving product-specific skills in those current operations and acquiring generic capability for more complex operations. The enhanced generic capability makes it profitable for firms to enter industries that use more valuable equipment per worker, that is, in industries with a higher capital/labor ratio.

For the sake of simplicity, consider an economy with a sequence of three sectors, light, heavy and high-tech, each operating under constant returns. Each industry is more complex than the last, which means a higher capital/labor ratio is used at any factor-price ratio. Entry into more complex industries is facilitated by the accumulation of generic industrial capability. The production process in any industry contributes to the accumulation of such competence. This is represented in Figure 6.4. The production process of each industry yields a threefold joint product: (i) the output, (ii) the specific skill that is useful in the same industry and (iii) the accumulation of generic industrial capability. The last one contributes to the operation of industries of greater complexity and hence capital intensity.

As in Van and Wan (1997), Figure 6.5 portrays the unit-value isoquants for the three industries, in both a developed economy and a 'pre-development' economy.

In the figure, there are three unit-value isoquants, shown as solid lines, labeled light industry, heavy industry and high-tech industry. Each shows the minimum labor–capital pairs that are needed to produce one unit value of output in the specific industry. Along the common tangent line ab (cd) for any pair of adjacent unit-value isoquants, the capital/labor ratio is higher in the heavy (high-tech) industry than in the light (heavy) industry. Points on

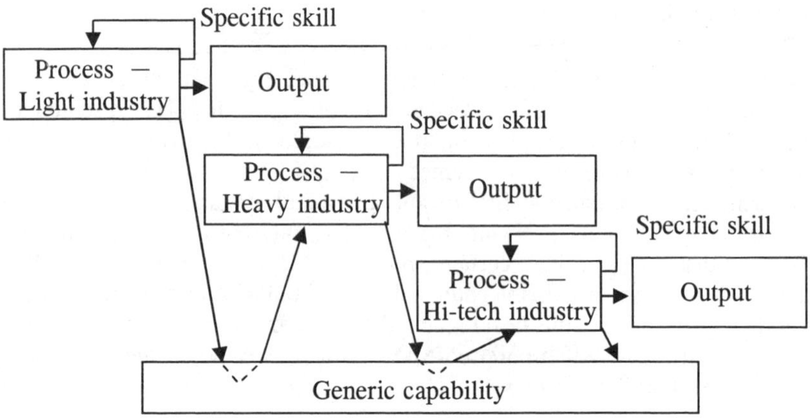

Figure 6.4 Specific and generic learning

any common tangent line represent the pairs of labor and capital inputs which can be so divided and allocated to the two adjacent industries, so that under constant returns, they will still produce one unit value of total output. The three isoquants together with the two common tangent lines become ee, the unit-value envelope for the pre-development economy. Only labor–capital pairs above or to the right of this envelope can produce one unit value of output. In contrast, in the developed economy, less input can still produce a unit value of output by using more advanced technology. This is depicted by

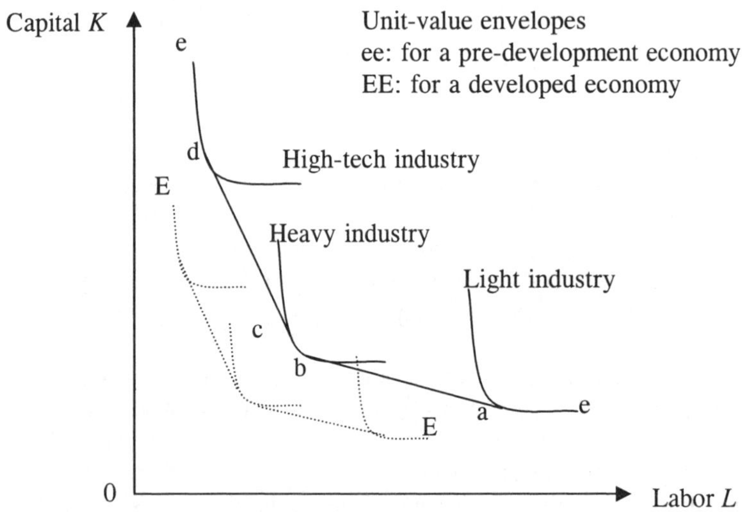

Figure 6.5 Unit-value isoquants and envelopes

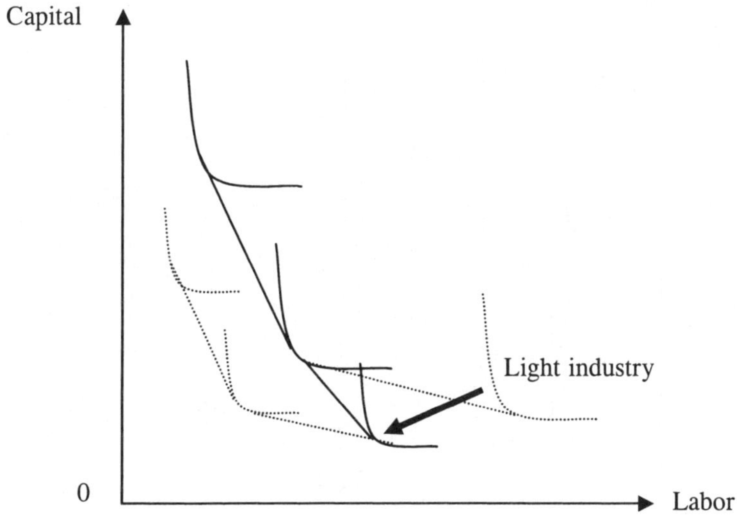

Figure 6.6 Early developing phase

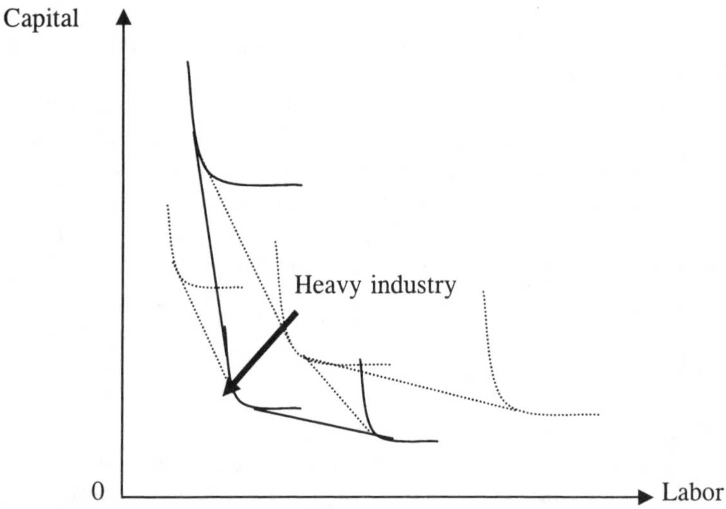

Figure 6.7 Late developing phase

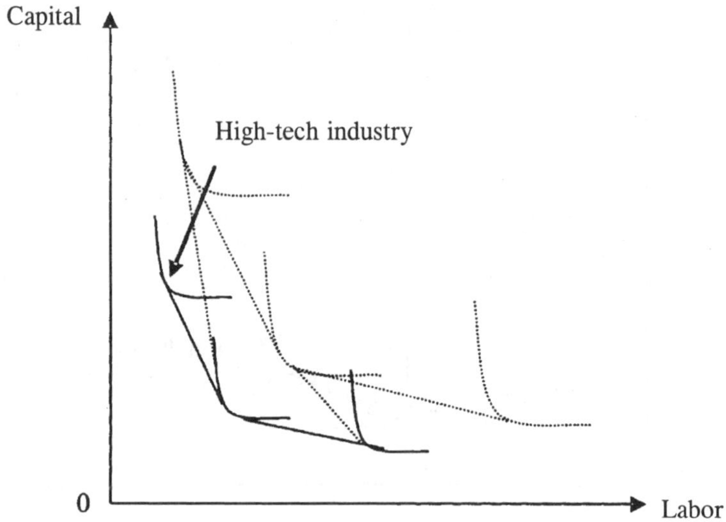

Figure 6.8 The developed economy

the unit-value industry-specific isoquants, their common tangent lines, as well as the envelope EE.

The development process allows the developing economy to assimilate foreign technology, but to do so for only one industry at a time. Moreover, progress will start from the simplest or the most labor-intensive sector, and move gradually into the more technically complex and the more capital intensive sectors. These are shown in Figures 6.6, 6.7 and 6.8. The envelope curve, shown as a solid line, joins the available unit-value isoquants with common tangent lines.

2.5 Summary

It is time now to take stock of the implications of the above analysis. Under the analysis described in Section 2.4, an economy enjoying rapid output growth would accumulate much generic capability, which will lead to a rapid shift of comparative advantage toward the capital-intensive industries. Under traditional growth accounting, capital accumulation would be regarded as the main source for growth, leaving little as the 'Solow residual'.[3] Now consider the analyses in Sections 2.2 and 2.3 together. Proportionately speaking, the NIEs are likely to have more industries that are new, with their firms paying the price of the first mover with heavier spending in sunk cost. There will also be more firms involved in the early phases of long-term plans, spending heavily during the gestation period of their plants. The 'pre-development' economies do not have to invest in such capital spending. Mature industrialized economies have already gone through this phase, and are presently enjoying the fruits of past endeavor. Thus, under the traditional growth accounting, the playing field is never level when one compares the NIEs against the other economies. Therefore, the actual productivity gain of the NIEs should be systematically larger than is found under growth accounting. This is true both in the relative sense, due to the analyses in Sections 2.2 and 2.3, and in the absolute sense as in Section 2.4. Although their productivity gain is less visible to the practitioners of growth accounting, it should be obvious to agents in those economies. According to the analysis in Section 2.1, such awareness will increase the rate at which they need to save in order to invest, in response to the encouraging prospects for growth. On the other hand, those drawing conclusions from their estimated TFPG would not look into what motivates investment, paying no heed to the Lucas critique (1976). In that sense, the role of efficiency gain (and what 'openness' has contributed to it) is systematically misrepresented, over and over again, all in the same direction of understatement.

3 AN ALTERNATIVE PERFORMANCE MEASURE

3.1 Motivation

Growth accounting was introduced to serve growth theory, which arose in the middle of the twentieth century. The growth theory has its focus on the *fully developed economies*; the premise is independent evolution, with influence from outside of the economy taken as given. By the end of the century, two trends become evident. First, the world economy has become increasingly integrated into a global system. As shown by data from the World Trade Organization, total trade has grown faster than total output, in almost all sectors, from agriculture to mining to manufacturing, and for all four post-Second World War subperiods, namely, 1950–63, 1963–73, 1973–90, and 1990–99.[4] Second, the growth literature, such as Lucas (1988, 1993), also cites the dramatic record of the NIEs[5] as evidence. Nowadays, growth theorists apply the same analytic approach to both the fully developed and other economies.

It is only natural that the new century will bring forth new research efforts, built upon the achievements of earlier theories, but also taking into account additional facts. The outline of such research is already predictable. It must capture a cardinal fact of this brave new world: the interdependence among the various economies, from the most advanced to the less developed. This, of course, is a theme already examined by Prebisch (1959) and Vernon (1966), and analyzed in the influential paper of Krugman (1979).

What has not been studied in depth is the fact that some economies of the developing South, like Japan, can reinvent themselves as members of the developed North. Logically, this process should be the most important matter in the field of development economics.

The new theory should also be empirically based. During the last dozen years or so, various types of endogenous growth model have arisen. Solow (2000) voiced his reservations, because each of these theories relies heavily upon highly specific assumptions. Now in all natural sciences, the presence of competing explanations of reality is commonplace. An example is whether global warming has already begun. In field after field, time after time, scientists eventually reach consensus by searching for testable implications and the observed evidence. There is every reason to believe that research in economics will proceed in a similar manner, rebuilding consensus on observations. Indeed, there is already a thriving literature on the convergence hypothesis. However, most such research is not based upon an overall conceptual framework. Consequently, the observed results often appear mutually contradictory, and defy interpretation. That is why we shall revisit such grounds anew.

3.2 The Technical Gap: The Concept and the Quantification

Having decided to study the interdependence of various economies empirically, we believe a good starting point is the series of per capita GNPs at international prices, as available in the data bank, namely, the World Development Index. There are 110 economies with uninterrupted data over those 24 years, 1975–98.[6] Set $N=110$, $T=24$. We shall call these $NT=2{,}640$ entries the *basic array*. Invoking a theme that has long been studied, namely, the 'technology gap,' the next step is to search for evidence for a theory about the interactions between the advanced 'center' and the followers in the 'periphery'. Our objective is to find for any 'following economy' at any instant, a measurement for this technology gap.

In principle, the problem can be quite complex. In real life, the center for technical progress is likely to cut across national boundaries. It may include both Tokyo, Japan and Silicon Valley, California, USA, but not Hokkaido, Japan or West Virginia, USA. Given the statistics available to us, our task becomes much simplified if we can approximate the center with a single economy.

In searching for one particular economy as a proxy for the center, it is preferable to follow some formal criteria. This might be done in two steps. First, over the era studied,[7] look *first* for a class of economies, each of which has enjoyed the highest per capita real GDP for at least one period. Call this class (of economies) the *dominant set*, and refer to its size as 'n'.

This set is said to be *properly dominant*, if $n<N$. The presence of a proper dominant set presumably implies a differentiated world. Second, find out in per capita real GDP, whether any of these n economies in this set ranks within the top n places, for all the N periods. If so, call this a *leading economy*. An economy fulfilling this 'ranking condition' must have access to a broad range of 'best practices'. Hence it can serve as the source of technology transfer. Finally, ask whether such economic leadership is unique. if the answer is positive, the technology gap can be computed in a straightforward manner.

The above discussion is lengthy but necessary. When working with many economies over a sufficiently long era, it seems to be too much to expect that there is only a single leader, and that particular economy is also the sole member of the dominant set. (See Appendix 6A for the five examples that clarify such concepts.)

For once, economists are quite lucky. Data show that together with Luxembourg, Switzerland and the United Arab Emirates, America belongs to a four-economy properly dominant set. Further, among these four, America alone is the economic leader.[8]

Overtaking the economic leader is neither impossible by logic, nor unprecedented in history. Yet, over the two and half centuries after the Industrial Revolution, the only clear case of such an event is America overtaking Britain. In that case, America, as an emerging leader, had exhibited tremendous technological precocity for a long period. The observations within our basic array offers few clues about *whether*, *when* and *how* the American economic leadership will be displaced by *which* other economy. In the recent past, there is as yet no other economy, beside America, that has exhibited such extraordinary technical vigor.

The presence of a consistent economic leader is convenient for studying those 106 economies outside the proper, dominant set.[9] Using concepts going back to Alexander Gerschenkron and Simon Kuznets, we may study a few purely arithmetical relationships between q_{it}, the per capita real GDP of a specific economy i and Q_t, the same for the leading economy. The ratio, $r_{it}=q_{it}/Q_t$, is sometimes referred to as the relative per capita real output (or GDP) and R is defined as the steady-state value of r_{it}. R may be assumed to be either unity, which means an actual catching-up with the leader, or it may take some other positive value, on account of certain other immutable facts. For example, one may consider the advantage of Singapore, as both a natural harbor and a defensible island at the head of the Malacca Strait, or the challenge for Finland of having the short growth season of 'Arctic farming'. Thus, ultimately Singapore may be somewhat richer than America and Finland somewhat poorer. In the late twentieth century, the rising output per capita has been the norm rather than the exception for most economies. Therefore in development economics, *international inequality*, rather than *poverty*, poses the popular challenge.

From this perspective, what is relevant are the expressions, $Q_t - q_{it}$, and perhaps even more appropriately, $g_{it} = (Q_t - q_{it})/Q_t = 1 - r_{it}$. These are specifically, the absolute and relative (per capita, real) output gaps of economy i, relative to the economic leader. At the same time, due to the non-rival nature of knowledge, emulation (or imitation) is often easier than innovation. The presence of an output gap is both a challenge, with its closing as the goal for development, and an opportunity. The presence of the gap makes it easier to improve the current practice toward the 'best practice'. Thus we shall refer to g_{it} as the *technological backlog*.

To recapitulate, in the mid-twentieth century, growth theory arose in order to study the advanced economies under *independent* evolution. At the dawn of the new millennium, a catching-up theory should be developed in this increasingly *interdependent* world, for the sake of all the technologically less advanced, whether in Bombay, Singapore, Sydney or Paris. After all, from laser to optical fiber, from the production of sub-micron semiconductors to Internet communication via the globally-positioned satellite system, from containerized shipping to bio-engineered food, most of such progress becomes implemented, if not also initiated, in a single economy. This fact poses specific economic choices for that 95 percent of the world's population residing elsewhere.

Speaking generally from the economic point of view, there are three parts of the current world: the developed North, the less-developed South, and the evolving East. The North and the South may appear poles apart. But there is never any East Pole. The East is a metaphor for those regions emerging from the ranks of the South to converge toward the North. Those converging at a fast pace largely rely on their close economic relationship with America, that economy in the North which is the incumbent economic leader. The observed performance of East Asia represents a phase of transformation. This process of transformation is not automatic, or instantaneous, or accessible to all. By themselves, the poorest economies may not attempt the transformation at all, or even if they try as hard as possible, not all may succeed. For others, conscious government action may be needed to overcome market failure. In any case, a self-sustained transformation may take time to bear fruit.

What made Japan (and Korea and Hong Kong) economically successful is not all that different from some more recent development episodes in the periphery of Europe along the great arc, from Israel (in the Near East) to Cyprus, from Malta to the Iberian Peninsula and thence to Ireland. Their record reflects the same general process at work. In that sense, both the wrong and the right steps taken by these economies are useful at least to those 95 percent of humankind referred to above.

The empirical findings on such issues are the subject matter of the on-going studies of Lau, Hong and Wan, and much of the historical and institutional analysis will be elaborated in the monograph of Wan (2004). In this chapter, we have two principal goals in mind: first, the catching-up rate, and second, the growth of total factor productivity (TFP), which serves as the workhorse in usual empirical macroeconomics.

We shall first present some analytic relationships between the catching-up rate, z_{it}, (which is the relative rate of change of g_{it}), and the growth rate, G_{it} (which is the relative rate of change of q_{it}), under some simple hypotheses. Next, we shall present some elementary findings by analyzing the evidence from the basic array. We find that the growth paths of several economies such as Japan and Singapore, as well as Malta, bear close resemblance to the predicted time paths for per capita product under one of our simple models. Furthermore, the findings in Lau and Wan (1994) imply that $R < 1$. In other words, the catching-up tends to be incomplete. This is in agreement with some of the simple models.

We then compare the rankings of 66 economies by Young (1994) with the average catching-up rates we have obtained from the basic array. The weak correlation between these two rates is related to the low TFP of the East Asian NIEs, as found by Kim and Lau (1994). Such paradoxical results can be explained by the nature of East Asian development, namely, the remedy of market failure during the launching of new industries. In this phase, massive investment is made prior to the initiation of industrial production. Due to the non-synchronized cost and benefit flows of such investment, the conventional procedure of growth accounting can easily lead to paradoxical results.

3.3 Some Basics about the Catching-up Models

We now focus attention on one economy at a time. Our purpose is to characterize the evolution of the income gap, for economies in the North (that is, among the developed economies), in the South (that is, among those in the pre-development phase) and in the East (that is, the 'emerging economies'). We shall provisionally assume that $R = 1$, so that every economy can exactly catch up with the leading economy. The notations can be greatly simplified by suppressing any subscripts for economy or time for the gap measure, $g = 1 - r$, which is always a positive fraction.

We then plot the gap $g(t)$ against time t in semilog scale and call it 'the economy curve' for convenience. Note that $\log g(t)$ always appears as negative magnitude, below the time axis. Our attention is on the proportional reduction rate of the gap,

$$(dg / dt) / g = d(\log g) / dt.$$

This is just the slope of the *economy curve*. The steeper the curve, the faster is the proportional rate of gap reduction. If the gap is eliminated for a particular period, the economy curve will diverge to negative infinity with a vertical slope. An exponential decay of the gap is represented as a negatively sloped straight line. A concave (convex) economy curve implies an increasing (decreasing) rate of proportional gap reduction. These concepts are illustrated below.

Figure 6.9(a) displays the economy curve for France, as an example of a developed economy. There is a very mild negative slope for the economy curve. By and large, the magnitude of the proportional income gap has not changed much at all for the quarter of a century being studied.

Figure 6.9(b) depicts the positively sloping economy curve for Côte d'Ivoire, which is falling behind relative to America, the leading economy. This is an example of a 'pre-development' economy. In spite of the gradual increase of the per capita real GDP, the income gap widened over the period of study.

Figure 6.9(c) shows four 'emerging economies', Korea and Singapore from Asia and Ireland and Malta from Europe. Over the period studied, all four have managed to narrow the income gap relative to America since each of these economy curves exhibits a general negative trend. For much of this period, up to the very end, the income gaps have been narrowed down at an increasing proportional rate. Only during the Asian financial crisis, do the economy curves of Korea and Singapore acquire a positive slope. Malta is steadily narrowing down the income gap between it and America, at an accelerating rate during the earlier years but at a decelerating rate at the very end. Among these four, Ireland alone maintains an increasing rate of gap reduction throughout the entire period.

To gain more perspective, we display the performance of Japan in Figure 6.9(d). The high growth period of Japan had passed by 1975. This figure shows the gap closing at a decreasing pace during the period shown. In the end, the gap between Japan and America remains at a certain magnitude, in spite of a sequence of seesaw movement. The broken line indicates the overall trend of catching-up. The third-degree polynomial trend line reveals the fact that there is a phase of accelerated growth for Japan, followed by deceleration, while the American growth rate is much more stable.

So far we have selected seven out of the 106 economies for display. From these, it is evident that the catching-up process is determined by three sets of factors: (a) the economy-specific factors; (b) the policy choices; and (c) the phase of the process.

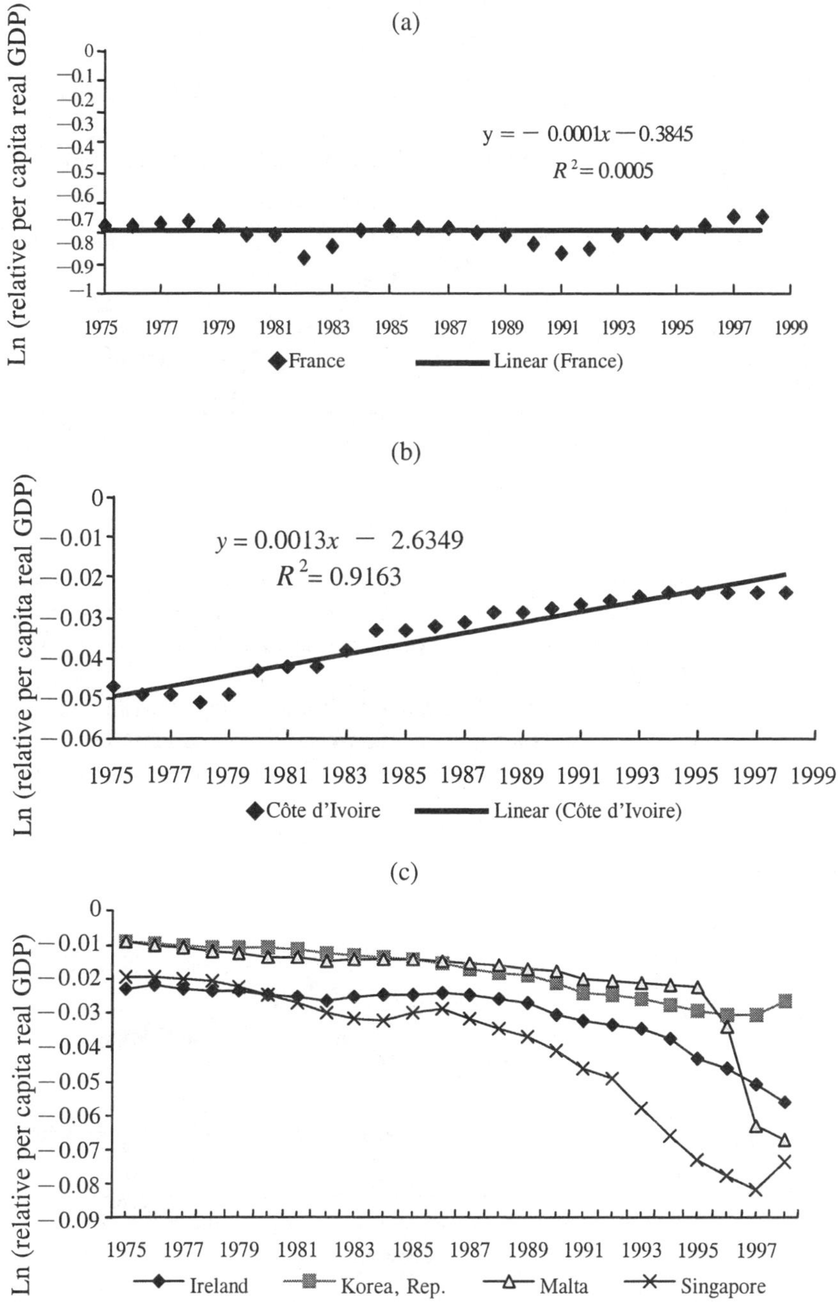
(a)
Ln (relative per capita real GDP)
y = − 0.0001x − 0.3845
R² = 0.0005
France
Linear (France)
(b)
Ln (relative per capita real GDP)
y = 0.0013x − 2.6349
R² = 0.9163
Côte d'Ivoire
Linear (Côte d'Ivoire)
(c)
Ln (relative per capita real GDP)
Ireland
Korea, Rep.
Malta
Singapore

(d)

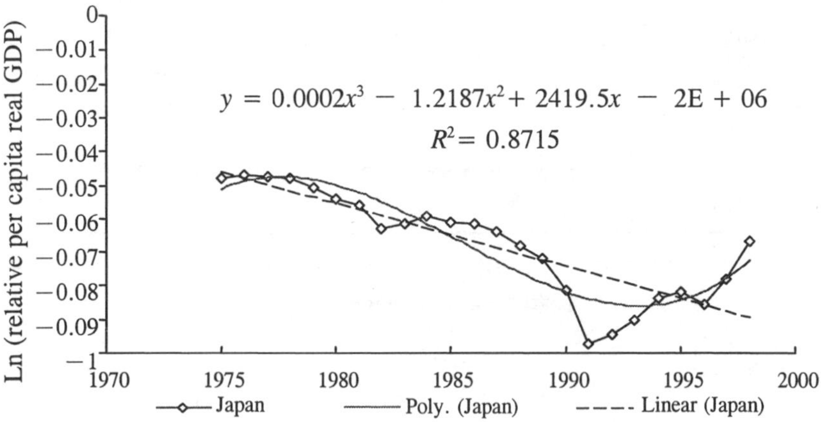

Figure 6.9 Gap in semilog

In this exploratory study, we have run 106 economy-specific linear equations regressing the logarithm of the gap against time. In such equations, the constant term is a measure of the average gap for an economy over the period of study, 1975–1998.

In Figure 6.10, we display a scatter diagram plotting the slope coefficients against the constants for those economy-specific equations. The figure requires some careful interpretation. For the 24 years in question, it shows that:

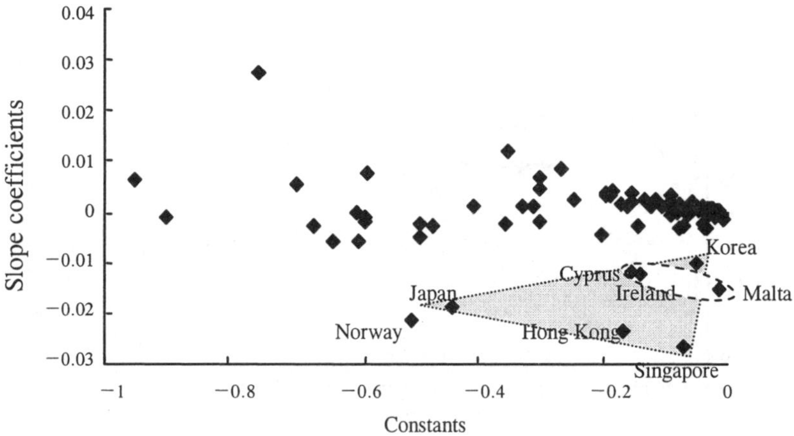

Figure 6.10 Scatter diagram for 106 economies

1. Of all the 106 economies, income gaps were widening (narrowing) for 64 (42) of them, over the period in question. Gap narrowing is not the usual pattern, let alone something automatic.
2. Those economies with the smallest initial gap (and therefore the most negative logarithmic values) correspond to observations near the left border of the figure. These economies are not associated with negative slopes that signify the trend for closing the gap further. This means that none of these 106 economies is catching up with America (the leader) in the near future.
3. Those 64 economies that are falling behind (that is, with positive slopes) have observations above the horizontal axis. The 'center of gravity' of this subset is near the right border. That is to say, their initial gap is very large so that the logarithmic values are negative, also close to 0. In other words, the typical economy that is falling behind is one with an initial gap approaching 1. That is to say, in purchasing power parity (PPP) terms, the values of their per capita GDPs are exceedingly small fractions relative to the American value.
4. In contrast, those 42 economies that are catching up with America have observations below the horizontal axis. Their 'center of gravity' is somewhat away from the right border. That is to say, the typical economy that is catching up is not among those with extremely low real GDP per capita relative to America.
5. In terms of the catching-up performance, the observations on the four East Asian economies have spanned a dotted triangle, and the observation on the three economies at the fringe of European Union (Ireland, Malta and Cyprus) are enclosed in an oval shape in dashed lines. The oval fits into the triangle like a hand into a glove. That is to say, for those who are successful in the catching-up process, similar economic forces seem to outdistance whatever differences might exist in cultural and historical spheres.

The last point is important. The scatter diagram seems to be almost a cloud, justifying the caution of Solow (2000) against cross-country comparisons in general. Nonetheless, for those that are successful in the process of catching-up, one can still describe the process in the manner used by Kuznets (1982). In short, a pattern amenable to research emerges. This pattern is applicable to both the developed economies (the North) and those economies that have somehow 'joined the club' (the East) in distinction to all the rest (the South). After all, Korea is the most recent member of the OECD, the group Solow focuses attention on. The result is an expanding horizon, with some hopeful regularity in the pattern of 'club' expansion.

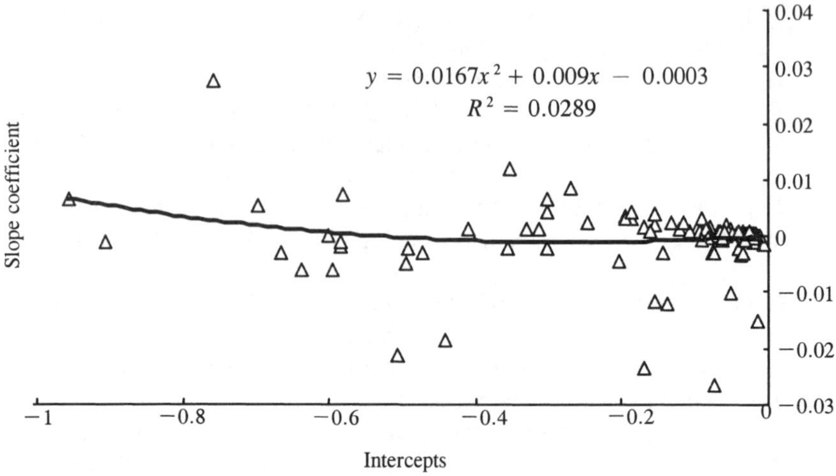

Figure 6.11 Scatter diagram with quadratic trend

With an added parabolic trend line, Figure 6.11 crystalizes points 3 and 4 above. The parabola is convex, with its apex below the horizontal axis. As observed by Lucas (1988) and discussed in Lau and Wan (1994), the poor economies have the least growth. This is presumably because of their limited capacity to exploit the available technological backlog. Rich economies have the greatest ability to learn from others, yet the amount of available technological backlog is minimal. The result is that the mid-income economies have the most impressive record in catching-up.

As a matter of fact, some more may be said. First, the leading economy has the most ability to imitate any near competitor, should the latter establish some local advantage over any limited range of the commodity spectrum. The revival of the American competitiveness against Japan in the last decade in areas such as quality control in auto making is a clear example. Second, as emphasized in Lau and Wan, catching-up is far from a free lunch. Resources must be committed even in the process of emulation. As Kuznets (1982) emphasized, poor economies cannot utilize the huge technological backlog, because there are various constraints blocking their progress. In market economies, investment decisions are usually made by private agents. Among these constraints, coordination failure is a crucial cause. The NIEs manage to have some success, often as a result of fortunate or judicious government action. In this process, long-term, massive investment has been made by either the government or the private sector, in the launching of new industries. See Itoh et al. (1991) and Miyajina et al. (1999).

4 RELATING THE TWO INDICES

We have now shown that the catching-up rate is an intuitive concept with some descriptive power over the empirical data. The concept of TFP has received wide attention in the recent literature, yet its use has also led to rather paradoxical conclusions. The question is, do economies showing strong growth in TFP also have outstanding records in catching up? From the 53 economies that appear in both the study of Young (1994) and our data for the catching-up ratio, we obtain Figure 6.12. Given the staggered period of coverage, one may ask whether the rate of TFP growth during 1970–85 can be a basis for predicting the ability of an economy to catch up for the 1975–98 period. Based upon the scatter diagram of Figure 6.12, the answer is clearly no. In fact, as highlighted by the twin blips in the figure, economies with low TFP growth, like Singapore, Japan and Korea, have reduced their income gap at proportional rates no slower than any other economy. Likewise, three of the four economies with the highest scores in TFPG – Egypt, Pakistan and Congo – have seen their income gap widened rather than reduced.[10]

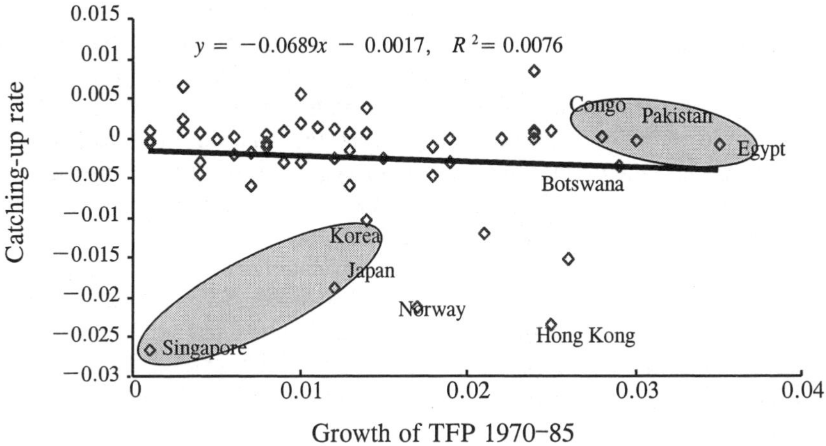

Source: Young (1994).

Figure 6.12 Relating two indices

5 CONCLUDING REMARKS

Economists are presumably interested in the *future* levels of per capita GDP, in real terms, rather than in the *current* figures of per capita GDP, or TFPG, or the rate of proportional gap reduction. *Current* rates of output growth are not heavily relied upon, because such growth rates are expected to vary from time to time. Solow (2000) explained the stand of the neoclassical growth theorists. For a country like America, one should first of all calculate the time path of TFP, and determine the implication of such an estimate for the economy. A separate 'theory of technology' can then be used to forecast the future trend of TFPG. The practitioners of growth accounting usually omit the formal forecasting of the future value of TFPG, as if its current value is assumed to last into the future. When the economy in question is a developing economy, enjoying the fruits of new-found mineral wealth, such an extrapolation is obviously prone to error.

The computation of the current relative rate of income gap reduction is certainly not an end in itself either, because as the past record shows us, this rate can also vary over time. On the other hand, it appears a much more useful intermediate step for research than TFPG. It helps to focus attention on the process of assimilating technology from abroad. This is both a principal link in the causal chain of growth, and is dependent upon policy regimes. For example, the effect of 'openness' should be explored in full. In all these, further study is needed.[11]

According to Young, East Asian high growth is based upon high investment; according to Krugman (1994), the high rate of investment that East Asian economies are engaging in may not be sustainable. Yet ten to 15 years after their period of study, the high performance of East Asian economies remains relatively strong, when the criterion of performance is 'catching-up' rather than the rate of growth, *per se*. The change in performance criterion here carries some importance. In particular, by using the catching-up criterion, it is not expected that any economy (say, Singapore), which is technologically no better than the 'leading economy', can maintain a higher rate of growth than the technological leader, when the gap is largely erased. Incidentally, on this catching-up basis, Japan has performed a good deal better than Korea. Their growth slowing down owes much to the exhaustion of the technological backlog rather than the saturation of capital investment.

APPENDIX 6A

Five Examples of the Search for the Leading Economy

Consider the case with three economies ($N = 3$) over three periods ($T = 3$). The values of per capita real GDP are tabulated below for Example 1. The highest value for any period is marked by an asterisk. In this case, each economy is the one with the highest per capita GDP in a different period. The dominant set is the same as the population of all economies, so that $n = 3 = N$. There is no proper, dominant set.

Example 1	No proper dominant set		
q_{it}	$t = 1$	$t = 2$	$t = 3$
$i = 1$	1	5	9*
$i = 2$	3*	4	7
$i = 3$	2	6*	8

Next, we consider Example 2, with the relevant data tabulated below. In all three periods, the peak value is associated with either economy 1 or economy 2. Again the highest value for any period is marked by an asterisk. In this case, the dominant set is {1, 2}, with two members, so that $n = 2 < N = 3$. This is a proper subset of the population of all economies. Therefore, we call {1, 2} a proper dominant set. However, each member of the proper dominant set fails in some period to rank within the first $n = 2$ places. specifically, economy 1 fails in period 1 and economy 2 fails in periods 2 and 3. In each case, a failure marked by a hash, #. Therefore there is no 'leader' in the population of is economies.

Example 2	No leader in the proper dominant set		
q_{it}	$t = 1$	$t = 2$	$t = 3$
$i = 1$	1#	6*	9*
$i = 2$	3*	4#	7#
$i = 3$	2	5	8

We next consider Example 3, where again the economies 1 and 2 form a proper dominant set, {1, 2} with two members. Only economy 3 fails to rank within the first $n = 2$ places. The use of * and # are the same as before. Now economies 1 and 2 rank within $n = 2$ places in every period. A 'leader economy' is marked by a dagger,†.

Example 3	No single leader		
q_{it}	$t = 1$	$t = 2$	$t = 3$
$i = 1^{\dagger}$	2	5	9*
$i = 2^{\dagger}$	3*	6*	8
$i = 3$	1#	4#	7#

In the next example, again both economies 1 and 2 form a proper dominant set, so that $n = 2 < 3$, but only economy 1 ranks within the first two places every period, so that there is a unique 'leader economy'.

Example 4 Existence of a single leader

q_{it}	$t = 1$	$t = 2$	$t = 3$
i = 1 †	2	5	9*
i = 2	3*	6*	7#
i = 3	1#	4#	8

Finally in the last of our five examples, we consider the case where the dominant set is a singleton, that is identical to the unique leader economy, namely economy 1.

Example 5 A single leader is the dominant set

q_{it}	$t = 1$	$t = 2$	$t = 3$
i = 1 †	3*	6*	9*
i = 2	1#	4#	8#
i = 3	2#	5#	7#

ACKNOWLEDGMENTS

The second author is most grateful for the comments of Dr. Simone Clemhout and the helpful assistance from Ms. Andrea Williams-Wan. All remaining errors are the responsibility of the authors.

NOTES

1. See Wan (2001) for more details.
2. An exception is Pack (2001).
3. It is also not clear how an aggregate production will be estimated under growth accounting as the observations come from a sequence generated by a mechanism depicted in Figures 6.5, 6.6, 6.7 and 6.8.
4. The exception is mineral products between 1973 and 1990.
5. These are not yet fully developed.
6. For political reasons, Russia, Germany and Taiwan do not have an unbroken data series over the 24 years. Both Hong Kong and the rest of China are represented.
7. Here an era covers more than one period, as is the usage in geology.
8. Simple logical examples can be constructed to show that the existence of neither the *properly dominant set,* nor an economic *leader* can be guaranteed in all possible worlds. Moreover, the *economic leadership* need not always be unique.

9. What can be said about the United Arab Emirates, Luxembourg and Switzerland will be dealt with later.
10. One might say that ten or 15 years do not represent the long run. How about another ten or 15 years? With due respect, the wait for a 'Congo Miracle' seems increasingly to look like the wait for Godot.
11. The ongoing work of Hong, Lau and Wan explores the effect of exports. For an empirical verification of the bias of the TFPG, see Park and Van (2001).

REFERENCES

Felipe, Jesus (1999), 'Total factor productivity growth in East Asia: a critical survey', *Journal of Development Studies*, **35**, 1–41.

Itoh, Motoshige, Kazuharu Kiyono, Masahiro Okuno-Fujiwara and Kotaro Suzumura (1991), *Economic Analysis of Industrial Policy*, San Diego, CA: Academic Press.

Kim, Jong-Il and Lawrence J. Lau (1994), 'The source of economic growth of the East Asian newly industrialized countries', *Journal of Japanese and International Economics*, **8** (3), 235–71.

Krugman, P. (1979), 'A model of innovation, technology transfer and the world distribution of income', *Journal of Political Economy*, **87** (2), 253–66.

Krugman, P. (1994), 'The myth of Asia's miracle', *Foreign Affairs*, **73** (6), 62–78.

Kuznets, S. (1982), 'Modern economic growth and the less developed countries', in Kwoh-ting Li and Tzong-shian Yu (eds), *Experience and Lessons of Economic Development in Taiwan*, Taipei: Academia Sinica.

Lau, Man-lui and Henry Y. Wan, Jr. (1994), 'On the mechanism of catching-up', *European Economic Review*, **38**, 952–63.

Lucas, Robert E., Jr. (1976), 'Econometric policy evaluation: a critique', *Journal of Monetary Economics*, **2**, Supplement, 19–46.

Lucas, Robert E., Jr. (1988), 'On the mechanics of economic development', *Journal of Monetary Economics*, **22** (1), 3–42.

Lucas, Robert E., Jr. (1993), 'Making a miracle', *Econometrica*, **61**, 257–72.

Miyajima, Hideaki, Takeo Kikkawa and Takashi Hikino (eds) (1999), *Policies for Competition*, New York: Oxford University Press.

Pack, Howard (2001), 'Technological change and growth in East Asia: macro versus micro perspectives', in Joseph E. Stiglitz and Shahid Yusuf (eds), *Rethinking the East Asian Miracle*, New York: Oxford University Press, 95–142.

Park, Ghunsu and Pham Hoang Van (2001), *Technological Change as a Series of Localized Technical Gains: Evidence from Korea, Singapore, and Taiwan,* Working Paper #01-06, University of Missouri, Columbia, MO.

Prebisch, Raul (1959), 'Commercial policy in underdeveloped countries', *American Economic Review, Papers and Proceedings*, **49**, 252–73.

Samuelson, Paul A. and Robert M. Solow (1956), 'A complete capital good model involving heterogeneous capital goods', *Quarterly Journal of Economics*, **70**, 537–62.

Solow, Robert M. (1956), 'A contribution to the theory of economic growth', *Quarterly Journal of Economics*, **70**, 5–94.

Solow, Robert M. (1957), 'Technical change and the aggregate production function', *Review of Economics and Statistics*, **39**, 312–20.

Solow, Robert M. (1966), 'Review of John R. Hicks, Jr., *Capital and Growth*',

American Economic Review, **56,** 1257–60.

Solow, Robert M. (2000), *Growth Theory, An Exposition*, 2nd edn, Oxford: Oxford University Press.

Stern, Joseph J., Ji-hong Kim, Dwight H. Perkins and Jung-ho Yoo (eds) (1995), *Industrialization and the State: The Korean Heavy and Chemical Industry Drive*, Cambridge, MA: Harvard University Press.

Van, Pham, H. and Henry Y. Wan, Jr. (1997), 'Interpreting East Asian growth', in B.S. Jenssen and K.Y. Wong (eds), *Dynamics, Economic Growth and International Trade*, Ann Arbor, MI Michigan University Press, 286–86.

Vernon, Raymond (1966), 'International investment and international trade in the product cycle', *Quarterly Journal of Economics*, **80**, 190–207.

Wan, Henry Y., Jr. (2004), *Economic development in a globalized environment: East Asian evidences*, Norwell MA: Kluwer Academic Publishers.

Young, Alwyn (1994), 'Lessons from the East Asian NICs: a contrarian view', *European Economic Review*, **38** (3–4), 964–73.

7. Indeterminacy in a Dynamic General Equilibrium Model of International Trade

Koji Shimomura

1 INTRODUCTION

Making use of a simple two(-country) by two(-tradable good) dynamic general equilibrium (DGE) model of international trade, we show that indeterminacy is possible without assuming any source of distortion such as technological externalities, increasing returns, government interventions or market imperfection.

Indeterminacy is a topic which has been paid much attention in the recent growth literature. In particular, the central question is under what conditions is it possible in a dynamic general equilibrium model. Authors commonly have assumed some kind of market distortion in their models, specifically: external increasing returns with perfect competition, some types of market imperfection, or government interventions.[1]

This chapter shows that indeterminacy is possible in a two(-country) by two(-tradable good) DGE model of international trade. We believe that the main result is new in the literature on indeterminacy. The DGE model in this chapter is completely standard in that production is subject to constant returns to scale, that there is neither inter- nor intranational externalities, either in production or in consumption, that perfect competition prevails in every market, and that there is no government intervention. The main message is that none of those distorting factors is necessary for the occurrence of indeterminacy.

As will be shown subsequently, two assumptions together contribute to the occurrence of indeterminacy. One of them is a strong negative income effect and the other is free trade between the two countries. Neither assumption implies market distortion.

The organization of this chapter is as follows. Section 2 describes the DGE model. Sections 3 secures tractability at the cost of some simplifications. By using a phase diagram which depicts a continuum of DGE paths, Section 4 proves the main indeterminacy proposition and discusses in what way the strong negative income effect contributes to the occurrence of indeterminacy. Section 5 makes clear why international trade is necessary for indeterminacy. Appendix 7A explains how to derive the phase diagram.

2 THE MODEL

The two by two DGE model is based on the model developed in Shimomura (1993) which was formulated in order to investigate the implications of time preferences for the trade pattern. The trading world consists of two countries, Japan and the United States, which produce two tradable goods, rice and cars. Rice is non-durable, while cars are durable. Both of them are consumption goods and neither is a factor of production. We assume that each car provides one unit of service flow per unit of time. Following the assumption on the investment good in Oniki and Uzawa (1965), we assume that newly produced cars are tradable, but existing ones are internationally immobile.

The infinitely-lived and perfectly farsighted representative agent in Japan maximizes the discounted sum of utility:

$$\int_0^\infty u(c,A)\exp(-\rho t)dt, \tag{7.1}$$

subject to:

$$\dot{A}\left(\equiv\frac{dA}{dt}\right)=Y(p)-pc-\delta A, \tag{7.2}$$

where c is the consumption of rice, A is the stock of cars owned by the agent, p is the price of rice in terms of cars, ρ is the rate of discount, δ is the rate of depreciation of cars, and $Y(p)$ is the GDP function.[2] We assume that the felicity function $u(c,A)$ is twice differentiable, increasing and strictly concave in c and A.

Define the Hamiltonian as:

$$\mathcal{H}=u(c,A)+\lambda[Y(p)-pc-\delta A] \tag{7.3}$$

where λ is the co-state variable, the shadow price of a car. The necessary conditions for optimality are:

$$\frac{\partial H}{\partial c} = u_c(c, A) - \lambda p = 0 \tag{7.4}$$

and

$$\dot{\lambda} = (\rho + \delta)\lambda - u_A(c, A), \tag{7.5}$$

where $u_c(c, A) \equiv \partial u(c, A)/\partial c$ and $u_A(c, A) \equiv \partial u(c, A)/\partial A$, and the transersality condition[3] is:

$$\lim_{t \to \infty} A(t)\lambda(t)\exp(-\rho t) = 0. \tag{7.6}$$

A parallel formulation is available for the representative agent in the US. Indicating the variables and functions belonging to the US by means of an asterisk (*), we have:

$$\dot{A}^* = Y^*(p) - pc^* - \delta^* A^* \tag{7.7}$$

$$\frac{\partial H^*}{\partial c^*} = u_c^*(c^*, A^*) - \lambda^* p = 0 \tag{7.8}$$

$$\dot{\lambda} = (\rho^* + \delta^*)\lambda^* - u_A^*(c^*, A^*) \tag{7.9}$$

and

$$\lim_{t \to \infty} A^*(t)\lambda^*(t)\exp(-\rho^* t) = 0. \tag{7.10}$$

Finally, the world market-clearing condition for rice is:

$$c + c^* = Y_p(p) + Y_p^*(p). \tag{7.11}$$

For simplicity, we assume away rental markets for existing cars.[4] The system, (7.2) and (7.4)–(7.11), is the DGE model of this chapter.[5]

3 SIMPLIFYING THE MODEL

The purpose of this chapter is not to derive a general sufficient condition for indeterminacy in a world economy without market distortion, but to provide an example of it. Thus, in order to derive clear results, we can simplify the model as follows.

First, the production technology for each good is assumed to be of Leontief type, which implies that the GDP functions are specified as $Y(p) = \alpha p + \beta$ and $Y^*(p) = \alpha^* p + \beta^*$, where α (resp. α^*) and β (resp. β^*) are the constant outputs of rice and car in Japan (resp. US). Moreover, we assume that the US is completely specialized to the production of cars, that is, $\alpha^* = 0$. Second, there is no international difference in the rates of discount and depreciation. Third, the felicity function of the US household is assumed to be quasi-linear:

$$u^*(c^*, A^*) = \eta^* \ln c^* + A^*. \tag{7.12}$$

Using these assumptions, the model can be rewritten as follows:

$$\dot{A} = p(\alpha - c) + \beta - \delta A \tag{7.13}$$

$$\dot{A}^* = -pc^* + \beta^* - \delta A^* \tag{7.14}$$

$$\dot{\lambda} = (\rho + \delta)\lambda - u_A(c, A) \tag{7.15}$$

$$\dot{\lambda}^* = (\rho + \delta)\lambda^* - 1 \tag{7.16}$$

$$u_c(c, A) - \lambda p = 0 \tag{7.17}$$

$$\frac{\eta^*}{c^*} - \lambda^* p = 0 \tag{7.18}$$

and

$$c + c^* = \alpha. \tag{7.19}$$

The dynamic system can be simplified further. First, from (7.13), (7.14) and (7.19), we have:

$$\frac{d(A + A^*)}{dt} = (\beta + \beta^*) - \delta(A + A^*), \tag{7.20}$$

which implies that the time profile $\{A(t) + A^*(t)\}_{t=0}^{t=\infty}$ depends only on $\left[A(0) + A^*(0)\right]$, $(\beta + \beta^*)$ and δ. Therefore, as far as those parameters are given, one of the time profiles, $\{A(t)\}_{t=0}^{t=\infty}$ and $\{A^*(t)\}_{t=0}^{t=\infty}$, is completely determined by the other one. Thus, without loss, we can concentrate on the time profile of $A(t)$.

Second, (7.16) means that $\lambda^*(t) = 1/(\rho + \delta)$, $\forall t > 0$, if $\lambda^*(0)$ is chosen as $1/(\rho + \delta)$. Since the Hamiltonian associated with the dynamic optimization by the representative household in the US is concave with respect to c^* and A^* under (7.12) and (7.14), the standard Mangasarian sufficiency condition ensures that the representative household behaves optimally under this choice of $\lambda^*(0)$ if $A^*(t)$ is bounded. Since (7.20) means that $A(t) + A^*(t)$ converges to $\beta + \beta^*/\delta$ for any $A(0) + A^*(0)$, the boundedness of $A^*(t)$ is guaranteed if that of $A(t)$ is guaranteed.

Let us assume that $\lambda^*(0)$ is chosen as $1/(\rho + \delta)$. Then, from (7.18) we derive the US demand function for rice, $c^* = (\rho + \delta)\eta^*/p$. Making use of the demand function, the above model can be much simplified as:

$$\dot{A} = (\rho + \delta)\eta^* + \beta - \delta A \tag{7.21}$$

$$\dot{\lambda} = (\rho + \delta)\lambda - u_A(c, A) \tag{7.22}$$

$$u_c(c, A) - \lambda p = 0 \tag{7.23}$$

and

$$c + \frac{(\rho + \delta)\eta^*}{p} = \alpha. \tag{7.24}$$

4 THE INDETERMINACY RESULT

Let us obtain the main result in this chapter. To do so, we derive the loci $\dot{A} = 0$ and $\dot{\lambda} = 0$ on the (λ, A)-plane. It immediately follows from (7.21) that the locus $\dot{A} = 0$ is a horizontal line like *fEFGf'* in Figure 7.1. Let us concentrate on deriving the locus $\dot{\lambda} = 0$.

First, note that (7.22)–(7.24) and $\dot{\lambda} = 0$ yield:

$$\frac{\eta^*}{\alpha - c} = \frac{u_c(c, A)}{u_A(c, A)} \tag{7.25}$$

and

$$\lambda = \frac{u_A(c, A)}{(\rho + \delta)}. \tag{7.26}$$

Totally differentiating (7.25) and (7.26) with respect to λ, c and A, we obtain:

$$\left.\frac{dA}{d\lambda}\right|_{\dot{\lambda}=0} = \frac{(\rho + \delta)\left[u_c^2 - (u_A u_{cc} - u_c u_{Ac})\eta^*\right]}{u_{AA}u_c^2 - u_A \eta^*(u_{cc}u_{AA} - u_{cA}^2)}. \tag{7.27}$$

Since we assume that $u(c, A)$ is increasing and strictly concave in c and A, the denominator of (7.27) is always negative. If the cross-partial derivative u_{Ac} is positive, the numerator of (7.27) is positive and therefore (7.27) is always negative. One can verify that the negatively-sloped locus $\dot{\lambda} = 0$ together with the horizontal locus $\dot{A} = 0$ generate a saddlepoint-stable stationary state on the (λ, A)-plane. On the other hand, if u_{Ac} is negative, the sign of the numerator is ambiguous. In fact, as is shown in Appendix 7A (A.1–A.3), under the following specification of $u(c, A)$ the cross-partial derivative u_{Ac} is negative and the locus $\dot{\lambda} = 0$ can be U-shaped on the (λ, A)-plane.

Lemma 1 Let us specify $u(c,A)$ as $v[\ln(c+A+1)+c]$, where $v(X)$ is a twice-differentiable, increasing and strictly concave function of $X \geq 0$. Then, this specified felicity function is also twice differentiable, increasing and strictly concave in c and A. There is a measurable set Γ in the parameter space (α, η^*) such that for any (α, η^*) in Γ the locus $\dot{\lambda} = 0$ is U-shaped on a part of the (λ, A)-plane in which a positive c maximizes the Hamiltonian.

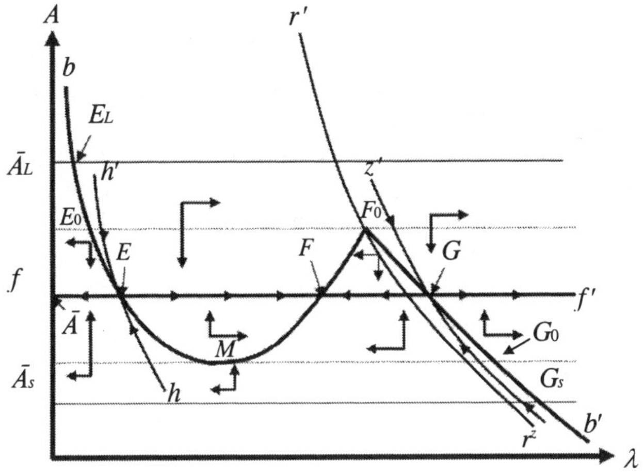

Notes:
Curve $bE_0EMFF_0GG_0G_sb'$ means $\lambda = 0$ curve $fEFGf'$ means $A = 0$.
Curve $h'Eh$, $z'Gz$ means the stable arms.
Curve $r'F_0r$ means the graph of $\tilde{\lambda}(A)$; curve $F_0GG_0G_s$ means the graph of $\hat{\lambda}(A)$.

Figure 7.1 The phase diagram

Appendix 7A (A.2 and A.4) shows that there is a border that divides the (λ, A)-plane in such a way that a positive c maximizes the Hamiltonian at one side of the border while $c = 0$ maximizes the Hamiltonian at the other side, and that the locus $\dot{\lambda} = 0$ is negatively sloped at the latter side. Combining the two loci $\dot{\lambda} = 0$, we derive the phase diagram (see Figure 7.1). Note that while the stationary-state value $\bar{A}_o \equiv (\rho+\delta)\eta^* + \beta/\delta$ depends on β, the locus $\dot{\lambda} = 0$ does not. Hence, by choosing an appropriate β, we can make the two loci intersect three times, that is, at *E*, *F* and *G*. Note that while *E* and *G* are saddlepoint stable, *F* is stable in the ordinary sense. Thus, indeterminacy and multiple stationary states occur simultaneously. That is, we find in Figure 7.1 that there is a continuum of DGE paths which commonly converge to point, *F*. Moreover, for a given initial value of the state variable A, the initial point, $A(0), \lambda(0)$, can be chosen either on hEh' or zGz' so that the DGE path converges to E or G. Thus, there are multiple stationary states. Let us state the main result.

Proposition 1 For appropriate values of the parameters, the DGE model not only has indeterminacy but also three stationary states in which A takes on a common value. Two of them are saddlepoints and the other is a stable point.

What are the main sources of the multiple stationary states and indeterminacy? First, the multiplicity is based on the fact that the locus $\dot{\lambda} = 0$ has an upward-sloping portion like MFF_0 in Figure 7.1 along which (7.27) is positive. Thus, what we need to explain is why the locus has the upward-sloping portion. Since A is equal to the service flow from the stock A and λ is the shadow price of cars, one can interpret the locus $\dot{\lambda} = 0$ as the home demand curve for the car service. To show why this interpretation is possible, consider the 'static' optimization problem as follows:

$$\max_{c,b} u\left(c, \frac{1}{\delta}b\right) \quad \text{subject to} \quad \lambda\beta + p\alpha \geq \lambda b + pc,$$

where p and λ are given. Let us solve the classroom exercise and obtain the demand function for the service flow, $b(\lambda, p)$. Then, one can verify that, at least near the stationary states,

$$sign\left[\left.\frac{dA}{d\lambda}\right|_{\dot{\lambda}=0}\right] = sign\left[\frac{\partial}{\partial\lambda}b(\lambda, p)\right]$$

as long as p satisfies the market-clearing condition (7.24) and ρ is very small.[6] Therefore, if the felicity function $u(.)$ is such that it generates a strong negative income effect so that b is a Giffen good for a range of its price λ, then the locus $\dot{\lambda} = 0$ has an upward-sloping portion. The above felicity function $v[\ln(c + A + 1) + c]$ is in fact one of such felicity functions.

Second, the negative cross-partial derivative of the home felicity function plays an important role for indeterminacy to occur. Suppose that the world economy is initially in a stationary state and that λ happens to jump at time zero. It is clear from (7.21) that A is unaffected by the jump and is kept at its stationary-state level. Now, let us focus on the shadow price λ. Other things being equal, in order for (7.22) to hold, a jump in $(\rho + \delta)\lambda$ has to have a positive direct effect on $\dot{\lambda}$, which means that the shadow price λ deviates further from the stationary state after time zero. At the same time, there is a negative indirect effect as follows. Denoting by $\bar{c}(\lambda p; A)$ the solution to (7.23), we can write the world market-clearing condition as:

$$\bar{c}(\lambda p; A) + \frac{(\rho+\delta)\eta^*}{p} = \alpha. \tag{7.24'}$$

Since $\bar{c}(\lambda p; A)$ is a decreasing function of $\lambda p,$ a rise in λ means that the LHS of (7.24′), the world demand function for rice, shifts down at time zero. It follows that both the home rice consumption, $\bar{c}(\lambda p; A)$, and the world market-clearing price, p, must be lowered at time zero. Then, if the cross-partial derivative u_{Ac} is negative, a decline in the home rice consumption raises the marginal felicity to cars, u_A. As is clear from (7.22), the decline in c reduces $\dot{\lambda}$. That is, the negative indirect effect of a jump in λ on $\dot{\lambda}$ If the negative indirect effect dominates the positive direct effect, $\dot{\lambda}$ becomes negative after the jump in $\lambda(0)$. As a result, λ declines toward its original steady-state level.

Let us check whether the indirect effect does dominate the direct effect. Denoting by $p(\lambda, A)$ the market-clearing price derived from (7.24′) and letting $c(\lambda, A) \equiv \bar{c}\left[\lambda p(\lambda, A); A\right]$, the DGE system (7.21)–(7.24) can be written as:

$$\dot{A} = (\rho+\delta)\eta^* + \beta - \delta A \tag{7.28}$$

and

$$\dot{\lambda} = (\rho+\delta)\lambda - u_A\left[c(\lambda, A), A\right]. \tag{7.29}$$

The characteristic equation of the system (7.28) and (7.29) is:

$$\begin{aligned} F(x) &\equiv \begin{vmatrix} x+\delta & 0 \\ u_{Ac}c_A + u_{AA} & x-(\rho+\delta)-u_{Ac}c_\lambda \end{vmatrix} \\ &= (x+\delta)[x-(\rho+\delta)-u_{Ac}c_\lambda] \\ &= 0, \end{aligned}$$

where $c_\lambda \equiv \partial c(\lambda, A)/\partial\lambda$, which is negative from (7A.5) in Appendix 7A(A.2). Thus, the characteristic equation has two negative real roots if $(\rho+\delta) - u_{Ac}c_\lambda < 0$, that is, if the negative indirect effect $-u_{Ac}c_\lambda$ dominates the positive direct effect $\rho+\delta$. The substitution of (7A.5) into the second root yields:

$$(\rho+\delta) - u_{Ac}c_\lambda = \frac{(\rho+\delta)\left[u_c^2 - (u_A u_{cc} - u_{Ac}u_c)\right]}{u_c^2 - u_A u_{cc}\eta^*}. \qquad (7.30)$$

Comparing (7.30) with (7.27), we find that (7.30) is negative if and only if the locus $\dot{\lambda} = 0$ is upward sloping. Figure 7.1 reveals that the indirect effect dominates the direct effect at the middle stationary state F and indeterminacy occurs around there.

5 CONCLUDING REMARKS

We have shown that some specific assumptions on preferences can generate indeterminacy in a standard convex DGE model without any distortive factor. Note that international trade or, more exactly, the existence of asymmetric households, is necessary for our result. If Japan is a closed economy, the domestic demand for rice c is always equal to its domestic supply α, which implies that (7.29) becomes:

$$\dot{\lambda} = (\rho+\delta)\lambda - u_A(\alpha, A).$$

Thus, a jump in λ induces only a positive direct effect on $\dot{\lambda}$. Therefore, indeterminacy is impossible.

It is our next research agenda to examine whether the present specific model can be generalized. In particular, we would like to check to what extent we can proceed without the specific assumptions like quasi-linearity.

APPENDIX 7A

A.1 The Properties of $v\left[\ln(c+A+1)+c\right]$

Let us show that if $v(X)$ is twice-continuously differentiable in $X \geq 0$, then $v\left[\ln(c+A+1)+c\right]$ is also strictly increasing and concave in c and A. The partial differentiation of $v[\ln(c+A+1)+c]$ with respect to c and A yields:

$$\begin{aligned} u_A &= v' \cdot (c+A+1)^{-1} > 0 \\ u_c &= v' \cdot \left[(c+A+1)^{-1} + 1\right] > 0 \\ u_{AA} &= (v'' - v')(c+A+1)^{-2} < 0 \\ u_{cc} &= [v'' \cdot (2+c+A)^2 - v'](c+A+1)^{-2} < 0 \\ u_{cA} &= [v'' \cdot (2+c+A) - v'](c+A+1)^{-2} < 0. \end{aligned} \tag{7A.1}$$

It follows that $u_{cc}u_{AA} - (u_{cA})^2 = -v''v'(c+A+1)^{-2} > 0$. Therefore, v [ln $(c$ $+A+1)+c]$ is increasing and strictly concave in c and A.

A.2 The Causality of the DGE Model (7.21)–(7.24)

First of all, let us check whether, under the above felicity function, p and c, which satisfy the first-order condition (7.23) and the market-clearing condition (7.24), at each point in time are uniquely determined for a given (A, λ). The first-order condition is specified as:

$$\begin{aligned} \lambda p &= u_c(c, A) \\ &= v' \left[\ln(c+A+1)+c \right] \times \left(\frac{c+A+2}{c+A+1} \right) \end{aligned}$$

or:

$$p = \frac{v' \left[\ln(c+A+1)+c\right]}{\lambda} \times \left[\frac{1}{(c+A+1)} + 1 \right] \equiv p_D(c; A, \lambda). \tag{7A.2}$$

Since $v(.)$ is strictly concave, $p_D(c; A, \lambda)$ is monotonically decreasing in c for a given (A, λ). Next, the market-clearing condition is:

$$p = \frac{(\rho+\delta)\eta^*}{\alpha - c} \equiv p_S(c), \tag{7A.3}$$

which is monotonically increasing and $\lim_{c \uparrow \alpha} p_S(c) = \infty$. Therefore, there exists a unique $c(A,\lambda) \in [0,\alpha]$ such that:

$$p_D\left[c(A,\lambda); A,\lambda\right] = p_S(c; A,\lambda),$$

if and only if $p_D(0; A,\lambda) \geq p_S(0)$ or:

$$\frac{v'\left[\ln(A+1)\right]}{\lambda} \times \left(\frac{1}{A+1}+1\right) \geq \frac{(\rho+\delta)\eta^*}{\alpha}$$

or

$$\lambda \leq \frac{\alpha v'\left[\ln(A+1)\right] \times \left(\frac{1}{A+1}+1\right)}{(\rho+\delta)\eta_*} \equiv \tilde{\lambda}(A).$$

$\tilde{\lambda}(A)$ is monotonically decreasing in A and depicted as rr' in the fourth quadrant of Figure 7A.1. For any (A, λ) below rr', p and c that satisfy the first-order condition and the market-clearing condition at each point in time are uniquely determined as interior solutions.

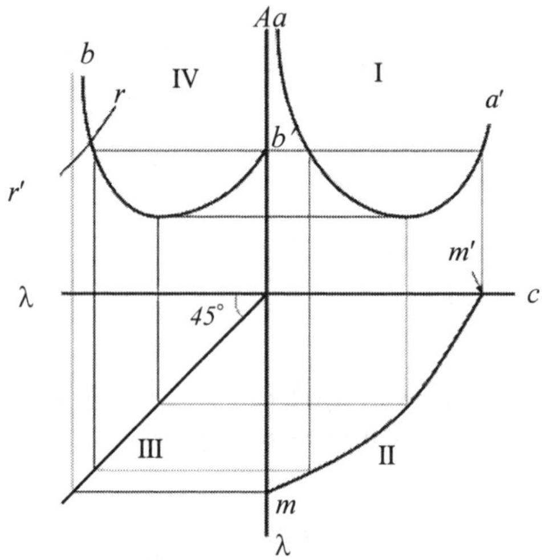

Figure 7A.1 The locus $\dot{\lambda} = 0$

Finally, let us derive the partial derivatives of $c\,(A, \lambda\,)$. If $u\,(.)$ is specified as $v\left[\ln(c+A+1)+c\right]$,

$$c_A \equiv \frac{\partial c(A,\lambda)}{\partial A} = \frac{u_A u_{cA} \eta^*}{u_c^2 - u_A u_{cc} \eta^*} < 0 \tag{7A.4}$$

and

$$c_\lambda \equiv \frac{\partial c(A,\lambda)}{\partial \lambda} = \frac{-u_c(\rho+\delta)\eta^*}{u_c^2 - u_A u_{cc} \eta^*} < 0. \tag{7A.5}$$

A.3 Deriving the Locus $\dot{\lambda} = 0$ on the Phase Diagram

Let us explain the construction of the locus $\dot{\lambda} = 0$ in the fourth quadrant of Figure 7A.1. When $u(c, A)$ is specified as $v[\ln(c + A + 1) + c]$, (7.28) can be simplified as:

$$A = \frac{\eta^*}{\alpha - c} - (c + 2) \equiv A(c). \tag{7A.6}$$

Since $\lim_{c \uparrow \alpha} A(c) = +\infty$, if $A(0) = \eta^*/\alpha - 2 > 0$ and $A'(0) = \eta^*/\alpha^2 - 1 < 0$ then the graph of $A(c)$ can be depicted like *aa'* in the first quadrant of Figure 7A.1. (See the parameter space of Figure 7A.2.) For any (α, η^*) inside the area *abh*, $A(0) > 0$ and $A'(0) < 0$. Let us denote by Γ the area *abh*.

Next, let us proceed to the second quadrant of Figure 7A.1, where we depict the graph of:

$$\begin{aligned} \lambda &= \frac{1}{\rho+\delta} u_A\left[c, A(c)\right] \\ &= \frac{1}{\rho+\delta} \frac{v'\left\{\ln\left[c + A(c) + 1\right] + c\right\}}{c + A(c) + 1} \\ &= \frac{v'\left[\ln\left(\frac{\eta^*}{\alpha - c} - 1\right) + c\right]}{(\rho+\delta)\left(\frac{\eta^*}{\alpha - c} - 1\right)} \equiv \lambda(c) \end{aligned} \tag{7A.7}$$

Since $\eta^*/(\alpha - c)$ is monotonically increasing and $v(.)$ is strictly concave, $\lambda(c)$ is monotonically decreasing for any $c \in [0, \alpha]$. Moreover, $\lambda(\alpha) = 0$ and, if $\eta^*/\alpha - 2 > 0$, $\lambda(0) = [v' \ln(\eta^*/\alpha - 1)]/[(\rho+\delta)(\eta^*/\alpha - 1)] > 0$. Thus, the graph of $\lambda(c)$ can be depicted as *mm'*.Then, depicting the 45°-line in the third quadrant and connecting those three graphs, we can derive the locus $\dot{\lambda} = 0$ in the fourth quadrant.

Now let us obtain:

$$\left.\frac{\partial \dot{\lambda}}{\partial \lambda}\right|_{\dot{\lambda}=0} = \frac{\partial}{\partial \lambda}\{(\rho+\delta)\lambda - u_A[c(\lambda, A), A]\}$$
$$= (\rho+\delta) - u_{Ac}c_\lambda$$
$$= (\rho+\delta) - \frac{u_{Ac}(\rho+\delta)\eta^*}{(\alpha-c)u_{cc} - u_c}$$
$$= \frac{(\rho+\delta)[(\alpha-c)u_{cc} - u_c - u_{Ac}(\rho+\delta)\eta^*]}{(\alpha-c)u_{cc} - u_c}$$
$$= \frac{(\rho+\delta)[u_c^2 - (u_A u_{cc} - u_c u_{cA})\eta^*]}{u_c^2 - u_A u_{cc}\eta^*}.$$

It follows from (7.29) that:

$$sign\left[\left.\frac{\partial \dot{\lambda}}{\partial \lambda}\right|_{\dot{\lambda}=0}\right] = sign\left[\left.\frac{dA}{dc}\right|_{\dot{\lambda}=0}\right] = -sign\left[\left.\frac{dA}{d\lambda}\right|_{\dot{\lambda}=0}\right]$$
$$= sign\left[u_c^2 - (u_A u_{cc} - u_c u_{cA})\eta^*\right].$$

Therefore, for any $(\alpha, \eta^*) \in \Gamma$, we can obtain a U-shaped locus $\dot{\lambda} = 0$ and a phase diagram like Figure 7.1.

A.4 The Case in which the Hamiltonian $\mathcal{H}$ has a Boundary Maximizer c=0

So far, we have focused on the case that (A, λ) is at the right-hand side of the curve *rbr'* in the fourth quadrant of Figure 7A.1, that is, that (A, λ) satisfies $\lambda < \tilde{\lambda}(A)$ which is defined in Appendix 7A(A.2). Let us consider the other side of it where the boundary solution $c = 0$. At that side, we have the locus $\dot{\lambda} = 0$ as follows:

$$\dot{\lambda} = (\rho+\delta)\lambda - u_A(0, A) = 0$$

or:

$$\lambda = \frac{u_A(0,A)}{\rho+\delta} \equiv \hat{\lambda}(A). \tag{7A.8}$$

Since u_{AA} is negative, the locus $\hat{\lambda}(A)$ is decreasing in A.

Let us compare $\hat{\lambda}(A)$ with $\tilde{\lambda}(A)$. Under the specification $u(c,A) \equiv v[\ln(c+A+1)+c]$ we obtain:

$$\tilde{\lambda}(A) - \hat{\lambda}(A) = \frac{v'[\ln(A+1)]}{(\rho+\delta)(A+1)}\left[\frac{\alpha}{\eta^*}A + (\frac{2\alpha}{\eta^*}-1)\right]. \tag{7A.9}$$

Now take a look at Figure 7.1. Along the locus E_0EMFF_0 except for F_0, $c>0$, and at F_0, $c=0$. Thus, we see that at $F_0, \tilde{\lambda}(A_{F_0}) = \hat{\lambda}(A_{F_0})$, or $\alpha/\eta^* A_{F_0} + (2\alpha/\eta^* - 1) = 0$, where A_{F_0} is the A-coordinate of the point F_0 in Figure 7.1. Therefore, under the assumption that the pair of parameters (α, η^*) is in the area *abh* in Figure 7A.2,

$$\frac{\alpha}{\eta^*}A + \left(\frac{2\alpha}{\eta^*} - 1\right) < 0 \text{ for any } A < A_{F_0}$$

or

$$\tilde{\lambda}(A) - \hat{\lambda}(A) < 0 \text{ for any } A < A_{F_0}.$$

Based on the foregoing argument, we derive the locus $\dot{\lambda} = 0$ as in Figure 7.1.

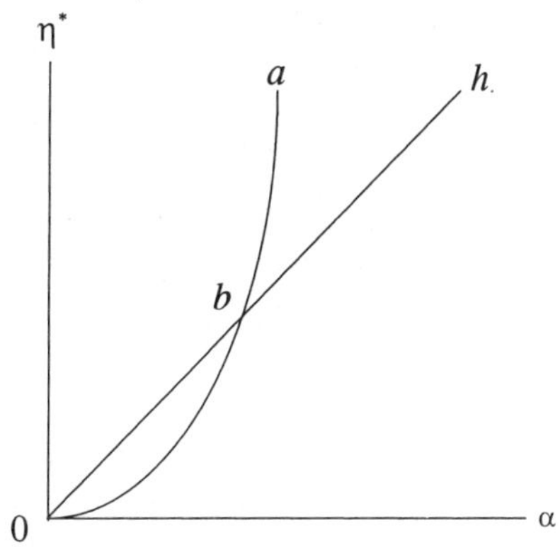

Notes:
Curve *Oba* means $\eta^* = \alpha^2$.
Curve *Obh* means $\eta^* = 2\alpha$.

Figure 7A.2 The area abh *where* $A(0) > 0$ *and* $A'(0) < 0$

ACKNOWLEDGMENTS

I am grateful to Michele Boldrin, Taiji Furusawa, Murray C. Kemp, Yoshio Kimura, Kazuo Mino, Takumi Naito, Kazuo Nishimura and Ping Wang for their valuable comments and insightful suggestions. Constructive suggestions from an anonymous referee have improved an earlier version. This research has been supported by the Grant in Aid for Research 09CE2002, 09730009 of the Ministry of Education, Science and Culture in Japan. All remaining errors are mine.

NOTES

1. See Benhabib and Farmer (1994, 1996), Boldrin and Rustichini (1994), Bond and Wang (1996), Farmer and Guo (1994) and Mino (2001), among others. Benhabib and Nishimura (1998) and Benhabib et al. (2000) show that social increasing returns are not necessary for indeterminacy if externality is assumed and sectors are multiple. Benhabib and Farmer (1999) provide a comprehensive survey of indeterminacy and related issues.
2. Suppose that there are m primary factors of production in Japan and rice and cars are produced by using a neoclassical constant returns to scale (CRS) production function, $f^x(l_1^x,\ldots,l_M^x)$, $x = rice, car$. The GDP function is defined as:

$$Y(p) \equiv \max[pf^{rice}(l_1^{rice},\ldots,l_M^{rice}) + f^{car}(l_1^{car},\ldots,l_M^{car})]$$
$$\text{subject to } l_i^{rice} + l_i^{car} \leq M_i, i = 1,\ldots,m$$

for given commodity price p and factor endowments $M_i, i = 1,\ldots,m.$ GDP and GNP functions have been popular in trade theory since a duality approach was introduced into the basic framework of trade theory. See Wong (1995) as a standard recent textbook of international trade that intensively uses a duality approach. Since there is no international rental market in the present model, GNP and GDP are identical here.
3. It is well known that there is an optimal control problem with an infinite time horizon such that an optimal solution does not satisfy the transversality condition. Kamihigashi (2001) provides a set of simple conditions under which the transversality condition is necessary for optimality. The present dynamic optimization problem satisfies the Kamihigashi conditions.
4. The main result in this chapter does not change even if domestic rental markets are assumed.
5. In the text we focus, for brevity, on the case in which a positive c maximizes the Hamiltonian $\mathcal{H}$. In Appendix 7A(A.4) the other case that $c = 0$ maximizes $\mathcal{H}$ is considered under a specification of the felicity function $u(c, A)$.
6. The proof is left to the reader.

REFERENCES

Benhabib, J. and R.E.A. Farmer (1994), 'Indeterminacy and growth', *Journal of Economic Theory*, **63**, 19–41.

Benhabib, J. and R.E.A. Farmer (1996), 'Indeterminacy and sector specific externalities', *Journal of Monetary Economics*, **37**, 397–419.

Benhabib, J. and R.E.A. Farmer (1999), 'Indeterminacy and sunspots in macroeconomics', in J.B. Taylor and M. Woodford (eds), *Handbook of*

Macroeconomics, **1**, Amsterdam: North-Holland, 387–448.

Benhabib, J., Q. Meng and K. Nishimura (2000), 'Indeterminacy under constant returns to scale in multi-sector economies', *Econometrica*, **68**, 1541–8.

Benhabib, J. and K. Nishimura (1998), 'Indeterminacy in a multi-sector model under social constant returns', *Journal of Economic Theory*, **81**, 58–96.

Boldrin, M. and A. Rustichini (1994), 'Indeterminacy of equilibria in models with infinitely-lived agents and external effects', *Econometrica*, **62**, 323–42.

Bond, E. and P. Wang (1996), 'A general two-sector model of endogenous growth with human and physical capital: balanced growth and transitional dynamics', *Journal of Economic Theory*, **68**, 149–73.

Farmer, R.E. and J.T. Guo (1994), 'Real business cycles and animal spirit hypothesis', *Journal of Economic Theory*, **63**, 42–72.

Kamihigashi, T. (2001), 'Necessity of transversality conditions for infinite horizon problems', *Econometrica,* **69**, 995-1012.

Mino, K. (2001), 'Indeterminacy and endogenous growth with social constant returns', to appear in *Journal of Economic Theory*, **97**, 203-22.

Oniki, H. and H. Uzawa (1965), 'Patterns of trade and investment in a dynamic model of international trade', *Review of Economic Studies*, **32**, 15–38.

Shimomura, K. (1993), 'Durable consumption goods and the pattern of international trade', in H. Herberg and N.V. Long (eds), *Trade, Welfare, and Economic Policies: Essays in Honor of Murray C. Kemp*, Ann Arbor, MT: Michigan University Press, 103–19.

Wong, Kar-yiu (1995), *International Trade in Goods and Factor Mobility*, Cambridge, MA: MIT Press.

8. Evaluating the Quantitative Effects of Import Restrictions — An Almost Neoclassical Benchmark

Chung Yi Tse

Then and now, it was recognized that trade policy was central to the overall design of policies for economic development (Krueger, 1997).

1 INTRODUCTION

There is by now widespread agreement that the adoption of liberal trade policies is a necessary element in any successful development strategies. The experiences of the East Asian miracle economies must be the best advertisement that there can be. More formal evidence in support of the positive influence of liberal trade policies on economic growth is abundant. The cross-country positive relationship between the growth rate of output and the share of export and import in GDP is almost always reconfirmed in every one of the countless number of studies.[1] But the questions of *how* liberal trade policies may promote growth and raise GDP are far from settled. There are many possible channels through which liberal trade policies could raise aggregate output, a few that have better-known neoclassical foundations and some more speculative. The goal of this chapter is to undertake a quantitative assessment of the positive influences of liberal trade policies on aggregate output in order to identify which channels may be potentially important and which may be safely ruled out as marginal. The confidence that we have in the accuracy of the exercise depends on how precisely we can pin down the parameters of the models. This consideration restricts our focus to models that may be readily parameterized. In particular, we shall study only explanations that may be incorporated into the neoclassical growth model with minimal additional parameterization and where the additional parameters have close empirical counterparts.

What may be such explanations?

Free trade raises the intensity of competition in the domestic economy. Firms that face more elastic demand restrict output less, raising employment and perhaps more importantly capital investment as a result. How much less the domestic monopolists produce and invest due to import restrictions would be a function of the markup of price over marginal cost — the key parameter in the model. Recent empirical evidence for the US has shown convincingly that the monopoly markup is merely around 1.03.[2] The US is relatively free of import restrictions and countries that practice more restrictive trade policies can be characterized by greater markups. Nevertheless, given the estimate for the US, the markup prevailing in a country with more restrictive trade policies is most likely bounded below 1.1.

The markup influences investment and employment incentives in a very intuitive manner. In particular, the markup is formally equivalent to a tax that raises the price of the investment good and the wage rate. A markup of 1.1, for example, would jack up the *implicit* price of the investment good and the wage rate by 10 percent. Now it is well known that only astronomical investment taxes may deliver big effects on output in the neoclassical growth model and a 10 percent tax, as will be seen in the following, has a long way to go to qualify as such. Somewhat surprisingly, the 10 percent rise in the wage rate would similarly not deliver big effects despite allowing for a fairly elastic labor supply.

In the neoclassical growth model with exogenous and disembodied technical change, the elasticity of output with respect to an investment tax is constant. This appears counterintuitive as it seems only reasonable that when the equipment price is higher to begin with, the same proportional tax should be more distortionary. Jovanovic and Rob (1999) show that switching to embodied technical change rectifies this shortcoming, and for this reason, I have followed their lead in assuming embodied technical change in this chapter. This simple change now makes it possible for us to squeeze bigger effects from import restrictions if we are willing to entertain a higher baseline investment good price. The choice for the baseline investment price is not entirely without discipline, however. Specifically, firms respond to a higher price by replacing capital equipment less often. My calculations show that for import restrictions to significantly lower investment and aggregate output, the required baseline investment good price is too large to be plausible as it would imply an undistorted replacement horizon far longer than may be deemed to be reasonable. The prudent conclusion then is that the implicit investment and employment taxes that arise from protected firms enjoying market power are not quantitatively important channels through which import restrictions inhibit economic development, in the absence of other considerations.

For one reason or another, capital equipment is often heavily taxed in developing countries. This has spawned a sizeable literature investigating the adverse effects of taxing capital equipment on aggregate output. Jones (1994) finds that the price of machinery is an empirically important determinant of equipment investment and growth. Parente and Prescott (1994), Schmitz (1993) and Jovanovic and Rob (1999) show that variations in taxes on capital equipment could generate large-level effects in variants of the neoclassical growth model if we are willing to entertain large differences in tax rates across countries. Yet, the difference in tax rates that is required to explain the observed differences in output and equipment investment across countries is often large – much larger than the observed differences in national tax codes. A common defense is that the official tax codes in poor countries could often vastly understate the true tax rates facing entrepreneurs. The distortion introduced by import restrictions is a potential source for such unobserved taxes. Now precisely because embodied technical change implies that the implicit investment tax associated with import restrictions is more distortionary when the equipment price is higher to begin with, import restrictions could conceivably make a given tax rate a significantly more serious distortion. My analysis indicates that the effects of taxing capital equipment could well double in size when there are also import restrictions. Nevertheless, the influence on aggregate output is far from impressive when we stick with a monopoly markup of 1.1 and restrict the baseline investment price to yield plausible replacement horizons.

The conclusion that we may draw from investigating the two channels discussed above is that with the distortions of import restrictions tightly tied to the monopoly markup, it does not appear possible for there to be a quantitatively important link between trade policies and aggregate output in the neoclassical growth model. The last channel I investigate breaks this correspondence. Firms operating under import protections in developing countries are often seen to be too inefficient to compete in the world market. In such economies, it would be left to firms in the open sector to export to generate the foreign exchange to finance domestic investment if capital equipment may only be imported from abroad.[3] Closing up more of the domestic economy shrinks the supply of funds available for investment. This mechanism can indeed be quantitatively important. There is no end to how much aggregate output may be lowered as the supply of investment funds is dried up by import restrictions. Admittedly, this channel has a less than impeccable neoclassical foundation as the assumption that firms selling in the protected sector are unable to export demands far more structure to substantiate than in the benchmark neoclassical growth model – thus the 'Almost Neoclassical' in the title of the chapter. Nevertheless, this is arguably far from being an unreasonable assumption, as causal empiricism would suggest. In the following, I shall provide somewhat more detailed defenses of the assumption.

This chapter belongs to the vast literature on the barriers to economic development that includes Parente and Prescott (1994, 1999) and Holmes and Schmitz (1995), among many others. In Parente and Prescott (1994), aggregate output is a very elastic function of some unobserved business capital, in addition to the usual dependence on physical capital. The government taxes both tangible physical capital investment and this unobserved business capital investment. The large effects on aggregate output predicted by their model are primarily through the distortions arising from taxing the unobserved business capital investment, which happens to be in the order of 40 percent of GDP. The present analysis largely sticks with standard neoclassical assumptions on technologies at the expense of maintaining an admittedly *ad hoc* assumption as to the behavior of firms in the protected industries. In particular, I have not derived the presumption that these firms choose not to export from first principles. The present chapter is also closely related to the arguments in Parente and Prescott (1999) and Holmes and Schmitz (1995), that market power protected by import restrictions could be an important distortion when the domestic monopolists with vested interests in inefficient technologies block the adoption of modern technologies. As an exercise of how monopoly may hinder economic development, this chapter complements my previous chapter (Tse, 2000), which assesses the quantitative effects of the holdup problem on aggregate output arising from market power.

The model of embodied technical change is based on Jovanovic and Rob (1999), to which I add monopolistic competition and assumptions on the trade regime. Jovanovic and Rob endogenize technical change by incorporating an equipment production sector that undertakes research to raise the productivity of machines. Since my analysis is concerned with less-developed countries, and most less-developed countries generally import all their capital equipment from abroad, I shall drop the machine production sector and instead assume that the country imports all its equipment from abroad. The model is presented in the next section. The relationship between aggregate output and trade policies is analyzed in Section 3. Section 4 provides some brief concluding comments. All proofs are omitted for the sake of brevity but are available in a technical appendix upon request.

2 MODEL

There is a continuum of intermediate goods with total measure equal to 1, indexed by $i \in [0,1]$. The production function of the final good is a constant elasticity of substitution (CES) aggregate of the intermediate goods:

$$Y(t) = \left[\int_0^1 y_i(t)^{\lambda} di \right]^{1/\lambda},$$

where $y_i(t)$ is the quantity of intermediate good i. The final good sector is assumed perfectly competitive throughout the analysis. The equilibrium price that allows firms to just break even would be.

$$P(t)=\left[\int_0^1 p_i(t)^{\lambda/(\lambda-1)}di\right]^{(\lambda-1)/\lambda} \tag{8.1}$$

where $p_i(t)$ is the price of intermediate good i. All intermediate goods are tradable. Normalizing the world price of each to 1, the world price of the final good would thus be $P(t)=1$ too. In the domestic economy, the production of each good i is monopolized by a single producer. The important assumption of this chapter is that a fraction $1-\alpha$ of all goods are open to foreign competition while the rest are closed to imports. Confronted with the competition from abroad, firms selling in the open sector have no real market power but may only sell at the world price of 1.[4] The monopolists in the closed sector may certainly choose to price above 1 when selling in the domestic economy. Specifically, firms in the protected sector face a downward-sloping demand curve when selling in the domestic-economy:

$$p_i(t)=\left[\frac{Y(t)}{y_i(t)}\right]^{1-\lambda}P(t). \tag{8.2}$$

Furthermore, I shall assume that these firms do not export at all and as such (8.2) comprises the entirety of its demand.[5]

Following Jovanovic and Rob (1999), I assume that the production of each intermediate good is governed by the same fixed coefficient technology that combines machines with workers in a one to one manner. The output of a worker is equal to $q(\tau)$, where τ is the vintage of the machine the worker is equipped with. All machines are purchased from abroad in a competitive world market. The world price of vintage τ machines is equal to $p_x q(\tau)$ for some p_x. Under this linearity assumption, all machine purchases will be for the latest vintage at the time the purchases are made.[6] Let $x_i(\tau)$ be the number of machines firm i buys at time τ, and z be the age of machines. Suppose the oldest vintage that the firm employs at time t is $t-T_i(t)$. If machines break down at the rate δ per unit of time, the output of the firm is:

$$y_i(t)=\int_0^{T_i(t)} x_i(t-z)q(t-z)e^{-\delta z}dz. \tag{8.3}$$

The variable T, being the age of the oldest machine in use, is equivalently how often the firm chooses to replace machines. Technical change is entirely embodied in machines of the latest vintage and vintage-specific productivity is assumed to grow at the exogenous rate $\dot{q}/q = g$. The firm's output may then be rewritten as:

$$y_i(t) = q(t) \int_0^{T_i(t)} x_i(t-z) e^{-(\delta+g)z} dz. \tag{8.4}$$

The firm's employment is equal to the number of machines in use:

$$n_i(t) = \int_0^{T_i(t)} x_i(t-z) e^{-\delta z} dz. \tag{8.5}$$

Each worker has the same lifetime utility function:

$$U = \int_0^{\infty} \left[c(t) l(t)^{\theta} \right] e^{-\rho t} dt, \tag{8.6}$$

where $c(t)$ and $l(t)$ are, respectively, consumption and leisure at time t, ρ is the discount rate and $\theta > 0$ a share parameter. Following Hansen (1985), I assume that labor is indivisible. Firms will offer employment contracts that pay the worker a wage that depends on the probability that the worker will be called upon to work. Specifically, a worker's wage income is given by $w(t)\eta(t)$ where $\eta(t) \leq 1$ denotes the probability of being called upon to work and $w(t)$ is the wage rate per unit of $\eta(t)$. If the worker is not working, the time available for leisure is 1. If the worker does work, the time available for leisure is given by some $l_0 \in [0,1]$. Workers also derive income from the ownership of a mutual fund which in turn owns all firms in the economy. Let $d(t)$ be the dividend per share of the fund, $a(t)$ the worker's share of the fund and $\mu(t)$ the price per share. The worker's intertemporal budget constraint is thus:[7]

$$P(t)c(t) = w(t)\eta(t) + d(t)a(t) - \mu(t)\dot{a}(t). \tag{8.7}$$

The utility maximization is over consumption $c(t)$ and labor supply $\eta(t)$ with $a(t)$ the state variable, taking $P(t)$, $w(t)$, $d(t)$, $\mu(t)$ and the worker's initial ownership of the mutual fund as given. To simplify, I shall assume that each worker owns an equal share of the fund to begin with. In equilibrium, there will be no trading of the shares of the mutual fund and so the ownership remains evenly distributed throughout.[8]

There is a continuum of worker types indexed by $j \in [0,1]$. Each type is made up of a continuum of workers of measure 1 as well. Type j workers can only work for firm $i = j$ as they are assumed to be completely unproductive elsewhere. The firms are therefore monopsonists in their respective labor markets. With a total population of workers equal to 1, each worker's capital income $d(t)a(t) = \Pi(t)$, that is, the aggregate profit net of the investment expenditure of all firms. In equilibrium the employment of the firm $n_i(t)$ would be equal to the probability that each worker chooses to work $\eta_j(t)$ for $i = j$. Utility maximization would then yield an upward-sloping labor supply curve facing each firm given by:[9]

$$n_i(t) = \frac{w_i(t) - v\Pi(t)}{2vw_i(t)}, \tag{8.8}$$

where $v = 1 - l_0^\theta > 0$. The labor supply is decreasing in the aggregate net profit of firms, which is due to the income effect of an increase in capital income.

The environments faced by the firms are different to the extent whether the firm happens to be within the open competitive sector or the protected monopolistic sector. We may then simplify notations by switching to indexing firms by c for firms in the competitive sector and m for firms in the monopolistic sector. For firms in the open sector, the revenue is simply equal to the firm's output as demand is perfectly elastic at the world price of 1. At each point in time, given the history of investment $\{x_c(t-z)\}_{z=0}^{\infty}$ and the aggregate net profit of all firms $\Pi(t)$, a given firm in the open sector chooses employment or equivalently the replacement horizon to maximize:

$$\pi_c(t) = \max_{T_c(t)} \{y_c(t) - w_c(t)n_c(t)\}. \tag{8.9}$$

In view of (8.2), the profit maximization for the firm in the protected sector is given by:

$$\pi_m(t) = \max_{T_m(t)} \left\{P(t)Y(t)^{1-\lambda} y_m(t)^{\lambda} - w_m(t)n_m(t)\right\}. \tag{8.10}$$

Then the firm chooses the time path of investment $\{x_s(\tau)\}_{\tau=t}^{\infty}$, $s = c$ or m to maximize the sum of discounted profits net of the investment in capital equipment:

$$V_s(t) = \int_t^{\infty} \left[\pi_s(\tau) - q(\tau)p_x x_s(\tau)\right] e^{-r(\tau-t)} d\tau,$$

taking as given the interest rate r which would be equal to the discount rate ρ in equilibrium given that utility is linear in consumption. Furthermore, the aggregate net profit would be given by:

$$\Pi(t)=(1-\alpha)\times\left[y_c(t)-\Pi(t)\frac{vn_c(t)}{1-2vn_c(t)}-q(t)p_x x_c(t)\right] + \alpha\left[P(t)Y(t)^{1-\lambda}y_m(t)^{\lambda}-\Pi(t)\frac{vn_m(t)}{1-2vn_m(t)}-q(t)p_x x_m(t)\right] \tag{8.11}$$

in equilibrium.

For tractability, I shall restrict attention to analyzing the steady-state equilibrium in which investment $x_s(t)$, $s=c$ and m stays constant over time. From (8.4) and (8.5), the steady-state output and employment of the firms are, respectively,

$$y_s(t)=q(t)x_s\frac{1-e^{-(\delta+g)T_s}}{\delta+g} \tag{8.12}$$

and

$$n_s=x_s\frac{1-e^{-\delta T_s}}{\delta}. \tag{8.13}$$

In the steady state, the output of firms in either sector grows at the exogenous growth rate of embodied technical change g and so aggregate output:

$$Y(t)=\left[\alpha y_m(t)^{\lambda}+(1-\alpha)y_c(t)^{\lambda}\right]^{1/\lambda} \tag{8.14}$$

will grow at g as well. Trade restrictions will then only have level but not growth effects. By (8.1) and (8.2) the price index is simplified to:

$$P(t)=\left\{\frac{1-\alpha\left[y_m(t)/Y(t)\right]^{\lambda}}{1-\alpha}\right\}^{(1-\lambda)/\lambda}, \tag{8.15}$$

which will be constant through time in the steady state. Solving (8.11) for $\Pi(t)$ and setting the employment of firms independent of time, the aggregate net profit in the steady state is given by:

$$\Pi(t) = \{(1-\alpha)\left[y_c(t) - x_c q(t) p_x\right] + \alpha\left[P(t)Y(t)^{1-\lambda} y_m(t)^{\lambda} - x_m q(t) p_x\right]\} \times \left[1 + (1-\alpha)\frac{vn_c}{1-2vn_c} + \alpha\frac{vn_m}{1-2vn_m}\right]^{-1} \quad (8.16)$$

which grows at the rate g. A technical appendix available upon request shows that the steady-state equilibrium $\{x_c, T_c, x_m, T_m\}$ may be characterized by the system:[10]

$$q(t)e^{-gT_c} = \Pi(t)\frac{v}{(1-2vn_c)^2}, \quad (8.17)$$

$$\lambda P(t)\left[\frac{Y(t)}{y_m(t)}\right]^{1-\lambda} q(t)e^{-gT_m} = \Pi(t)\frac{v}{(1-2vn_m)^2}, \quad (8.18)$$

$$\frac{1-e^{-(\delta+r)T_c}}{\delta+r} - e^{-gT_c}\frac{1-e^{-(\delta+r-g)T_c}}{\delta+r-g} = p_x, \quad (8.19)$$

and

$$\lambda P(t)\left[\frac{Y(t)}{y_m(t)}\right]^{1-\lambda}\left[\frac{1-e^{-(\delta+r)T_m}}{\delta+r} - e^{-gT_m}\frac{1-e^{-(\delta+r-g)T_m}}{\delta+r-g}\right] = p_x. \quad (8.20)$$

With the levels of employment and output in the two sectors pinned down by $\{T_c, T_m, x_c, x_m\}$, the above is a system of four equations in these four variables. Equations (8.16) and (8.18) are, respectively, the equilibrium conditions for T_c and x_c. When vintage-specific productivity is growing at the rate g, the left-hand side of (8.16) is merely $q(t-T_c)$, which is the output of the last machine employed by a firm in the open competitive sector. At an output price of 1, this is also the marginal revenue generated by bringing this last machine into production. Doing so requires hiring an additional worker and this increases wage expenditure by $\partial(w_c n_c)/\partial n_c$, given by the right-hand side of (8.16). The right-hand side of (8.18) is the cost of purchasing a machine at time t divided by $q(t)$. The left-hand side is the discounted net revenue generated by the employment of the machine over its lifetime, similarly divided by $q(t)$.

The other two conditions, (8.17) and (8.19), are the respective equilibrium conditions for T_m and x_m. The cost sides of these conditions are identical to the corresponding conditions for the open competitive sector, as they should be. The differences in the revenue sides are due to the fact that firms in the protected monopolistic sector face downward-sloping demand curves. The factor $\lambda P(Y/y_m)^{1-\lambda}$ that augments the revenue sides of the conditions, by virtue of (8.2), is the marginal revenue associated with the demand curve facing the firm. There is an alternative interpretation of these two equilibrium conditions if the factor is moved to the right-hand sides. The factor $\lambda P(Y/y_m)^{1-\lambda}$ would fall below one in equilibrium and hence firms in the monopolistic factor would behave as if they were operating under a higher marginal cost of raising employment and a higher investment good price. As such, import protections, by making the industry monopolistic, would lower employment and investment. To conclude the section, we note the existence and uniqueness of a steady-state equilibrium.

Proposition 1 A unique equilibrium exists if $\lambda/(r+\delta) > p_x$ for all $\alpha \in [0,1]$.

3 TRADE RESTRICTION AND AGGREGATE OUTPUT

I now come to the central question of the chapter — in what way and how much can import restrictions affect aggregate output? In Subsection 3.1, I establish formally the adverse influence of import protections on investment and employment incentives noted in the last section and assess its quantitative importance. Subsection 3.2 examines how import restrictions magnify the distortion from taxing imported capital. Subsection 3.3 discusses and evaluates the repercussion of import restrictions on the supply of investment funds.

3.1 Investment and Employment Incentives

First we shall establish that firms in the protected sector restrict employment and investment, lowering aggregate output as a result.

Proposition 2 Firms in the monopolistic sector (a) replace machines less often, that is, $T_m > T_c$, (b) purchase fewer machines at each point in time, that is,

$x_m < x_c$, (c) hire fewer workers, that is, $n_m < n_c$, and (d) produce a lower level of output, that is, $y_m < y_c$.

Facing downward-sloping demand curves, firms in the protected sector restrict output to maximize profits. When producing at lower output levels, they hire fewer workers and have less incentive to update technologies as often as firms whose objective is to maximize output. As a result, they end up having an older and less productive capital stock.

How may the equilibrium depend on the degree of import protections α? First, varying α has a compositional effect on aggregate output in transforming a larger trunk of the economy into output-restricting monopolies. The employment, investment and output of firms in each sector may also be affected by the degree of import protection. In particular, the parameter α may enter the system of equations (8.16)–(8.19) characterizing the steady-state equilibrium through the factor $\lambda P(Y/y_m)^{1-\lambda}$ which is the marginal revenue of firms within the protected sector and the aggregate net profit of firms $\Pi(t)$. However, the factor $\lambda P(Y/y_m)^{1-\lambda}$ turns out to be independent of α. This can be seen by combining (8.13) and (8.14) to yield:

$$\lambda P(t)\left[\frac{Y(t)}{y_m(t)}\right]^{1-\lambda} = \lambda\left[\frac{y_c(t)}{y_m(t)}\right]^{1-\lambda} \tag{8.21}$$

and so α drops out altogether. This may appear counterintuitive since when more industries are transformed into output-restricting monopolies, aggregate output Y should decline, lowering the marginal revenue of the monopolistic firms. This is indeed the case in partial equilibrium when we ignore the effects of α on the price of the final good P. When more of the goods in the economy sell at the higher monopolistic price, P rises. Under the CES technology, the opposite effects of α on $(Y/y_m)^{1-\lambda}$ and P happen to exactly cancel out.

This leaves $\Pi(t)$ the only channel through which α may affect the investment, employment and output of firms in each sector. Firms in the protected sector certainly earn greater profits than firms in the competitive sector since the former are at liberty to mimic the investment, employment and output decisions of the latter. By virtue of (8.11), $\Pi(t)$ is a weighted average of the profits of firms in the two sectors and so a marginal increase in α would raise $\Pi(t)$. The income effect of the increase in capital income would then lower the labor supply and in turn the output of firms in both sectors.

Proposition 3 An increase in α lowers the investment, employment and output of firms in both sectors.

The effects of α on aggregate output are thus unambiguously negative with the effect on the sectoral output reinforcing the negative compositional effect. With aggregate output lowest in the most restrictive economy, to obtain an upper bound on the effects of import restrictions, it suffices to compare the levels of output between the completely closed economy with $\alpha = 1$ and the completely open economy with $\alpha = 0$. Figures 8.1 and 8.2 plot the ratio of output of these two economies for various values of the monopoly markup $1/\gamma$ and the machine price p_x, respectively. The baseline parameters for these plots are set according to $\delta = 0.1$, $r = 0.04$, $g = 0.02$, $p_x = 0.84$ and $v = 0.435$. The choices for δ and r are standard in the business cycle literature and a g equal to 0.02 is the long-run growth rate of most advanced economies. Taking the United States as the benchmark of the completely open economy, the choice for p_x calibrates a competitive replacement horizon of $T_c = 12$, whereas the choice for v calibrates a competitive labor force participation rate of $n_c = 0.671$ to match the average service life of capital equipment in the US as reported in Coen (1980) and the US labor force participation rate in 1999, respectively.[11] The quantitative exercise is thus an exercise that asks how much aggregate output would be lowered in an economy which is otherwise identical to the US but practices a restrictive trade policy. With these parameter values, the labor supply in the benchmark competitive economy which can be calculated from (8.8) turns out to be quite elastic at 0.71. This suggests that the distortions arising from monopoly pricing can be potentially important.

Even though the intermediate goods are imperfect substitutes in the production of the final good, firms in the completely open economy have no real market power to speak of because of the import competition. As such the monopoly markup $1/\gamma$ does not affect the equilibrium of the completely open economy. The markup certainly does affect the equilibrium of the closed economy. Figure 8.1 confirms that as the markup increases, the output of the closed economy falls. How distortionary import restrictions can be then is a question of what may be a reasonable value for the markup. Recent empirical studies by Burnside (1996) and Basu and Fernald (1997) have shown that the US economy is characterized by a minimal markup of around 1.03. This value of the markup, however, is not directly applicable to the present exercise, because our interest is in establishing what the markup may be in a closed economy but not the markup that prevails in the fairly open US economy. Nevertheless, an upper bound of around 1.1 is not unreasonable given the US observation. Figure 8.1 shows that import restrictions may only lower aggregate output by less than 5 percentage points. Even if we are willing to entertain a markup of 1.2, the decline in output increases to no more than 8 percentage points. Hence, variations of the markup within a range that is deemed reasonable do not appear to imply that the distortions of import restrictions can be important.

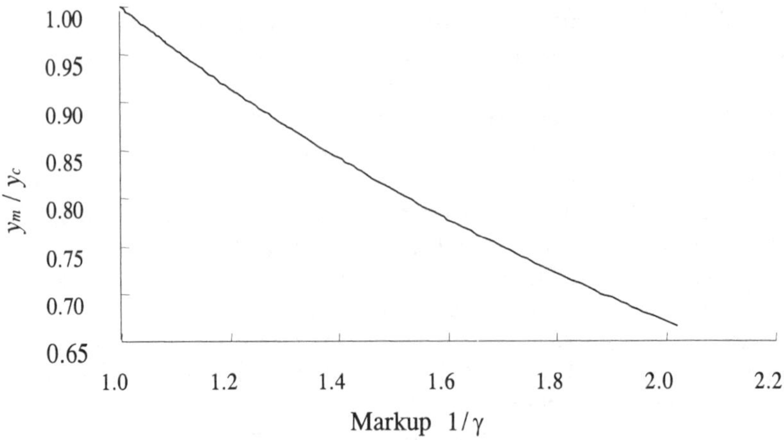

Figure 8.1 The effect of import restrictions on aggregate output for various markups

Import restrictions lower aggregate output through raising the implicit price of the investment good and the wage rate. In particular, firms in the closed economy see an implicit machine price increase to p_x/λ and the labor supply curve similarly shifted in by the multiple $1/\lambda$. If a reasonable upper bound for the markup is around 1.1–1.2, the effect of import restrictions would be such that firms would see a machine price and a wage rate that are about 10–20 percent higher than otherwise. It is perhaps not too surprising that the 10–20 percent increase in the price of the investment good would not significantly affect aggregate output. That should be the case since aggregate output is not particularly sensitive to the price of the investment good in the neoclassical growth model with exogenous and disembodied technical change.[12] There is no compelling reason why merely switching to assuming embodied technical change should turn the conclusion around in any significant way. However, given that the parameterization implies an elasticity of labor supply as high as 0.71 in the open economy benchmark, it is somewhat unexpected that import restrictions would not be more distortionary. Specifically, at markups equal to 10 and 20 percent, respectively, my calculations show that labor inputs in the closed economy fall by merely 4 and 7 percent from the level of labor input in the open economy. This is more remarkable given the fact that import restrictions, in raising the profits of firms and thereby workers' capital income, would turn on an income effect to lower labor supply further from the initial decline associated with the fall in investment.

In Figure 8.2, I examine the effects of varying the machine price p_x on how much output may be lowered by import restrictions, keeping the markup fixed at 1.1. The competitive replacement horizon is increasing in p_x since at a higher p_x, firms cut down investment and replace equipment less often. For an easier interpretation, I plot the competitive replacement horizons T_c implied by the various machine prices on the x-axis of the figure. The downward-sloping curve shows that import restrictions are more distortionary at higher machine prices. Nevertheless, the quantitative effects are minuscule. In particular, even when p_x increases to the extent that the competitive replacement horizon doubles to 24 years from the benchmark of 12 years, the output decline rises to less than 7 percent from the initial decline of about 5 percent. In all unless we are willing to entertain an unreasonably large markup of price over marginal cost in the closed economy, the model would not predict large differences in aggregate output among economies adopting different degrees of import restrictions.

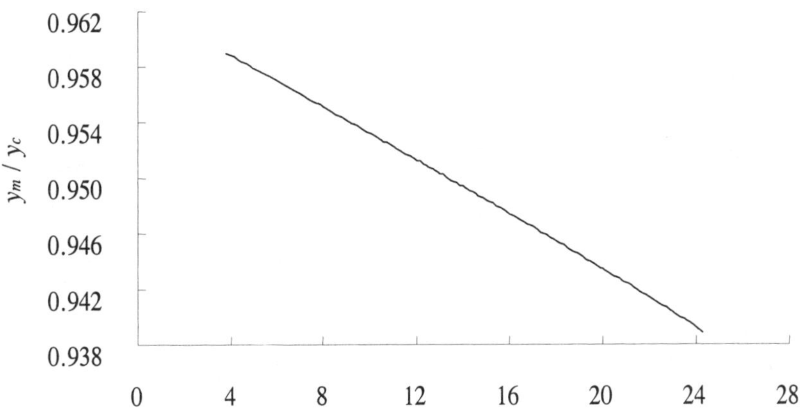

Figure 8.2 The effect of import restrictions on aggregate output for various competitive replacement horizons

In the open (closed) economy, the worker is called upon to work with probability n_c (n_m) in which case leisure is given by $l_0^\theta = 1 - v$ and not required to work with probability $1 - n_c$ $(1 - n_m)$ in which case leisure is given by 1. In equilibrium, each worker's consumption is the difference between output and investment. In view of (8.6) the expected utility is:

$$Eu_s(t) = \left[y_s(t) - x_s p_x q(t)\right](1 - vn_s), \tag{8.22}$$

where $s = c$ for the worker in the open economy and $s = m$ for the worker in the closed economy. Figures 8.3 and 8.4 show how the ratio $Eu_m(t)/Eu_c(t)$ varies with the monopoly markup and the machine price. As in Figures 8.2, I plot the competitive replacement horizons T_c implied by the various machine prices on the x-axis in Figures 8.4 for an easier interpretation. Not unexpectedly, the effects of trade restrictions on the welfare of workers are similarly not important. In fact, the effects are even more subdued than the effects on aggregate

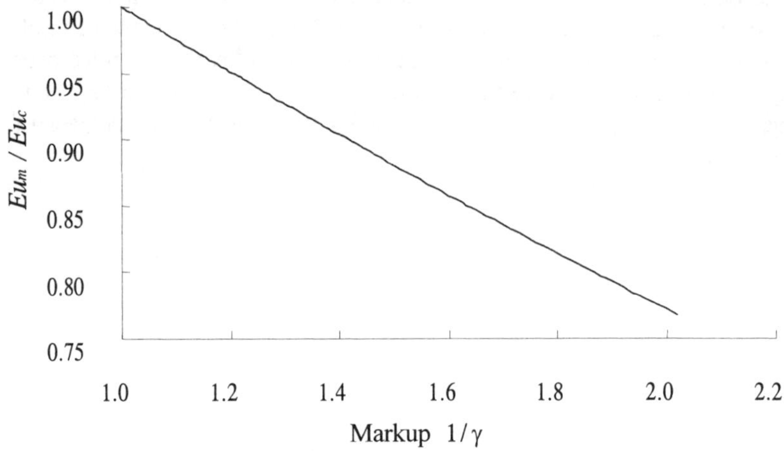

Figure 8.3 The effect of import restrictions on welfare for various markups

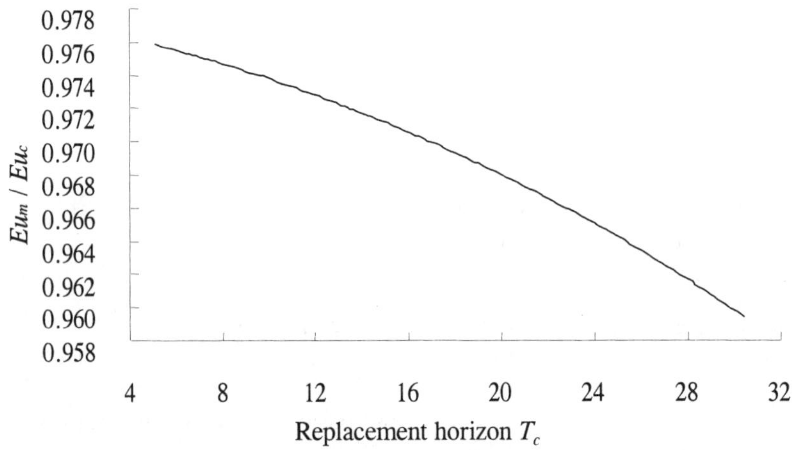

Figure 8.4 The effect of import restrictions on welfare for various competitive replacement horizons

output. In the benchmark of a monopoly markup equal to 1.1 and a machine price that implies a competitive replacement horizon of 12 years, the level of utility is lowered by no more than 3 percentage points compared to an output decline of about 5 percentage points. That should be the case since the greater consumption of leisure enjoyed by workers in the closed economy partially compensates for the fall in consumption.

3.2 Interaction with Taxes on Investment Goods

Quite obviously, taxing capital equipment, in raising the price of investment goods, lowers investment and aggregate output. The analysis of Jovanovic and Rob (1999), from which follows the specification of embodied technical change in this chapter, shows that the same investment tax is proportionally more distortionary when the price of the investment good is higher to begin with. Specifically, the percentage decline in output in response to the same tax-induced increase in the price of investment goods is greater at a higher pre-tax investment good price. Now, if import restrictions affect investment incentives in a way that is equivalent to raising the effective price of equipment for firms in protected industries, the same investment tax would be more distortionary in the closed than in the open economies. And this could well be a potentially important channel through which restrictive trade policies lower aggregate output.

Table 8.1 shows how much taxing capital equipment may lower aggregate output in the completely open and the completely closed economies for various investment good prices and two different monopoly markups. The first column shows the ratio of the investment good price under consideration to the benchmark of $p_x = 0.81$ that is associated with a competitive replacement horizon of 12 years. The second, fourth and sixth columns show that as p_x rises, firms in both the open and the closed economies replace machines less often. The third, fifth and seventh columns show how much aggregate output would decline in response to a 1 percent tax-induced increase in the investment good price. As expected, the absolute value of the elasticities are larger in the closed economies than in the open economy and are largest at the higher markup of 1.2. Hence a given tax on capital equipment is indeed more distortionary if the country also practices restrictive trade policies at the same time. Furthermore, both the percentage and the absolute differences in the elasticities between the two economies are larger at a higher initial investment good price.

The elasticities in the third, fifth and seventh columns show that taxing capital equipment can be almost three times more distortionary in the closed economy that has a monopoly markup of 1.2 than in the open economy when the investment good price is four times the benchmark of 0.81. But such a high investment good price would have to be associated with a competitive re placement horizon of around 38 years, which is for all purposes too long to be

Table 8.1 The effects of taxing capital equipment

$\frac{p_x}{0.81}$	T_c	$\left\lvert\frac{\partial \log y_c}{\partial \log p_x}\right\rvert$	T_m	$\left\lvert\frac{\partial \log y_m}{\partial \log p_x}\right\rvert$	T_m	$\left\lvert\frac{\partial \log y_m}{\partial \log p_x}\right\rvert$
			$\left(\frac{1}{\gamma}=1.1\right)$		$\left(\frac{1}{\gamma}=1.2\right)$	
(1)	(2)	(3)	(4)	(5)	(6)	(7)
0.25	5.13	0.024	5.45	0.027	5.71	0.030
0.50	7.71	0.036	8.22	0.040	8.65	0.044
1.00	12.00	0.052	12.90	0.060	13.64	0.067
2.00	19.90	0.073	21.70	0.090	23.22	0.106
3.00	28.26	0.089	31.28	0.123	33.96	0.160
4.00	37.85	0.110	42.72	0.185	47.22	0.274

plausible. For more plausible competitive replacement horizons, say atthe benchmark of 12 years, the price elasticities in the closed economy with monopoly markups equal to 1.1 and 1.2 are only, respectively, 1.15 and 1.29 times higher than the price elasticity in the open economy.[13] Furthermore, the absolute increases in both cases are minimal. Perhaps that should not be surprising. First under the essentially neoclassical assumptions made in the analysis, aggregate output is not quite responsive to small changes in the investment good price. Furthermore, as shown in the previous section, a small markup of 1.1 to 1.2 would not deliver big effects on equilibrium quantities despite assuming a fairly elastic labor supply. Hence when the model is restricted to predict plausible competitive replacement horizons, taxing capital equipment turns out to be not particularly more distortionary in the closed than in the open economies.

3.3 Supplies of Investment Funds

We have so far assumed that the entire output of the intermediate good firms is sold to domestic final good producers. And then, if capital equipment may only be purchased from abroad, the final good would have to play the role of the sole exportable to generate the foreign exchange to finance the purchase of investment goods from abroad. Is this a feasible arrangement? Protecting the upstream intermediate good producers raises the costs of the final good producers, resulting in the final good costing more to produce in the domestic economy than the cost of producing it elsewhere. Specifically, the domestic final good producers only break even if they may charge $P = \left\{(1-\alpha)/\left[1-\alpha(y_m/Y)^{\lambda}\right]\right\}^{(\lambda-1)/\lambda} > 1$ as long as $\alpha > 0$ and $Y > y_m$. And hence these firms can never be competitive in the world market and there actually has to be a tariff equal to at least $P-1$ for them to survive the import competition in the domestic economy. If the final good cannot qualify as an exportable and with our assumption that the protected firms would not bother to export, firms in the open competitive sector will have to bear the entire responsibility of earning the foreign exchange to finance domestic investment. Our previous assumption that the output of firms in this sector is only sold to domestic final good producers is, strictly speaking, not a valid assumption. In equilibrium, only a fraction of the output of these firms is sold to domestic final good producers and the rest is exported to finance the investment of capital equipment. Our next task is to examine how this consideration may change the assessment of the quantitative effects of import restrictions.

In the steady state, if every economy in the world grows at the same rate g, there cannot be any borrowing or lending among countries in the world's equilibrium given our assumption of homothetic preferences. The country's external account must then balance at each point in time, from which it follows that the sum of consumption and investment expenditure is identically equal to aggregate income:

$$Y(t) = C(t) + X(t). \tag{8.23}$$

In turn, aggregate income is equal to the sum of the revenues of firms in the two sectors:

$$Y(t) = \alpha p_m(t)x_m(t) + (1-\alpha)y_c(t), \tag{8.24}$$

where p_m denotes the price charged by firms in the closed sector in terms of the output of firms in the open sector. Aggregate investment is equal to the sum of the investment in the two sectors:

$$X(t) = q(t)p_x\left[\alpha x_m(t) + (1-\alpha)x_c(t)\right]. \tag{8.25}$$

It is now necessary to distinguish between how much of the output of firms in the open competitive sector is sold to domestic final good producers and how much is exported. Denote $y_c^d(t)$ as the domestic demand. With the domestic production of the final good purely for consumption and the fact that in equilibrium final good producers earn zero profit, aggregate consumption expenditure may be written as:

$$C(t) = \alpha p_m(t) y_m(t) + (1-\alpha) y_c^d(t). \tag{8.26}$$

Combining (8.22)—(8.25):

$$X(t) = (1-\alpha)\left[y_c(t) - y_c^d(t)\right]. \tag{8.27}$$

Equation (8.26) is the key equation of this section. It states that the entirety of domestic investment has to be financed by the export of firms within the open competitive sector. Formally, the model is an otherwise standard two-sector model in which one sector produces both consumption and investment goods while the other produces consumption good only. What is not standard is that the relative size of the two sectors is fixed by the trade policy variable α rather than being allowed to vary according to preferences and technologies.

The only change to the equilibrium conditions is that the marginal revenue of firms producing in the protected industries is now equal to:

$$\lambda P(t)\left[\frac{Y^d(t)}{y_m(t)}\right]^{1-\lambda} = \lambda\left[\frac{y_c^d(t)}{y_m(t)}\right]^{1-\lambda} \tag{8.28}$$

where Y^d denotes the domestic production of the final good. Other than the second-order effect on the labor supply arising from changes in the capital income, the equilibrium in the open competitive sector is left unaffected.

The negative effects of an increase in α on the employment, investment and output of firms within each sector that work through the increase in the aggregate net profit of firms and consequently workers' capital income established in proposition 3 remain operative. But now closing up more of the economy to import competition would affect the investment and output of firms to an even greater extent. That is the case since only firms in the open sector export to earn the foreign exchange to finance investment, closing up more industries to import competition would dry up the supply of investment funds. We may similarly think in terms of the effect of trade policies on the implicit price of the investment good that affects the protected firms' incentive to invest. Specifically, by virtue of (8.19) and (8.27), the implicit price of investment good for firms in the protected sector is $p_x/\lambda\left(y_m/y_c^d\right)^{1-\lambda}$. The next task is to check how it would respond to changes in the trade policy variable α. To this end, combine (8.24) and (8.26) to yield:

$$y_c^d(t) = y_c(t) - q(t)\,p_x\left(x_c + \frac{\alpha}{1-\alpha}x_m\right).$$

For a given (y_c, x_c, x_m) triple, y_c^d is decreasing in α and so the implicit investment good price should be increasing in α. As a result, firms in the protected sector, facing a higher implicit price of the investment good, may only invest less when import protections are extended to more industries. Indeed, as α approaches 1, y_c^d tends to 0 and therefore the implicit price could become arbitrarily large. When an economy approaches complete closedness, the supply of funds available for capital investment would be completely dried up. The effects on aggregate output could conceivable become very dramatic.

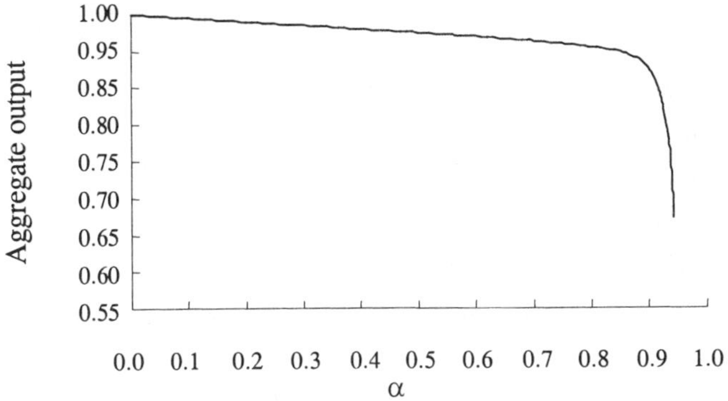

Figure 8.5 The effects of increasing trade restrictions on output

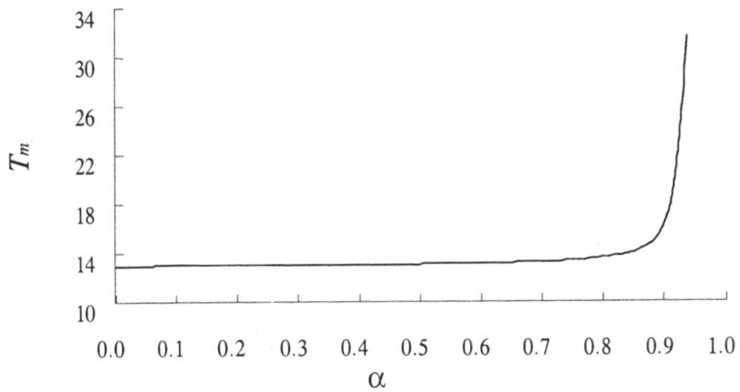

Figure 8.6 The effects of increasing trade restrictions on replacement horizon

These effects are depicted in Figures 8.5 to 8.9. In these plots, I stick with a monopoly markup of 1.1 and an investment good price of 0.81 that is associated with a competitive replacement horizon of 12 years. Each figure shows how the variable of interest varies with the degree of import restrictions α. Specifically, Figure 8.5 shows that as import restrictions are extended to about 90 percent of the economy, output starts falling rapidly. When the economy reaches 95 percent closedness, aggregate output has fallen by around 25 percent and there is no end as to how much more output will decline as α increases further. Figure 8.6, 8.7 and 8.8, respectively, show that the rapid output decline is caused by rapid increases in the replacement horizon and declines in investment and employment. In all, this channel can indeed be quantitatively important even when we stick with a modest markup of 1.1.

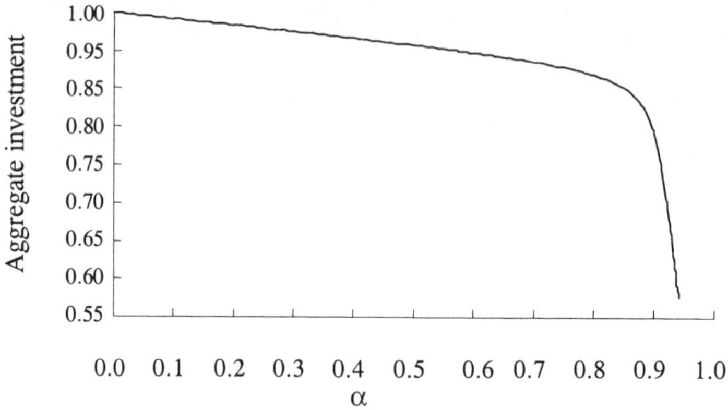

Figure 8.7 The effects of increasing trade restriction on investment

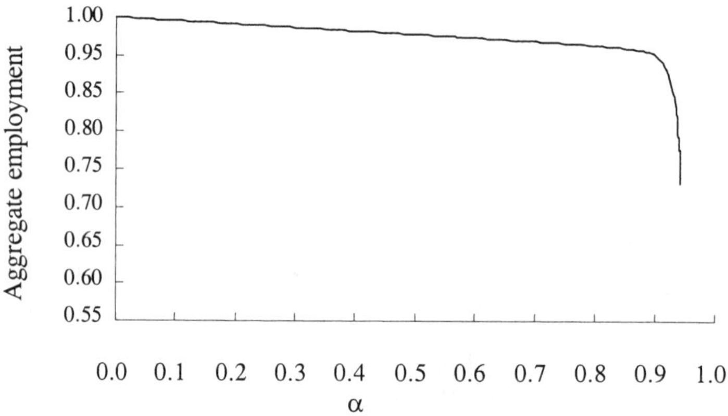

Figure 8.8 The effects of increasing trade restriction on employment

As to the effects on welfare, we may first define the average expected utility enjoyed by workers in a partially closed economy as:

$$Eu(t;\alpha) = \alpha Eu_m(t) + (1-\alpha) Eu_c(t), \tag{8.29}$$

where $Eu_s(t)$, $s = m$ or c is the expected utility of workers employed in sector s. In view of (8.21), $Eu_s(t)$ may be defined as:

$$Eu_s(t) = c_s(1 - vn_s) = \frac{w_s(t)n_s + \Pi(t)}{P(t)}(1 - vn_s).$$

Figure 8.9 shows how $Eu(t;\alpha)$ as defined in (8.28) varies as α increases. The effect is similar to the effect on output, with the decline in utility accelerating rapidly when the economy reaches 90 percent closedness. Nevertheless, the decline is less pronounced than the decline in output given that workers are partially compensated for greater leisure as employment falls.

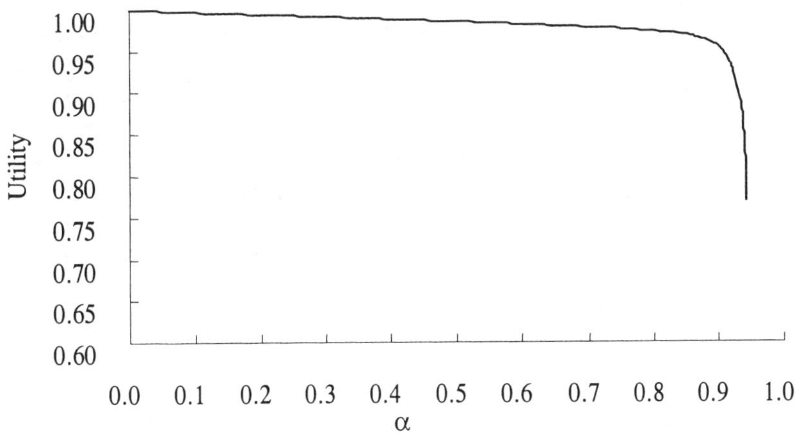

Figure 8.9 The effects of increasing trade restriction on utility

In the two channels considered in the earlier sections, the magnitudes of the distortions arising from import restrictions are tightly linked to the monopoly markup. There, unless we are willing to entertain markups that are very rarely seen in practice, the increases in the implicit investment good price and wage rate may never approach the magnitudes that would cause important distortions on aggregate output. The analysis depicted in Figure 8.2 suggests that import restrictions may deliver bigger effects on aggregate output if we start with some very high baseline investment good price. The switch to assuming embodied technical change has the advantage that it instills more discipline in the choice of the baseline investment good price. Whether the particular choice makes sense can be ascertained by checking the implied competitive replacement horizon. The investment good prices that may deliver big effects on output are not plausible precisely because they would be accompanied by hugely unreasonably long replacement horizons.

The general equilibrium effects that work through shrinking the supply of investment funds free up the tight relationships between the increase in the implicit investment good price and wage rate and the monopoly markup. Thus the markup may remain moderate for the distortions from import restrictions to yield sufficiently large increases in the implicit investment good price and wage rate to deliver big effects on aggregate output. However, this result crucially depends on the assumption that firms in the protected sector would not bother to export. Without this assumption, the protected firms will also be earning foreign exchange that may finance domestic investment. The general equilibrium effects that arise from the shortage of investment funds would then vanish. There is, however, reason to believe that the assumption of the protected firms choosing not to sell in the world market should not be too objectionable. First, the country's trading partners would impose similar trade restrictions as retaliatory measures in many realistic situations. Also, it is often argued that most protected firms in poor countries are too inefficient to compete in the world market. I have not modeled how this can be the case in this chapter. But there has been some promising work on this front. The paper by Goh (2000) is a case in point. She assumes that firms may only start production after having spent some time on improving its technology. Import protections raise the opportunity cost of time by making the domestic market more lucrative and consequently lower firms' incentives to invest in technology improvements. Indeed, if firms may only compete in the world market after having reached some minimum technical competence, they may well choose not to bother.

4 CONCLUDING REMARKS

Import restrictions are formally equivalent to investment and employment taxes. With not unreasonable assumptions on the monopoly markup, the taxes may raise the price of investment goods and the wage rate that protected firms see by only around 10 percent when we ignore the general equilibrium effects that arise from a shrinking supply of investment funds due to closedness. When the latter effect is taken into account, the implicit investment good price and wage rate rise a great deal more. Only then may import restrictions deliver big effects on aggregate output in the neoclassical growth model.

Finally, it should be mentioned that there are several prominent hypotheses as to why import restrictions may be important distortions that I have chosen not to analyze in this chapter. First, several authors have argued that opening up the domestic economy to competition from abroad could be an effective means to reduce X-inefficiencies.[14] Second, interactions with overseas producers may stimulate the learning of the world's best-practice technologies by domestic firms.[15] Finally, a free trade regime, by enlarging the markets of domestic producers, raises the total factor productivity if production exhibits increasing returns to scale.[16] As to the first two arguments, the quantitative assessments obviously require choosing parameter values that we have little confidence in their accuracy. The problem is certainly not insurmountable but it would be beyond the scope of this chapter. As to the last argument, there is in fact a sizeable literature that comes under the heading of 'computable general equilibrium' studying how much aggregate output may be lowered by import restrictions,[17] and so it would be redundant to repeat the analysis in this chapter.

NOTES

1. The usual criticism that such a relationship cannot be taken as evidence in support of the merits of liberal trade policies is that trade shares are endogenous. Frankel and Romer (1999) rise to this challenge by using geography variables as instruments in their cross-country regression of GDP against trade share, among other independent variables. The relationship turns out to be even stronger than that obtained from simple OLS (ordinary least squares) regressions. In an earlier study, Leamer (1988) confronts the issues directly by regressing aggregate output against measures of trade policies that are constructed independently from the information contained in actual trade shares. The positive relationship is similarly confirmed.
2. Burnside (1996) and Basu and Fernald (1997).
3. By comparing data on import and equipment investment, De Long and Summers (1993) conclude that in developing countries, the bulk of capital equipment is purchased from abroad.
4. The idea that imports serve to raise the elasticity of demand facing domestic producers dated back to the import discipline hypothesis in the old industrial organization literature. Its use in modern trade theory began in Krugman (1979).
5. The assumptions made here imply that they would like to do so, however. The role played by this assumption and its justification will be discussed in more detail.
6. See note 5 of Jovanovic and Rob (1999) for why that is the case under the assumption that the cost of a machine is linear in quality and the restriction that each worker may only be combined with one machine at any one time.
7. Borrowing may be accomplished by short-selling shares of the mutual fund and arbitrage would ensure that the cost would be identical to the interest rate and so the market for loans is spurious.
8. That there is no trading of the shares is due to the assumption of homothetic preference and the fact that in equilibrium the wage income of all workers will grow at the same rate.
9. The calculations are in an appendix available upon request. Equation (8.8) assumes an interior solution to the worker's utility maximization. If $w_i \leq \nu\Pi(t)$, $n_i(t) = 0$ and if $w_i(t) \geq [\nu\Pi(t)]/(1-2\nu)$, $n_i(t) = 1$. The case of $n_i(t) = 0$ is clearly not equilibrium. In the quantitative exercises that follow, I pick parameter values to ensure interior solutions throughout. It is perhaps surprising that $P(t)$ drops out from the labor supply curve. With a multiplicative utility function, the income and substitution effects of a higher price level apparently cancel out.
10. Equations (8.16) and (8.17) presume an equilibrium with $\{n_c, n_m\} < (1,1)$. If the equilibrium happens to involve full employment in one or both sectors, the equalities in the equations concerned would be replaced with inequalities.
11. Although the model is not calibrated to match the investment–output ratio in the US, the parameter values chosen happen to imply an investment–output ratio of 0.127 which matches the invest-

ment–output ratio of the US quite closely.

12. See Schmitz (1993) for an analysis of how much aggregate output would respond to increases in the price of investment goods in the neoclassical growth model with disembodied and exogenous technical change.
13. As noted previously, an investment good price of 0.81 not only matches the average service life of capital equipment in the US, but also implies a competitive investment–output ratio of 0.12 that is quite close to the actual investment–output ratio in the US. On the other hand, an investment good price that is four times the benchmark value would predict not only an implausibly long competitive replacement horizon but also a competitive investment–output ratio of almost 0.4, which is similarly too large to be taken seriously.
14. Heitger (1987), among others.
15. Edwards (1992), among others.
16. Krugman (1979) first advanced the argument.
17. The efficacy of this channel has been questioned in a recent study by Tybout and Westbrook (1995). They report evidence that gains due to scale economy are minor and not correlated with increases in import competition in the Mexican trade liberation of the 1980s.

REFERENCES

Basu, Susanto and John G. Fernald (1997), 'Returns to scale in U.S. production: estimates and implications', *Journal of Political Economy*, **105**, 249–83.

Burnside, Craig (1996), 'Production function regressions, returns to scale and externalities', *Journal of Monetary Economics*, **37**, 177–201.

Coen, R.M. (1980), 'Alternative measures of capital and its rate of return in United States manufacturing', in D. Usher (ed.), *The Measurement of Capital. Studies in Income and Wealth*, **45**, Chicago: University of Chicago Press, 121–149.

De Long, J. Bradford and Lawrence H. Summers (1993), 'How strongly do developing economies benefit from equipment investment?', *Journal of Monetary Economics*, **32**, 395–415.

Edwards, S. (1992), 'Trade orientation, distortions and growth in developing countries', *Journal of Development Economics*, **39**, 31–57.

Frankel, Jeffrey A. and D. Romer (1999), 'Does trade cause growth?', *American Economic Review*, **89**, 378–99.

Goh, A. (2000), 'Opportunity cost of time, trade policies and the efficiency of firms', *Journal of Development Economics*, **62**, 363–83.

Hansen, Gary D. (1985), 'Indivisible Labor and Business Cycle', *Journal of Monetary Economics*, **16**, 309–27.

Heitger, Bernhard (1987), 'Import protection and export performance: their impact on economic growth', *Weltwirtschaftliches Archiv.*, **123**, 249–61.

Holmes, Thomas J. and James A. Schmitz (1995), 'Resistance to technology and trade between areas', *Federal Reserve Bank of Minneapolis Quarterly Review,* **19**, 2–17.

Jones, Charles I. (1994), 'Economic growth and the relative price of capital', *Journal of Monetary Economics*, **34**, 359–82.

Jovanovic, Boyan and Rafael Rob (1999), 'Solow vs. Solow', memo, New York University.

Krueger, Anne O. (1997), 'Trade policy and economic development: how we learn', *American Economic Review*, **87**, 1–22.

Krugman, Paul (1979), 'Increasing returns, monopolistic competition and international trade', *Journal of International Economics*, **9**, 469–80.

Leamer, Edward E. (1988), 'Measures of openness', in R.E. Baldwin (ed.), *Trade Policy Issues and Empirical Analysis*, Chicago: University of Chicago Press, 147–200.

Parente, Stephen L. and Ed C. Prescott (1994), 'Barriers to technology adoption and development', *Journal of Political Economy*, **102**, 298–321.

Parente, Stephen L. and Ed C. Prescott (1999), 'Monopoly: barriers to riches', *American Economic Review*, **89**, 1216–33.

Schmitz, James A. (1993), 'Early progress on the problem of economic development', *Federal Reserve Bank of Minneapolis Quarterly Review*, **17**, 17–35.

Tse, Chung Yi (2000), 'Monopoly, human capital accumulation and development', *Journal of Development Economics*, **61**, 137–74.

Tybout, James R. and M. Daniel Westbrook (1995), 'Trade liberation and the dimensions of efficiency change in Mexican manufacturing industries', *Journal of International Economics*, **39**, 53–78.

9. Innovation in a Shrinking World

Amy Jocelyn Glass

1 INTRODUCTION

This chapter explores the implications of reductions in tariffs or transport costs on the rate of innovation in a quality ladders model where firms from both countries innovate. If a country raises its tariffs, its wage rises relative to the other country and its firms become technology leaders for a larger fraction of products, but the aggregate rate of innovation falls. If transport costs fall symmetrically everywhere, then the aggregate rate of innovation rises, with no distributional consequences across countries. Additionally, diffusion of innovation technology to firms in the foreign country generates effects similar to a unilateral reduction in the protection of domestic markets through tariffs.

This chapter uses a North–North quality ladders model to consider the effect of trade barriers on economic growth. In this model, successful innovators from similar countries export their products to markets abroad. Product cycle models generally have focused on a North–South setting, where firms in the developed North innovate and firms in the less-developed South imitate. However, the bulk of trade, and especially of intraindustry trade, occurs *between developed countries* and the largest reductions in trade barriers have been *among developed countries*. Consequently, the role of reductions in trade barriers in a North-North growth model needs to be addressed. The contribution of this chapter is to analyze the effects of freer trade in a product cycle model where firms from more than one country innovate.

Segerstrom et al. (1990) show that tariffs protecting dying industries raise wages at the expense of thwarting economic growth. The reduction in profits due to reduced access to foreign markets cause firms to reduce their research and development (R&D) effort (a costly activity). But access to foreign markets might be less important for rich countries with large domestic markets, which suggests that the results for developed countries may differ from those for developing countries. Ades and Glaeser (1999) examine whether the degree that openness leads to faster growth is greatest in the poorest countries. The measure of openness used for the sample of the US states in the nineteenth century – proximity to major ports or railways – depicts transportation costs, whereas the measure used in the sample of poor countries in the late twentieth century – share of trade relative to GDP – captures both natural and artificial barriers to trade.

Rivera-Batiz and Romer (1991) show that economic integration between two developed countries can accelerate economic growth when innovations introduce new varieties. Grossman and Helpman (1991a) have shown that a quality ladders model may exhibit results that differ from a varieties-based model. Thus, it remains to be seen whether different results are obtained in a North–North setting when innovations improve the quality of existing products.

Comparison of a North–North quality ladders model to North–South ones or to North–North varieties models can be useful for examining the theoretical robustness of the effect of openness on economic growth. The potential for underlying fragility in the theoretical predictions is suggested by the fragility of empirical studies of the effects of trade reform on economic growth. Lee (1993) finds empirical evidence of the damage done by tariffs to the growth rate of per capita income across countries. Harrison (1996) finds broad support for a positive link between different measures of openness and economic growth in a cross-section and in panel data. Frankel and Romer (1999) use an instrumental variables approach – using geographic characteristics as instruments for openness – to estimate the effects of trade on growth, controlling for the possibility of reverse causality. But O'Rourke (2000) finds that tariffs were *positively* related to growth for a panel of ten countries between 1875 and 1914.

Similar to Ben-David and Loewy (1998), the differences between the effects of unilateral versus bilateral tariff reductions (or reductions in transport costs) can be examined. The trend toward freer trade has occurred through both improvements in transportation and reductions in government-imposed barriers to trade. Natural barriers to trade have been declining throughout recent history. Harley (1988) finds that metal ships and steam engines caused a major decline in freight rates after 1850. Finger and Yeats (1976) find that for US imports in 1965, international transportation costs imposed a degree of protection at least as great as did tariffs for most goods, especially for bulky goods with low unit values. The General Agreement on Tariffs and Trade (GATT) and its successor, the World Trade Organization (WTO), have achieved substantial reductions in tariffs and non-tariff barriers to trade over the past 50 years through multilateral negotiations, especially among developed countries.

The model is based on the quality ladders model of endogenous innovation by Grossman and Helpman (1991a) but with firms from both countries innovating. Changes in tariffs or transport costs alter the rate of innovation, relative wages and aggregate spending through the incentive to create quality improvements of existing products. A small increase in tariffs reduces profits and thus *reduces the rate of innovation but improves the relative wage*, as in Segerstrom (1991). Reducing tariffs (or transport costs) to the same degree in both countries can speed innovation while maintaining a constant relative wage. Liberalization, whether unilateral or multilateral, increases steady-state growth of all trading partners. Unilateral liberalization redistributes income away from the liberalizing country, whereas bilateral liberalization does not when both countries liberalize to the same degree. Unilateral liberalization may therefore be difficult to achieve, as the growth effects of faster innovation would need to dominate the level effect of lower income for a country to benefit from unilaterally lowering its tariffs. Unilateral liberalization also involves transitional dynamics that are eliminated if both countries reduce their tariffs to the same degree.

In addition to falling barriers to trade, the world has also been shrinking through improved communications and other links that may speed the spread of knowledge (which may in turn be related to expanding trade or foreign direct investment). An enhanced flow of information between countries may lead to a faster diffusion of technologies, including the knowledge of how to develop new products or better versions of existing products.

Suppose one country's innovation technology is superior to another country's (for all products) and consider the effects of an improvement in the innovation technology of the lagging country. Unilateral improvements in innovation technology generate effects that bear close similarity to the effects of a unilateral reduction in trade barriers by the trading partner: innovation rises and the relative wage falls. Falling trade barriers operates on the benefit side — a given innovation earns a greater reward — while a reduction in innovation difficulty operates on the cost side — a given innovation is cheaper to make.

While the effects of a unilateral improvement in innovation technology seem quite plausible, a potential implication of these findings is more startling. The GATT (and now the WTO) have achieved substantial tariff reduction over the past 50 years. In the Uruguay Round, an agreement was reached that is leading to tougher standards for intellectual property rights protection. By curtailing the diffusion of innovation technology (or at least making the use of the superior technology of others illegal), the recent agreement on intellectual property rights may in fact work against the previous tariff reductions by reducing the incentives for innovation. More work needs to be done in this area, such as allowing for foreign direct investment as in Glass and Saggi (2002a, 2002b) or for technologies to differ across industries so that technological diffusion can occur bilaterally.

Section 2 establishes the behavior of firms choosing their efforts at innovation. Section 3 characterizes the steady-state equilibrium where firms serve markets abroad through exporting and Section 4 determines how increases in tariff or transportation costs (and increases in the difficulty of innovation) have an impact on the variables of the model, including the rate of innovation. Section 5 concludes.

2 PRODUCT CYCLE MODEL

Suppose that there are two developed countries in the world. Firms in each country can design improved versions of existing products and sell them both at home and abroad (after paying a tariff or transport cost). All consumers share the same preferences and value quality improvements to the same degree. The willingness of consumers to pay for quality improvements generates the incentive for innovation.

2.1 Consumers

The specification of consumer preferences follows that in Grossman and Helpman (1991a, 1991b). Consumers live in one of two countries, domestic or foreign $i \in [D, F]$, and choose from a continuum of products indexed by j, available in discrete quality levels indexed by m. Consumers view quality level m of product $j \in [0,1]$ as being better than the previous quality level $m-1$. Quality level m of product j provides quality $q_m(j) \equiv \lambda^m$. All products start at time $t = 0$ at quality level $m = 0$, so the base quality is $q_0(j) = (\lambda^{\omega})^0 = 1$. By the definition of quality improvement, all consumers agree that new generations are better than the old: $q_m(j) > q_{m-1}(j) \rightarrow \lambda^m > \lambda^{m-1} \rightarrow \lambda > 1$. Firms know the magnitude of the quality increment λ, which is assumed to be the same across all products.

A consumer has additively separable intertemporal preferences given by lifetime utility:

$$U_i = \int_0^{\infty} e^{-\rho t} \log u_i(t) dt, \tag{9.1}$$

where instantaneous utility is:

$$\log u_i(t) = \int_0^1 \log\left[\sum_m \lambda^m x_{im}(j,t)\right] dj, \tag{9.2}$$

Where ρ is the common subjective discount factor, λ^m is the assessment by consumers of quality level m and $x_{im}(j,t)$ is consumption by consumers in country i of quality level m of product j at time t.

A consumer maximizes lifetime utility (9.1) by choosing an optimal time path for expenditure and by allocating expenditure optimally at each point of time across products and to quality levels of the products. Since preferences are homothetic, the aggregate demand of consumers in each country is found by maximizing lifetime utility subject to the aggregate intertemporal budget constraint:

$$\int_0^\infty e^{-R(t)} E_i(t)dt \le A(0) + \int_0^\infty e^{-R(t)} Y_i(t), \tag{9.3}$$

which equates the present value of lifetime expenditure to the value of initial asset holdings plus the present value of lifetime income. The aggregate income of consumers in country i is $Y_i(t) = L_i w_i(t)$, the aggregate spending of consumers in country i is:

$$E_i(t) = \int_0^1 \left[\sum_m p_m(j,t) x_{im}(j,t) \right] dj . \tag{9.4}$$

$R(t) = \int_0^t r(s)ds$ is the cumulative interest rate up to time t, $A(0)$ is the value of any initial asset holdings, $w_i(t)$ is the wage rate in country i at time t, L_i is the exogenous labor supply in country i, and $p_m(j,t)$ is the price of quality level m of product j at time t.

The consumer's maximization problem can be broken into three stages: allocation of lifetime wealth across time, allocation of expenditure at each instant across products, and allocation of expenditure at each instant for each product across available quality levels. Each consumer evenly spreads lifetime spending for each product across time, evenly spreads spending at each instant across products, and allocates spending for each product at each instant to the quality level that has the lowest quality-adjusted price p_m/λ^m.

The logic for these arguments is the same as in Grossman and Helpman (1991a, 1991b). In the final stage, to maximize instantaneous utility (9.2), the representative consumer allocates spending for each product at each instant to the quality level $\tilde{m}(j,t)$ offering the lowest quality-adjusted price, $p_m \cdot (j,t)/\lambda^m$. Indifference is settled in favor of the higher quality level so the quality level selected is unique. In the second stage, the representative consumer then evenly spreads spending across the unit measure of all products, $E_i(j,t) = E_i(t)$, as the elasticity of substitution is constant at unity. Consumers demand $x_{\tilde{m}}(j,t) = E_i(t)/p_{\tilde{m}}(j,t)$ units of quality level $\tilde{m}(j,t)$ of product j and no units of other quality levels of that product. Thus lifetime utility (9.1) becomes:

$$U_i = \int_0^\infty e^{-\rho t} \left\{ \log E_i(t) + \int_0^1 \left[\tilde{m}(j,t) \log \lambda - \log p_{\tilde{m}}(j,t) \right] dj \right\} dt \tag{9.5}$$

by substituting for instantaneous utility and demand. The consumer is assumed able to borrow and lend at an endogenous instantaneous interest rate r, which the representative consumer views as given. In the first stage, the consumer chooses the optimal time profile of expenditure to maximize (9.5) subject to the intertemporal budget constraint (9.3). As is well known, the solution to this problem requires the time path of expenditure to satisfy $\dot{E}/E = r - \rho$. In equilibrium, the representative consumer will evenly spread lifetime spending across time, $E_i(t) = E_i$, as the utility function is time separable and the aggregate price level will not vary across time $\log p_{\tilde{m}}(j,t) = \log p_{\tilde{m}}(j)$. Since aggregate spending is constant across time, the interest rate at each point in time reflects the discount rate $r(t) = \rho$, so $R(t) = \rho t$ in the intertemporal budget constraint.

2.2 Incentives to Innovate

Innovation here takes the form of the unique knowledge of how to produce a higher quality level of a product than any other firm. Modeling innovation as a continuous Poisson process follows Grossman and Helpman (1991a, 1991b) but without any imitation. No imitation occurs if imitation costs are close enough to innovation costs as the profits from imitation would be smaller than from innovation. As opposed to Segerstrom (1991), here collusion between an imitator and an innovator is not possible due to delays in retaliation following a deviation or antitrust regulations.

Innovation races occur simultaneously for all products, with all firms able to target the quality level above the current highest quality level. Undertaking innovation intensity $\tilde{\iota}_i$ for a time interval dt requires $a_i \tilde{\iota}_i dt$ units of labor at a cost of $w_i a_i \tilde{\iota}_i dt$ and leads to success with probability $\tilde{\iota}_i dt$ for any industry. Innovation resembles a lottery: firms endure a cost for a chance at winning a payoff. An innovation success means that the firm discovers how to produce the quality level m, where the previous quality level in the industry was $m-1$. A higher investment in innovation yields a higher probability of success, but no level of investment in innovation can guarantee success. Only the current level of innovation activity determines the chance of innovation success, since innovation is memory-less for simplicity. Assume free entry into innovation, with an endless pool of potential innovators.

Given the innovation intensity ι of other firms, a firm's strategy is to pick an innovation intensity $\tilde{\iota}_i$ and a price p to charge for its product, once successful in innovation. I look for the steady-state equilibrium in stationary strategies, where firms' strategies are time invariant (but may depend on the current state of the economy). Firms already producing a quality level of a product can be shown to not engage in further innovation on that product — the proof mirrors that in Grossman and Helpman (1991a, 1991b). Producing firms lose value when subsequent innovation is successful, so other firms stand to gain more (net) and undertake innovation. Once a quality level of a product has been developed, another firm never invents the same quality level due to Bertrand competition in the product market, as a second innovation would earn no profits to compensate for the innovation costs.

A firm's problem can be broken down into two stages. First, when undertaking innovation, the firm chooses its intensity of innovation to maximize its expected value, given the innovation intensities of other firms. Once successful in innovation, the firm then chooses the price of its product to maximize its value, given prices and innovation intensities of other firms. Each nonproducing firm chooses its intensity of innovation to maximize its expected value, given the innovation intensities of other firms.

In the innovation stage, a firm endures innovation costs of $w_i a_i \tilde{\iota}_i dt$ and gains an expected reward of $v_i \tilde{\iota}_i dt$ (enjoys gains v_i with probability $\tilde{\iota}_i dt$). Each nonproducing firm chooses its intensity of innovation $\tilde{\iota}_i$ to maximize its expected gain from innovation, which is the difference between the expected reward and the costs of innovation. These expected values from engaging in innovation have an upper bound of zero; otherwise, if expected gains exceeded costs, innovation intensities would be infinite. On the other hand, if expected gains fall short of costs, innovation intensities are zero. To generate finite rates of innovation, expected gains must not exceed their cost, with equality when innovation occurs with positive intensity:

$$v_i \leq w_i a_i, \tilde{\iota}_i > 0 \quad \longleftrightarrow \quad v_i = w_i a_i, \tag{9.6}$$

where v_i is the value a firm gains from successful innovation. I focus on equilibria where the domestic and foreign intensities of innovation are positive, so that firms from both countries have leadership in some industries. This case will arise if the labor supply of each country is large enough.

Once successful in innovation, each producing firm then chooses the price of its product to maximize its value, given the prices and innovation intensities of other firms. All firms are exposed to further innovation by firms from both countries. Let:

$$\iota \equiv \iota_D + \iota_F \quad \longleftrightarrow \quad \iota_F = \iota - \iota_D, \tag{9.7}$$

denote the aggregate rate of innovation, the sum of the intensity of innovation by firms from each country. The mixture of the domestic and foreign innovation intensities in the aggregate rate of innovation influences the likelihood that any given innovation will be made by a domestic versus a foreign firm.

At each instant, a producer earns instantaneous profits $\pi_i dt$ and its value appreciates by $\dot{v}_i dt$ if no innovation occurs. With probability ιdt, an innovation occurs and the current producer suffers a capital loss of $v_i dt$ as it is priced out of the market by the firm that just innovated the next generation of that product. This risk is idiosyncratic and can be averaged out by a consumer holding a diversified portfolio of shares. Consequently, consumers require the expected rate of return to equal the risk-free interest rate r. Using (9.6) and $\dot{E}/E = r - \rho$, the no-arbitrage condition can be rewritten as requiring:

$$\frac{\dot{E}}{E} = \frac{\pi_i}{w_i a_i} + \frac{\dot{w}_i}{w_i} - \rho - \iota. \tag{9.8}$$

The rate of growth of expenditure increases with the level of expenditure (through profits) and decreases with the aggregate rate of innovation. In a steady-state equilibrium, the no-arbitrage condition can be rewritten to specify that the reward to innovation is the discounted stream of profits from production:

$$v_i = \frac{\pi_i}{\rho + \iota}. \tag{9.9}$$

As in Grossman and Helpman (1991b), aggregate expenditure is a jump variable that immediately takes its equilibrium value.

2.3 Product Market Profits

Consumers spend E on each product and are willing to pay a premium λ for a one quality level improvement in a product. Of the total spending, $E_D = f_D E$ is spent by domestic consumers and the remaining $E_F = f_F E$ is spent by foreign consumers (subscripts denote country i). Suppose in each industry, one firm can produce the highest quality level and another firm (from the same country) can produce the quality level one below. Normalize prices by the foreign wage and normalize the unit labor requirement in production to one in each country. The relative wage $w \equiv w_D/w_F = w_D$ is the domestic wage relative to the foreign wage. The relative wage is always (weakly) greater than one $w \geq 1$ by choice of country labels. The marginal cost of producing one unit of output of any quality is $c_D = w$ (the relative wage) in the domestic country and $c_F = 1$ in the foreign country.

Under Bertrand competition, the market outcomes depend on the extent of competition from rivals priced out of the market in equilibrium. Firms maximize profits by engaging in limit pricing. The most recent innovator for each product is the only firm able to produce the highest quality level available of that product due to assumed perfect patent protection. A firm just successful in innovation has a one quality level lead over its closest rival (the firm able to produce the next highest quality level of that product). The firm engages in limit pricing to keep its closest rival from earning a positive profit from production. Choosing a price equal to the quality increment λ times the closest rival's marginal cost just keeps the rival out of the market and thus maximizes the value of a firm. Given its rival's price, if the firm were to raise its price, consumers would buy from its rival. If the firm were to lower its price, it would not gain because industry demand functions are unit elastic. Similarly, if the rival were to lower its price, it would make negative profits and any higher price would not matter since it does not have any sales.

A market is *domestic led* if a domestic firm made the most recent innovation (and thus can produce the highest quality level of that product) and *foreign led* otherwise. The closest rivals when selling to foreign consumers will be foreign firms, with a marginal cost of one. A foreign firm could potentially license the technology from the domestic owner of the old technology if necessary (as when the current foreign firm had successfully targeted a domestic firm's product for improvement). Similarly, the closest rivals when selling to domestic consumers will be domestic firms, with marginal cost of w, as a domestic firm could potentially license the old technology from a foreign firm if necessary. Free access to old technologies was also assumed in Glass (1997). Licensing of old technologies need never actually take place since the old technologies are never actually produced in equilibrium. The potential marginal cost of producing the old technologies merely ties down the maximum price the new innovator can charge for the state of the art.

Prices will be $p_D = \lambda w$ when selling to domestic consumers and $p_F = \lambda$ when selling to foreign consumers, each a markup of the quality increment relative to local marginal costs. With these prices, sales are $x_D = E_D/(\lambda w)$ when selling to domestic consumers and $x_F = E_F/\lambda$ when selling to foreign consumers. Thus, a domestic exporter earns instantaneous profits of the form $\pi = (p - c)x$, which are:

$$\begin{aligned}\pi_D &= E_D(1-\delta) + E_F(1-\tau_F - w\delta) \\ &= E\left[1 - f_F\tau_F - (f_D + f_F w)\delta\right],\end{aligned} \tag{9.10}$$

where τ_i is the *ad valorem* tariff on imports into country i and $\delta \equiv 1/\lambda$. The two terms in the initial profit expression reflect profits from sales to the domestic and foreign consumers, respectively. The foreign tariff must not be too large $\tau_F < 1 - w\delta$ if the domestic firm is to serve the foreign market through exports. A foreign exporter earns instantaneous profits:

$$\begin{aligned}\pi_F &= E_F(1-\delta) + E_D\left(1 - \tau_D - \frac{\delta}{w}\right) \\ &= E\left[1 - f_D\tau_D - \left(\frac{f_D}{w} + f_F\right)\delta\right].\end{aligned} \tag{9.11}$$

Similarly, the domestic tariff must not be too large $\tau_D < 1 - \delta/w$ if the foreign firm is to serve the domestic market through exports. The tariff τ_i (or transport cost) places a wedge between the price consumers pay and the revenue the firm receives net of the tariff. As can be seen from the profit expressions (9.10) and (9.11), an import tariff cuts into the profits of firms from the other country: a domestic tariff lowers foreign firm profits while a foreign tariff lowers domestic firm profits. Changes in these profits influence the incentives for firms to innovate.

3 STEADY-STATE EXPORTING EQUILIBRIUM

In equilibrium, consumers in both countries maximize their intertemporal utility subject to the intertemporal budget constraint, firms in both countries maximize their value given prices and innovation intensities of other firms, and labor markets in both countries clear. This section characterizes the unique steady-state equilibrium with exporting.

3.1 Labor Constraints

Firms from both countries produce in their home market and export to serve the market abroad. As common in product cycle models, the labor supply in each country is assumed to be fixed. The fixed supply of labor is allocated between innovation and production in each country: for equilibrium in the labor market, the demand for labor must equal the supply of labor in each country. Under two-way exporting, the domestic resource constraint is:

$$a_D\iota_D + n_D\left(\frac{f_D}{w} + f_F\right)E\delta = L_D, \tag{9.12}$$

and the foreign resource constraint is:

$$a_F \iota_F + n_F \left(\frac{f_D}{w} + f_F \right) E\delta = L_F. \tag{9.13}$$

The first term of each labor constraint is demand for labor in innovation and the second term is demand for labor in production. The identity of the technology leader for each product dictates where production of that product occurs.

3.2 Constant Leadership Measures

Let n_i denote the percentage of markets where a firm from country i is the technology leader. Whether a product is produced by a domestic or a foreign firm changes over time as innovation occurs. Successful innovation by domestic firms that targets foreign-led markets increases domestic leadership, while successful innovation by foreign firms that targets domestic-led markets decreases domestic leadership. Thus the fraction of products that are domestic-led must obey the differential equation:

$$\dot{n}_D = \iota_D n_F - \iota_F n_D. \tag{9.14}$$

The solution is:

$$n_D(t) = \bar{n}_D + \left[n_D(0) - \bar{n}_D \right] e^{-\iota t}. \tag{9.15}$$

The fraction of markets that are domestic led is a state variable that is determined by past innovation intensities. Its steady-state value is:

$$\bar{n}_D = \frac{\iota_D}{\iota_D + \iota_F} = \frac{\iota_D}{\iota}. \tag{9.16}$$

More markets are domestic led when domestic innovation is higher relative to foreign innovation.

To achieve a steady-state equilibrium, the same fraction of products must become domestic led as become foreign led (and hence no longer domestic led) at each point in time so the extent of domestic leadership remains constant $\dot{n}_D = 0$. The flows into domestic leadership are $\iota_D n_F$ while the flows out are $\iota_F n_D$, and these flows must be equal:

$$\iota_D n_F = \iota_F n_D. \tag{9.17}$$

Additionally, the measures of market leadership must sum to one:

$$n_D + n_F = 1 \quad \longleftrightarrow \quad n_F = 1 - n_D. \tag{9.18}$$

While the fraction of products where domestic firms are the technological leaders remains constant in the steady-state equilibrium, each product cycles between domestic and foreign leadership. The equilibrium will determine the steady-state extent of domestic leadership. When domestic leadership increases, domestic firms have the ability to produce the state-of-the-art quality level for a larger fraction of all markets.

3.3 Steady-state System of Equations

Firms from each country serve the other country through exports. The first two equations are the domestic and foreign resource constraints (9.12) and (9.13):

$$wa_D n_D \iota + n_D\left(f_D + wf_F\right)E\delta - wL_D = 0 \tag{9.19}$$

and

$$wa_F\left(1-n_D\right)\iota + \left(1-n_D\right)\left(f_D + wf_F\right)E\delta - wL_F = 0. \tag{9.20}$$

The remaining two equations are the innovation valuation conditions (9.6) with the producing firm valuation equations (9.9) and profits (9.10) and (9.11) inserted:

$$E\left[1 - f_F\tau_F - \left(f_D + wf_F\right)\delta\right] - wa_D\left(\rho + \iota\right) = 0 \tag{9.21}$$

and

$$E\left[w - wf_D\tau_D - \left(f_D + wf_F\right)\delta\right] - a_F\left(\rho + \iota\right) = 0. \tag{9.22}$$

I substituted $\iota_F = \iota - \iota_D$, $n_F = 1 - n_D$ and $\iota_D = n_D \iota$ from the market measures conditions (9.17) and (9.18) to convert the system into only the four variables: the relative wage, aggregate spending, domestic leadership, and the aggregate rate of innovation $\{w, E, n_D, \iota\}$.

3.4 Uniqueness and Stability

The laws of motion for the share of products with domestic leadership (9.14) can be used to demonstrate the stability of the steady-state equilibrium. Solve the foreign resource constraint (9.20) and the foreign valuation condition (9.22) for the relative wage w and aggregate expenditure E. The remaining domestic resource constraint (9.19) and domestic valuation condition (9.21) then determine the share of domestic leadership n_D and the aggregate rate of innovation ι.

The economy must be at a point on the resource constraint because labor demand can never exceed labor supply. The law of motion can be rewritten as:

$$\dot{n}_D = \iota_D (1 - n_D) - \iota_F n_D \tag{9.22}$$

So long as the leadership measures sum to one ($n_F = 1 - n_D$). A steady-state equilibrium requires $\dot{n}_D = 0$. When the measure of domestic leadership is above its equilibrium value $\bar{n}_D$, domestic leadership will fall as more foreign innovation will successfully target domestic leaders than domestic innovation will displace foreign leadership $\dot{n}_D > 0$ (the second term will be larger than the first term). Similarly, domestic leadership that is too low $n_D < \bar{n}_D$ will result in domestic leadership rising $\dot{n}_D > 0$. Thus, the world economy will move along the labor constraint in the direction needed to achieve the equilibrium values of domestic leadership and the aggregate rate of innovation which also solve the domestic valuation condition. Only one pair (n_D, ι) solves the domestic resource constraint and domestic valuation condition for a positive aggregate rate of innovation $\iota > 0$ and a measure of domestic leadership that is strictly between zero and one $0 < n_D < 1$ so that some markets are led by domestic firms while others are led by foreign firms.

4 EFFECTS OF A SHRINKING WORLD

A shrinking world may manifest itself along several dimensions. First, transport costs may fall, making international trade easier. Second, governments may negotiate the removal of artificial impediments to trade such as tariffs; the reduction in tariffs may be unilateral (undertaken by one country) or bilateral (undertaken by both countries). Both countries lowering tariffs but to differing degrees would be equivalent to both lowering tariffs by the lesser degree combined with one country additionally lowering its tariffs by the remaining difference. A third way in which the world may shrink is through improvements in communication. Better communication may result in greater spread of knowledge, including the knowledge of how best to innovate. Any superiority of firms in one country over firms elsewhere in the ability to innovate may lessen over time as word spreads of any special methods. This section explores the effects of changing the magnitude of tariffs or transport costs τ_i and of international technology diffusion lowering the foreign resource requirement in innovation a_F.

4.1 Unilateral Tariffs

To determine the effects of a domestic or a foreign tariff τ_D or τ_F on the steady-state equilibrium values of these four variables, the above system of four equations was totally differentiated; details of this procedure appear in Appendix 9A. Assuming that firms serve markets abroad through exports, the following main result was obtained:

Proposition 1 An increase in the domestic tariff decreases the aggregate rate of innovation and increases domestic leadership, aggregate expenditure, and the relative wage; an increase in the foreign tariff decreases the aggregate rate of innovation, domestic leadership, aggregate expenditure and the relative wage.

The adverse effect of tariffs on the rate of innovation is natural: by reducing the realized gains from exchange, tariffs reduce the reward to innovation. Tariffs are protectionist and bad for growth since they reduce the reward to innovation. However, when the domestic tariff is increased, the reward to innovation is most severely reduced for foreign firms, so the fraction of products where domestic firms are the market leaders increases. Also, domestic tariffs achieve a positive level effect through a higher relative wage. Since I normalized by the foreign wage, the higher aggregate expenditure indicates a lower foreign wage, and a negative level effect for the foreign country when the domestic country increases its tariff.

As for the transition path, the domestic labor constraint is unaffected by tariffs since tariffs do not consume real resources. An increase in the domestic tariff causes the valuation condition to shift down to require a lower aggregate rate of innovation for any value of domestic leadership. The transition occurs by a movement along the labor constraint as domestic leadership adjusts smoothly toward its new equilibrium, such as described by (9.15). Because the labor constraint does not shift, the transition for all variables is simply a gradual move toward the values in the new steady-state equilibrium.

In a steady-state equilibrium, instantaneous utility is given by:

$$\log u_i(t) = \log E_i + \overline{m} \log \lambda - \log \overline{p}_i, \qquad (9.23)$$

where the expected number of innovations arriving in time period t is $\overline{m} = \iota t$ and the average price paid by consumers is $\overline{p}_i = \lambda$ (under $w = 1$). Instantaneous utility can be written as:

$$\log u_i(t) = \log E_i + (\iota t - 1) \log \lambda. \qquad (9.24)$$

Lifetime utility takes the form:

$$U_i = \frac{\log E_i + (\iota/\rho - 1) \log \lambda}{\rho}. \qquad (9.25)$$

The expression for lifetime utility enables weighing the benefits of a faster rate of innovation against the cost of a lower level of real expenditure. If the discount rate is slight enough, indeed the rate of innovation is the most crucial determinant of national welfare. Nonetheless, the negative level effect of tariff reductions may make them politically difficult to achieve.

4.2 Bilateral Tariffs or Transport Costs

Let $\partial\tau = \partial\tau_D = \partial\tau_F$ represent an equal change in both tariff (or transport cost) wedges. A direct implication of proposition 1 is that if transportation costs fall everywhere, the rate of innovation rises. A reduction in tariffs or transportation costs in a country raises innovation according to proposition 1. If both countries lower their tariffs equally, as through bilateral negotiations, innovation rises all the more.

Corollary 1 A reduction in transportation costs or tariffs, anywhere or everywhere, increases the aggregate rate of innovation.

In addition, the relative wage remains constant, so distributive effects between countries are absent when both countries lower their tariffs equally. Also, domestic leadership remains constant since innovation incentives increase for domestic and foreign firms to the same degree. Since the leadership measures do not need to adjust, the transition from the old to the new steady-state equilibrium is immediate:

the rate of innovation jumps to its new level. The same phenomenon that could occur through bilateral tariff reductions can also arise through a 'shrinking world' — a reduction in transport costs due to improved transportation technologies (which are likely to be similar across all developed countries).

4.3 International Diffusion of Innovation Technology

In addition to declining trade barriers (both natural and artificial) another way that the world can shrink is through the international diffusion of technology. The model already supposes that the knowledge of innovation in itself diffuses across countries sufficiently that firms can improve upon an existing innovation regardless of their location.

However, improvements in communication may also lead to a narrowing of any gaps in the ability to engage in innovation. The foreign resource requirement in innovation may exceed that of the domestic economy $a_F > a_D$, implying that any given effort at innovation yields success with a lower probability abroad. Many aspects of a shrinking world may lead to the foreign resource requirement in innovation falling as foreigners learn some of what makes the domestic economy more productive at innovation.

Similar techniques to those used to address tariffs may be used to examine the effects of a reduction in the foreign resource requirement in innovation a_F. Appendix 9A provides expressions for the derivatives to support the following result.

Proposition 2 A decrease in the resource requirement in foreign innovation increases the aggregate rate of innovation and decreases domestic leadership, aggregate expenditure and the relative wage.

Comparison to proposition 1 indicates that international diffusion of the technology for engaging efficiently in innovation, by reducing the resource requirement in innovation abroad, leads to effects that are similar, at least in direction, to those of a unilateral lowering of tariffs. Providing freer access to the domestic market works through the benefit side to increase the incentives for innovation abroad, while providing for easier innovation works on the cost side. An implication of this analysis is that negotiating for stronger protection of intellectual property abroad may be a substitute for protection of domestic markets from imports: innovation abroad becomes more difficult and consequently there are fewer foreign products that can effectively compete with domestically produced goods.

5 CONCLUSION

This chapter has constructed a dynamic model of endogenous innovation to determine the impact of tariffs or transport costs on innovation, where similar developed countries trade with each other. A tariff raises a country's relative wage, a positive level effect, but reduces the rate of innovation, a negative growth effect. This trade-off between positive level effect and negative growth effect indicates that protection may be adopted if discounting is sufficiently severe. Equal tariff reductions allow the positive growth effect to be enjoyed by both countries without the negative level effect that occurs through the relative wage when a tariff reduction is unilateral. Additionally, restrictions on the diffusion of innovation technology abroad may act like increases in tariffs in that both generate positive level effects but reduce innovation. Given the predictions of this model, perhaps it is no coincidence that the substantial negotiated reductions in tariffs have been followed by efforts to strengthen the protection of intellectual property worldwide.

APPENDIX 9A

The proof is seen by totally differentiating the system:

$$\begin{bmatrix} a_D n_D w & b_{12} & b_{13} & b_{14} \\ w a_F n_F & b_{22} & b_{23} & b_{24} \\ -w a_F & 0 & b_{33} & b_{34} \\ -w a_D & 0 & b_{41} & b_{41} \end{bmatrix} \begin{bmatrix} \partial \iota \\ \partial n_D \\ \partial E \\ \partial w \end{bmatrix} = \begin{bmatrix} 0 \\ 0 \\ w f_D E \partial \tau_D \\ f_F E \partial \tau_F \end{bmatrix}$$

where:

$$b_{12} = w a_D \iota + E\delta\left(f_F w + f_D\right)$$

$$b_{13} = n_D \delta\left(f_F w + f_D\right)$$

$$b_{14} = a_D n_D \iota + f_F n_D E\delta - L_D$$

$$b_{22} = -w a_F \iota - E\delta\left(f_F w + f_D\right)$$

$$b_{23} = \delta n_F \left(f_F w + f_D\right)$$

$$b_{24} = a_F \iota n_F + E\delta f_F n_F - L_F$$

$$b_{33} = w\left(1 - f_D \tau_D - f_F \delta\right) - f_D \delta$$

$$b_{34} = E\left(1 - f_D \tau_D - f_F \delta\right) - a_F \left(\rho + \iota\right)$$

$$b_{43} = 1 - f_F \tau_F - \left(f_D + f_F w\right)\delta$$

and

$$b_{44} = -f_F E\delta - a_D \left(\rho + \iota\right)$$

to find the derivatives:

$$\frac{\partial \iota}{\partial \tau_D} = -\frac{\iota \delta f_D f_F \left(n_D w + n_F\right)}{1 - \delta} < 0$$

$$\frac{\partial n_D}{\partial \tau_D} = \frac{\delta f_D f_F n_D n_F \left(w - 1\right)}{1 - \delta} > 0$$

$$\frac{\partial E}{\partial \tau_D} = \frac{f_D E\left[1 - \delta + f_D n_D \delta\left(w - 1\right)\right]}{1 - \delta} > 0$$

$$\frac{\partial w}{\partial \tau_D} = \frac{w f_D \left(1 - f_D \delta - f_F w \delta\right)}{1 - \delta} > 0$$

and

$$\frac{\partial \iota}{\partial \tau_F} = -\frac{\iota \delta f_D f_F (n_D w + n_F)}{w(1-\delta)} < 0$$

$$\frac{\partial n_D}{\partial \tau_F} = -\frac{\delta f_D f_F n_D n_F (w-1)}{w(1-\delta)} < 0$$

$$\frac{\partial E}{\partial \tau_F} = -\frac{\delta E f_D f_F n_D (w-1)}{w(1-\delta)} < 0$$

$$\frac{\partial w}{\partial \tau_F} = -\frac{f_F \left[w(1-\delta) + f_D \delta (w-1) \right]}{1-\delta} < 0$$

where:

$$|B| = \frac{wE^3(1-\delta)}{\iota} > 0$$

and impose $\tau_D = \tau_F = 0$ initially and take the limit as $\rho \to 0$ to simplify the expressions. The model can be further simplified by assuming that the two countries are exactly identical: same labor supplies, same innovation technologies and same tariffs always. In that special case, the relative wage would always be one and domestic leadership would always be exactly one-half. If the common tariff were set to zero, the model would then reduce to the one-country quality ladders model (for a country with its labor supply equal to the world labor supply).

Total differentiation also generates the following effects of an increase in the foreign resource requirement in innovation:

$$\frac{\partial \iota}{\partial a_F} = -\frac{\iota^2 \left[f_F n_D \delta w + n_F (1-\delta f_D) \right]}{E(1-\delta)} < 0$$

$$\frac{\partial n_D}{\partial a_F} = \frac{\iota n_D n_F \left[1-\delta(f_D + f_F w) \right]}{E(1-\delta)} > 0$$

$$\frac{\partial E}{\partial a_F} = \frac{\iota n_D\left[1-\delta\left(f_D + f_F w\right)\right]}{\left(1-\delta\right)} > 0$$

and

$$\frac{\partial w}{\partial a_F} = \frac{\iota w\left[1-\delta\left(f_D + f_F w\right)\right]}{E\left(1-\delta\right)} > 0.$$

The signs of the derivatives are of course reversed for a reduction in a_F.

One possible extension of the model would be if labor–leisure choice led to an upward-sloping labor supply curve instead of the fixed labor supply assumed in the base model. Suppose labor supply in country i is $L_i\left(w_i\right)$ and is an increasing function of the wage in country $i: \partial L_i/\partial w_i > 0$. A unilateral increase in the domestic tariff increases the relative wage, which would then increase the domestic relative labor supply. The resulting increase in the domestic relative labor supply will in turn increase domestic innovation relative to foreign innovation and thus increase the measure of domestic leadership. The additional effect on the aggregate rate of innovation would depend on the second derivative of the labor supply curve, which determines whether the increase in domestic labor supply exceeds the decrease in the foreign labor supply. Compared to the base model with exogenous labor supplies, only the magnitude of the effects, not their direction would be affected.

REFERENCES

Ades, Alberto F. and Edward L. Glaeser (1999), 'Evidence on Growth, Increasing Returns, and the Extent of the Market', *Quarterly Journal of Economics*, **114**, 1025–45.

Ben-David, Dan and Michael B. Loewy (1998), 'Free Trade, Growth and Convergence', *Journal of Economic Growth*, **3**, 143–70.

Finger, J.M. and Alexander J. Yeats (1976), 'Effective Production by Transportation Costs and Tariffs: A Comparison of Magnitudes', *Quarterly Journal of Economics*, **90**, 169–76.

Frankel, Jeffrey A. and David Romer (1999), 'Does Trade Cause Growth?', *American Economic Review*, **89**, 379–99.

Glass, Amy J. (1997), 'Product Cycles and Market Penetration', *International Economic Review*, **38**, 865–92.

Glass, Amy J. and Kamal Saggi (2002a), 'Licensing versus Direct Investment: Implications for Economic Growth', *Journal of International Economics*, **56**, 131–53.

Glass, Amy J. and Kamal Saggi (2002b), 'Intellectual Property Rights and Foreign Direct Investment', *Journal of International Economics*, **56**, 387–410.

Grossman, Gene M. and E. Helpman (1991a), 'Quality Ladders and Product Cycles',

Quarterly Journal of Economics, **106**, 557–86.

Grossman, Gene M. and E. Helpman (1991b), 'Quality Ladders in the Theory of Growth', *Review of Economic Studies*, **58**, 43–61.

Harley, C. Knick (1988), 'Ocean Freight Rates and Productivity, 1710–1913: The Primacy of Mechanical Invention Reaffirmed', *Journal of Economic History*, **48,** 851–76.

Harrison, Ann (1996), 'Openness and Growth: A Time-Series, Cross-Country Analysis for Developing Countries', *Journal of Development Economics*, **48,** 419–47.

Lee, Jong Wha (1993), 'International Trade, Distortions, and Long-Run Economic Growth', *IMF Staff Papers*, **40**, 299–328.

O'Rourke, Kevin H. (2000), 'Tariffs and Growth in the Late 19th Century', *Economic Journal*, **110**, 456–83.

Rivera-Batiz, Luis A. and Paul M. Romer (1991), 'Economic Integration and Endogenous Growth', *Quarterly Journal of Economics*, **106**, 531–55.

Segerstrom, Paul S. (1991), 'Innovation, Imitation, and Economic Growth', *Journal of Political Economy*, **99**, 807–27.

Segerstrom, Paul S., T.C.A. Anant and Elias Dinopoulos (1990), 'A Schumpeterian Model of the Product Life Cycle', *American Economic Review*, **80,** 1077–91.

Part III

Public Policy

10. Long-run Effects of Financial Policy in an Endogenously Growing Economy

Been-Lon Chen, Yeong-Yuh Chiang and Ping Wang

1 INTRODUCTION

This chapter develops an overlapping generations model with an active financial sector, where human capital accumulation is the engine of endogenous growth and firms' physical capital investments require external financing. It evaluates the long-run growth effects of three financial policies — a reserve requirement policy, a loan rate control policy (which is often associated with a financially repressed economy) and a deposit rate ceiling policy (Regulation Q). Under our economic environment with diminishing net marginal benefit of education, an increase in the required reserve ratio in an unconstrained equilibrium tends to lower savings in kind and retard economic growth, whereas a loan rate control or a deposit rate ceiling policy in a constrained equilibrium may induce savings in kind and hence promote growth. Further comparative statics concerning the effects of financial policies on the loan and deposit rates as well as the long-run consequences of changes in external financing efficacy and pecuniary education cost are also examined.

Since the birth of the new growth theory one and a half decades ago, economists have undertaken numerous studies on long-run growth consequences of macro policies, such as tax, education, public investment and monetary policies, to name but a few. Yet, despite its increasing importance, few have investigated how various forms of financial policy may affect the long-run performance of an economy within the endogenous growth framework.[1] Our chapter attempts to fill this gap by examining the long-run macroeconomic consequences of financial policy in an economy where human capital accumulation is the engine of endogenous growth and firms' physical capital investments require external financing, as observed in several rapid-growing newly industrialized countries. We evaluate, in particular, three forms of financial policy that have been implemented in those economies at various stages of development: (i) a reserve requirement policy, (ii) a loan rate control policy that is commonly observed in financially repressed economies, and (iii) a deposit rate ceiling policy (Regulation Q).

We construct an endogenous growth model of financial intermediation with overlapping generations of optimizing households and external financing firms to examine the long-run growth effects of financial policies. There are four theaters of economic activity involving households, firms, banks and the government. For analytic convenience and without loss of generality, we consider savings in kind via intergenerational human capital accumulation as the engine of growth. Each household lives two periods, works when young and consumes when old. In the presence of parental altruism, a young household decides the division of time to work or to educate the next generation, where the latter enables intergenerational accumulation of human capital. Due to forced savings in goods, a household deposits the entire wages, net of the pecuniary cost of education, to a bank at the young age for consumption at the old age. Firms are infinitely lived, utilizing effective labor and physical capital, which is financed externally with bank loans, to produce a single final good. Perfectly competitive banks accept deposits from households and make loans to producers to achieve maximum periodic profits. The model is closed with a government sector, which is passive except for exercising financial policies on reserve requirements and loan and deposit rate controls. The central feature of the model is the development of an active financial sector and the separation of the behaviors of the lenders and the borrowers, which are crucial for a complete examination of the three financial policies mentioned above. Although our framework is highly stylized, it offers a parsimonious structure enabling analytical solution and characterization of the equilibrium.

Under this setup, we can show that there is a unique unconstrained (in the case with reserve requirement policy) and a unique constrained (in the case with loan or deposit rate controls) balanced growth equilibrium. We then characterize unconstrained and constrained balanced growth equilibrium in response to financial policy as well as selected economic parameter changes. The main findings are summarized as follows. First, in an unconstrained equilibrium, an increase in the required reserve ratio raises the loan rate. Under a regularity condition that the net marginal benefit of education is diminishing, a tightened reserve requirement policy tends to lower both savings in kind and the rate of economic growth. Second, along an unconstrained balanced growth path, the effects of less effective transformation from loan services to physical capital accumulation are to reduce economic growth. Third, when the loan rate is controlled below the market equilibrium level as found in the case of financial repression, the constrained equilibrium rates of human capital accumulation and economic growth are higher than those under the unconstrained equilibrium. Finally, a Regulation Q policy that sets a deposit rate ceiling may also help to reallocate available resources to savings in kind within our framework and hence promote economic growth.

There are a few related studies, evaluating the reserve requirement policy or examining financial repression within the dynamic general equilibrium framework. Freeman (1987) develops a model of optimizing agents who choose to hold deposits at financial intermediates in which fractional required reserves can be regarded as a tax on deposits with positive inflation. Thus, the optimal policy when reserves are required is a mix of the reserve requirement ratio and the monetary expansion rate. Recently, Haslag and Young (1998) constructed an AK model of endogenous growth with a bank and an informal bank to quantitatively assess the impact of changes in the rate of money creation and reserve requirements on real seigniorage revenue and economic growth. Reserves are required only in the bank (rather than the informal bank), but the informal bank also serves to intermediate savings. They show that higher reserve requirements reduce the return to deposits, thereby reducing the incentives to save as well as lowering the rates of capital accumulation and economic growth. Finally, Roubini and Sala-i-Martin (1995) study an economy where tax evasion is extensive and hence the government represses the financial sector to increase seigniorage tax revenues. They find that such a financially repressing policy may reduce the efficiency of financial intermediation and reduce the economic growth rate.

It may be informative to compare our findings with those in previous studies so as to highlight the contributions of our chapter. While both Haslag and Young (1998) and our chapter find tightened reserve requirements to suppress economic growth, their result is mainly driven by discouragement of savings in goods but ours is due to a reduction in human capital accumulation. Due to this very different setting, the rate of deposit in Haslag and Young responds negatively to reserve requirements, but ours may respond positively if the effect through the loan rate is dominant. More specifically, under our setup, higher reserve requirements are accompanied by tightened funds available for loans, raising the loan rate and, via banks' zero profit condition, increasing the deposit rate. In contrast with Roubini and Sala-i-Martin (1995) where a negative relationship between the financial repression policy and economic growth is obtained in the presence of tax evasion, we find that such a loan rate control policy increases the net rate of returns on savings in kind and enhances economic growth. In contrast to previous work, we examine both required reserve and loan rate control policies in an endogenously growing economy. Moreover, the long-run consequences of a deposit rate regulation are also evaluated in a dynamic general equilibrium setting, which is, to our knowledge, the first attempt in the literature.

The remainder of the chapter is organized as follows. In Section 2, we describe the structure of the overlapping generations model with endogenous growth via intergenerational human capital accumulation. Section 3 analyzes the individual optimizing behavior for households, firms and banks, and solves for the balanced growth equilibrium. Section 4 performs comparative-static analysis with respect to the three financial policies on reserve requirements and the loan and deposit rates. Finally, a brief summary of our theoretical findings and possible extensions of interests is provided in Section 5.

2 THE MODEL

In this section, we construct an endogenous growth model of financial intermediation with overlapping generations (OG) of optimizing households to examine the long-run macroeconomic effects of financial policies. In the model economy, there are four theaters: households, firms, banks and the government. There is a continuum of each type of economic agent (households, firms and banks) with unit mass. The consideration of an active financial sector is crucial for an adequate evaluation of interest tax policies. We begin by constructing a model with only savings in kind (intergenerational human capital accumulation) yet in the concluding section making remarks on the consideration of savings in goods. This savings-in-kind setup provides a parsimonious analytic structure capturing the spirit of the human capital-based endogenous growth model developed by Lucas (1988) and Glomm and Ravikumar (1992). Moreover, the OG framework is not only analytically tractable, allowing for a complete characterization of the equilibrium and analysis of the policy effects, but also sufficient to ensure the active role of the financial sector via forced savings in goods.

Each household lives two periods, young and old.[2] Each household works when young and consumes when old. Each household is endowed with one unit of labor supply when young in which a fraction ν is devoted to 'home activity' in educating its next generation and the remaining fraction, $1-\nu$, is to market activity in production. The wage rate (per unit of effective labor) is w and, in the presence of forced savings, a household deposits the entire wages, net of the pecuniary cost for intergenerational human capital transfer, ϕh, in a bank. To be consistent with a perpetual growth framework, the real resource cost of education is assumed to be proportional to the level of human capital. In contrast with the endogenous growth model of Lucas (1988), we allow for both time and real resource costs of education. The household redeems its deposits (with interest) in the second period of its lifetime and consumes the entire amount in the absence of intergenerational transfer in goods.

Although there is no bequest in cash, parental altruism is allowed via home education and intergenerational human capital transfer, as a household cares for not only its own consumption when old but also the consumption of its next generation. For illustrative purposes, we shall call $(1-v)wh$ and ϕh, , respectively, the time/effort cost and the pecuniary cost of intergenerational human capital accumulation. Each household has an identical logarithmic preference that is monotonically increasing in consumption. Let $c_{t+1}(c_{t+2})$ be the consumption of the generation $t(t+1)$ when old. Then the utility of generation t is given by: $U_t = \ln c_{t+1} + 1/(1+\rho)\ln c_{t+2}$, where $\rho > 0$ is an intergenerational discount rate in order to capture less than 100 percent altruism.

A generation t household receives a wage income of $w_t(1-v_t)h_t$ when young where h_t is the level of human capital for the household born in t. Since each representative household only works when young and consumes when old, this results in forced savings and, in the absence of bond or capital market, a generation t household has all wage income channeled through the banking sector to earn positive interest. Thus, the total deposit by each household of generation t, denoted a_t, can be written as:

$$a_t = w_t(1-v_t)h_t - \phi h_t. \tag{10.1}$$

Using (10.1), the amount of consumption when old is measured by:

$$c_{t+1} = (1+r_t)[w_t(1-v_t)h_t - \phi h_t], \tag{10.2}$$

where r_t is the deposit interest rate between t and $t+1$.

Firms are owned by capitalists. Each representative firm in the economy uses capital, k_t and effective labor, $(1-v_t)h_t$, together with external finance or bank loans, x_t, to produce a single final good, y_t. Assuming complete capital depreciation, the output is allocated to capital, $k_t + 1$ (which equals investment) and consumption. The production function is given by:

$$y_t = A\min\left\{k_t^{\alpha}, (bx_t)^{\alpha}\right\}\left[(1-v_t)h_t\right]^{1-\alpha} \tag{10.3}$$

where $A > 0$, $b > 0$ and $\alpha \in [0,1]$.

The above setup of production technology highlights the significance of financial instruments for a firm's capital formation, which has been emphasized in the finance literature.[3] We consider, in particular, that physical capital and loan services are perfect complements, consistent with a fractional loan-in-advance constraint on investment purchases. Indeed, our framework can be regarded as a generalization of imposing a loan-in-advance constraint on investment: by assuming $b > 1$, (10.3) implies that only a fraction of capital investment is externally financed via the banking sector. Moreover, should one consider $b < 1$, it may be postulated that in a primitive credit market, there is 'red tape' in the borrowing and lending process along which only a fraction of bank loans are transformed into effective loan services for purchases of investment projects. In general, one may regard b as measuring the efficacy of loan services in transforming available funds for productive investment uses. Moreover, we follow Diamond and Yellin (1990) in assuming that the goods producer (capitalist) is a residual claimer in the sense that it ingests the unsold consumption goods (denoted z_t, which can be thought of as the conventionally modeled profit flow) in a fashion consistent with lifetime firm value maximization.[4] The net profit flow of a representative firm is,

$$\begin{aligned}\pi_t &= A\min\left\{k_t^{\alpha},(bx_t)^{\alpha}\right\}\left[(1-v_t)h_t\right]^{1-\alpha} \\ &\quad -(1+\delta_t)x_t - w_t(1-v_t)h_t - k_{t+1}.\end{aligned} \tag{10.4}$$

We now study the activity of the financial intermediation in which each bank accepts deposits from households and makes loans to producers in order to make periodic profits. Denote δ_t as the loan rate and μ as the unit bank operation cost. We assume the banking industry is competitive and is free to enter. In any given period t, the profit of a bank is the revenue flow from loan receipts, $\delta_t x_t$, net of interest payments to its depositors, $r_t a_t$, and the bank operation costs, μx_t, which is: $(\delta_t - \mu)x_t - r_t a_t$. To close the model, we must specify the intergenerational human capital accumulation process. As in the conventional wisdom (for example, Lucas, 1988; Stokey, 1991; Glomm and Ravikumar, 1992), the stock of human capital of generation $t+1(h_t 1)$ can be specified as:

$$h_{t+1} = \left[1+g(v)\right]h_t, \tag{10.5}$$

in which g measures the rate of human capital accumulation (and hence the rate of growth of the economy) with $g_v > 0$ and $g_{vv} \leq 0$. Thus, when $g_{vv} = 0$, the human capital accumulation process reduces to that in Lucas (1988).

3 OPTIMIZATION AND BALANCED GROWTH EQULIBRIUM

We start with the optimization of banks. Under perfect competition, the optimization of banks is consistent with the zero profit condition,

$$(\delta_t - \mu)x_t = r_t[w_t(1-v_t)h_t - \phi h_t]. \tag{10.6}$$

That is, under a nonnegativity constraint on the deposit (that is, the square bracket on the right-hand side of the zero profit condition), operative banking in the sense that the deposit rate is positive (see condition R to be established below) will ensure that the loan rate exceeds the variable bank operation cost. The transformation of deposits into loans, under loan market equilibrium in the absence of central bank intervention on deposit and loan rates of interest, takes a simple form:

$$x_t = (1-\eta)a_t, \tag{10.7}$$

where η measures the rate of reserve requirements. Notably, the required reserves, ηa_t, may be thought of as idle funds or funds used in the creation of seigniorage revenues to finance nonproductive government spending. That is, under either setup, the entirety of the reserves is regarded as a tax on the private sector without general equilibrium redistribution or public good benefits.

In this model with forced savings in good, households' consumption and savings decision is trivial. Thus, the main task is to determine the fraction of time devoted to working $1-v_t$ by maximizing the dynastic utility function subject to constraints (10.2) and (10.5), taking v_{t+1} and prices (deposit interest and wage rates) as given.[5] The first-order necessary condition is:

$$w_t = \frac{\zeta(v_t)}{v_t}[w_t(1-v_t) - \phi], \tag{10.8}$$

where $\zeta(v) = \varepsilon(v)/(1+\rho)$ and $\varepsilon(v) = v/(1+g)\cdot d(1+g)/dv > 0$ is the education elasticity of human capital accumulation. For analytical convenience, we assume throughout the chapter that εv is independent of v and thus ζ is constant. In (10.8), the left-hand side is the marginal cost of education investment by reducing a unit of working time. The right-hand side is the generationally discounted marginal benefit, where the first term measures the net gain from educating the next generation multiplied by the deposit rate of interest and the second term is associated with a reduction in the real resource cost of education.

Finally, we solve the optimization of a representative firm. Facing a given rate of interest on loans, δ, the representative producer in any given period t chooses loan demand, labor demand and consumption goods supply to maximize its lifetime value V (the sum of present discounted gross profit flows). Thus, the discounted sum of profit flows can be specified as:

$$V(k_t) = \max_{\{x_t, 1-v_t\}} \sum_{\tau=t}^{\infty} \Delta_\tau \pi_\tau, \text{ where } \Delta_\tau = \Pi_{j=t}^{\tau} \left(\frac{1}{1+\delta_j} \right).$$

In the absence of credit market imperfections, optimal loan must satisfy:

$$\frac{k_t}{h_t} = b \frac{x_t}{h_t}. \tag{10.9}$$

Under (10.9), optimization Vk_t with respect to $1-v_t$ leads to:

$$Ab^{\alpha}(1-\alpha)(1-v_t)^{-\alpha} \left(\frac{x_t}{h_t} \right)^{\alpha} = w_t. \tag{10.10}$$

Substituting (10.10) into π_t to eliminate x_t, the discounted sum of profits can be written in Bellman equation form as:

$$\begin{aligned} V(k_t) = \max_{k_{t+1}} & \left[A^{1/\alpha} \alpha \left(\frac{1-\alpha}{w_t} \right)^{(1-\alpha)/\alpha} - \left(\frac{1+\delta_t}{b} \right) \right] k_t \\ & - k_{t+1} + \frac{1}{1+\delta_{t+1}} V(k_{t+1}). \end{aligned} \tag{10.11}$$

We proceed with standard dynamic programming techniques, combining the first-order condition and the Benveniste–Scheinkman condition to obtain:

$$A\alpha \frac{b^{\alpha}}{1+b} (1-v_t)^{1-\alpha} \left(\frac{x_t}{h_t} \right)^{\alpha-1} = 1 + \delta_t. \tag{10.12}$$

Thus, the value function can be shown proportional to the amount of physical capital and the transversality condition for the firm's maximization is guaranteed by:

Condition T (Transversality) $\delta > g$.

Finally, from (10.3) and (10.9), the material balance condition of the goods market can be written as:

$$Ab^{\alpha} x_t^{\ \alpha}[(1-v_t)h_t]^{1-\alpha} = c_t + z_t + k_{t+1}. \tag{10.13}$$

We are now ready to solve for the balanced growth equilibrium. First, we define the concept of a balanced growth path (BGP). Then we prove the existence and uniqueness of a BGP.

Definition A BGP is a tuple

$$\{c_t/h_t, z_t/h_t, k_t/h_t, a_t/h_t, x_t/h_t; v_t, w_t, r_t, \delta_t\}$$

such that:

1. households, firms and banks all optimize subject to relevant constraints: (10.2) (for households); (10.9), (10.10), (10.12) (for firms); (10.1), (10.6) and (10.7) (for banks);
2. material balance: (10.13);
3. intergenerational human capital accumulation: (10.8) is satisfied; and
4. each of the variables is constant over time.

Obviously, by Walras's law and by our setup wherein the deposit market is automatically clear, once the goods market is material balanced, the loan market must also be clear (that is, loan demand obtained from the firm side must be equal to loan supply from the bank side). To characterize the BGP, we can transform the system in balanced growth into stationary ratios, in particular, focusing on x/h, δ and r due to the recursive nature of the model to be elaborated below.

First, the amount of loans x in equation (10.7) can be regarded as loan demand or loan supply. Hence, from banks' zero profit condition (10.6) and the deposit–loan transformation and loan market equilibrium relationship (10.7), we get the loan and deposit rate relationship as:

$$\delta = \mu + \frac{r}{1-\eta}. \tag{10.14}$$

That is, the deposit rate is positive (that is, the banking sector is operative) if and only if the loan rate exceeds the bank's unit operation cost. However, it is important to note that, in the presence of central bank regulation on either the deposit or the loan rate, equation (10.7) only represents loan supply, not necessarily loan demand, where the latter enters all the conditions on the firm side. That is, in solving for equilibrium under the central bank regulation, we will not use the relationship specified in (10.7) and instead apply one of the two central bank financial policy constraints:

$$\delta = \bar{\delta} < \mu + \frac{r}{1-\eta} \tag{10.15}$$

and

$$r = \bar{r} < (1-\eta)(\delta-\mu), \tag{10.16}$$

where (10.15) is applicable in the case of financial repression (that is, setting up a loan rate below the market equilibrium level) and (10.16) is for Regulation Q (that is, imposing a deposit rate ceiling).

Rewriting the Benveniste–Scheinkman condition for firms' optimization (10.12), we get the following relationship:

$$\left(\frac{x}{h}\right)^{1-\alpha} = Ab^{\alpha}(1-v)^{1-\alpha}\left(\frac{\alpha}{1+b}\right)\left(\frac{1}{1+\delta}\right). \tag{10.17}$$

Substitution of firms' first-order condition (10.10) into the Benveniste–Scheinkman condition for firms' optimization (10.12) to eliminate x/h yields the factor price frontier:

$$w = [(1-\alpha)A]^{1/1-\alpha}\left(\frac{\alpha}{1-\alpha}\frac{b}{1+b}\frac{1}{1+\delta}\right)^{\alpha/1-\alpha}. \tag{10.18}$$

As a result of Pareto complementarity between labor skill and physical capital, the factor price frontier possesses the standard downward-sloping property. Moreover, when a firm relies more on external financing as a result of lower efficacy of loan services (smaller b), induced demands for production inputs decrease, thus shifting the factor price frontier inward.

Note that both relationships specified above involve only a firm's optimization without assuming the clearance of the loan market. Substituting (10.17) and (10.18) into banks' zero profit condition (10.6) and manipulating, we can obtain:

$$r = (\delta - \mu) \cdot \left\{ (1-\alpha)\frac{(1+b)(1+\delta)}{\alpha} - \left[\frac{1}{Ab^{\alpha}}\frac{(1+b)(1+\delta)}{\alpha}\right]^{1/1-\alpha}\frac{\phi}{1-v}\right\}^{-1}. \quad (10.19)$$

Tedious but straightforward differentiation shows that the deposit rate is increasing in both the loan rate and intergenerational human capital investment as long as the loan rate exceeds the variable bank operation cost. Intuitively, under perfect competition, a higher loan rate enables a higher deposit rate while maintaining banks' zero profit condition. To ensure that the banking sector is operative, the deposit rate must be strictly positive, which is guaranteed by,[6]

Condition R

$$v < v_{\max} \equiv 1 - \frac{\phi}{1-\alpha}\left(Ab^{\alpha}\right)^{-1/1-\alpha}.$$

This condition will hold if the pecuniary education cost, ϕ, is not too large or if the degree of efficacy of loan services, b, is not too low.

Define $G(v) = uiv\{1/[(1-v) - v/\zeta(v)]\}$, which is positive under,

Condition N

$$\zeta(v) > \frac{v}{1-v}.$$

This condition is necessary to ensure nondegenerate solution for intergenerational human capital investment decision. Utilizing the labor supply and the labor demand schedules, (10.8) and (10.10), respectively, together with (10.17), we can derive the following labor market equilibrium relationship (referred to as the LE locus):

$$G(v) = \frac{1}{\phi}\left[A(1-\alpha)b^{\alpha}\right]^{1/1-\alpha}\left(\frac{\alpha}{1-\alpha}\frac{1}{1+b}\frac{1}{1+\delta}\right)^{\alpha/1-\alpha}(1+r) \quad (10.20)$$

which is downward sloping in (δ, v) space. It is important to note in our OG economy, that the intergenerational human capital accumulation activity is the sole determinant of economic growth. One may regard the left-hand side of equation (10.20) as the (transformed) net marginal cost of education, whereas the right-hand side is the (transformed) marginal benefit from incremental productivity across generations. Intuitively, given the downward-sloping factor price frontier (10.18), an increase in the loan rate discourages borrowing and physical capital accumulation and lowers the real wage rate. As G is monotonically increasing in v, this in turn reduces the incentive to save in kind.

Equations (10.14), (10.19) and (10.20) jointly determine the BGP equilibrium human capital investment as well as the loan and the deposit rates. These values can then be substituted into (10.17) to pin down the equilibrium loan–human capital ratio, which, together with (10.1), (10.2), (10.9), (10.10) and (10.13), in turn determine the deposit–human capital ratio, the consumption–human capital ratio, the physical–human capital ratio, the wage rate and the firm owner's consumption to human capital ratio, respectively, in balanced growth equilibrium. Therefore, we can conclude,

Proposition 1 (Existence) Under conditions T, N and R, there is a perfect foresight balanced growth equilibrium.

4 FINANCIAL POLICY ANALYSIS

There are three cases to be discussed: (i) reserve requirement policy, (ii) loan rate control (suppressed at the below market equilibrium level as found in the situation of financial repression), and (iii) deposit rate ceiling (that is, Regulation Q). Except for the first case, the loan market need not be in equilibrium as a result of price inflexibility.

4.1 Reserve Requirement Policy

In the absence of interest rate controls, the loan market clears and the loan–deposit interest rate differential is pinned down by (10.14), yielding the financial markup ratio:

$$\frac{\delta - \mu}{r} = \frac{1}{1 - \eta}, \tag{10.21}$$

which is increasing in the reserve requirement ratio. This can then be substituted into (10.19) to obtain:

$$\frac{1}{1-\nu}=\frac{1}{\phi}[A(1-\alpha)b^{\alpha}]^{1/1-\alpha}$$
$$\cdot\left[\left(\frac{\alpha}{1-\alpha}\frac{1}{1+b}\frac{1}{1+\delta}\right)^{\alpha/1-\alpha}-\left(\frac{\alpha}{1-\alpha}\frac{1}{1+b}\frac{1}{1+\delta}\right)^{1/1-\alpha}\frac{1}{1-\eta}\right], \quad (10.22)$$

which may be referred to as banks' zero profit relationship given external financing efficiency and loan-market equilibrium (or, in short, the BZ locus). Notably, should there be any interest-control policy, equation (10.22) need not hold up because in such cases the loan market is no longer in equilibrium. Consider the case where the labor income share (or the output elasticity of the effective labor input), $1-\alpha$, is not too large, though it is plausible to restrict the labor income share to exceed the capital labor share,

Condition LS $\alpha<1-\alpha<1/(1+b)\cdot 1/(1+\delta)$.

It can be easily shown that under the second inequality of condition LS, the right–hand side of (10.22) is strictly increasing for all $\delta>\mu$. In this case, the BZ locus is upward sloping in (δ,ν) space.

Combining (10.20) and (10.22), we can solve the unconstrained equilibrium loan rate and intergenerational human capital investment jointly. For ease of illustration, Figure 10.1 depicts the LE and BZ loci, where point E indicates the unconstrained equilibrium. Define $M\equiv\alpha/(1-\alpha)\cdot 1/(1+b)\cdot 1/(1+\mu)$ in order to guarantee the existence of an interior equilibrium, consider:

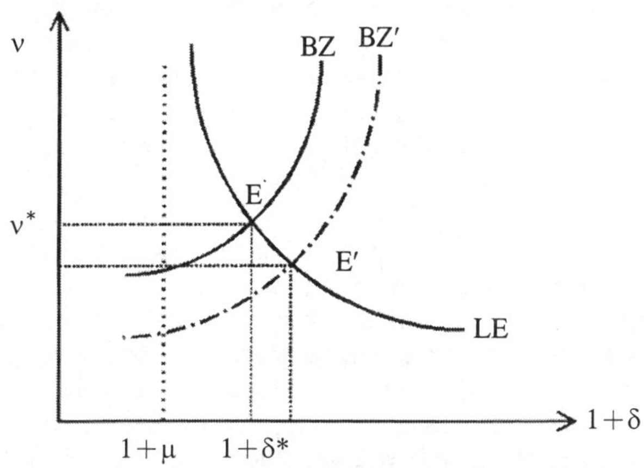

Figure 10.1 Equilibrium and effects of reserve requirement policy

Condition E

$$\zeta > \zeta_{\min} \equiv \frac{[A(1-\alpha)(bM)^{\alpha}]^{\frac{1}{1-\alpha}}\left(1-\frac{M}{1-\eta}\right)-\phi}{\frac{1}{\phi}[A(1-\alpha)(bM)^{\alpha}]^{\frac{2}{1-\alpha}}\left(1-\frac{M}{1-\eta}\right)-\phi}.$$

Under condition E, the value of v corresponding to $\delta = \mu$ for the LE locus is larger than that for the BZ locus and thus guarantees an interior intersection of the loci as in Figure 10.1. Substituting the equilibrium (δ^*, v^*) into (10.17) and (10.19), we can solve the equilibrium loan–human capital ratio and the equilibrium deposit rate.

Consider now a tightened reserve requirement policy that increases in the required reserve ratio, η. While the LE locus remains unaffected, the BZ locus shifts downward because for given human capital investment, the tightened loanable funds market requires the loan rate to rise in order to maintain banks' zero profit condition (see the BZ′ locus and point E′ in Figure 10.1). As a consequence, the equilibrium loan rate is higher whereas the rates of human capital investment and economic growth are lower. Recall from (10.19) that the reduction in human capital accumulation suppresses the deposit rate but the increase in the loan rate raises it. Thus, the net effect on the deposit rate is ambiguous. Intuitively, in response to a tightened reserve requirement policy, fewer resources will be devoted to intergenerational human capital accumulation, thus lowering the rate of economic growth. Although this detrimental growth effect corroborates the findings in Haslag and Young (1998), their findings are obtained for a very different reason: a tightened reserve requirement policy lowers the rate of returns on deposit, thus reducing saving, capital accumulation and economic growth. We can also examine the comparative statics of (i) an decrease in the degree of external financing efficacy (a smaller b) and (ii) an increase in the unit pecuniary education cost (a larger ϕ). The results are reported in Table 10.1. Both shift the LE and BZ loci downward (not shown in figure 10.1), leading to a smaller human capital investment and an ambiguous effect on the loan rate. When a firm relies more on external financing as a result of lower efficacy of loan services, incremental productivity across generations becomes lower as physical capital accumulation becomes more restricted under the generalized fractional loan-in-advance setup. Hence, less time is devoted to human capital accumulation, which leads to a lower rate of economic growth. A decrease in the efficacy of external finance raises the demand for loans and reduces the marginal cost for education investment, making the effect of the loan rate ambiguous and, under banks' zero profit condition, the effect on the deposit rate ambiguous as well. Moreover, it also has an ambiguous effect on the loan–human capital ratio due to a negative direct effect together with a positive indirect effect via the reduction in the

Table 10.1 Comparative statics under various policy regimes

	Human capital investment ν	Deposit rate r	Loan rate δ	Loan-human capital ratio x/h	Growth rate g
I. Reserve Requirement Policy					
Tightened reserve requirement $\eta \uparrow$	$(-)$[a]	?	+	$(-)$[b]	$(-)$[a]
Decrease in external financing efficacy $b \downarrow$	–	?	?	$(-)$[b]	–
Increase in pecuniary education cost $\phi \uparrow$	–	?	?	?	–
II. Loan Rate Control					
Tightened loan rate control $\bar{\delta} \downarrow$	+	–	–	–	+
Decrease in external financing efficacy $b \downarrow$	–	–	0	$(-)$[b]	–
Increase in pecuniary education cost $\phi \uparrow$	–	+	0	+	–
III. Deposit Rate Ceiling					
Tightened deposit rate ceiling $\bar{r} \downarrow$	$(+)$[a]	–	$(-)$[c]	$(-)$[c]	$(+)$[c]
Decrease in external financing efficacy $b \downarrow$	$(-)$[a]	0	$(-)$[c]	$(-)$[b, c]	$(-)$[c]
Increase in pecuniary education cost $\phi \uparrow$	$(-)$[c]	0	$(+)$[c]	$(+)$[c]	$(-)$[c]

Notes:

a. Under Condition LS.

b. If the direct effect dominates.

c. Under Condition 5.

home education activity. The effect of an increase in the unit pecuniary education cost has a similar effect to a decrease in the degree of external financing efficacy, as a higher education cost reduces the incentive to save in kind. In summary, we have,

Proposition 2 (Characterization of Reserve Requirement Policy) Under conditions T, N, R, LS and E, there is a perfect foresight balanced growth equilibrium possessing the following properties:

1. a tightened reserve requirement, a decrease in external financing efficacy, or a higher unit pecuniary education cost reduces the human capital investment and economic growth;
2. while a tightened reserve requirement increases the loan rate, a decrease in external financing efficacy or a higher unit pecuniary education cost has an ambiguous effect on the loan and deposit rates.

4.2 Loan Rate Control

An effective control of the loan rate would suppress it below the equilibrium level, as indicated by (10.15). To illustrate the effects, consider that the central bank control a loan rate at a level $\bar{\delta}$ lower than the equilibrium rate δ^* (see Figure 10.2). It is clear that in such a financially repressed economy, there are fewer funds available for investment purchases. Thus, the unconstrained BZ locus is now replaced by the vertical loan rate control (LC) locus, which together with the LE locus pin down the constrained equilibrium E′ and the value of human capital investment $\bar{v}$.

In response to a lower loan rate, the marginal product of labor as well as the real wage rate increase, thus encouraging savings in kind. As the intergenerational human capital accumulation rate is higher, the rate of economic growth also rises. Moreover, to maintain banks' zero profit condition, the rate of deposit is also lower. Our results contrast with Roubini and Sala-i-Martin's (1995) in which a negative relationship between the financially repressing loan rate control policy and economic growth is obtained due to tax evasion.

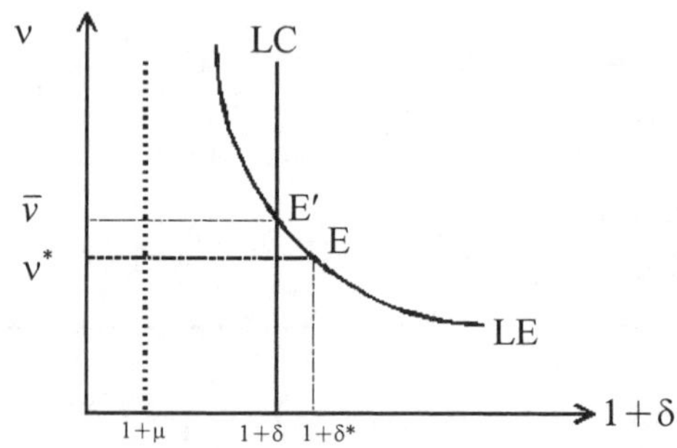

Figure 10.2 Constrained equilibrium under loan rate control

In response to lower efficacy of loan services, the firm relies more on external financing and its physical capital accumulation becomes more restrictive. Therefore, incremental productivity across generations is lower, as are the rates of human capital accumulation and economic growth. As a result of the reduced rate of returns on loans, a bank must lower the deposit rate to maintain the zero profit condition. Similar to the case of reserve requirement policy, the response of the loan–human capital ratio to a reduction in external financing efficacy is ambiguous due to the negative direct effect offsetting the positive indirect effect via the reduction in the home education activity.

When the unit pecuniary education cost is higher, the incentive to save in kind reduces. As a result, human capital accumulation and economic growth rates are both lower. Since the loan rate is fixed, there exist only a positive direct effect and a negative indirect effect via human capital investment on the deposit rate. It is not difficult to show that as long as the bank is operative, the direct effect always dominates and hence the deposit rate rises unambiguously. In summary, we have,

Proposition 3 (Characterization of Loan Rate Control Policy) Under conditions T, N and R, there is a perfect foresight constrained balanced growth equilibrium with the loan rate below the market equilibrium level, possessing the following properties:

1. a tightened loan rate control tends to increase human capital investment and economic growth and lowers the deposit rate and human capital investment and economic growth;
2. both a decrease in external financing efficacy and an increase in the unit pecuniary education cost tend to reduce human capital investment and economic growth;
3. while a decrease in external financing efficacy lowers the deposit rate, an increase in the unit pecuniary education cost raises it.

4.3 Deposit Rate Ceiling

Regulation Q, which sets a deposit rate ceiling at $\bar{r}$, is effective if the ceiling is below the market equilibrium level, as described by (10.16). In this case, it is more convenient to characterize the steady-state results in (v, r) space, in which the deposit rate control is captured by a vertical line, the DC locus. More specifically, we can modify condition R to ensure the monotonic property between the loan and the deposit rates,

Condition R′ $\quad v < v'_{max} = 1 - \frac{\phi}{(1-\alpha)^2}\left(Ab^{\alpha}\right)^{-1/1-\alpha}.$

We can now express (10.19) as an implicit function $\delta = D(r, v; \phi, b)$ with $D_r > 0$, $D_v < 0$, $D_\phi < 0$ and $D_b > 0$. This implicit function can then be substituted into (10.20) to obtain:

$$G(v) = \frac{1}{\phi}\left[(1-\alpha)Ab^{\alpha}\right]^{1/1-\alpha}\left(\frac{\alpha}{1-\alpha}\frac{1}{1+b}\frac{1}{1+D(r,v;\ \phi,b)}\right)^{\alpha/1-\alpha}. \quad (10.23)$$

It is obvious that the right-hand side of (10.23) is monotonically decreasing in r. However, since both the left-hand and the right-hand sides of (10.23) are increasing in v, it is useful for us to consider a benchmark case assuming a dominant direct effect via the marginal cost of education (that is, the left-hand side net of the right-hand side is strictly increasing in v),

Condition V $\frac{G_v(v)}{G(v)} > \frac{\alpha}{1-\alpha}\frac{-D_v(v)}{1+D(v)}$.

Under condition V, (10.23), referred to as the LD locus, specifies a negative relationship between the deposit rate and education investment given labor market equilibrium. The DC and LD loci together determine the constrained equilibrium in $(r,\ v)$ space (see point E′ in Figure 10.3). Under an effective Regulation Q policy, the deposit rate control is pinned at a level $\bar{r}$ lower than the equilibrium rate r^*. Figure 10.3 shows that the associated intergenerational human capital accumulation rate is higher, as is the rate of economic growth. Intuitively, when the deposit rate is fixed at its ceiling, it is no longer a driving force of households' savings in kind. Rather, this lower deposit rate (compared to the unconstrained equilibrium) via banks' zero profit condition implies a lower loan rate, which in turn encourages firms' physical capital accumulation. As a consequence, there is a substitution from labor to capital and households find it more profitable to accumulate intergenerational human capital, thereby leading to a higher rate of economic growth.

When firms rely more on external financing as a result of lower efficacy of loan services, incremental productivity across generations decreases because physical capital accumulation is now more restricted. Thus, the economy is associated with less human capital investment and thus slower economic growth. Next, utilizing (10.19), as firms rely more on external financing while the deposit rate is fixed at its ceiling, banks can suppress the loan rate while maintaining zero profit. As in the case of reserve requirement policy, the negative direct effect and the positive indirect effect via the reduction in the home education activity lead to an ambiguous result on the loan–human capital ratio.

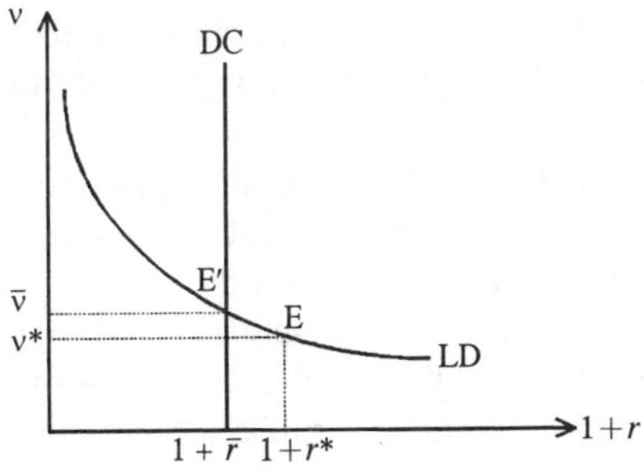

Figure 10.3 Constrained equilibrium under deposit rate ceiling

Finally, it is noted that as in previous cases, an increase in pecuniary education cost always discourages human capital accumulation and hence reduces economic growth. However, since the deposit rate is fixed at the ceiling, the loan rate responds to an increased education cost only through the negative direct and positive human capital investment channels. It turns out that as long as banks are operative (that is, condition R is satisfied), the human capital investment effect is the dominant force. Thus, the loan rate rises in response to an increase in the unit pecuniary education cost.

The above discussion can be compactly summarized as follows:

Proposition 4 (Characterization of Deposit Rate Ceiling Policy) Under conditions T, N, R, and V, there is a perfect foresight constrained balanced growth equilibrium with the deposit rate below the market equilibrium level, possessing the following properties:

1. a tightened deposit rate ceiling tends to raise human capital investment and economic growth, whereas a decreased external financing efficacy or an increased unit pecuniary education cost tends to reduce them;
2. while a tightened deposit rate ceiling or a decreased external financing efficacy suppresses the deposit rate, an increased unit pecuniary education cost raises it.

5 SUMMARY AND EXTENSIONS

We have evaluated the long-run macroeconomic consequences of three financial policies, a tightened reserve requirement, a tightened loan rate control and a tightened deposit rate ceiling. We have characterized both the uniquely determined unconstrained (in the case with reserve requirement policy) and constrained (in the case with loan or deposit rate controls) balanced growth equilibria in response to changes in financial policy on reserve requirements and interest rates. In a prototypical economy with diminishing marginal benefit of education, a tightened reserve requirement policy is growth retarding, accompanied by a higher rate of interest on loans.

When the loan rate is controlled below the market equilibrium level as found in the case of financial repression, the constrained economic growth rate exceeds the unconstrained one. Thus, when the underlying driving force of economic growth is primarily human capital based, it is possible that a financially repressed economy will grow more rapidly than a market economy, as experienced by the Asian Tigers. For similar arguments, in an economy where human capital accumulation is the main driving force of economic growth, a Regulation Q policy that sets a deposit rate ceiling may reallocate available resources to savings in kind. Thus, such a policy is likely to be growth enhancing, particularly in an economy where there are excessive savings in funds, as in the case of Taiwan in the 1980s. It is, however, important to recognize that the growth-enhancing effects of these interest rate control policies are obtained in those economies where human capital accumulation is the engine of endogenous growth and firms' physical capital investments require external financing. Moreover, it is clear that if human capital and physical capital are completely complementary in the Leontief sense, a financial repression policy would not generate any positive growth effect. This implies that the potential gains from a loan rate control may diminish if productive capitals are more complementary in the process of production. Therefore, one should not draw general conclusions prematurely about the effectiveness of government intervention in the financial market.

There are several ways to extend our analysis. For brevity, we shall discuss only four. First, one may consider savings in goods and perpetual physical capital accumulation over time. This would enrich the characterization of economic growth as long-run development is no longer a monotonically increasing function of human capital investment alone. Of course, one must realize that in our chapter, there are three optimizing agents (instead of one as in the standard representative-agent framework). Thus, the analysis cannot be carried out successfully without further simplification of the model structure. Second, one may follow the Romer (1986)–Lucas (1988) convention of allowing for uncompensated positive spillovers in productive capitals. In this case, the free-rider problem is present, thereby resulting in social inefficiency. One may then ask whether a financial policy that better facilitates external financing may play a positive a role in rectifying this social inefficiency. Third, if required reserves can be used, via seigniorage revenues, to support a public good, the distortionary effect of such a policy may be partly offset. One may then compare the findings with those obtained by Espinosa and Yip (1999) in which the interactions between fiscal and monetary policies are explicitly models via reserve requirements. Finally, our framework may be used to re-examine the macroeconomic effects of financial policy in the presence of credit market imperfections. For example, one may incorporate the moral hazard problem discussed in Chen, et al. (2000) in which incentive compatibility requires competitive banks to set the loan and deposit rates above the market equilibrium level. This result would certainly change if there is a loan rate control or deposit rate ceiling in practice.

ACKNOWLEDGMENTS

We have benefited from invaluable comments and suggestions made by Joe Haslag and Rody Manuelli. This research was initiated while the third author was a visiting research fellow at the Institute of Economics, Academia Sinica, which provided financial support to facilitate this international collaboration. Needless to say, the usual disclaimer applies.

NOTES

1. There is a small but growing literature on the emergence of financial intermediation within the endogenous growth framework, focusing on the role of the financial sector rather than policy issues. See a survey by Becsi and Wang (1997).
2. Implicitly, one may imagine that each household lives three periods with a passive childhood period, a working middle age and a retirement period. Since there is no economic decision to be made during childhood, it can be omitted without loss of generality.
3. For example, Vinala and Berges (1988) illustrate that financial services have the potential to affect real investment decisions by making available to firms cheaper or flexible external financing sources and by allowing firms to make better investment decisions through monitoring.
4. This is the simplest way to avoid the Arrow–Debreu redistribution of firm profits to consumers while maintaining the general equilibrium nature.
5. Substituting (10.2) and (10.3) into the dynastic utility function yields the following objective:

$$u_t^0 + \ln[w_t(1-v_t) - \phi] + (1+\rho)^{-1}\ln[1+g(v_t)],$$

   where:

$$u_t^0 \equiv \ln(1+r_t)h_t + (1+\rho)^{-1}\ln(1+r_{t+1})h_t[w_{t+1}(1-v_{t+1}) - \phi].$$

6. When $\delta > \mu$, (10.19) implies: $r > 0$ if:

$$(1-\alpha)(1+b)(1+\delta)/\alpha > [(1+b)(1+\delta)/(\alpha A b^{\alpha})]^{1/(1-\alpha)}\,\phi/(1-v).$$

   Since:

$$[(1+b)(1+\delta)/\alpha]^{1/(1-\alpha)} > (1+b)(1+\delta)/\alpha > 1,$$

   condition R is sufficient to guarantee that the above inequality will hold.

REFERENCES

Becsi, Zsolt and Ping Wang (1997), 'Financial Development and Growth', *Federal Reserve Bank of Atlanta, Economic Review*, **82**(4), 46–62.

Chen, Been-Lon, Yeong-Yuh Chiang and Ping Wang (2000), 'Financial Intermediation, Credit Rationing and Economic Growth', Working Paper, Department of Economics, Vanderbilt University, Nashville, TN.

Diamond, Peter and Joel Yellin (1990), 'Inventories and Money Holdings in a Search Economy', *Econometrica*, **58** (4), 929–50.

Espinosa, Marco and Chong K. Yip (1999), 'Fiscal and Monetary Policy Interactions in an Endogenous Growth Model with Financial Intermediaries', *International Economic Review*, **40** (3), 595–615.

Freeman, Scott (1987), 'Reserve Requirements and Optimal Seigniorage', *Journal of Monetary Economics*, **19**, 307–14.

Glomm, Gerhard and B. Riavikumar (1992), 'Public versus Private Investment in Human Capital: Endogenous Growth and Income Inequality', *Journal of Political Economy*, **100** (4), 818–34.

Haslag, Joseph and Eric Young (1998), 'Money Creation, Reserve Requirement and Seigniorage', *Review of Economic Dynamics*, **1**, 677–98.

Lucas, Robert E., Jr. (1988), 'On the Mechanism of Economic Development', *Journal of Monetary Economics*, **22** (1), 3–42.

Romer, Paul M. (1986), 'Increasing Returns and Long Run Growth', *Journal of Political Economy*, **64** (5), 1002–37.

Roubini, Nouriel and Xavier Sala-i-Martin (1995), 'A Growth Model of Inflation, Tax Evasion and Financial Repression', *Journal of Monetary Economics*, **35**, 275–301.

Stokey, Nancy L. (1991), 'Human Capital, Product Quality and Growth', *Quarterly Journal of Economics*, **106** (2), 587–616.

Vinala, Jose and Angel Berges (1988), 'Financial Innovation and Capital Formation', in Arnold Heertje (ed.), *Innovation, Technology and Finance*, New York, NY: Basil Blackwell, 158–202.

11. Credit Rationing, Public Borrowing and Endogenous Growth

Wai-Hong Ho

1 INTRODUCTION

This chapter investigates the role of public borrowing in a financial market with credit rationing problem. Two kinds of borrowing activities coexist in the economy, one from the public sector and the other from the private. Public borrowing is funded with no obligations to pay any interest. Under such circumstances, we found that the credit rationing problem is escalating with the amount of public borrowing. In addition, the presence of public borrowing can generate two opposing effects on economic growth. Surprisingly, we find that the growth rate of an economy with public borrowing activities can be higher than one without, even if these activities assume no productive purpose. A numerical example is given to illustrate the result.

How a financial market allocates funds to their best use has recently attracted much attention from macroeconomists. This interest is aroused by the concern that the problem of asymmetric information (and credit rationing thus generated) can hinder the optional flow of financial resources to borrowers/producers. Rothchild and Stiglitz (1976) published one of the pioneering papers which contributes to our better understanding of this problem. Stimulated by their work, a host of literature focusing on the pros and cons of credit rationing *vis-à-vis* growth emerged in the 1990s. Bencivenga and Smith (1993) presume a negative impact of credit rationing on economic growth. In Bose and Cothren (1996), screening, rationing and a combination of these two characterize alternative forms of contracts to be chosen by the lender. But the equilibrium contracts do not support maximum economic growth in general. Shi (1996) reaches a conclusion that is in stark contrast to that of previous papers. He suggests that credit rationing may stimulate agents to undertake high-quality and high-risk projects whose success may create positive spillovers of new knowledge and hence the possibility of high economic growth.

This chapter differs from the other papers by introducing public borrowing activities into an endogenous growth model with financial market frictions.

This kind of borrowing is guaranteed sufficient funding and no interest payments are required. To be specific, we call the kind of borrowing activities proposed by a private borrower a 'private borrowing' and that proposed by the government a 'public borrowing'. Incorporating these structural differences into an endogenous growth model, I shall examine the macro- and the microeconomic implications of credit rationing.

To design discriminatory policies in favor of public sector activities is a common government practice. Real-world examples abound. For instance, lenders may find it more secure to lend to state-owned enterprises rather than private enterprises since the latter have a smaller chance of repaying old debts in the event of bankruptcy, (see Perotti, 1993 for a related discussion). Further, a low interest rate can help mitigate state-owned enterprises', inclination to undertake high-risk projects under the influence of soft-budget constraints. This is because in the presence of high interest rates a small expected profit will motivate managers to switch to high-return and high-risk projects – if the projects fail, the government will cover the loss, if the projects succeed, the profits will go to the managers (see Zou and Sun, 1996). In our chapter, this practice is captured by the privileges enjoyed by the public sector in obtaining interest-free funds. In order to redeem the loss, lenders have to set higher interest rates which will 'crowd out' some of those low-risk private borrowers who should be able to borrow funds.

Stiglitz and Weiss (1981) develop a credit rationing model with two groups of people, safe and risky, borrowing money from lenders. The risky group is willing to pay a higher interest rate than the safe group for funds. Stiglitz and Weiss show that, even if the interest rate increases slightly in the market, the mix of loan applicants will change in such a drastic way that all low-risk borrowers may withdraw from the market. In our chapter, the increase in interest rate is provoked by the presence of public borrowing. Further, the separating equilibrium contracts will show that low-risk borrowers have a lower equilibrium probability of getting funds than in the case without public borrowing. High-risk private borrowers can avoid this adverse effect since their probability of getting funds is always unity.[1] Though most of the 'good' private projects in the sense of Stiglitz and Weiss do not materialize due to the high interest rate, long-run economic growth will still be possible if the effect exerted by the presence of public borrowing on lenders' behavior can overwhelm its side effect on labor supply. More to the point, the presence of public borrowing which tightens the financial market induces more lenders to keep their funds for internal use. The average firm will benefit from such behavior if lenders can convert their funds into capital stock efficiently. But this positive effect on capital stock accumulation will be eroded by the growing labor supply, which is composed of low-risk borrowers whose loan applications cannot be fulfilled.

How economic growth will be affected by the interplay of these two opposing forces is the main theme of this chapter.

We shall compare the growth rates of two economies in the following — one with public borrowing and one without. Interestingly, we find that the growth rate of the economy with public borrowing can be higher than the other one, even if they assume no productive purpose. Further, the aggregate capital stock accumulation of this economy will also be higher eventually even if it is smaller than the other one at the initial stage. Thus, a counterintuitive conclusion is obtained — the economy with *fewer* financial resources can experience higher economic growth.

The rest of this chapter will proceed as follows. In Section 2, the basic model will be developed. The separating equilibrium contracts will be presented in Section 3. In Section 4, we shall discuss the growth of the economy. Section 5 will give a numerical example to illustrate the main results. The last section will conclude and discuss some possible extensions.

2 THE MODEL

The overlapping generations framework developed in Bose and Cothren (1996) will be adopted as the vehicle to convey our theory. In the following, the model without public borrowing is the benchmark case. All variables and parameters in this benchmark will be denoted with a 'hat'('^').

The economy consists of an infinite sequence of *two-period lived* overlapping generations in which each generation has an identical population size that is normalized to one.

Young agents in each period are divided into lenders and borrowers. Lenders who endow a limited amount of funds are the only financial source in the economy. Each of these borrowers is born with a potential project that needs funds to be implemented.

Each private project is of either a high-risk (H) or a low-risk (L) type. A high-risk project has a lower possibility of success. Otherwise, the two types of project are alike. I assume that a fraction λ of private borrowers has an H-type project. By utilizing one unit of labor, each investment project can convert consumption goods into capital goods.

The *i*-type, $i=H, L$ investment project can with probability P_i convert x units of time t outputs and one unit of labor into $Q \cdot x$ units of time $t+1$ capital. The project may fail with probability $1-P_i$. We further assume that $1 \geq P_l > P_h \geq 0.$ Young borrowers who choose to quit the projects provide one unit of labor to the market to earn a wage. Alternatively, they can make use of their labor to run the project. If a loan application is denied, H-type borrowers will consume nothing for the rest of their life and L-type borrowers can sustain their life by supplying labor in exchange for wages.[2] Their output can be stored for consumption in the next period and provide a return of $\beta_l \leq 1$ per unit of output. Borrowers will consume only in the second period.

If a private borrower's project is implemented successfully, he/she will become a firm owner in the next period. This owner is able to rent capital and hire labor at the rental rate, ρ_t, and the wage rate, w_t, determined competitively by the market. Each firm assumes the following production function: $y_t = \psi_t^{\alpha} k_t^{\theta} L_t^{1-\theta}$, where:

y_t = units of output at time t,
ψ_t = average capital stock per firm at time t,
k_t = units of capital at time t,
L_t = units of labor at time t.

For simplicity, we assume that $\alpha = 1-\theta$.

Each young lender is endowed with one unit of labor force which is supplied inelastically to the market to earn a wage. The lender can convert his/her time t and wage w_t into $Q \cdot \varepsilon \cdot w_t$ units of capital in time $t+1$ and can rent this amount to firms. Or, the lender can lend the wage to a borrower in exchange for capital in $t+1$.[3] ε is assumed to be sufficiently smaller than P_h to guarantee that loans between borrowers and lenders occur. Borrowers and lenders are both risk neutral. Lenders cannot observe the risk level of private investment projects. It is this problem of asymmetric information that leads to the existence of credit rationing.

Each young lender is required by the government to allocate an amount of funds q_u from his/her expected revenue to the public sector. q_u is a time-invariant parameter which can be observed by all parties in the economy.[4] Thereafter, the lender will announce a set of contracts. If these contracts are not dominated by the others, one borrower will approach the lender and select a contract. By following Bose and Cothren (1996), we assume that each lender will be approached by one private borrower only and the competition in the credit market will drive the lender's economic profit to the reservation level, which is normalized to zero.

The type-H private borrowers have an objective function of the form: $P_h \Pi_{ht}(Q\rho_{t+1} - R_{ht})q_{ht}$, where Π_{ht} is the probability of getting funds from lenders. If the borrower obtains q_{ht} amount of funds, he/she will produce Qq_{ht} units of capital at time $t+1$ with probability P_h. $Qq_{ht}\rho_{t+1}$ is the rent he/she can earn and R_{ht} is the interest rate. But if he/she cannot borrow anything, he/she will consume nothing in the next period.

A type-L private borrower's objective function assumes the following functional form: $P_l \Pi_{lt}(Q\rho_{t+1} - R_{lt})q_{lt} + (1-\Pi_{lt})\beta_l w_t$. Recall that, if the type-L private borrower cannot borrow anything, he/she will provide his/her labor effort to earn a wage. We assume the condition $P_i(Q\rho_t - R_t) > \beta w_t > 0$ in what follows to ensure that private borrowers' expected payoff is increasing with Π_{it}.

3 THE SEPARATING EQUILIBRIUM CONTRACT

The loan contract at time t is in the form $(R_{it}, q_{it}, \Pi_{it})$ where $i = H, L$, R_{it} is the gross real rate of interest and q_{it} is the amount of loan offered to the borrower. Since the maximum amount of funds at period t is w_t, we have $w_t \geq q_{it}$. Π_{it} is the probability that the private borrower can obtain funds from the lender.

In equilibrium, a lender will offer the approaching borrower a menu of contracts $\{C_L, C_H\}$ from which this borrower will choose the contract that matches with his/her interest (type-L borrower accepts C_L and type-H borrower accepts C_H). In other words, these contracts will be incentive compatible.

For high-risk private borrowers, the optimal loan contract can be derived from solving the following program (HR):

$$\max_{\{q_{ht}, R_{ht}, \Pi_{ht}\}} P_h \Pi_{ht}(Q\rho_{t+1} - R_{ht})q_{ht}$$

$$\text{s.t.} \begin{cases} \Pi_{ht}(P_h R_{ht} q_{ht} - Q\varepsilon\rho_{t+1} q_{ht}) - Q\varepsilon\rho_{t+1} q_u = 0 \\ w_t \geq q_{ht} \quad \text{and} \quad 1 \geq \Pi_{ht} \geq 0. \end{cases}$$

The lender will maximize the type-H private borrower's objective function subject to three constraints: (i) the lender's zero economic profit condition, (ii) specifies the maximum amount of available funds, and (iii) stipulates the feasible range for the probability Π_{ht}. Since the second inequality constraints must be binding, the maximum loan amount for a high-risk private borrower q_{ht} is w_t. The gross rate of interest is $R_{ht} = 1/P_h[Q\varepsilon\rho_{t+1}(1 + q_u/q_{ht})]$ and the probability of getting funds is $\Pi_{ht} = \Pi_h = 1$. Since $q_u > 0$, a high-risk private borrower needs to pay a higher interest rate to obtain funds than in the benchmark case.[5] Note that R_{ht} is an increasing function of q_u.

The optimal contract for low-risk private borrowers is the solution of the following program (LR):

$$\max_{\{q_{lt}, R_{lt}, P_{lt}\}} P_l \Pi_{lt} (Q\rho_{t+1} - R_{lt}) q_{lt} + (1 - \Pi_{lt}) \beta_l w_t$$

$$\text{s.t.} \begin{cases} \Pi_{lt}(P_l R_{lt} - Q\varepsilon\rho_{t+1}) q_{lt} - Q\varepsilon\rho_{t+1} q_u = 0 \\ P_h (Q\rho_{t+1} - R_{ht}) q_{ht} \geq \Pi_{lt} P_h (Q\rho_{t+1} - R_{lt}) q_{lt} \\ w_t \geq q_{lt}, 1 \geq \Pi_{lt} \geq 0, \end{cases}$$

$$\text{with } q_{ht} = w_t \quad \text{and} \quad R_{ht} = \frac{1}{P_h}\left[Q\varepsilon\rho_{t+1}\left(1 + \frac{q_u}{q_{ht}}\right)\right].$$

Besides the zero economic profit condition and the feasibility conditions, an incentive compatibility constraint is required to induce a type-H private borrower to tell the truth regarding his/her investment risk. This is the second constraint in program LR.

From the first constraint, we find that $R_{lt} = 1/P[Q\varepsilon\rho_{t+1}(1 + q_u / \Pi_{lt} q_{lt})]$. The second and the third constraints must be binding since q_{lt} appears only on their right-hand side. Therefore, we have:

$$q_{lt} = \frac{(Q\rho_{t+1} - R_{ht}) q_{ht}}{(Q\rho_{t+1} - R_{lt}) \Pi_{lt}} \Leftrightarrow \Pi_{lt} = \frac{(Q\rho_{t+1} - R_{ht})}{(Q\rho_{t+1} - R_{lt})}.$$

Similar to high-risk borrowers, low-risk borrowers also need to pay an interest rate which is positively correlated to q_u. Note that R_{ht} and R_{lt} are linked because of the binding incentive compatibility constraint.

In order to derive the value of Π_{lt} as a function of parameters of this model, we substitute the values for R_{ht} and R_{lt} into $\Pi_{lt} = (Q\rho_{t+1} - R_{ht})/(Q\rho_{t+1} - R_{lt})$. We find :

$$\Pi_{lt} = \frac{1 - \frac{\varepsilon}{P_h} - \frac{\varepsilon q_u}{w_t}\left(\frac{1}{P_h} - \frac{1}{P_l}\right)}{\left(1 - \frac{\varepsilon}{P_l}\right)}.$$

Note that if $q_u = 0$, $\Pi_{lt} = (1 - \varepsilon/P_h)/(1 - \varepsilon/P_l)$, which is the low-risk private borrowers' probability of getting funds in Bose and Cothren (1996).

The following lemmas will discuss some properties of this probability.

Lemma 1 The probability of getting funds for low-risk private borrowers, Π_{lt}, is smaller than 1.

Proof Since $P_l > P_h$, we have:

$$\frac{\varepsilon}{P_h} > \frac{\varepsilon}{P_l} \rightarrow 1 - \frac{\varepsilon}{P_l} > 1 - \frac{\varepsilon}{P_h}.$$

Given $q_u > 0$,

$$1 - \frac{\varepsilon}{P_l} > 1 - \frac{\varepsilon}{P_h} - \frac{\varepsilon q_u}{w_t}\left(\frac{1}{P_h} - \frac{1}{P_l}\right).$$

Lemma 2 Low-risk private borrowers have a smaller probability of getting funds than in the case when $q_u = 0$.

Proof We need to compare the probabilities of getting funds in two different cases — the one with public borrowing $(q_u > 0)$ and the one without $(q_u = 0)$:

$$\frac{1 - \frac{\varepsilon}{P_h} - \frac{\varepsilon q_u}{w_t}\left(\frac{1}{P_h} - \frac{1}{P_l}\right)}{1 - \frac{\varepsilon}{P_l}} - \frac{1 - \frac{\varepsilon}{P_h}}{1 - \frac{\varepsilon}{P_l}} = - \frac{\frac{\varepsilon q_u}{w_t}\left(\frac{1}{P_l} - \frac{1}{P_h}\right)}{1 - \frac{\varepsilon}{P_l}} < 0$$

since $P_l > P_h > \varepsilon > 0$.

In order to simplify the subsequent discussion on economic growth, we make the following assumption on q_u:

Assumption 1 $q_u / w_t = \bar{q}$ is a constant.

That is, the government asks for the same ratio of financial support from lenders at each period of time. Based on this assumption, $\Pi_{lt} = \bar{\Pi}$ becomes time independent. Lemma 3 gives another property of $\bar{\Pi}$ based on Assumption 1.

Lemma 3 The probability of getting funds for low-risk private borrowers is strictly decreasing with $\bar{q}$.

Proof

$$\frac{\partial \bar{\Pi}}{\partial \bar{q}} = \frac{-\varepsilon\left(\frac{1}{P_h} - \frac{1}{P_l}\right)}{1 - \frac{\varepsilon}{P_l}} < 0$$

since $P_l > P_h > \varepsilon > 0$.

Therefore the problem of credit rationing will escalate if the amount of public borrowing increases. This is called the 'crowding-out' effect in the model. The economic intuition of this effect is the following. The higher q_u (or $\bar{q}$) and hence the smaller amount of funds available in the financial market, the higher is the expected opportunity cost of lending and the contractual rate of interest. It is this relation between q_u and the probability of getting funds for low-risk borrowers that forms the core part of our analysis. However, this effect does not apply to high-risk borrowers due to their probability of being funded is equal to 1.

The following proposition summarizes the optimal contracts to be offered by the lenders:

Proposition 1 The lender will offer the following contracts C_H and C_L in the economy:

$$C_L \begin{cases} R_{lt} = \dfrac{1}{P_l}\left[Q\varepsilon\rho_{t+1}\left(1 + \dfrac{q_u}{\Pi_{lt} q_{lt}}\right)\right] \\ q_{lt} = w_t \\ \bar{\Pi} = \dfrac{1 - \dfrac{\varepsilon}{P_h} - \varepsilon\bar{q}\left(\dfrac{1}{P_h} - \dfrac{1}{P_l}\right)}{1 - \dfrac{\varepsilon}{P_l}} \end{cases}$$

$$C_H \begin{cases} R_{ht} = \dfrac{1}{P_h}\left[Q\varepsilon\rho_{t+1}\left(1 + \dfrac{q_u}{q_{ht}}\right)\right] \\ q_{ht} = w_t \\ \Pi_h = 1. \end{cases}$$

This proposition shows that the optimal contracts depend on the rate of return of capital, ρ_{t+1}. In the following section, I shall show that the optimal growth rate depends on two effects exerted by the presence of public borrowing activities.

4 THE GROWTH RATE

In this section, we shall discuss the growth rate of the economy. To do so, we first need to compute the quantity of labor employed by each firm. Those private borrowers (low and high risk) who can successfully borrow funds will become firms in the second period of their lives. Therefore, we have $1/2[\lambda P_h + (1-\lambda)P_l\bar{\Pi}]$ firms operating at period t. $1/2(1-\lambda)(1-\bar{\Pi})$ of low-risk private firms are credit rationed. So, the total labor supply in the economy is $1/2+1/2(1-\lambda)(1-\bar{\Pi})$. In other words, the quantity of labor employed by each firm is:

$$L_t = \frac{\frac{1}{2}+\frac{1}{2}(1-\lambda)(1-\bar{\Pi})}{\frac{1}{2}[\lambda P_h + (1-\lambda)P_l\bar{\Pi}]} = \frac{1+(1-\lambda)(1-\bar{\Pi})}{\lambda P_h + (1-\lambda)P_l\bar{\Pi}} = \bar{L}.$$

From the production function as defined in Section 2, we can derive the marginal product of labor and the marginal product of capital as follows:

$$w_t = \frac{\partial y_t}{\partial L_t} = (1-\theta)\psi_t^{\alpha} k_t^{\theta} L_t^{-\theta} = (1-\theta)k_t\bar{L}^{-\theta}$$

and

$$\rho_t = \frac{\partial y_t}{\partial k_t} = \theta\psi_t^{\alpha} k_t^{\theta-1} L_t^{1-\theta} = \theta\bar{L}^{1-\theta}.$$

Since $\bar{L} = [1+(1-\lambda)(1-\bar{\Pi})]/[\lambda P_h + (1-\lambda)P_l\bar{\Pi}]$, we have

$$\rho_t = \theta \bar{L}^{1-\theta} = \theta \left[\frac{1+(1-\lambda)(1-\bar{\Pi})}{\lambda P_h + (1-\lambda)P_l\bar{\Pi}} \right]^{1-\theta}$$

and

$$w_t = (1-\theta)\left[\frac{1+(1-\lambda)(1-\bar{\Pi})}{\lambda P_h + (1-\lambda)P_l\bar{\Pi}} \right]^{-\theta} k_t.$$

The capital stock at $t+1$ comes from those funded borrowers who can run their projects successfully and from the lenders who converted their wages into capital stock after they credit rationed the low-risk private borrowers. Algebraically, their contributions are equal to $1/2[\lambda P_h + (1-\lambda)P_l\bar{\Pi}]Qw_t$ and $1/2(1-\lambda)(1-\bar{\Pi})Q\varepsilon w_t$ respectively.

Therefore, the aggregate capital stock accumulation at time $t+1$ is:

$$K_{t+1} = \frac{1}{2}\{[\lambda P_h + (1-\lambda)P_l\bar{\Pi}] + (1-\lambda)(1-\bar{\Pi})\varepsilon\}Qw_t.$$

The capital stock owned by each firm at time $t+1$ is equal to the following:

$$k_{t+1} = \frac{\frac{1}{2}\{[\lambda P_h + (1-\lambda)P_l\bar{\Pi}] + (1-\lambda)(1-\bar{\Pi})\varepsilon\}Qw_t}{\frac{1}{2}[\lambda P_h + (1-\lambda)P_l\bar{\Pi}]}$$

$$= \left[1 + \frac{(1-\lambda)(1-\bar{\Pi})\varepsilon}{\lambda P_h + (1-\lambda)P_l\bar{\Pi}} \right] Qw_t.$$

Define

$$1 + \frac{(1-\lambda)(1-\bar{\Pi})\varepsilon}{\lambda P_h + (1-\lambda)P_l\bar{\Pi}} = (1+\bar{\varepsilon}).$$

Then, $k_{t+1} = (1+\bar{\varepsilon})Qw_t$. Since $w_t = (1-\theta)k_t\bar{L}^{-\theta}$,

$$\bar{g} = \frac{k_{t+1}}{k_t} = Q(1-\theta)(1+\bar{\varepsilon})\bar{L}^{-\theta},$$

where $\bar{g}$ is the growth rate of the economy. In addition, it must be that $k_t = (\bar{g})^t k_0$ where k_0 is the initial capital stock. Therefore, the aggregate capital stock at time t is $K_t = 1/2[\lambda P_h + (1-\lambda)P_l\bar{\Pi}](\bar{g})^t k_0$. To facilitate the following comparison, we display the economic growth rate of the benchmark case (see Bose and Cothren 1996):

$$\hat{g} = Q(1-\theta)(1+\hat{\varepsilon})(\hat{L})^{-\theta}.$$

In order to understand how the presence of public borrowing affects the growth rate of the economy, we need the results of the following two lemmas.

Lemma 4 Given a $\bar{q} > 0$, $\bar{\varepsilon} > \hat{\varepsilon}$. That is $1+\bar{\varepsilon} > 1+\hat{\varepsilon}$.

Proof $\bar{\varepsilon} = [(1-\lambda)(1-\bar{\Pi})\varepsilon]/[\lambda P_h + (1-\lambda)P_l\bar{\Pi}]$ and $\bar{\varepsilon}$ is strictly decreasing with any $\bar{\Pi} \in [0,1]$. Since $\bar{\Pi} < \hat{\Pi}$ where $\hat{\Pi} = (1-\varepsilon/P_h)/(1-\varepsilon/P_l)$ from lemma 2, $\bar{\varepsilon} > \hat{\varepsilon}$ follows.

The result of lemma 4 has the following interpretation. Under the influence of the crowding-out effect, more lenders choose to ration private borrowers as compared to the case with no public borrowings and thus more lenders convert their own wages into capital stocks instead of lending out their funds.

Lemma 5 Given a $\bar{q} > 0$, $\bar{L} > \hat{L}$ and hence $\bar{L}^{-\theta} < (\hat{L})^{-\theta}$.

Proof $\bar{L} = [1+(1-\lambda)(1-\bar{\Pi})]/[\lambda P_h + (1-\lambda)P_l\bar{\Pi}]$ and $\bar{L}$ is strictly decreasing with any $\bar{\Pi} \in [0,1]$. Since $\bar{\Pi} < \hat{\Pi}$ from lemma 2, $\bar{L} > \hat{L} \rightarrow \bar{L}^{-1} < (\hat{L})^{-1} \rightarrow \bar{L}^{-\theta} < (\hat{L})^{-\theta}$ follows.

To explain $\bar{L} > \hat{L}$, recall that those low-risk borrowers who are credit rationed will supply their labor force to the market. Therefore, in the case with public borrowing, as the number of firms is smaller, the labor supply must be bigger, implying, the labor force per firm must also be bigger.

Combining the results of lemmas 4 and 5 gives rise to the following proposition.

Proposition 2 $\bar{g} > \hat{g}$ if the growth-enhancing effect being discussed in lemma 4 can dominate the growth-retarding effect being discussed in lemma 5. Otherwise, the reverse is true.

The crowding-out effect spawns two opposing effects on economic growth. The positive effect described by lemma 4 is about the capital stock in the average firm. It is possible for each firm to produce more capital stocks than in the benchmark since a smaller number of firms will share the aggregate capital stock and more lenders will convert their wages into capital. The growth-retarding effect described by lemma 5 is about the growing labor supply introduced by the crowding-out effect. Whether $\bar{g} > \hat{g}$ depends on which effect can dominate.

Now, we can see how the crowding-out effect may worsen the aggregate capital stock accumulation. We know that $K_t = \{1/2[\lambda P_h + (1-\lambda)P_l\bar{\Pi}]\}(\bar{g})^t k_0$. In the case with public borrowing, the number of firms producing capital stocks in the economy is smaller because a smaller number of borrowers can obtain funds. This is represented by a $\bar{\Pi}$ that is smaller than $\hat{\Pi}$. Therefore, even if the economy with public borrowing has a higher economic growth rate, the aggregate capital stock accumulation of this economy may not be higher than the benchmark case.

5 A NUMERICAL EXAMPLE

A numerical example will be used to illustrate the crowding-out effect on the aggregate capital stock accumulation and economic growth. Let us consider an economy where $P_h = 0.4$, $P_l = 0.7$, $\lambda = 0.75$, $\varepsilon = 0.25$, $\theta = 0.2$, $Q = 2$ and $\bar{q} = 0.2$. With the exception of those for θ and $\bar{q}$, these numerical values are adopted from Bose and Cothren (1996). In addition, when we calculate the aggregate capital stocks, we assume that the initial capital stock k_0 equals 1. Table 11.1 presents the results of our calibration.

Table 11.1 Calibration results

	Benchmark	Model with $\bar{q} > 0$
Π	0.580	0.500
L	2.750	2.900
$1+\varepsilon$	1.060	1.080
g	1.392	1.397
K_5	1.051	1.031
K_{10}	5.490	5.490
K_{20}	149.930	155.520

It is clear that in the public borrowing case, low-risk borrowers have a smaller probability of getting funds, which is 0.5 in the example. The labor force employed by each firm is 2.9, which is higher than that in the benchmark.

However, there are more lenders who choose to credit ration low- risk borrowers, which makes the value of $1+\varepsilon$ higher in this case. As a result, the model with $\bar{q}$ exhibits a higher economic growth rate. Note that K_5, the aggregate capital stock accumulation when $t=5$, is 1.031, which is smaller than that in the benchmark. But eventually, the positive economic growth effect overwhelms the negative crowding-out effect. Finally, the aggregate capital stock accumulation becomes bigger in the model with $\bar{q}$ after the tenth period.

The above results are sensitive to the value of θ. For any $\theta \in [0.3,1]$, the benchmark model always has higher economic growth and aggregate capital stocks. A low θ contributes to higher economic growth in the model with $\bar{q}$ because it helps mitigate the adverse effect exerted by the increasing labor force in each firm.

We have discussed and compared two different economies. One with public borrowing activities and one without. By using a numerical example, we find that the former can have a higher economic growth rate and eventually higher aggregate capital stocks without specifying how the funds, $\bar{q}$, are used. Therefore, the economy that has fewer financial resources can experience higher economic growth. At first glance, this conclusion is rather counterintuitive. But this seemingly counterintuitive conclusion can be explained in the following intuitive way. Indeed, how efficiently the lenders can convert their wages into capital stocks is the crucial element. After the government has extracted some resources from lenders, the financial market becomes tight in the sense that lenders are more hesitant to lend their funds to borrowers. Instead, they have a higher incentive to produce capital at home by using a technology which is more primitive compared to those private investment projects. The productivity of this 'home' technology is measured by the value of ε. When this value is not too much smaller than P_h and the value of θ is not too big, the whole economy can gain from a more frequent use of this home technology and hence the higher economic growth.

As shown, this positive growth rate can eventually offset the adverse crowding-out effect which worsens the aggregate capital stock accumulation.

6 CONCLUSION

This chapter provides an analysis on the role of public borrowing activities in an endogenous growth model. As an economy evolves with private projects of good or bad quality and the credit rationing contract is the only means to induce self-selection, the government can 'borrow' from the private sector strategically to promote growth at the expense of some low-risk private investment projects. To achieve this objective, two conditions must be met. First, lenders must have some less primitive home production technologies. Second, the amount of labor supply being expelled from the credit market cannot be too abundant. This conclusion can be considered as supplementary to the view that economic growth is still possible when there is asymmetric information problem in the economy, for example, Shi (1996). In Shi's paper, the possibility for borrowers to switch their project types is the main mechanics whereby a higher rate of growth is possible. The policy implication of our chapter is that when the financial market involves high risk investment projects, the government can deliberately increase the interest rate so as to restrict financial activities. As a result of this policy, lenders will retain their funds for other productive uses, which may turn out to be growth enhancing.

The 'crowding-out' effect discussed in this chapter refers to the smaller probability of obtaining funds for low-risk private borrowers when there are public borrowing activities in a credit market with informational frictions. Note that the meaning of this term is not exactly the same as the one in standard macroeconomic textbooks (see Barro, 1997). Even if there is no credit rationing, the government expenditure will still crowd out some economic activities from the private sector. Yet, in this situation, we cannot tell the quality of the activities being expelled.

One conceivable extension of this chapter is to endogenize q_u. It will be interesting to study whether there exists an optimal amount of funds for public projects which maximizes the economic growth rate and if it exists, what properties does it have?

ACKNOWLEDGMENTS

I would like to thank my advisor, Hans Haller for his valuable comments and encouraging me to pursue this line of research. Insightful comments from participants of the Taipei International Conference on Economic Growth, seminar participants at the Chinese University of Hong Kong and one anonymous referee are also gratefully acknowledged. Any remaining errors are my own.

NOTES

1. Therefore, my model is of a stochastic credit rationing type: a portion of loan applicants get the credit they want, whereas the others do not get any.
2. This asymmetric treatment of borrowers, which can help simplify the algebra and maintain the same qualitative results, is adopted from Bose and Cothren (1996).
3. As pointed out by one referee, it is common to observe that people utilize their own savings to

start up business in developing countries. But in order to study the problem of asymmetric information in financial markets, we have to assume that borrowers need some external funds to finance their projects. For simplicity, they do not have any internal sources of finance such as savings in the model.

4. q_u can also be interpreted as a tax to be collected by the government. This way of this interpretation will not affect the economic meanings of our theoretical results.
5. The interest rate is $Q\varepsilon\rho_{t+1}/P_i$, $i = h,l$ when there is no public borrowing in the economy.

REFERENCES

Barro, Robert J. (1997), *Macroeconomics*, 5th edn, Cambridge, MA and London: MIT Press.

Bencivenga, Valerie R. and Bruce D. Smith. (1993), 'Some Consequences of Credit Rationing in an Endogenous Growth Model', *Journal of Economic Dynamics and Control*, **17**, 97–122.

Bose, Niloy and Richard Cothren (1996), 'Equilibrium Loan Contracts and Endogenous Growth in the Presence of Asymmetric Information', *Journal of Monetary Economics*, **38**, 363–76.

Perotti, Enrico (1993), 'Bank Lending in Transition Economies', *Journal of Banking and Finance*, **17**, 1021–32.

Rothchild, M. and J. Stiglitz (1976), 'Equilibrium in Competitive Insurance Markets: An Essay on the Economics of Imperfect Information', *Quarterly Journal of Economics*, **80**, 629–49.

Shi, Shouyong (1996), 'Asymmetric Information, Credit Rationing, and Economic Growth', *Canadian Journal of Economics*, **29**, 665–87.

Stiglitz, Joseph E. and Andrew Weiss (1981), 'Credit Rationing in Markets with Imperfect Information', *American Economic Review*, **71**, 393–410.

Zou, Liang and Laixiang Sun (1996), 'Interest Rate Policy and Incentives of State-owned Enterprises in the Transitional China', *Journal of Comparative Economics*, **23**, 292–318.

12. Government Expenditure and Social Status in a Two-sector Model of Endogenous Growth

Jhy-yuan Shieh, Wen-ya Chang and Ching-chong Lai

1 INTRODUCTION

It is widely believed in the literature that government expenditure plays an important role in affecting the economic growth rate. However, empirical studies show an inconsistent conclusion on this subject. For example, Ram (1986) finds a positive relationship between government size and economic growth. Kormendi and Meguire (1985) show an insignificant relationship between government spending and growth. Landau (1983), Grier and Tullock (1989) and Barro (1990, 1991) even conclude a negative effect of government spending on economic growth.

In the hope of reconciling inconsistent empirical evidence, a number of papers provide a useful theoretical framework to examine the growth effect of fiscal expansion. They often categorize government spending into two distinct groups in their analyses. One is government consumption expenditure, which is modeled as utility enhancing to households, such as national parks, national defense, libraries and various social security programs. Barro (1990) and Faig (1995) develop a typical endogenous growth framework incorporating government consumption expenditure into the household's utility, and find that government consumption expenditure has no effect on the long-run growth rate. The other is government infrastructure expenditure, which is modeled as an input to the private production process, such as education, bridges, highways, airplanes, and other infrastructure programs. Barro (1990), Futagami et al. (1993), and Greiner and Hanusch (1998) set up theoretical frameworks to highlight the importance of government infrastructure in the aggregate production technology. They find that government infrastructure expenditure enhances the long-run growth rate.[1]

In reality such a dichotomous classification of government expenditure does not fit the facts. Take government expenditure on national defense as an example. On the one hand, a rise in the national defense enhances the home country's security and hence increases the representative agent's utility. On the other hand, the defense sector provides a variety of public infrastructure (for example, dams, communication networks, roads, airports, highways and other transportation networks), and hence has a positive externality effect on private production. Moreover, defense spending promotes economic growth since it provides both internal and external security, and hence boosts private investment and attracts foreign investment. Based on this observation, some public goods not only increase the private sector's output production, but also enhance the private agent's utility in nature. Hence, it is more reasonable that some public goods enter into not only the utility function of the household, but also the firm's production function.

Among the literature, Arrow and Kurz (1970) put the role of public goods into both the private production function and the private utility function, and use an exogenous growth model to discuss the impact of government expenditure on the economy. Using an exogenous growth model embodying the fact that the stock of public capital simultaneously affects the private production function and the private utility function, Baxter and King (1993) quantitatively examine the impact of government spending on output multipliers. However, as in the conventional wisdom of exogenous growth setting, both studies confine themselves to the analysis of the level effect of government spending. They clearly downplay the role of government expenditure on the economic growth rate. This chapter instead sets out an endogenous growth model with public goods affecting utility and production of the private sector so as to address the linkage between public spending and economic growth. The emphasis is placed on identifying the main channels that might explain the inconsistent empirical evidence.

Departing from the aforementioned literatures, the role of social culture differences is also taken into consideration. As documented by Zou (1994, p. 280), 'the culture differences among countries, in addition to technology, play an important role in the determination of economic growth'. In order to capture the socio-cultural aspect, following Kurz (1968), Zou (1994, 1995) and Bakshi and Chen (1996), we propose the role of desire for a wealth-induced social status when analyzing government expenditure's impact on the economic growth rate.

The basic argument of a wealth-induced social status is that individuals accumulate wealth not only for its implied consumption reward, but also for its induced social status. As highlighted by Weber (1958) and further elaborated by Zou (1994, 1995), Bakshi and Chen (1996), Corneo and Jeanne (1997), Futagami and Shibata (1998) and Chang et al. (2000), individuals pursue capital accumulation in order to advertise their wealth and thereby achieve a social position and power. Seeking greater social status thus provides incentives for individuals to perform growth-enhancing activities. Consequently, the agent's preference should depend on one's wealth holdings (the accumulating stocks of physical capital) as well as one's consumption. Based on our model, it is found that although social status may have interesting effects on growth, a crowding-out effect resulting from an increase in government spending causes individuals to leave growth-enhancing activities, hence lowering economic growth. As a result, the consideration of social status is essential for examining the government spending effect on economic growth.

The remainder of the chapter is organized as follows. Section 2 presents the analytical framework and uses it to examine how the economic growth rate will react following a change in government expenditure. Some concluding perspectives are presented in Section 3.

2 THE MODEL

Consider an economy consisting of a representative household and a government. The household produces two types of commodity. The first one is the civilian good, which can be consumed, accumulated as capital, and paid for as a tax. The second one is the public good, which can only be sold to the government to accumulate the public capital stock.

The representative household derives positive utility from consumption of the civilian good, c, the public capital stock, G, and the private capital stock, k.[2] The positive linkage between the household's utility and the capital stock stems from the viewpoint of social status proposed by Kurz (1968), Zou (1994, 1995) and Bakshi and Chen (1996). The representative household's objective is to maximize the discounted sum of future instantaneous utilities, which is given by:

$$\int_0^\infty U(c,G,k)e^{-\rho t}dt, \qquad (12.1)$$

where U is the utility function and ρ is the subjective time preference rate. Furthermore, the instantaneous utility function is specified as follows:

$$U(c,G,k) = [(cG^{\theta}k^{\beta})^{1-\sigma} - 1]/(1-\sigma);\ \sigma > 0,\ \theta > 0,\ \beta > 0. \qquad (12.2)$$

In equation (12.2), σ is the inverse of the intertemporal elasticity of substitution, which measures the utility function's curvature. The instantaneous utility function reduces to $U(c,G,k) = \ln c + \theta \ln G + \beta \ln k$ when $\sigma = 1$. In equation (12.2), the parameters θ and β measure the impact of the public capital stock and wealth-induced social status on household welfare, respectively. To satisfy the requirement that consumption, the public capital stock and the private capital stock yield a positive, but diminishing marginal utility, we impose the restrictions $\sigma, \theta, \beta > 0$, $\theta(1-\sigma) < 1$ and $\beta(1-\sigma) < 1$. Moreover, $\sigma > (\theta + \beta)(1-\sigma)$ is assumed to ensure that the utility function is concave in the quantities *c*, *G* and *k*.

In line with the specification of the government infrastructure expenditure model (for example, Grossman and Lucas, 1974; Barro, 1981, 1990; Aschauer, 1988; Baxter and King, 1993; Turnovsky and Fisher, 1995; and Fisher and Turnovsky, 1998), the public sector is assumed to have a positive externality on the civilian sector. Hence, the civilian output y is produced by using the fraction u of the productive private capital stock k, the public capital stock G, and inelastically-supplied labor. Moreover, we assume that the production function exhibits constant returns to scale with a diminishing return with respect to uk and G, that is:

$$y = ukf(G/uk); \; f' > 0, f'' < 0. \tag{12.3}$$

The representative household also produces a public good, namely *d*, using an analogous production function:

$$d = (1-u)k\phi[G/(1-u)k]; \; \phi' > 0, \; \phi'' < 0. \tag{12.4}$$

The relative price of the public good in terms of the civilian output p is taken as exogenously given by the representative household, and is determined by the economy's market-clearing condition. In addition, physical capital is freely mobile between the two sectors.

One point should be noted here. Our model decomposes production into public goods and civilian goods, while existing studies treat public and civilian goods as a homogeneously-collective good. Public goods, like weapons, national parks and dams, are common in the real world and share production resources with civilian goods, and so it is quite natural to decompose production into public goods and civilian goods. Given this observation, a two-sector model seems more reasonable. The household budget constraint can thus be expressed by:

$$\dot{k} = y + pd - c - T, \tag{12.5}$$

where an overdot denotes the rate of change with respect to time, and T is a lump-sum tax.

The representative household chooses both consumption and the fraction of physical capital allocated to the civilian sector so as to maximize the discounted sum of utility defined in equation (12.1), subject to equations (12.2), (12.3), (12.4) and (12.5). The current-value Hamiltonian function, H, is given by:

$$\begin{aligned} H &= [(cG^{\theta}k^{\beta})^{1-\sigma} - 1]/(1-\sigma) \\ &+ \lambda\{ukf(G/uk) - c + p(1-u)k\phi[G/(1-u)k] - T\}, \end{aligned}$$

where λ is the co-state variable which can be interpreted as the imputed value of the physical capital stock.

The optimal conditions necessary for this optimization problem are given by:

$$(cG^{\theta}k^{\beta})^{1-\sigma}(1/c) = \lambda, \tag{12.6a}$$

$$f - f'G/uk = p[\phi - \phi'G/(1-u)k], \tag{12.6b}$$

$$\begin{aligned} -\dot{\lambda} + \rho\lambda &= \{uf - f'G/k + p[(1-u)\phi - \phi'G/k]\}\lambda \\ &+ \beta(cG^{\theta}k^{\beta})^{1-\sigma}/k, \end{aligned} \tag{12.6c}$$

together with the representative household's budget constraint (equation (12.5)), and the transversality condition $\lim_{t\to\infty} \lambda k e^{-\rho t} = 0$. Equation (12.6a) expresses that the marginal utility of civilian good consumption equals the shadow value of the physical capital stock λ. Equation (12.6b) states that the marginal revenue product of private capital between the two sectors is equal. Equation (12.6c) is the Euler equation, which describes the evolution of λ.

The government is assumed to collect its lump-sum tax revenue to finance its expenditure. In order to sustain an equilibrium with steady-state growth, following Devereux and Love (1995), Turnovsky (1995) and Bruce and Turnovsky (1999), we assume that the government sets its expenditure g as a fixed fraction of civilian output, that is:[3]

$$g = \psi y = \psi ukf(G/uk); \; 0 < \psi < 1. \tag{12.7}$$

The parameter ψ is the share of civilian output devoted to government spending. Assume that the government maintains a continuous balanced budget, and that government spending is entirely on the public goods procurement pd. The government budget constraint can then be expressed as:

$$T = g = \psi ukf(G/uk) = pd = p(1-u)k\phi\left[G/(1-u)k\right]. \tag{12.8}$$

Hence, the stock of public capital evolves according to:

$$\dot{G} = d = (1-u)k\phi\left[G/(1-u)k\right]. \tag{12.9}$$

Substituting equations (12.4) and (12.8) into (12.5), the resource constraint of the whole economy is:

$$\dot{k} = ukf(G/uk) - c. \tag{12.10}$$

Differentiating equation (12.6a) with respect to time and substituting equations (12.6b), (12.6c), (12.9) and (12.10) into the resulting equation, the optimal change in consumption is given by:

$$\begin{aligned}\dot{c}/c &= \{\theta(1-\sigma)(1-u)(G/k)^{-1}\phi \\ &\quad + [1+\beta(1-\sigma)u]f - f'G/uk - \rho\}/\sigma + \beta c/k.\end{aligned} \tag{12.11}$$

The public goods market must clear at each instant of time. Given that the public good is supplied by the representative household and is exclusively demanded by the government, equation (12.8) thus represents the public goods market-clearing condition. Therefore, using equation (12.8), the relative price of public goods in terms of civilian goods is given by:

$$p = \psi uf/(1-u)\phi. \tag{12.12}$$

Along a balanced growth path, private consumption, private capital stock and public capital stock will grow at the same rate. Thus, following Futagami et al. (1993), Barro and Sala-i-Martin (1995) and Faig (1995), we define $x \equiv G/k$ and $z \equiv c/k$. As a consequence, from equations (12.9), (12.10) and (12.11), the dynamic system in terms of the transformed variables, x and z, can be summarized by the following equations:

$$\dot{x}/x \equiv \dot{G}/G - \dot{k}/k = (1-u)x^{-1}\phi - uf + z \tag{12.13a}$$

and

$$\begin{aligned}\dot{z}/z &\equiv \dot{c}/c - \dot{k}/k \\ &= \{\theta(1-\sigma)(1-u)x^{-1}\phi + [1+\beta u - \sigma u(1+\beta)]f \\ &- xf'/u - \rho\}/\sigma + (1+\beta)z.\end{aligned} \tag{12.13b}$$

In addition, substituting equation (12.12) into (12.6b), the momentary equilibrium condition is:

$$f - xf'/u = \psi uf[\phi - x\phi'/(1-u)]/(1-u)\phi. \tag{12.13c}$$

Accordingly, the economy's dynamic behavior can be restated by differential equations (12.13a) and (12.13b) and the momentary equilibrium condition (12.13c).

The analysis proceeds as follows. Totally differentiating equation (12.13c), it is easy to derive a reduced-form solution for the share of capital stock allocated to the civilian sector in terms of x and ψ:

$$u = u(x, \psi), \tag{12.14}$$

where:

$$\begin{aligned}u_x &= [\psi f'\Lambda_1 - \phi'\Lambda_2 - xu\psi f\phi''/(1-u)^2 + x\phi f''(1-u)/u^2]/\Omega, \\ u_\psi &= uf\Lambda_1/\Omega < 0, \\ \Lambda_1 &= \phi - x\phi'/(1-u) > 0, \\ \Lambda_2 &= f - f' \quad x/u > 0, \\ \Omega &= x^2 f''\phi\cdot(1-u)/u^3 + x^2 u\psi f\phi''\cdot/(1-u)^3 - (1+\psi)\Lambda_1\Lambda_2 < 0.\end{aligned}$$

Let superscript '$*$' denote the stationary values of relevant variables. Substituting equation (12.4) into (12.13a) and (12.13b) and linearizing the resulting equations around the steady-state equilibrium, we then have:

$$\begin{bmatrix} \dot{x} \\ \dot{z} \end{bmatrix} = \begin{bmatrix} a_{11} & a_{12} \\ a_{21} & a_{22} \end{bmatrix} \begin{bmatrix} x - x^* \\ z - z^* \end{bmatrix} + \begin{bmatrix} b_1 \\ b_2 \end{bmatrix} (\psi - \psi_0), \tag{12.15}$$

where:

$$\begin{aligned}
a_{11} &= -[(1 - u^* + u_x x^*)\Lambda_1 x^{*-2} + \Lambda_2 u_x + f']x^*, \\
a_{12} &= x^*, \\
a_{21} &= \{[\beta - \sigma(1+\beta)](\Lambda_2 u_x + f') - \theta(1-\sigma)(1 - u^* + u_x x^*)\Lambda_1 x^{*-2} \\
&\qquad - (u^* - u_x x^*)x^* f'' / u^{*3}\} z^* / \sigma, \\
a_{22} &= (1+\beta)z^*, \\
b_1 &= -\left(\Lambda_1 x^{*-1} + \Lambda_2\right) u_\psi x^*, \\
b_2 &= \{[\beta - \sigma(1+\beta)]\Lambda_2 - \theta(1-\sigma)\Lambda_1 x^{*-1} + x^* f'' / u^{*3}\} u_\psi z^* / \sigma.
\end{aligned}$$

Let s_1 and s_2 be the two characteristic roots of the dynamic system. From equation (12.15) we have:

$$\begin{aligned}
s_1 s_2 &= x^* z^* \{[\theta(1-\sigma) - \sigma(1+\beta)](1 - u^* + u_x x^*)\Lambda_1 x^{*-2} \\
&\quad + (u^* - u_x x^*)x^* f'' / u^{*3} - \beta(f' + \Lambda_2 u_x)\} / \sigma.
\end{aligned} \tag{12.16}$$

As addressed in the literature of dynamic rational expectations models including Burmeister (1980), Buiter (1984) and Turnovsky (1995), the dynamic system exists with a unique perfect-foresight equilibrium if the number of unstable roots equals the number of jump variables. Since the dynamic system reported in equation (12.15) has one jump variable z, in what follows we impose $s_1 s_2 < 0$ to assure such a unique perfect-foresight equilibrium.

We now consider the effects of a rise in public spending on the steady-state growth rate. First, with $\dot{x} = \dot{z} = 0$ in equation (12.15), we can easily derive the following steady-state relationships:

$$\begin{aligned}
&\partial x^* / \partial \psi = \\
&\{[\sigma(1+\beta) - \theta(1-\sigma)]\Lambda_1 x^{*-1} + x^{*2} f'' / u^{*3} + \beta\Lambda_2\} x^* z^* u_\psi / \sigma s_1 s_2,
\end{aligned} \tag{12.17a}$$

$$\partial z^* / \partial\psi =$$
$$\{[x^{*2} f' + u^* x^* \Lambda_2 + \Lambda_1] f'' / u^3 + x^{*-2} \Lambda_1 [(\beta+\theta)(1-\sigma) - \sigma] \quad (12.17b)$$
$$\cdot [(1-u^*)\Lambda_2 - x^* f']\} x^* z^* u_\psi / \sigma s_1 s_2 .$$

Next, let γ^* be the steady-state growth rate and note that $(\dot{c}/c)^* = (\dot{k}/k)^* = (\dot{d}/d)^* = (\dot{G}/G)^* = (\dot{y}/y)^* = \gamma^*$ is held in the steady-state growth equilibrium. From equations (12.10), (12.14), (12.17a) and (12.17b), we can easily obtain:

$$\begin{aligned} &\partial\gamma^* / \partial\psi \\ &= \Lambda_2 u_\psi + \Lambda_2 u_x \cdot \partial x^* / \partial\psi + f' \cdot \partial x^* / \partial\psi - \partial z^* / \partial\psi \\ &= -x^{*-1} z^* \Lambda_1 \left[\beta(1-u^*)\Lambda_2 - \beta x^* f' + x^{*2} f'' / u^{*3}\right] u_\psi / \sigma s_1 s_2 . \end{aligned} \quad (12.18)$$

Equation (12.18) reveals the main finding. It indicates that a permanent rise in public spending has an ambiguous effect on the steady-state growth rate. As shown in the first line in equation (12.18), a rise in the public expenditure affects the balanced growth rate through four channels. The net effect depends on the relative strength of these four channels.

The first channel is the 'direct crowding-out effect', whereby an increase in government expenditure will *directly* reduce the share of physical capital allocated to the civilian sector. This channel tends to lower private output production and the available resources for investment hence decrease.

The second channel is the 'resource allocation effect' between two sectors, whereby an increase in public spending will alter the relative marginal revenue product of private capital between two sectors, and hence *indirectly* changes the share of physical capital allocated to the civilian sector. To be specific, a rise in government expenditure will change the public good–private capital ratio, and the relative marginal revenue product of private capital between two sectors will hence alter. With such an adjustment, the representative household tends to redistribute the allocation of physical capital between two sectors. Given that the relationship between the public good–private capital ratio and the allocation of physical capital between two sectors (u_x) is ambiguous, this channel has an ambiguous effect on private investment.

The third channel is the 'spin–off effect', whereby an increase in government spending has a positive externality to civilian goods production. This channel has a positive externality to civilian goods production and tends to boost investment.

The fourth channel is the 'resource mobilization effect', whereby a rise in government expenditure governs the behavior of private consumption. A rise in government expenditure leads to more public capital accumulation, and a higher value of future public capital stock is associated with a higher value of $cG^{\theta}k^{\beta}$, leading to changes in the marginal utility of both future consumption and future social status. The marginal utility of both future consumption and future social status will increase if the substitution between intertemporal consumption is elastic ($\sigma < 1$). Faced with this scenario, the representative consumer lowers his/her current consumption and current investment to gain higher future utility. Conversely, the representative agent tends to boost current consumption and current investment if the substitution between intertemporal consumption is inelastic ($\sigma > 1$). Accordingly, the fourth channel has an ambiguous effect on private investment.

In order to sharpen the role of both social status and the production externality of public goods on the linkage between fiscal spending and the balanced growth rate, in what follows we address some special situations. First, if the effect of the wealth-induced social status is absent, $\beta = 0$, then equation (12.18) reduces to:

$$\partial\gamma^* / \partial\psi\big|_{\beta=0} = -\Lambda_1 x^* z^* f'' u_{\psi} / \sigma s_1 s_2 u^{*3} > 0. \qquad (12.18a)$$

This implies that, when the representative agent does not care about social status, a rise in fiscal spending makes a positive contribution to the economy's long-run growth rate. This result confirms the empirical result of Ram (1986).

The second special situation we deal with is that the public sector has no externality effect on the civilian sector. In such a scenario, to sustain balanced growth the production function is specified to take the Ak technology. Hence, from equation (12.18) with $f = A$, $f' = 0$ and $f'' = 0$, we have:

$$\partial\gamma^* / \partial\psi\big|_{f=A} = -x^{*-1} z^* \Lambda_1 \beta (1 - u^*) A u_{\psi} / \sigma s_1 s_2 < 0. \qquad (12.18b)$$

It is easy to conclude from equation (12.18b) that a rise in government spending negatively affects the economy's long-run growth rate if only the effect of social status enters the picture. This result conforms with the empirical findings of Landau (1983), Grier and Tullock (1989) and Barro (1990, 1991).

The results in equations (12.18a) and (12.18b) can be explained as follows. In equation (12.18a), if the representative household does not care about social status, then the spin-off effect outweighs the sum of the resource allocation effect, the direct crowding-out effect and the resource mobilization effect, and hence the economy is characterized by a higher growth rate of output. On the other hand, the spin-off effect will disappear when the externality effect for the civilian sector stemming from the public sector is terminated. As indicated in equation (12.18b), the sum of the resource allocation effect, the direct crowding-out effect and the resource mobilization effect tends to lower the representative household's investment, if the desire for social status is present, but the externality effect is absent. Hence, expansionary fiscal spending contributes a negative impact on growth.

The third special situation is that the public's desire for social status and the production externality effect of public goods are both absent. Under this situation, it is easy to infer from equation (12.18) that the public burden is totally incapable of influencing the economic growth rate, implying that the sum of the resource allocation effect, the crowding-out effect and the resource mobilization effect is zero.

3 CONCLUDING PERSPECTIVES

This chapter presents an endogenous growth model in which public goods enter both the household's utility function and the private production function. Contrary to the existing literature, like Barro (1990), Devereux and Love (1995), Faig (1995) and Greiner and Hanusch (1998), the role of wealth-induced social status is taken into account to capture social culture difference in the economy. In addition, our model decomposes production into public goods and civilian goods, while existing studies treat public and civilian goods as a homogeneously-collective good. Within such a framework, we focus on highlighting the question of whether a rise in public spending tends to speed up or reduce the economy's balanced growth rate. Given that the government sets its expenditure as a fixed fraction of output as proposed by Turnovsky (1995) and Bruce and Turnovsky (1999), we find that both the desire for social status and the production externality of public goods are two important factors that determine the effectiveness of a rise in fiscal spending on the sustained growth rate. Specifically, if the desire for social status is absent and the production externality of public goods is present, then an increase in public expenditure tends to favor the steady-state growth rate. On the other hand, when the public sector has no externality on the civilian sector, but the desire for social status is present, an increase in government expenditure will lower the balanced growth rate.

ACKNOWLEDGMENTS

The authors are deeply indebted to Professor Ping Wang and two anonymous referees for their helpful suggestions and insightful comments on an earlier version of this chapter. We alone are responsible for all the views and any remaining shortcomings herein.

NOTES

1. The definition of government consumption expenditure and government infrastructure expenditure is adopted from Turnovsky and Fisher (1995). Barro (1993, ch.12) has a similar classification, however, he does not give a clear appellation.
2. Alternatively, we may follow Bakshi and Chen (1996), Corneo and Jeanne (1997) and Futagami and Shibata (1998) to specify that the individual is interested in the relative level of his or her position in society. A relative social position depends on his/her capital stock k relative to the aggregate stock of capital K. As a consequence, the instantaneous utility function stated in equation (12.2) can be modified as follows: $U(c,G,k/K)=\{[cG^{\theta}(k/K)^{\beta}]^{1-\sigma}-1\}/(1-\sigma)$; $\sigma>0$, $\theta>0$, $\beta>0$. The representative household treats the aggregate stock of capital as given when solving its optimization problem. Given that our framework is a representative agent model, $k=K$ holds in the aggregate market equilibrium. In such a scenario, our main results remain true.
3. In fact, our results hold if the government sets its expenditure as a fixed fraction of private total income, that is, $g=\psi(y+pd)$.

REFERENCES

Arrow, K.J. and M. Kurz (eds) (1970), *Public Investment, the Rate of Return, and Optimal Fiscal Policy*, Baltimore, M.D: Johns Hopkins University Press.

Aschauer, D.A. (1988), 'The equilibrium approach to fiscal policy', *Journal of Money, Credit, and Banking*, **20**, 41–62.

Bakshi, G.S. and Z. Chen (1996), 'The spirit of capitalism and stock-market prices', *American Economic Review*, **86**, 133–57.

Barro, R.J. (1981), 'Output effects of government purchases', *Journal of Political Economy*, **89**, 1086–121.

Barro, R.J. (1990), 'Government spending in a simple model of endogenous growth', *Journal of Political Economy*, **98**, 103–25.

Barro, R.J. (1991), 'Economic growth in a cross-section of countries', *Quarterly Journal of Economics*, **56**, 407–43.

Barro, R.J. (1993), *Macroeconomics*, 4th edn, New York: John Wiley.

Barro, R.J. and X. Sala-i-Martin (1995), *Economic Growth*, New York: McGraw-Hill.

Baxter, M. and R.G. King (1993), 'Fiscal policy in general equilibrium', *American Economic Review*, **83**, 315–34.

Bruce, N. and S.J. Turnovsky (1999), 'Budget balance, welfare, and the growth rate: "Dynamic scoring," of the long-run government budget', *Journal of Money, Credit, and Banking*, **31**, 162–86.

Buiter, W.H. (1984), 'Saddlepoint problems in continuous time rational expectations models: a general method and some macroeconomic examples', *Econometrica*, **52**, 665–80.

Burmeister, E. (1980), 'On some conceptual issues in rational expectations modeling', *Journal of Money, Credit, and Banking*, **12**, 800–812.

Chang, W.Y., Y.N. Hsieh and C.C. Lai (2000), 'Social status, inflation, and endogenous growth in a cash-in-advance economy', *European Journal of Political Economy*, **16**, 535–45.

Corneo, G. and O. Jeanne (1997), 'On relative wealth effects and the optimality of growth', *Economics Letters*, **54**, 87–92.

Devereux, M.B. and D.R.F. Love (1995), 'The dynamic effects of government spending policies in a two-sector endogenous growth model', *Journal of Money, Credit, and Banking*, **27**, 232–56.

Faig, M. (1995), 'A simple economy with human capital: transitional dynamics, technology shocks, and fiscal policies', *Journal of Macroeconomics*, **17**, 421–46.
Fisher, W.H. and S.J. Turnovsky (1998), 'Public investment, congestion, and private capital accumulation', *Economic Journal*, **108**, 399–413.
Futagami, K., Y. Morita and A. Shibata (1993), 'Dynamic analysis of an endogenous growth model with public capital', *Scandinavian Journal of Economics*, **95**, 607–25.
Futagami, K. and A. Shibata, (1998), 'Keeping one step ahead of the Joneses: status, the distribution of wealth, and long run growth', *Journal of Economic Behavior and Organization*, **36**, 109–26.
Greiner, M. and H. Hanusch (1998), 'Growth and welfare effects of fiscal policy in an endogenous growth model with public investment', *International Tax and Public Finance*, **5**, 249–61.
Grier, K.B. and G. Tullock (1989), 'An empirical analysis of cross-sectional economic growth: 1950–1980', *Journal of Monetary Economics*, **24**, 259–77.
Grossman, H.I. and R.F. Lucas (1974), 'The macro-economic effects of productive public expenditure', *Manchester School*, **42**, 162–70.
Kormendi, R.C. and P.G. Meguire (1985), 'Macroeconomic determinants of growth: cross country evidence', *Journal of Monetary Economics*, **16**, 141–63.
Kurz, M. (1968), 'Optimal economic growth and wealth effects', *International Economic Review*, **9**, 348–57.
Landau, D.L. (1983), 'Government expenditure and economic growth: a cross-country study', *Southern Economic Journal*, **49**, 783–92.
Ram, R. (1986), 'Government size and economic growth: a new framework and some evidence from cross-section and time series data', *American Economic Review*, **76**, 191–203.
Turnovsky, S.J. (1995), *Methods of Macroeconomic Dynamics*, Cambridge, MA: MIT Press.
Turnovsky, S.J. and W.H. Fisher (1995), 'The composition of government expenditure and its consequences for macroeconomic performance', *Journal of Economic Dynamics and Control*, **19**, 747–86.
Weber, M. (1958), *The Protestant Ethic and the Spirit of Capitalism*, New York, NY: Charles Scribner's Sons.
Zou, H.F. (1994), 'The spirit of capitalism and long-run growth', *European Journal of Political Economy*, **10**, 279–93.
Zou, H.F. (1995), 'The spirit of capitalism and savings behavior', *Journal of Economic Behavior and Organization*, **24**, 131–43.

13. Economic Growth and the Environmental Kuznets Curve in Taiwan: A Simultaneity Model Analysis

Ming-Feng Hung and Daigee Shaw

1 INTRODUCTION

This chapter uses panel data on Taiwan to examine the environmental Kuznets curve (EKC) relationship between per capita income and air pollution. In the EKC literature, EKC is always estimated in the form of a single equation. However, since both income and environmental quality are endogenous variables, that is, they impact upon each other, the estimation of single-equation relationships where simultaneity exists will produce biased and inconsistent estimates. We specify the channels through which *Y* (income) affects *P* (pollution) and *P* affects *Y* in a conceptual model and then formulate a two-equation simultaneous model for empirical research. We test for exogeneity with the Hausman test and estimate the simultaneity model using the two-stage least squares method. The inverted U-shaped relationships are found between NO_2/CO and per capita income in Taiwan. As income grows, there is first an increase in the levels of NO_2 and CO, followed by a decrease. Air pollution, however, does not significantly affect income.

Many countries have clearly demonstrated extraordinary levels of economic performance over the last century, but the question remains as to the costs of such success. An important question is whether economic growth is achieved through the sacrifice of environmental quality, and in turn, growth eventually ceases, or whether economic growth will be accompanied by environmental awareness and technology progress, which finally create a win–win situation in environment and economics? Many recent studies of the EKC have tried to answer this question.

The EKC hypothesizes that there is an 'inverted-U' relationship between the various indicators of environmental quality, and levels of per capita income. This hypothesis draws its inspiration from the income distribution theory developed by Kuznets (1955) in which he discovered an inverted-U relationship between an indicator of income inequality and the level of income.

Following Grossman and Krueger's (1991) path-breaking study, an extensive literature has developed, reporting EKC estimates and discussing their implication.[1] Earlier papers by Shafik and Bandyopadhyay (1992), Panayotou (1993), Selden and Song (1994) and Grossman and Krueger (1995) presented initial evidence that some pollutants followed an EKC pattern. These findings then led to some naive idea that economic growth is, by nature, the remedy to environmental problems. However, recent research has focused on the effect of using different indicators, the use of a wider range of explanatory variables than income alone and the estimation of different models (see surveys in De Bruyn, 2000, p. 86 and Panayotou, 2000, pp. 20–21). The EKC results are not generally reproduced by this recent research.

One important critique for the empirical studies of the EKC is that they are based on a reduced-form model where there is no feedback effect from the environment to economic growth and therefore environmental quality is invariably viewed as the outcome of economic growth (for example, Pearson, 1994; Stern et al., 1996; Stern, 1998; Borghesi, 2002; De Bruyn, 2000). In all of the EKC empirical literature, the effect of economic growth on environmental quality is estimated directly. However, it is well known that, in addition to the effect of economic growth on environmental quality, environmental degradation may directly impact upon economic growth through a restriction or reduction in production (Barbier, 1994; Pearce and Warford, 1993, pp. 19–20) and adverse effects upon production factors (Van Ewijk and Van Wijnbergen, 1995; De Bruyn, 2000).[2] Environmental degradation may also indirectly impact upon economic growth through higher emission reduction costs resulting from environmental regulations. Generally, the economic growth and the environment are jointly determined (Perrings, 1987). It is therefore inappropriate to estimate a single-equation model of unidirectional causality from economy to environment. As Stern (1998) concluded, 'estimating single equation relationships by ordinary least squares where simultaneity exists produces biased and inconsistent estimates'(p.181). Hence, 'a simultaneous-equation model may be more appropriate for understanding the environment–income relationship' (Borghesi, 2002, p.213).

However, there is no empirical study that estimates the simultaneous relationship between economic growth and environmental quality, due to the difficulty in model specification and the demanding data requirements (De Bruyn, 2000). The first purpose of this chapter is therefore to formulate a simultaneity model between income and the environment and then to estimate the EKC. The theoretical growth model concerning the environment serves as a good starting point for model specification. There have been a number of theoretical models developed that generate the EKCs under appropriate assumptions (see the survey paper of Panayotou, 2000). In this class of models (for example, López, 1994; Stokey, 1998; Munasinghe, 1999; Smulders and Bretscher, 2000), pollution generally affects utility function with a negative effect and serves as an input of the production of consumption goods. At the optimal, the marginal benefit and marginal cost of pollution are equal. Because of the elasticity of the marginal utility of consumption, the elasticity of substitution in production between conventional factor and pollution, and environmental regulations, these theoretical models can generate the inverted-U income–environment relationship.

However, if we were to specify an empirical model according to the above theoretical models, the specified equations of marginal benefit and marginal cost of pollution could not be empirically estimated because we generally do not have time-series or cross-sectional data on them. In this chapter, we therefore first develop a conceptual model of the simultaneous relationship between income and pollution[3] and then formulate two equations for empirical research: the income and pollution equations. Even though we are not able to estimate the full structural model because its estimation requires data over a large number of years, not only for pollution and income but also for all intermediate variables, such as policy, technological progress and structural changes, we take a more flexible approach by estimating a simultaneous two-equation model. The integration of theoretical and empirical models provides us with an enhanced understanding of the relationship between economic growth and the environment.

A Hausman test for income endogeneity is used to determine the econometric justification of the model specification. When Holtz-Eakin and Selden (1995) and Cole et al. (1997) tested the income exogeneity, they found no evidence of simultaneity for their data. However, the results of this analysis reject the income exogeneity hypothesis for two pollutants and thus, we go on to estimate pollution and income equations simultaneously.

The second purpose of this chapter is to investigate the contribution of pollution to production and, consequently, to growth. In recently developed endogenous growth models, human capital accumulation,[4] fertility choice, research and development (R&D), pollution and so on, have been proposed as a means of explaining output growth. Although in these studies pollution has been theoretically considered — the role of inputs, the adverse impacts on labor, man-made inputs and production — no studies have yet examined the effects of pollution on production empirically. In this chapter, we capture the effects of pollution on production in Taiwan based on the estimates of pollution on income.

Our third purpose is to test the EKC hypothesis for the case of Taiwan. Moving from cross-country to single-country studies is a new line for EKC research.[5] Until now, Wu (1998) has provided the only paper estimating an

EKC relationship between suspended particulate matter/dust fall and per capita income in Taiwan. Here, we study three other air pollutants and include additional important pollution control policy measures as the explanatory variables. The consistency of the relevant data defining air quality across time is also considered. Furthermore, we use 'air basin' rather than 'county' as the unit of observation for airborne and gaseous pollutants. We believe that the regional dispersion pattern of these pollutants makes the use of 'county' an inappropriate management unit for determining air quality.

The remainder of this chapter is organized as follows. Section 2 specifies the model for examining the relationship between economic growth and environmental quality, with a description of the variables and the data. Section 3 provides empirical estimates and their subsequent analysis. Section 4 concludes.

2 MODEL SPECIFICATION AND DATA

We shall study the interactions between air quality and per capita income. Air quality is examined because no one can escape the impacts of poor air quality,[6] and its data and environmental regulation measures are more complete and sound. The panel data set provides us with a greater number of data points than time-series or cross-sectional data sets.

2.1 Model specification

A conceptual model of the two-way relationship between income (Y) and the environment (P) is given in Figure 13.1. There are many driving forces behind the two-way relationship between Y and P. First, income influences the environmental quality directly because pollution is its byproduct. In addition, income can also influence the environmental quality indirectly. Income growth is accompanied by increasing demand for improvements in environmental quality and, through such driving forces as public and private control measures, technological progress, international trade, and structural changes in consumption, production and institutions, pollution level changes.

Second, the role of pollution on production is also multiple:

1. Pollution may act as a negative externality, directly reducing output and productivity of man-made capital and labor (for example, López, 1994; Smulders, 1999; De Bruyn, 2000). Examples are the loss of days worked due to health problems, the corrosion of industrial equipment due to polluted air or water, and product deterioration due to being polluted. In this case, if pollution is reduced (increased), output will increase (decrease).

2. Pollution may act like a factor of production. To reduce pollution, we need to input human and man-made capital for pollution control. Therefore, if there is no pollution control, part of the output can be viewed as the contribution of pollution to production. In this case, if pollution is reduced (increased), output will decrease (increase).

In addition to the driving forces mentioned above, the income–environment relationship can also be influenced by exogenous variables such as traditional production factors, policies, population density and site-specific variables.

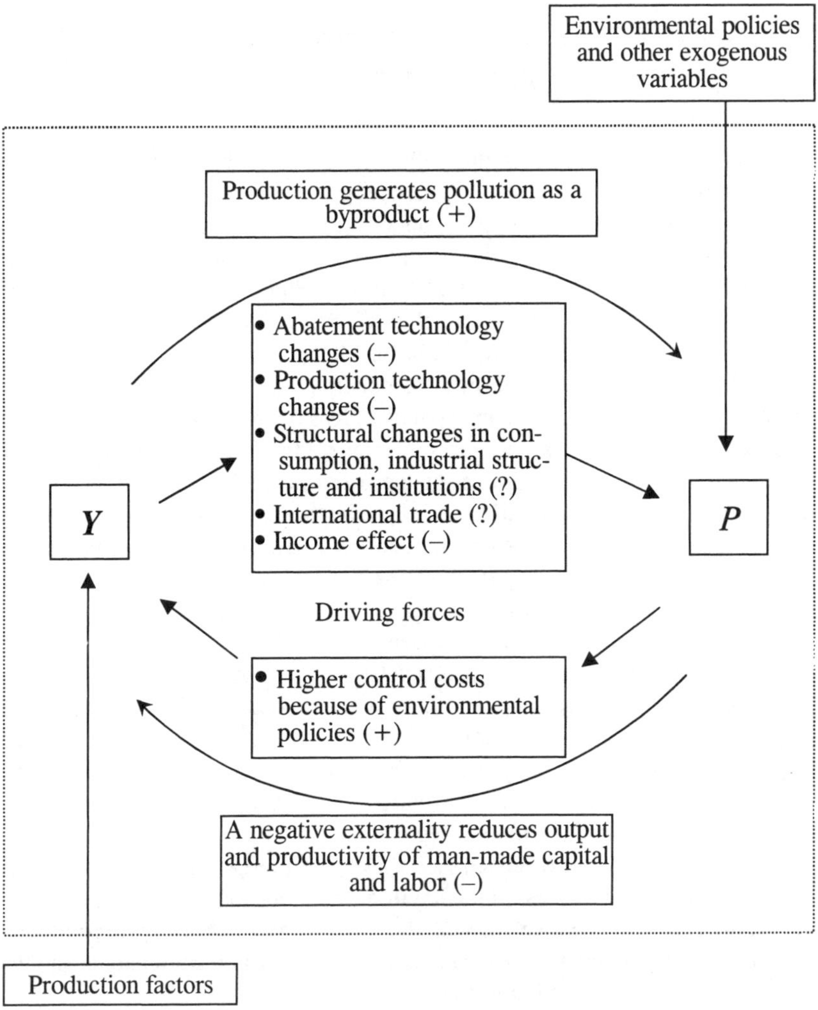

Figure 13.1 The relationship between income and the environment

Based upon the conceptual model in Figure 13.1, we specify the simultaneity model of income and the environment as follows to estimate the relationship between pollution and per capita income in Taiwan:

$$\ln P_{it} = \mu_i + \gamma_1 \ln Y_{it} + \gamma_2 (\ln Y_{it})^2 + \omega \ln X_{it} + e_{it} \tag{13.1}$$

and

$$\begin{aligned} \ln Y_{it} &= \alpha_i + \beta_1 \ln P_{it} + \beta_2 \ln K_{it} + \beta_3 \ln L_{it} \\ &\quad + \beta_4 \ln H_{it} + \beta_5 \ln G_{it} + \varepsilon_{it}. \end{aligned} \tag{13.2}$$

Equation (13.1) represents the pollution equation, where P_{it} denotes air pollution in air basin *i* for year *t*; Y_{it} denotes per capita income in air basin *i* for year *t*; and μ_i is the specific effect on air basin *i*. Here income Y_{it} acts as a surrogate variable representing the aggregate effects of some direct and indirect driving forces on pollution. The time path of pollution may display different shapes as a result of relative weights of every driving force. If $\gamma_1 > 0$ and $\gamma_2 < 0$, we expect that there will be an EKC relationship.[7]

In addition to the income terms, the pollution equation is often studied by including other variables such as population density and site-specific variables. The inclusion of other variables aims to improve the fit of the estimations and to provide additional explanations for the pattern of pollutants with economic development. Many recent EKC studies have focused on examining possible determinants of the EKC relationship, such as trade, political freedom, policy variables and so on, to investigate the impact of various exogenous variables on the EKC relationship (De Bruyn, 2000, p. 86; Panayotou, 2000, pp. 20–21). Here, X_{it} represents this kind of exogenous variable.

Taking into consideration the data availability, we include in X_{it} the population density, a dummy for the data irregularity, the number of specialists involved in air quality protection within the government, and air pollution inspection rates on stationary and mobile sources as exogenous variables, which might be closely related to pollution in Taiwan. The last two variables are supposed to represent pollution-regulation efforts.

Equation (13.2) is an extended Cobb–Douglas production function. In this specification, income Y_{it} is a function of air pollution P_{it}, man-made capital K_{it}, raw labor L_{it}, human capital H_{it} and local government expenditure G_{it}. It is expected that man-made capital, raw labor and human capital should contribute positively to output growth.

Local government expenditure is included as an explanatory variable because government is an important factor in economic growth. The provision of infrastructure services, the protection of property rights, and the taxation of economic activities can affect income. It should therefore not be ignored as an omitted variable. However, there is a limitation in the data available. Because the definitions and contents of data were revised in 1990,[8] we can obtain the total government expenditures composed of government transfer payments and government investments. Theoretically, government transfer payments have a negative effect, while government investments have a positive effect on economic growth. Due to this weakness, the estimates of local government expenditure on economic growth might be tentative.

Pollution P_{it} acts as a surrogate variable representing the aggregate effects of some direct and indirect driving forces on production. We expect that the aggregate effects of air pollution on production might not be significant for two reasons. First, relative to other kinds of environmental problem, such as deforestation, desertification and land erosion, air pollution dissipates more rapidly. Since people could also adopt averting behavior, the negative impacts of air pollution on production would therefore not be serious. Second, although the environmental protection authorities in Taiwan have applied many environmental policies during the past decade, the impacts of policies on firms might not be particularly significant. Under pressure from industrial interest groups, not only can the air pollution emission fees not be set high enough to attain the environmental goals, but also the tax-allowance subsidies for the abatement costs of firms are always extended following their expiry date (see Shaw and Hung, 2001). However, even if we expect that the estimates might not be significant, it is interesting to know the aggregate effect of air pollution on production empirically in the case of Taiwan.

The simultaneity model of income and the environment is checked by the order and rank conditions for identification and each equation is identified. A Hausman test for income endogeneity is performed to determine the econometric justification of the simultaneity model specification for the data set.[9] Holtz-Eakin and Selden (1995) and Cole et al. (1997) tested for income exogeneity, and found no evidence of simultaneity. Here we employ a single-equation version of the Hausman specification test, as devised by Spencer and Berk (1981), to test the null hypothesis of exogeneity of per capita income in the pollution equation. We estimate the simultaneous model using the two-stage least squares method when the exogeneity hypothesis is rejected to get the unbiased estimates.[10]

The simultaneity model of income and the environment is tested and estimated using panel data. We estimate all of the equations using a fixed-effects rather than a random-effects specification, since there are only six air basins, and in accordance with Hsiao (1986), the effects of air basins can be assumed fixed, with the inferences based on the model being confined to Taiwan. Moreover, all of the likelihood ratio (LR) tests reject the null hypothesis of ordinary least squares specification against the fixed-effects specification for each regression.

2.2 Data

Table 13.1 provides the descriptions of the variables and the data sources. All monetary terms with regard to per capita income, capital and local government expenditure are deflated by the consumer price index with the base year of 1996.

Table 13.1 Description of variables and data sources

Variables	Description	Mean (std.dev.) (air-quality standard)	Source
PM_{10} ($\mu g/m^3$)	Particulate matter (diameter <10 μm)	73.319 (24.601) (65 $\mu g/m^3$)	*Yearbook of Environmental Protection Statistics,* Taiwan Area, ROC (1990–97, EPA)
SO_2 (ppm)	Sulfur dioxide	0.020 (0.014) (0.03 ppm)	*Yearbook of Environmental Protection Statistics,* Taiwan Area, ROC (1988–97, EPA)
NO_2 (ppm)	Nitrogen dioxide	0.024 (0.006) (0.05 ppm)	
CO (ppm)	Carbon monoxide	1.354 (0.824) (NA)	
POP_DEN (persons/km^2)	Population density	1730.099 (1398.167)	*Urban and Regional Development Statistics* (1988–97).
SPECIALIST (%)	Number of specialists of air quality protection as percentage of population	6.953 (5.755)	*Yearbook of Environmental Protection Statistics,* Taiwan Area, ROC (1988–97, EPA)
INSPECT_RATE (%)	Air pollution inspection rates of stationary sources and motor vehicles	52.909 (55.689)	
D94	Dummy for year 1994		D94=0, year 1988–93; =1, year 1994–97

Variables	Description	Mean (std.dev.) (air-quality standard)	Source
Y (NT$1,000)	Per capita income (annual per capita current receipts)	230.418 (61.133)	*Report on the Survey of Family Income and Expenditure,* Taiwan Province, ROC; *Report on the Family Income and Expenditure Survey,* Taipei City; *Report on the Survey of Family Income and Expenditure,* Kaohsiung Municipality (1988–97)
K (NT$1,000)	Per capita man-made capital stock for population aged 15 and over (measured by dividing total capital of business registration with population aged 15 and over)	167.780 (277.512)	*Statistical Yearbook of Taiwan Province,* Statistical Abstract of Taipei Municipality, *Statistical Yearbook of Kaohsiung Municipality* (1988–97)
L (%)	Employed persons as percentage of population aged 15 and over	57.232 (1.747)	*Urban and Regional Development Statistics* (1988–97)
H (%)	Persons with educational level of senior high school and above as percentage of population aged 15 and over	51.650 (5.533)	
G (NT$1,000)	Per capita government expenditure	21.583 (6.233)	

Air pollutants examined include the airborne PM_{10} and the gaseous pollutants (SO_2, NO_2, and CO). Post-1987 data are available and expressed as average annual concentrations. The air basin is used as the unit of observation because the dispersion pattern of those pollutants makes county an inappropriate observation unit for air quality.[11] Ignoring this factor may provide us with incorrect or unreliable empirical results.[12] However, because the Taiwanese Environmental Protection Administration (EPA) does not provide air-basin data for these air pollutants, their values are calculated by averaging the concentrations of counties in the same air basin.

One dummy variable, *D94*, is used to take account of the differences in the pre- and post-1994 data sets. The system of air-quality monitoring stations was renovated and expanded in 1993. From 1994, stations with monitoring hours of less than 6000 are excluded from the statistics. We observe that there are substantial differences between pre- and post-1994 monitoring data due to technical differences in the two systems of measurement. Despite this irregularity, all monitoring data are of good quality with respect to air pollution. A dummy variable is therefore used to control the data difference without dropping the data before 1994.

The EPA's *Environmental Protection Statistics Year book* also provides some useful data, such as environmental-loading variables (population, factories and motor vehicles density) [13] and policy variables (inspection rate,[14] number of specialists or staff involved in pollution control).

3 EMPIRICAL ESTIMATION AND RESULTS ANALYSIS

Estimates of the simultaneity model of income and environment are provided in Table 13.2, with the upper set of regressions being the pollution equations. Ambient concentrations of air pollutants are functions of income, population density and control variables. The second (lower) set of regressions is for the income equation. We regress income on four commonly used production input variables (man-made capital, labor, human capital and government expenditure) as well as ambient air quality.

First, a Hausman test is employed to test the exogeneity of income in the pollution equations. In the estimated pollution equations, the test shows that there exist significant feedback effects between NO_2/CO and income. Thus, the single-equation estimates of models 3 and 5 are both inconsistent and biased, and it is necessary to estimate simultaneous-equation models as in models 4 and 6 (see Table 13.2).

In the two simultaneously estimated equations (NO_2_SIM and CO_SIM), the two income terms are significant and their signs imply inverted U-shaped relationships between income and pollutants that follow the EKC hypothesis. The turning points of per capita income in the inverted U-shaped relation are NT$384,000 (approx. US$12,800) for NO_2 and NT$205,000 (approx. US$6,833) for CO, respectively.

Comparing each region's per capita income, we find that CO is now decreasing as income increases in all regions within Taiwan. However, decreasing NO_2 levels are currently being experienced only in the richer Taipei-Keelung region. We do not find it surprising that the NO_2 turning point is at the higher end of the distribution of per capita income across different air basins and years, as NO_2 is more expensive to control. Similar results are found in Cole et al. (1997). Both NO_2 and CO mainly come from the transport sector. As income increases, people can afford better cars that are also more environmentally friendly. But CO is easier to control because even the earliest form of catalytic converters could tackle CO, while only more recent versions are able to reduce NO_2 emissions.

Table 13.2 Regression results (air-basin data, 1988–97)

Variables \ Models	1	2	3	4	5	6
	PM_{10}	SO_2	NO_2	NO_2_SIM	CO	CO_SIM
Y	7.987	–4.660	6.865**	8.415**	12.514**	14.303**
	(1.348)	(–1.034)	(3.265)	(3.693)	(5.231)	(5.554)
Y^2	–0.793	0.470	–0.570**	–0.707**	–1.169**	–1.344**
	(–1.461)	(1.091)	(–2.834)	(–3.244)	(–5.110)	(–5.467)
POP_DEN	–4.729**	2.276	–0.650	–0.952	–0.936	–0.690
	(–2.305)	(1.190)	(–0.744)	(–1.043)	(–0.957)	(–0.682)
D94	0.109	–1.725**	–0.157**	–0.163**	–0.462**	–0.436**
	(1.160)	(–14.880)	(–2.902)	(–2.887)	(–7.462)	(–6.827)
SPECIALIST	0.084	–0.217*	–0.063	–0.062	–0.005	0.004
	(0.975)	(–1.958)	(–1.208)	(–1.164)	(–0.092)	(0.063)
INSPECT_RATE	0.062	–0.145*	–0.030	–0.042	0.024	0.020
	(1.018)	(–1.855)	(–0.848)	(–1.166)	(0.600)	(0.491)
Adj. R^2	0.818	0.941	0.859	0.855	0.930	0.930
LR TEST	43.488**	76.850**	27.509**		90.241**	
EXOGENEITY	0.865	1.985	5.333**		4.457**	
	Y	Y	Y	Y_SIM	Y	Y_SIM
PM_{10}	–0.033					
	(–0.696)					
SO_2		–0.017				
		(–1.015)				
NO_2			0.103	0.036		
			(1.474)	(0.410)		
CO					0.004	–0.032
					(0.085)	(–0.700)
K	0.161**	0.099	0.136**	0.117*	0.108*	0.091
	(2.463)	(1.642)	(2.161)	(1.784)	(1.687)	(1.399)
L	–0.241	–0.494	–0.594	–0.527	–0.491	–0.477
	(–0.543)	(–1.007)	(–1.211)	(–1.058)	(–0.990)	(–0.954)
H	1.352**	2.337**	2.295**	2.388**	2.442**	2.403**
	(3.515)	(6.947)	(6.915)	(6.959)	(7.455)	(7.265)
G	0.270**	0.095	0.092	0.100	0.106	0.097
	(3.212)	(1.141)	(1.116)	(1.206)	(1.260)	(1.148)
Adj. R^2	0.942	0.933	0.934	0.933	0.931	0.930
LR TEST	64.509**	84.957**	68.041**		85.357**	

Notes:

1. *t*-statistics are in parentheses under the coefficient estimates.
2. ** (*) indicates that the estimate is significantly different from null hypothesis at the 5 (10) percent level.
3. All variables are in natural log form.

In order to visualize the observed relationship between income and air pollution, we calculate the simultaneous solutions of these two equations for both income and NO_2/CO, given a fixed set of values for all exogenous variables except man-made capital, *K*. With different values for *K*, the relationships between income and NO_2 (CO) are plotted in Figure 13.2 (Figure 13.3). We can see that the income–pollution relationships are inverted U-shaped curves as expected.[15]

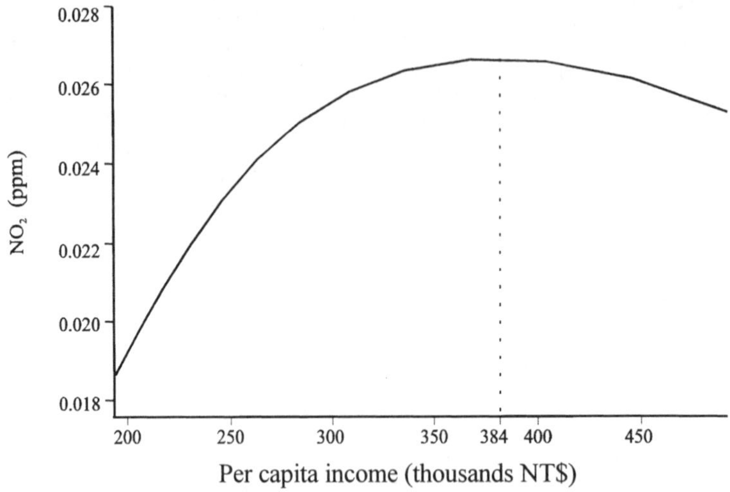

Figure 13.2 EKC relationship between per capita income and NO_2 concentrations

Although per capita income has significant effects on NO_2 and CO concentrations in the pollution equations, the estimates of income equation show that the effects of air pollutants on income are not significantly different from zero. This is expected for several reasons. First, the multiple roles of air pollution on production tend to counteract each other. On the one hand, pollution is an externality causing negative effects on outputs *per se* and on the productivities of other inputs. Improving the environmental quality therefore could increase production. On the other hand, environmental variables affect production via environmental policies that raise the production costs and reduce outputs. Improving the environmental quality therefore reduces production. These two forces counteract each other such that the aggregate effects of air pollutants on income are small and the direction is ambiguous.

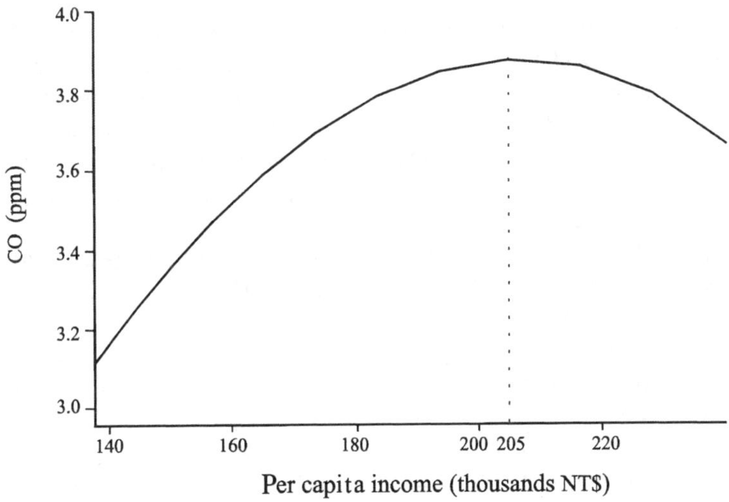

Figure 13.3 *EKC relationship between per capita income and CO concentrations*

Second, Table 13.1 shows that concentrations of these air pollutants in Taiwan are not high enough to produce a noticeable effect on per capita income. It requires high concentrations to cause serious damages to production and human health, for example, 'killer fog' in London (1952), 'excess death' in New York (1953, 1962, 1966), serious air pollution in Yokkaichi, Japan (1961–65), and the recent Southeast Asian haze (1997). Although none of these lasted for a long period, they not only had an immediate impact, but also caused chronic diseases, such as asthma, heart trouble, respiratory diseases and so on, that degrade labor productivity in the long run. There are no such serious air pollution problems in Taiwan, however. Moreover, as people often undertake behavioral measures of avoidance and adjustment, the impacts of air pollution on outputs and inputs are deflated.

Third, polluters do not have to pay for all their control costs and external costs so that total production was not affected significantly in Taiwan. Although many environmental policies have been applied to reduce air pollution, the external costs are only partially internalized because of the pressure of economic interest groups and the growth-oriented policies of the government. For example, the air pollution emission fee is not set sufficiently high to give enough economic incentives to firms. Furthermore, there are many subsidy programs including tax allowances, soft loans and technical assistance for enterprises to reduce abatement costs under the Statute for the Encouragement of Investment and the later Statute for Upgrading Industries. These three reasons explain why the aggregate effects of air pollutants on income are not significant in Taiwan.

All other production input variables generally behave as expected. Human and man-made capital are the two most significant production inputs of this decade, with human capital particularly making a significant contribution to production in all models. The coefficients of government expenditure are positive and sometimes significant, which means that the government investments on infrastructure services, education and transportation have positive effects on the economy. However, due to the fact that we cannot differentiate between government transfer payments and government investments in total government expenditure, as expressed in Chen and Chou (1993), the coefficients are generally not significant.

Raw labor is always an insignificant determinant of income and contrary to our expectation. This might be caused by the limitation of the data set. Our data set covers only ten years (1988–97) and the economy has been transformed to a much more service and high-tech-oriented economy. As human capital becomes more important in production, raw labor becomes correspondingly less important.

Returning to the pollution equations, *D94* are negative and significant for almost all pollutants; this is because the entire network of the air quality monitoring stations was renovated and expanded in 1994. The new monitoring equipment significantly reduces the measured concentration levels of most pollutants, particularly SO_2, NO_2 and CO; in the absence of this consideration, we might gain the incorrect impression that air quality has been improving significantly since 1994.

Instead of the income, *Y*, the explicit EPA policy variables (the number of specialists involved in air quality protection and air pollution inspecting rates) are the significant factors that reduce SO_2. This may be due to the fact that the EPA has been charging air pollution emission fees based on SO_2 emissions since 1995, and at the same time, the EPA has upgraded its enforcement efforts toward SO_2 emissions. Other driving forces that income surrogates do not affect SO_2 significantly.[16]

Population density exhibits significant effects only on PM_{10}. Among airborne and gaseous pollutants, PM_{10} is invariably the first one to be controlled since it is the most visible and the cheapest to control. The tighter control in the urban areas is a response to the urban population's demand for better air quality and, consequently, political pressure. Thus, the estimate shows significant negative effect with regard to population density.

Finally, let us examine the effects of variations in exogenous variables. Given the simultaneity model estimates and a fixed set of values for all exogenous variables except one in either of the two equations, we can solve the simultaneity model over some range of the exogenous variable to yield values of the two endogenous variables. The solutions can provide us with valuable insights into the effects of these exogenous variables.

First, the effects of varying one exogenous variable in the pollution equation are examined. In Figure 13.4, PE_0 is the pollution equation and *IE* is the income equation given some specific values of exogenous variables. Because the estimated effect of NO_2/CO on income is not significantly different from zero, the slope of *IE* is very steep, though it is positive between NO_2 and income; and negative, between CO and income. Assume E_0 is the initial simultaneous solution of the two equations.

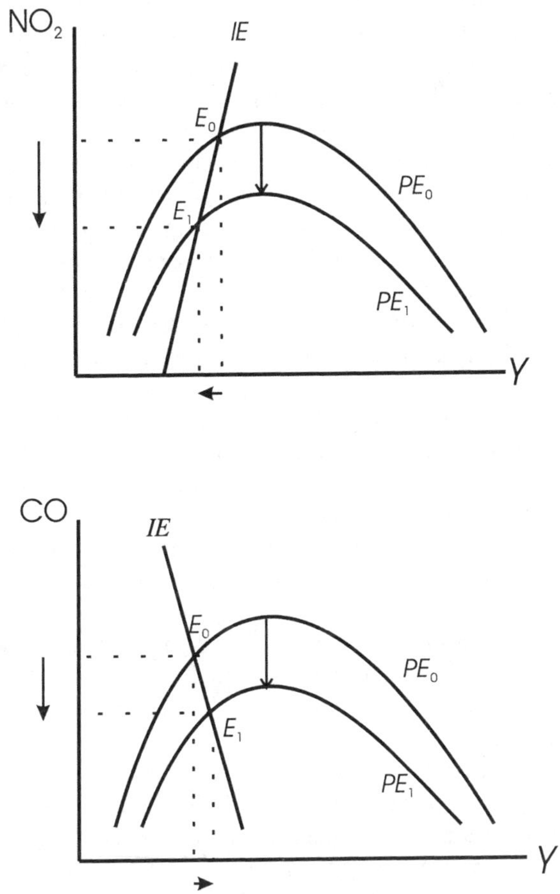

Figure 13.4 Effects of an exogenous variable in the pollution equation

Suppose the environmental authority now applies a control policy (for example, increasing the inspection rate) that could reduce NO_2/CO concentrations directly.[17] This policy would move PE_0 vertically downward to PE_1, which, 'tunnels through' the original inverted U-shaped pollution equation and the new solution is E_1.

Comparing E_0 and E_1, we find that the control of NO_2 and CO has different effects on income. On the one hand, the positive slope of *IE* in the upper diagram in Figure 13.4 implies that environmental policies can increase the abatement costs of firms (NO_2 decreases and output decreases) and this force outweighs the negative external effects of NO_2 on production (NO_2 decreases and output increases). Therefore if the environmental policy is enforced, NO_2 emission will decrease and at the same time firms' abatement costs rise and outputs decrease. This is consistent with the fact that NO_2 is expensive to control. On the other hand, the negative slope of *IE* in the lower diagram in Figure 13.4 implies that the negative externalities of pollution on production (CO decreases and output increases) outweigh the production reduction effects from increases in abatement costs (CO decreases and output decreases). This is consistent with the fact that CO is easy and inexpensive to control. In this case, if the environmental policy is enforced, CO emission will decrease and the better environmental quality increases production. It is worth noting that when the estimated effects of pollution on production are smaller (that is, the slope of *IE* is very steep), the impacts of environmental policy on income are smaller as well.

Next, the effects of varying an exogenous variable in the income equation (for example, man-made capital) are examined. In the first quadrant of Figure 13.5, PE_0 is the pollution equation and IE_0 is the income equation for the simultaneity model between income and NO_2, which can be drawn given some specific values of other exogenous variables and man-made capital (K_0). We assume that E_0 is the initial simultaneous solution of the two equations.

When the accumulation of man-made capital is increased to K_1 and K_2, *ceteris paribus*, the income equation is moved to IE_1 and IE_2; and the corresponding simultaneous solutions are E_1 and E_2, respectively. We see that as man-made capital increases, income increases and the pollution first increases and then decreases.

There is a policy implication derived from the EKC relationship that economic growth is good for the environment. Accelerated economic growth can speed up the mitigation of environmental problems. However, this policy implication has been viewed as naive (Arrow et al., 1995). Here we consider this policy issue with respect to the time effects.

In order to examine the time effects, it is necessary to add a time scale in the x-axis called 'year' in Figure 13.5. We assume originally at the fifth year, that the level of man-made capital is K_0 and the simultaneous solution is (Y_0, P_0) in the first quadrant. When man-made capital increases to the level of K_1 at the thirteenth year, the simultaneous solution is (Y_1, P_1). The accelerating line in the second quadrant means that if it takes 5 (13) years to be at the levels of K_0 and Y_0 (K_1 and Y_1), then when we accelerate investment in man-made capital, it will now takes a shorter period of time — 3 (8) years — to achieve the same levels of man-made capital and income.

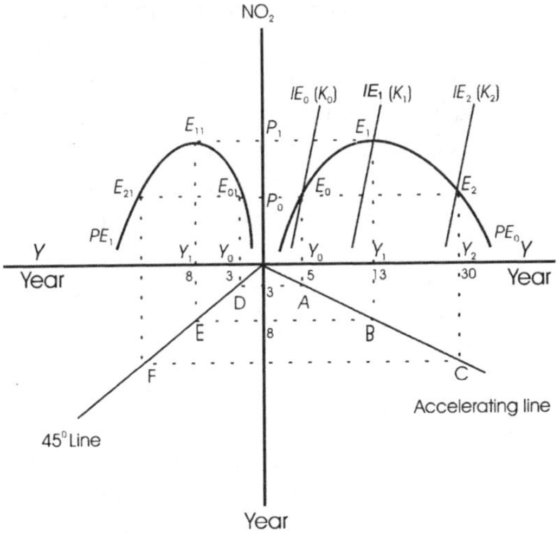

Figure 13.5 Effects of an exogenous variable in the income equation

The inverted U-shaped curve in quadrant 4 is derived by dropping vertical lines from points on PE_0 in quadrant 1 to the accelerating line in quadrant 2 (points E_0, E_1 and E_2 to A, B and C, respectively), drawing horizontal lines from those intersections to points D, E and F on the 45° line in quadrant 3, and then drawing vertical lines to intersect with the horizontal lines from points E_0, E_1 and E_2. The intersections (points E_{01}, E_{11} and E_{21}) in quadrant 4 develop an accelerated EKC curve, PE_1.

Comparing PE_0 and PE_1, we find that NO_2 increases from P_0 to P_1 in eight years originally (quadrant 1). It takes only five years to reach the same level of pollution when a policy of accelerating the investment of man-made capital is applied (quadrant 4). This is a very dangerous development paradigm since the carrying capacity of the environment may be reduced to a low level in a short time such that the resource base is irreversibly damaged. In addition, serious environmental problems might result in social-costly environmental and human-health losses that lead to social confrontations and economic catastrophe.

4 CONCLUSIONS

It is generally acknowledged that the economy and its environment are jointly determined. However, there are no empirical studies that estimate the simultaneous relationship between economic growth and environmental quality due to the difficulties of model specification and data requirements. In this chapter, we make a modest attempt to incorporate explicitly the simultaneity between income and pollution as a first step towards better understanding of the income–environment relationship. Our empirical results confirm that the hypothesis of simultaneity exists in some air pollutants. Estimating a single equation where simultaneity exists will therefore produce biased and inconsistent estimates. With simultaneously estimated equations, we found that the magnitudes of the estimates of income coefficients become larger and more significant.

An EKC relationship does exist for NO_2 and CO in Taiwan. This result is consistent with the underlying driving forces. In order to meet people's increasing demand for better air quality due to higher income, the Taiwanese EPA instituted a new regulation in 1990 that requires every new car to be fitted with a catalytic converter that can dramatically reduce NO_2 and CO emissions from the transport sector. The policy effects, however, were not embodied in the two policy variables – inspection rate and number of specialists for air quality protection – since its enforcement does not require many specialists to inspect the cars regularly.

The turning points of per capita income in the inverted U-shaped relation are much higher for NO_2 than for CO, because the transport sector accounts for the majority of CO emissions and only half of NO_2 emissions, and the EPA did not require stationary sources to control NO_2 emissions until 1998 because it is more expensive to control.

In addition to the effects of income on the environment, environment also has impacts on income. We know of no study, however, that has empirically attempted to estimate the impacts of pollution on income. Basically, pollution affects production via two channels: negative externalities on output and productivity, and higher abatement costs. These two forces counteract each other, and we estimate the aggregate effects of pollution on production. We found that although income does have an effect on some cases of air pollution, air pollution statistically has no impact on income in Taiwan. This is consistent with our expectations because the concentrations of these air pollutants are not high enough and polluters do not have to pay all their control costs and external costs. It is also possible that not all the effects of the environment on income are caught because the time span of our data set is not long enough.

Natural resource-based environmental problems, such as land erosion and deforestation, are other topics that deserve in-depth investigation in the future.

These kinds of environmental problem have caused heavy damage to the economy during the typhoon season. Because of climate change and population growth, they will surely become serious problems.

ACKNOWLEDGMENTS

We are grateful to my colleagues B. L. Chen, C. H. Huang, K. Kan, W. J. Tsay and conference participants for their valuable comments and help, and the referees for helpful comments.

NOTES

1. For example, two recent special issues on EKC have appeared, *Environment and Development Economics* (1997) and *Ecological Economics* (1998), in addition to many articles appearing in other journals and books.
2. Environmental degradation not only reduces the productivity of workers and man-made capital, it also reduces the quality or quantity of natural resources as inputs.
3. This model is similar to De Bruyn's structural model specification for simultaneously estimating the two-way relationship between economic growth and environmental quality (De Bruyn, 2000, model (a) in Figure 1.1).
4. Several empirical studies have shown that human capital accumulation is a very important factor in Taiwan's economic growth (Chen and Chou, 1993; Lee et al., 1994; Tallman and Wang, 1994).
5. Vincent (1997) argues that cross-country EKC may merely reflect the 'juxtaposition' of two opposite trends, rather than describe the process of evolution of a single economy over time. Stern et al. (1994), and De Bruyn and Heintz (1999) suggest that more could be learned from an examination of the experiences of individual countries. Carson et al. (1997) also argue that the study of a single country eliminates the problems associated with data comparison from different countries.
6. Air pollution affects people more directly relative to other kinds of pollution. For example, the water used in our everyday life is pretreated. If we do not swim in a polluted river, water pollution does not affect us directly. Therefore, air pollution is usually the first one to be regulated and with sounder control measures in most countries.
7. A cubic specification for the pollution equation has also been considered since the pollution-reducing forces counteracting the negative impact of economic growth on the environment may be less effective in the long run (Borghesi, 2002). However, since our data set may not be long enough to exhibit the cubic relationship between income and the environment, we do not employ a cubic form.
8. The definitions and contents of total government expenditures were revised in 1990; it is impossible to identify and distinguish consistent data of government transfer payments and investments, respectively, for the time span of the data set.
9. 'The Cowles Foundation approach to simultaneous equations held the view that causality and exogeneity cannot be tested. These are things that have to be specified a priori. In recent years it has been argued that if some variables are specified as exogenous and the equation is identified, one can test whether some other variables considered endogenous are indeed endogenous or not' (Maddala, 1992, p. 395). In addition, a Granger causality test is not performed because the data analyzed is panel data which have only ten periods. 'Granger noncausality is neither necessary nor sufficient for exogeneity as understood in the usual simultaneous equations

literature' (Maddala, 1992, p. 394).

10. A further econometric question which may need to be answered, is whether to test the null hypothesis that each individual time series contains a unit root, against the alternative hypothesis that each time series is stationary, when using panel data. Levin and Lin (1993) considered this question and indicated that it is not necessary to test the unit root hypothesis because the normal distribution provides an excellent approximation of the empirical distribution of the test statistics in relatively small samples, and the panel framework can provide dramatic improvements in statistical power as compared to performing a separate unit root test for each individual time series.
11. According to the Taiwanese EPA, there are eight air basins, namely, Taipei-Keelung; Taoyuan-Hsinchu-Miaoli; Taichung-Changhwa; Nantou; Yunlin-Chiayi; Tainan-Kaohsiung-Pingtung; Hualien-Taitung; and Ilan. Among these, PM_{10}, SO_2, CO and NO_2 data for Nantou and Ilan are not used because there are too many missing data points. The demarcation of air basins is based mainly on meteoric and geographic considerations.
12. Not only air pollutants, but also labor can easily move to neighboring counties. By using the air basin as the unit – usually comprising adjacent counties with one major city at the center–we alleviate both pollutant dispersion and human movement problems.
13. Factory density and motor vehicle density are not used in the regression because they are highly correlated with population density. Population density provides information on the environmental loads in each air basin.
14. The data in the EPA yearbooks are the inspected numbers of air pollution from stationary sources and motor vehicles. We combine these data as a variable of air pollution inspection rate of stationary sources and motor vehicles. First, we divide the inspected numbers from stationary sources (motor vehicles) by the numbers of registered factories (motor vehicles). Then, we use the air pollution contributions of stationary sources and motor vehicles as weights to produce the variable of inspection rate used in the estimation.
15. The income levels where turning points occur are the same as those calculated directly using the estimates of the simultaneous equations.
16. Kaufmann et al. (1998) also find that it is not income that provides the impetus for SO_2 reduction. In their results, the spatial intensity of economic activity is the factor that reduces SO_2 significantly.
17. The estimates of both EPA policy variables are not significantly different from zero. In order to examine the effect of an exogenous variable in the pollution equation, however, we assume that raising the inspection rate is a very effective policy for NO_2/CO control.

REFERENCES

Arrow, K., B. Bolin, R. Costanza, P. Dasgupta, C. Folke, C.S. Holling, B.-O. Jansson, S. Levin, K. Maler, C. Perrings, and D. Pimental (1995), 'Economic Growth, Carrying Capacity, and the Environment', *Science*, **268**, 520–21.

Barbier, E.B. (1994), 'Natural Capital and the Economics of Environment and Development', in A. Jansson, M. Hammer, C. Folke and R. Costanza (eds), *Investing in Natural Capital: The Ecological Economics Approach to Sustainability*, New York: Columbia University Press, 291–322.

Borghesi, S. (2002), 'The Environmental Kuznets Curve: A Survey of the Literature', in Franzini (eds), *Economic Institutions and Environmental Policy*, Aldershot: Ashgate, 201–24.

Carson, R.T., Y. Jeon and D.R. McCubbin (1997), 'The Relationship between Air Pollution Emissions and Income: US Data', *Environment and Development Economics*, **2**, 433–50.

Chen, B.L. and L.C. Chou (1993), 'Human Capital and Income Growth in Taiwan: Theory and Empirical Study', in *Proceedings of the Annual Meeting of the Chinese*

Economic Association, Chinese Economic Association, 143–65 (in Chinese).

Cole, M.A., A.J. Rayner and J.M. Bates (1997), 'The Environmental Kuznets Curve: An Empirical Analysis', *Environment and Development Economics*, **2** (4), 433–50.

De Bruyn, S.M. (2000), *Economic Growth and the Environment: An Empirical Analysis*, Dordrecht: Kluwer Academic Publishers.

De Bruyn, S.M. and R.J. Heintz (1999), 'The Environmental Kuznets Curve Hypothesis', in J.C.J.M. van den Bergh, (ed.), *Handbook of Environmental and Resource Economics*, Cheltenham, UK and Northampton, MA, USA: Edward Elgar, 656–77.

Grossman, G.M. and A.B. Krueger (1991), 'Environmental Impacts of a North American Free Trade Agreement', National Bureau of Economic Research Working Paper 3914, NBER, Cambridge, MA.

Grossman, G.M. and A.B. Krueger (1995), 'Economic Growth and the Environment', *Quarterly Journal of Economics*, **112**, 353–78.

Holtz-Eakin, D. and T.M. Selden (1995), 'Stoking the Fires? CO_2 Emissions and Economic Growth', *Journal of Public Economics*, **57**, 85–101.

Hsiao, C. (1986), *Analysis of Panel Data*, Cambridge: Cambridge University Press.

Kaufmann, R.K., B. Davidsdottir, S. Garnham and P. Pauly (1998), 'The Determinants of Atmospheric SO_2 Concentrations: Reconsidering the Environmental Kuznets Curve', *Ecological Economics*, **25**, 209–20.

Kuznets, S. (1955), 'Economic Growth and Income Inequality', *American Economic Review*, **49**, 1–28.

Lee, M.L., B.C. Liu and P. Wang (1994), 'Growth and Equity with Endogenous Human Capital: Taiwan's Economic Miracle Revisited', *Southern Economic Journal*, **61** (2), 435–44.

Levin, A. and Chien-Fu Lin (1993), 'Unit Root Tests in Panel Data: New Results', University of California San Diego Working Paper 93–56, San Diego, CA.

López, R. (1994), 'The Environment as a Factor of Production: The Effects of Economic Growth and Trade Liberalization', *Journal of Environmental Economics and Management*, **27**, 163–84.

Maddala, G.S. (1992), *Introduction to Econometrics*, 2nd edn, New York: Macmillan.

Munasinghe, M. (1999), 'Is Environmental Degradation an Inevitable Consequence of Economic Growth: Tunneling through the Environmental Kuznets Curve', *Ecological Economics*, **29**, 89–109.

Panayotou, T. (1993), 'Empirical Tests and Policy Analysis of Environmental Degradation at Different Stages of Economic Development', Working Paper, Technology and Environment Programme, International Labour Office, Geneva.

Panayotou, T. (2000), 'Economic Growth and the Environment', CID Working Paper No. 56, (Center for International Development at Harvard University.) in K.G. Mäler and J. Vincent (eds), *Handbook of Environmental Economics*, North-Holland, forthcoming.

Pearce, D.W. and J.J. Warford (1993), *World without End: Economics, Environment and Sustainable Development*, Oxford: Oxford University Press.

Pearson, P. (1994), 'Energy, Externalities and Environmental Quality: Will Development Cure the Ills It Creates?', *Energy Studies Review*, **6** (3), 199–215.

Perrings, C.A. (1987), *Economy and Environment: A Theoretical Essay on the Inter-dependence of Economic and Environmental Systems*, Cambridge: Cambridge University Press.

Selden, T.M. and D. Song (1994), 'Environmental Quality and Development: Is There a Kuznets Curve for Air Pollution Estimates?', *Journal of Environmental Economics and Management*, **27**, 147–62.

Shafik, N. and S. Bandyopadhyay (1992), 'Economic Growth and Environmental Quality: Time Series and Cross-country Evidence', Background Paper for World Development Report 1992, World Bank, Washington, DC.

Shaw, D. and M.F. Hung (2001), 'Evolution and Evaluation of Air Pollution Control Policy in Taiwan', *Environmental Economics and Policy Studies*, **4**, 141–66.

Smulders, S. (1999), 'Endogenous Growth Theory and the Environment', in J.C.J.M. van den Bergh, (ed.), *Handbook of Environmental and Resource Economics*, Cheltenham, UK and Northampton, MA, USA: Edward Elgar, 610–21.

Smulders, S. and L. Bretschger (2000), 'Explaining Environmental Kuznets Curves: How Pollution Induces Policy and New Technologies', Tilburg University CentER Working Paper No. 2000-95, CentER, Tilburg University, Netherlands.

Spencer, D. and K. Berk (1981), 'A Limited Information Specification Test', *Econometrica*, **49**, 1079–85.

Stern, D.I. (1998), 'Progress on the Environmental Kuznets Curve?', *Environment and Development Economics*, **3**, 173–96.

Stern, D.I., M.S. Common and E.B. Barbier (1994), 'Economic Growth and Environmental Degradation: A Critique of the Environmental Kuznets Curve', Discussion Paper in Environmental Economics and Environmental Management, No. 9409, University of York.

Stern, D.I., M.S. Common and E.B. Barbier (1996), 'Economic Growth and Environmental Degradation: The Environmental Kuznets Curve and Sustainable Development', *World Development*, **24**, 1151–60.

Stokey, N. (1998), 'Are There Limits to Growth?', *International Economic Review*, **39** (1), 1–31.

Tallman, E.W. and P. Wang (1994), 'Human Capital and Endogenous Growth: Evidence from Taiwan', *Journal of Monetary Economics*, **34** (1), 101–24.

Van Ewijk, C. and S. Van Wijnbergen (1995), 'Can Abatement Overcome the Conflict between the Environment and Economic Growth?', *De Economist*, **143**, 197–216.

Vincent, J.R. (1997), 'Testing for Environmental Kuznets Curves within a Developing Country', *Environment and Development Economics*, **2**, 417–31.

Wu, P.I. (1998), 'Economic Development and Environmental Quality: Evidence from Taiwan', *Asian Economic Journal*, **12** (4), 395–412.

Index